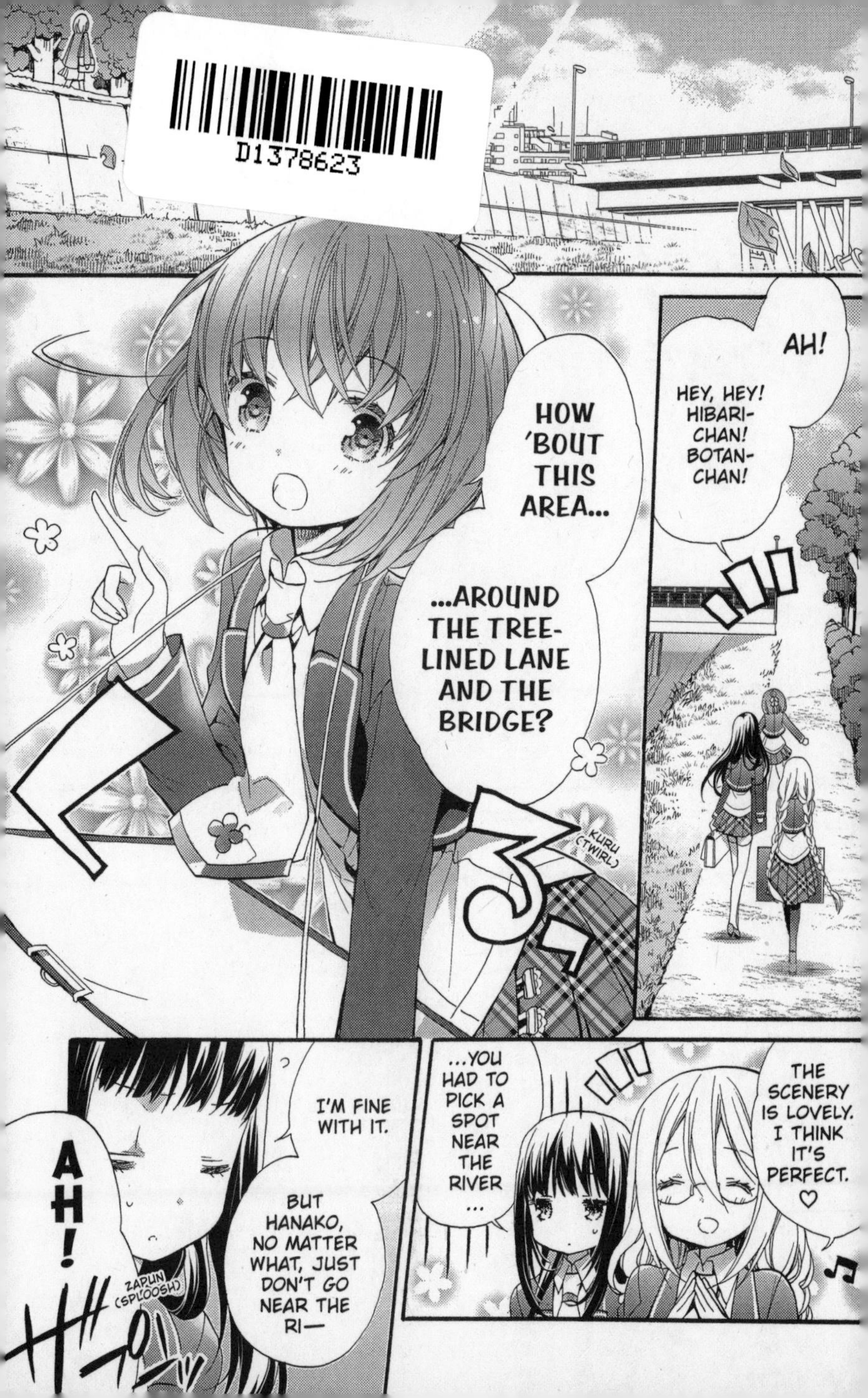
AH!
HEY, HEY! HIBARI-CHAN! BOTAN-CHAN!
HOW 'BOUT THIS AREA...
...AROUND THE TREE-LINED LANE AND THE BRIDGE?
KURU (TWIRL)
THE SCENERY IS LOVELY. I THINK IT'S PERFECT. ♡
...YOU HAD TO PICK A SPOT NEAR THE RIVER ...
I'M FINE WITH IT.
BUT HANAKO, NO MATTER WHAT, JUST DON'T GO NEAR THE RI—
AH!
ZAPUN (SPLOOSH)

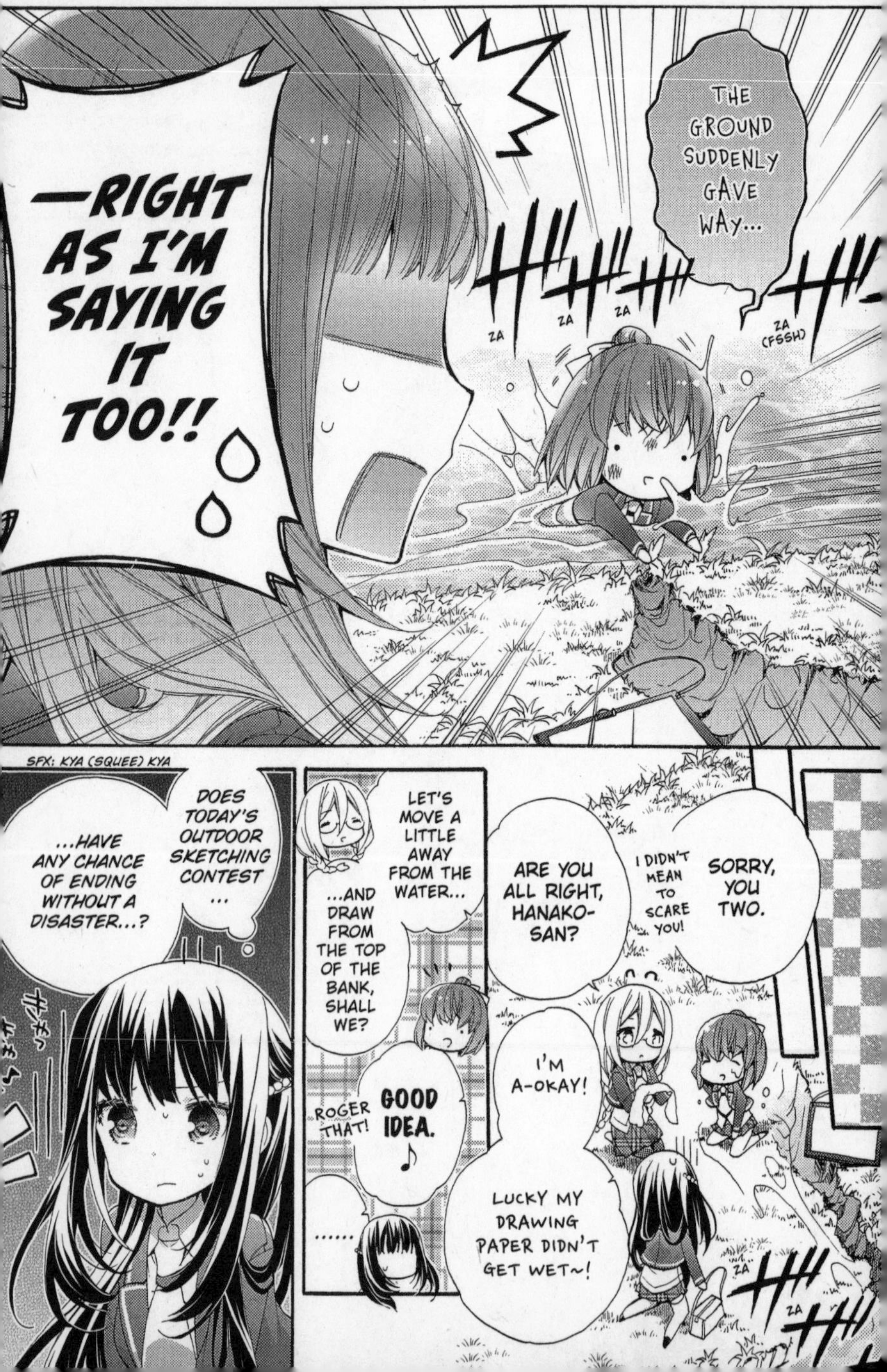
THE GROUND SUDDENLY GAVE WAY...
ZA
ZA
ZA
ZA (FSSH)
—RIGHT AS I'M SAYING IT TOO!!
SFX: KYA (SQUEE) KYA
SORRY, YOU TWO.
I DIDN'T MEAN TO SCARE YOU!
ARE YOU ALL RIGHT, HANAKO-SAN?
I'M A-OKAY!
LUCKY MY DRAWING PAPER DIDN'T GET WET~!
ZA
ZA
LET'S MOVE A LITTLE AWAY FROM THE WATER...
...AND DRAW FROM THE TOP OF THE BANK, SHALL WE?
GOOD IDEA. ♪
ROGER THAT!
......
DOES TODAY'S OUTDOOR SKETCHING CONTEST...
...HAVE ANY CHANCE OF ENDING WITHOUT A DISASTER...?

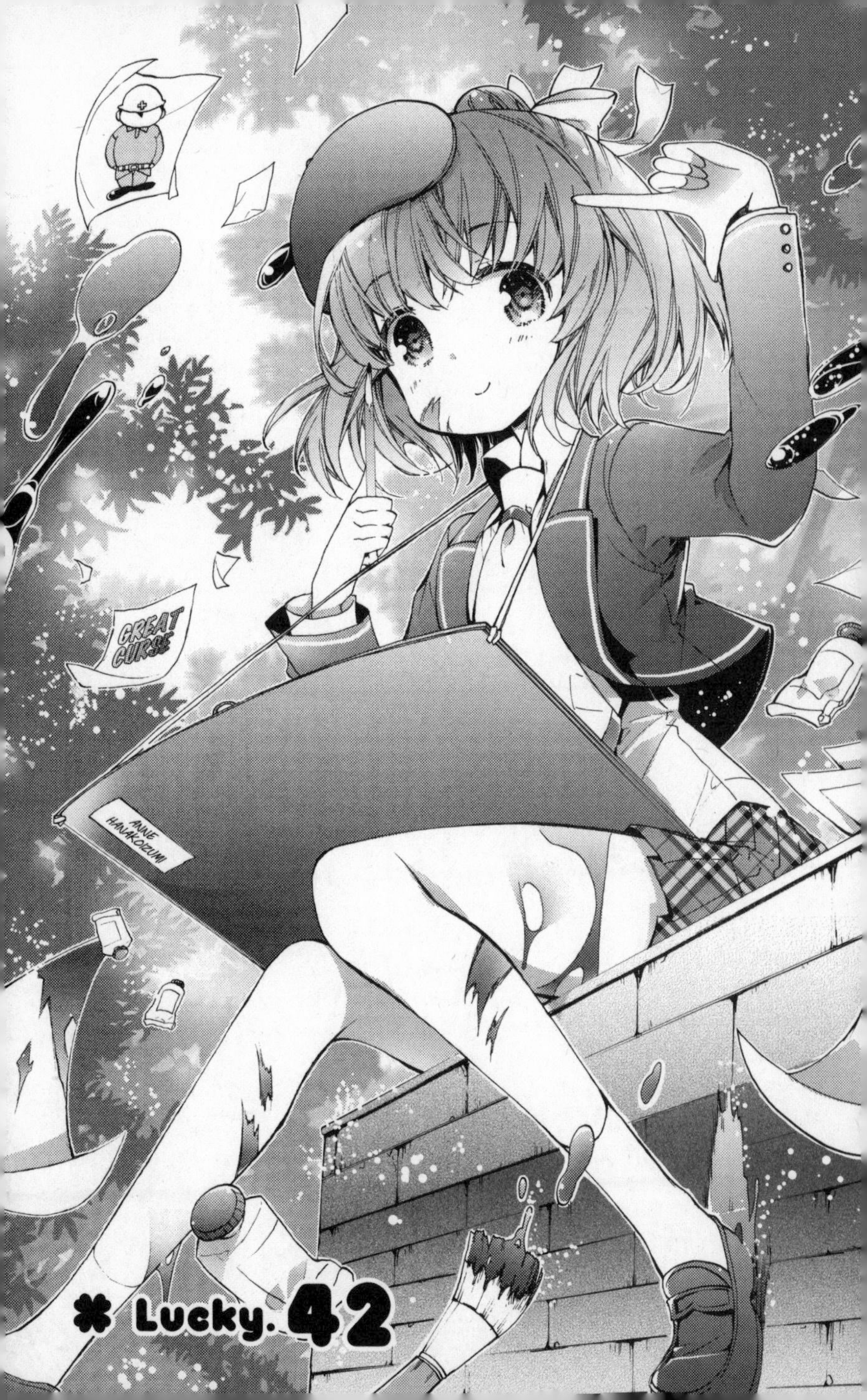
GREAT CURSE
ANNIE HANAKOIZUMI
* Lucky. 42

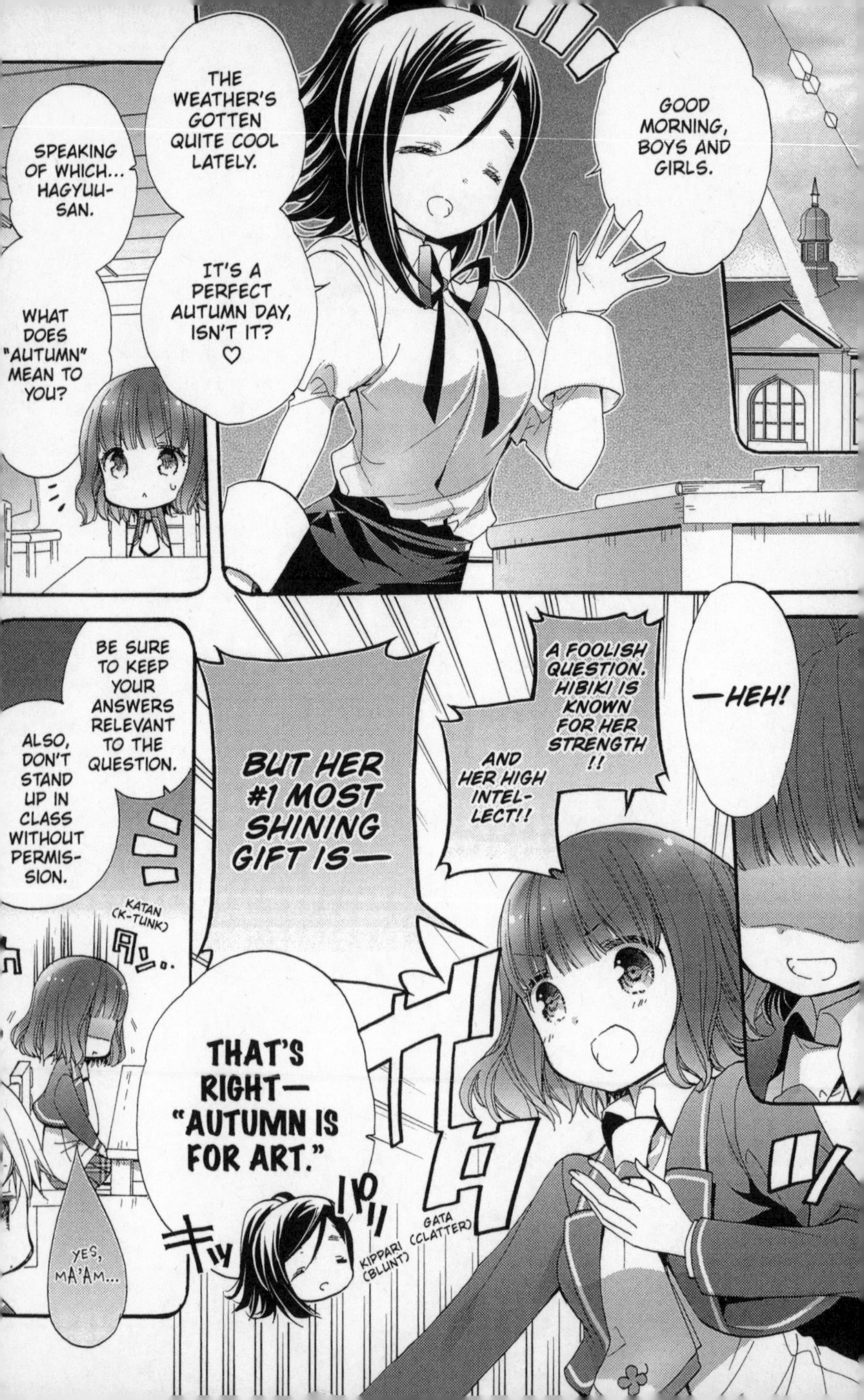
GOOD MORNING, BOYS AND GIRLS.
THE WEATHER'S GOTTEN QUITE COOL LATELY.
IT'S A PERFECT AUTUMN DAY, ISN'T IT? ♡
SPEAKING OF WHICH... HAGYUU-SAN.
WHAT DOES "AUTUMN" MEAN TO YOU?
—HEH!
A FOOLISH QUESTION. HIBIKI IS KNOWN FOR HER STRENGTH!!
AND HER HIGH INTELLECT!!
BUT HER #1 MOST SHINING GIFT IS—
GATA (CLATTER)
THAT'S RIGHT— "AUTUMN IS FOR ART."
KIPPARI (BLUNT)
BE SURE TO KEEP YOUR ANSWERS RELEVANT TO THE QUESTION.
ALSO, DON'T STAND UP IN CLASS WITHOUT PERMISSION.
KATAN (K-TUNK)
YES, MA'AM...

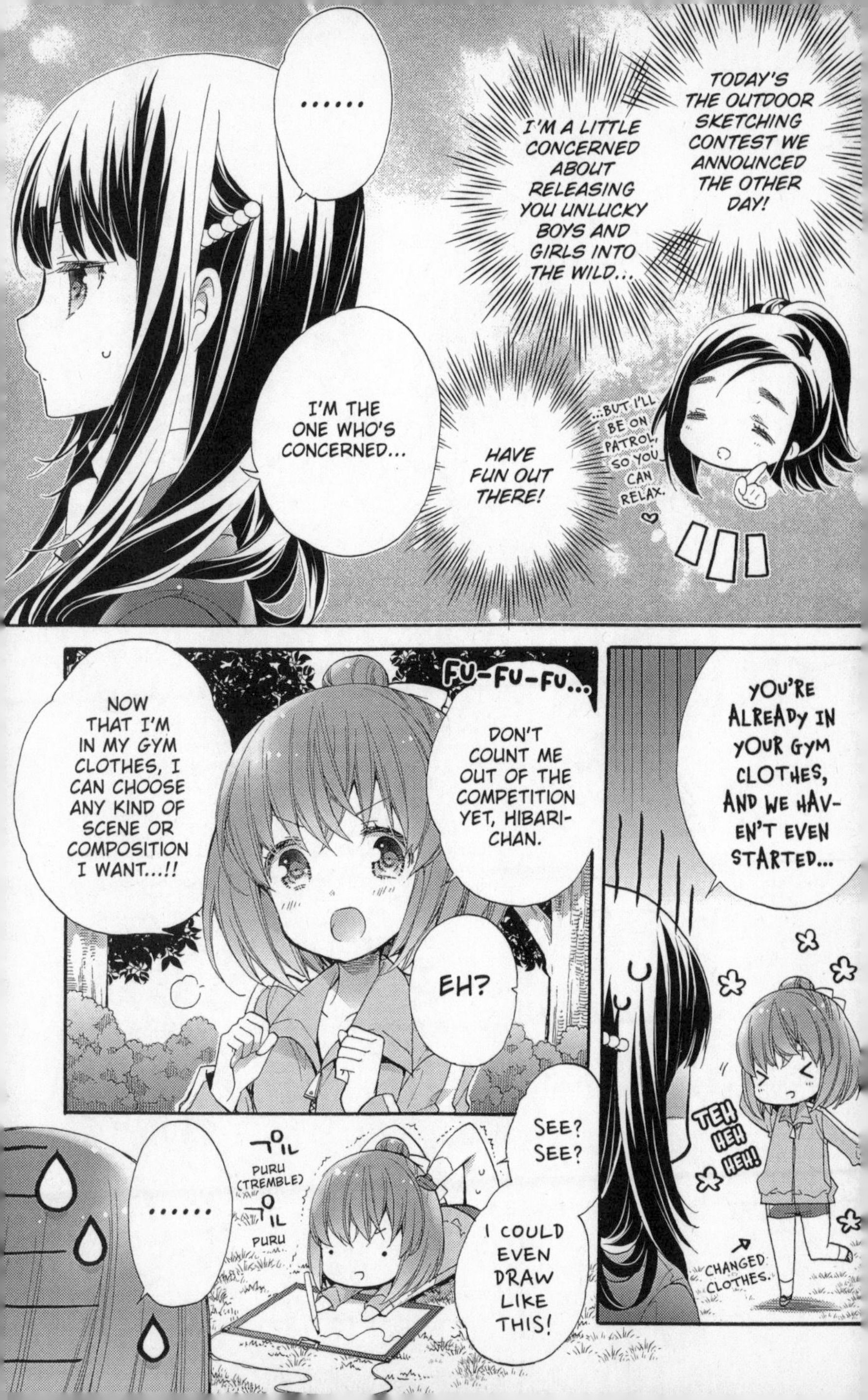
TODAY'S THE OUTDOOR SKETCHING CONTEST WE ANNOUNCED THE OTHER DAY!
I'M A LITTLE CONCERNED ABOUT RELEASING YOU UNLUCKY BOYS AND GIRLS INTO THE WILD...
...BUT I'LL BE ON PATROL, SO YOU CAN RELAX.
HAVE FUN OUT THERE!
I'M THE ONE WHO'S CONCERNED...
......
YOU'RE ALREADY IN YOUR GYM CLOTHES, AND WE HAV-EN'T EVEN STARTED...
TEH HEH HEH!
CHANGED CLOTHES.
FU-FU-FU...
DON'T COUNT ME OUT OF THE COMPETITION YET, HIBARI-CHAN.
NOW THAT I'M IN MY GYM CLOTHES, I CAN CHOOSE ANY KIND OF SCENE OR COMPOSITION I WANT...!!
EH?
SEE? SEE?
I COULD EVEN DRAW LIKE THIS!
PURU (TREMBLE)
PURU
......

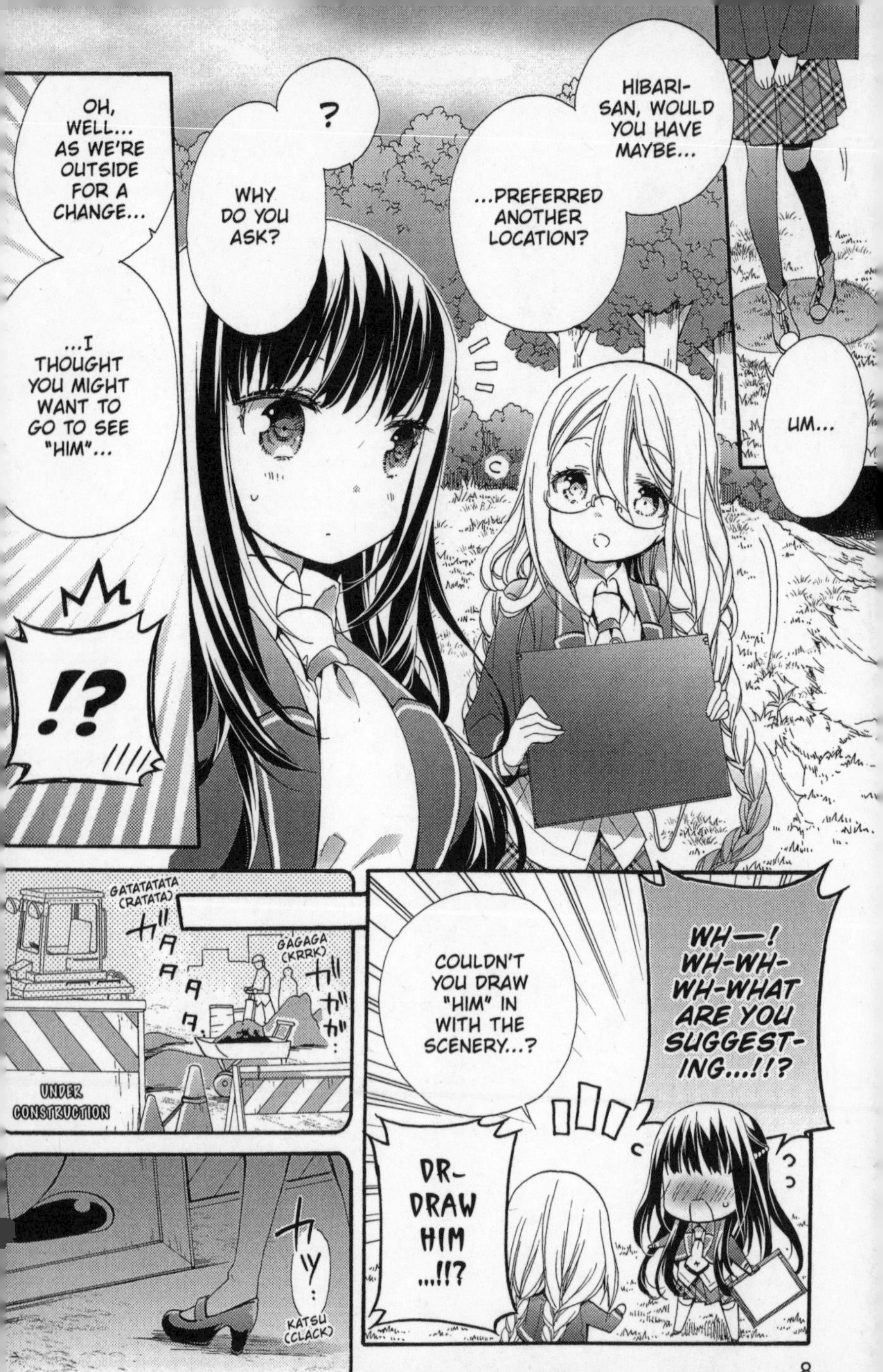
UM...
HIBARI-SAN, WOULD YOU HAVE MAYBE...
...PREFERRED ANOTHER LOCATION?
?
WHY DO YOU ASK?
OH, WELL... AS WE'RE OUTSIDE FOR A CHANGE...
...I THOUGHT YOU MIGHT WANT TO GO TO SEE "HIM"...
!?
WH—! WH-WH-WH-WHAT ARE YOU SUGGEST-ING...!!?
COULDN'T YOU DRAW "HIM" IN WITH THE SCENERY...?
DR-DRAW HIM ...!!?
GATATATATA (RATATA)
GAGAGA (KRRK)
UNDER CONSTRUCTION
KATSU (CLACK)

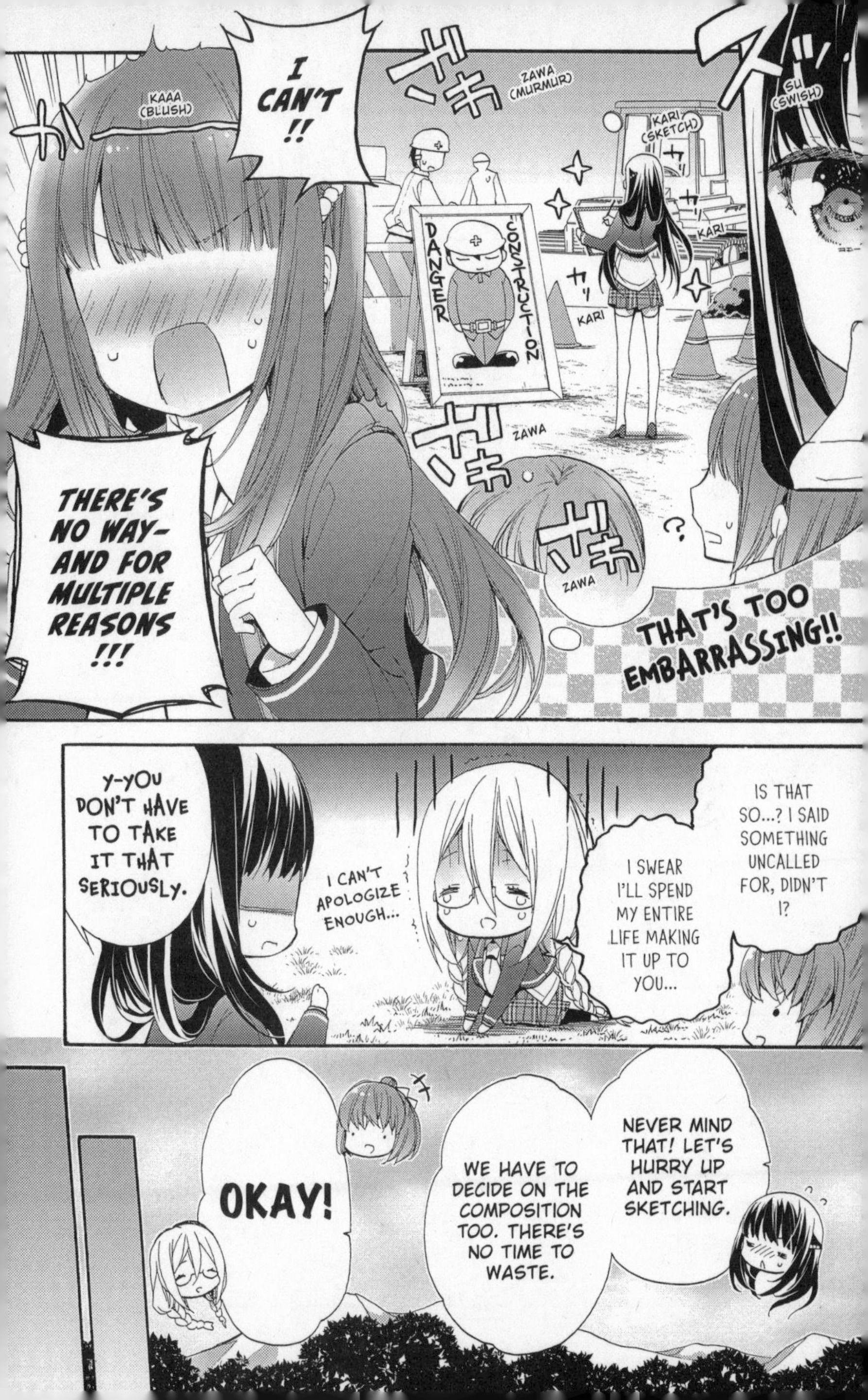
SU (SWISH)
KARI (SKETCH)
KARI
ZAWA (MURMUR)
I CAN'T!!
KAAA (BLUSH)
DANGER
CONSTRUCTION
KARI
ZAWA
ZAWA
THAT'S TOO EMBARRASSING!!
THERE'S NO WAY—AND FOR MULTIPLE REASONS!!!
IS THAT SO...? I SAID SOMETHING UNCALLED FOR, DIDN'T I?
I SWEAR I'LL SPEND MY ENTIRE LIFE MAKING IT UP TO YOU...
I CAN'T APOLOGIZE ENOUGH...
Y-YOU DON'T HAVE TO TAKE IT THAT SERIOUSLY.
NEVER MIND THAT! LET'S HURRY UP AND START SKETCHING.
WE HAVE TO DECIDE ON THE COMPOSITION TOO. THERE'S NO TIME TO WASTE.
OKAY!

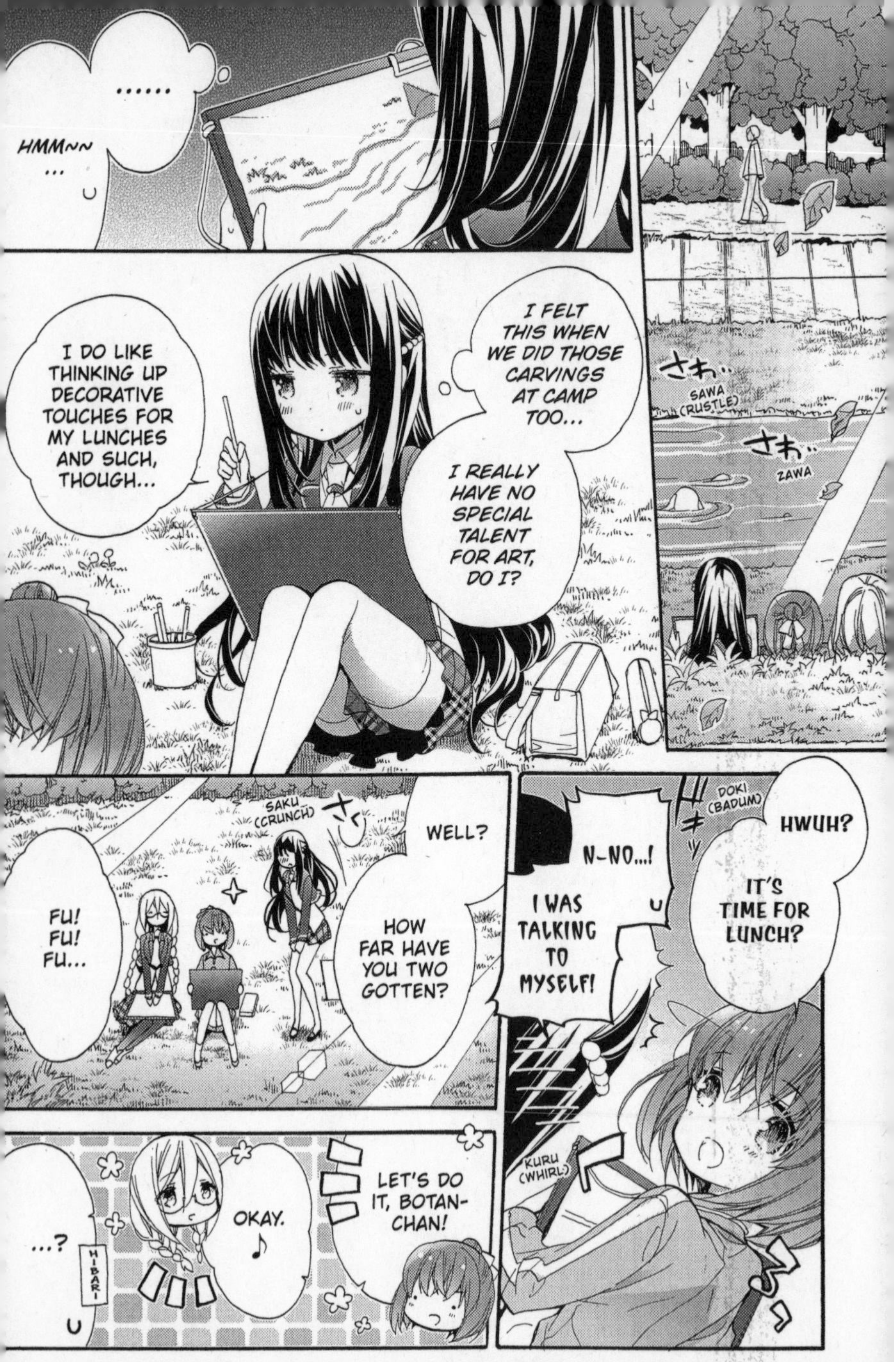
SAWA (RUSTLE)
ZAWA
......
HMM~~ ...
I FELT THIS WHEN WE DID THOSE CARVINGS AT CAMP TOO...
I REALLY HAVE NO SPECIAL TALENT FOR ART, DO I?
I DO LIKE THINKING UP DECORATIVE TOUCHES FOR MY LUNCHES AND SUCH, THOUGH...
DOKI (BADUM)
HWUH?
IT'S TIME FOR LUNCH?
N-NO...!
I WAS TALKING TO MYSELF!
KURU (WHIRL)
SAKU (CRUNCH)
WELL?
HOW FAR HAVE YOU TWO GOTTEN?
FU! FU! FU...
LET'S DO IT, BOTAN-CHAN!
OKAY. ♪
...?
HIBARI

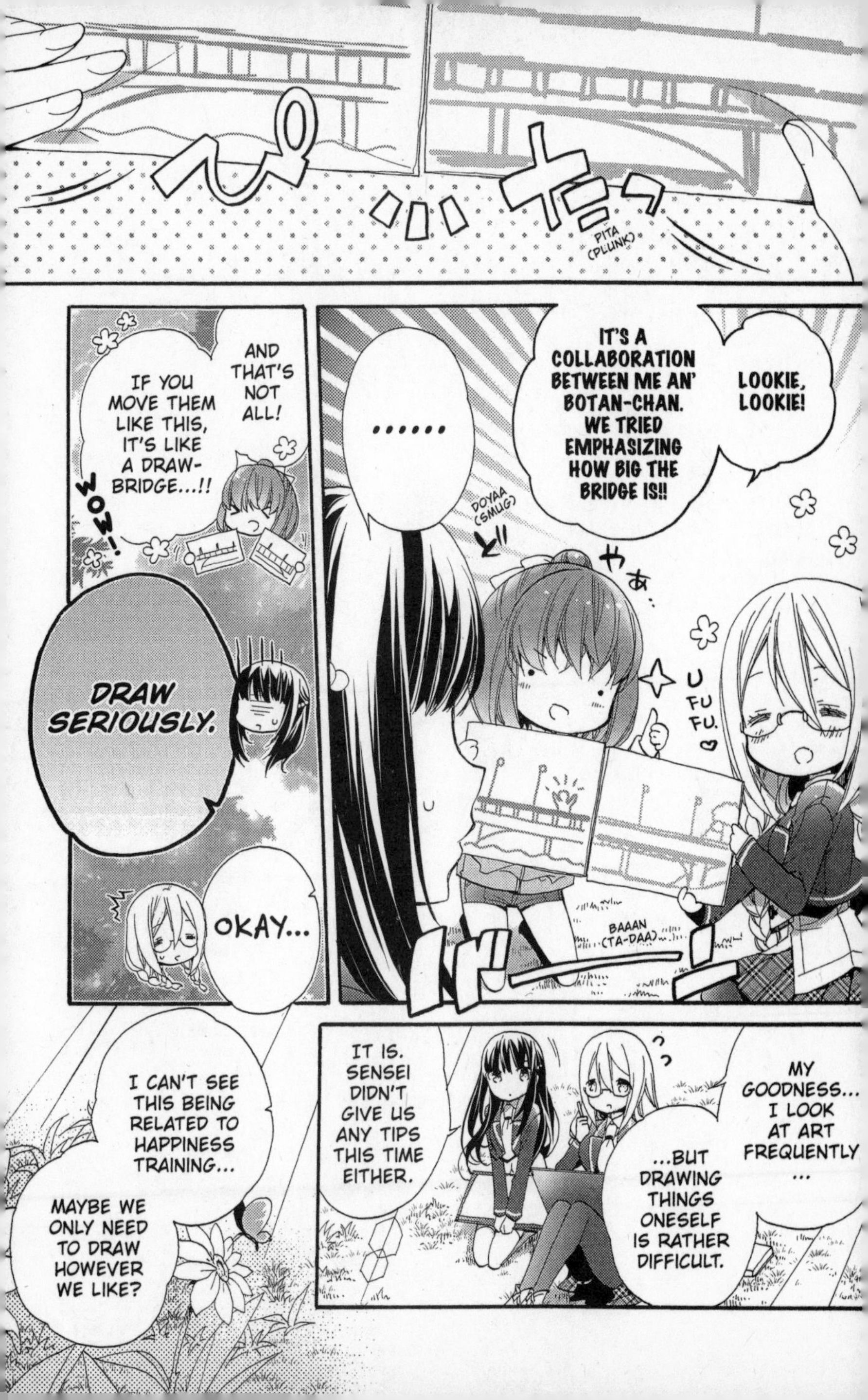
PITA (PLUNK)
LOOKIE, LOOKIE!
IT'S A COLLABORATION BETWEEN ME AN' BOTAN-CHAN. WE TRIED EMPHASIZING HOW BIG THE BRIDGE IS!!
UFUFU.
DOYAA (SMUG)
......
BAAAN (TA-DAA)
AND THAT'S NOT ALL!
IF YOU MOVE THEM LIKE THIS, IT'S LIKE A DRAW-BRIDGE...!!
WOW!
DRAW SERIOUSLY.
OKAY...
MY GOODNESS... I LOOK AT ART FREQUENTLY...
...BUT DRAWING THINGS ONESELF IS RATHER DIFFICULT.
IT IS. SENSEI DIDN'T GIVE US ANY TIPS THIS TIME EITHER.
I CAN'T SEE THIS BEING RELATED TO HAPPINESS TRAINING...
MAYBE WE ONLY NEED TO DRAW HOWEVER WE LIKE?

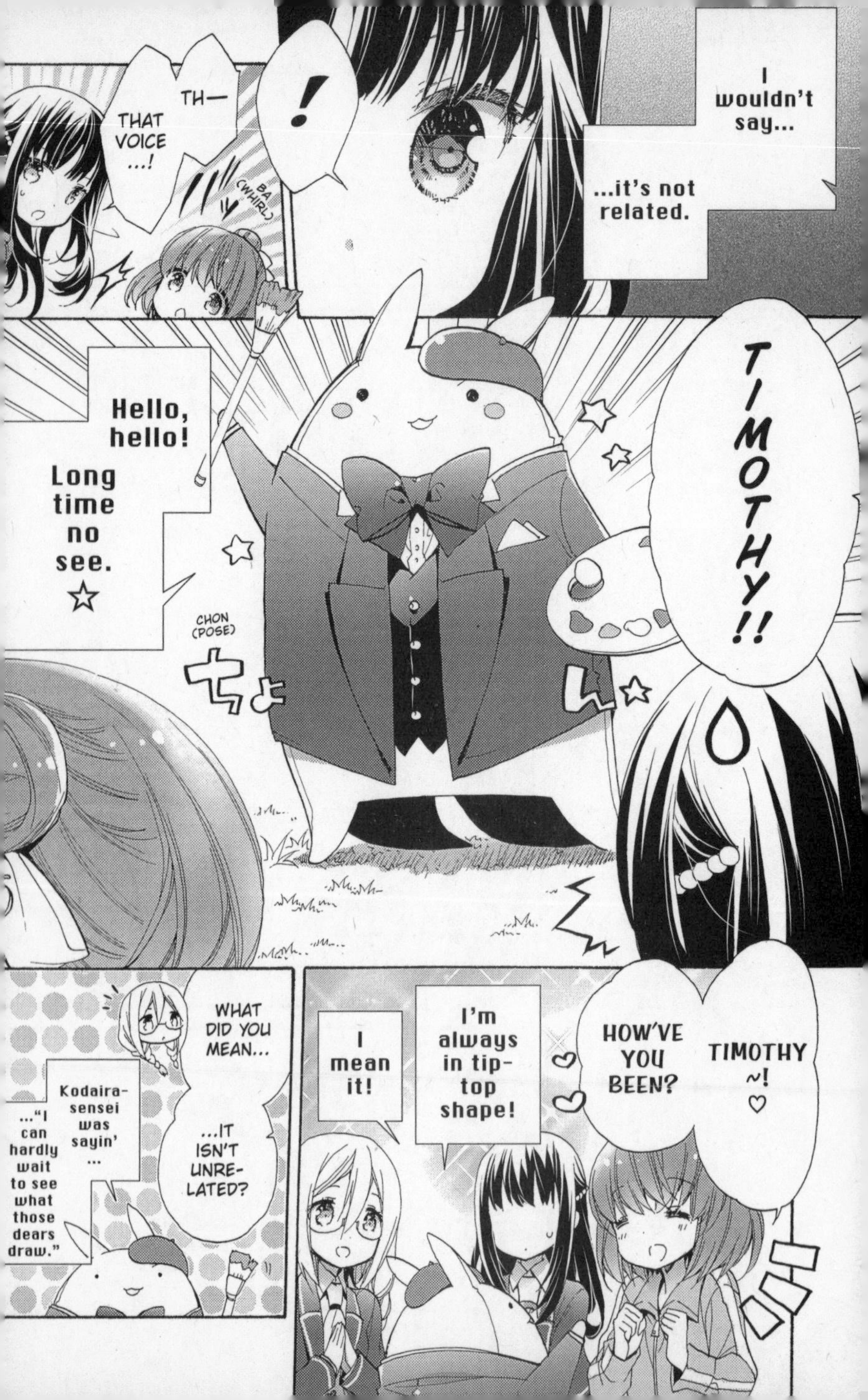
I wouldn't say...
...it's not related.
!
TH—
THAT VOICE ...!
BA (WHIRL)
TIMOTHY!!
Hello, hello!
Long time no see. ☆
CHON (POSE)
TIMOTHY ~! ♡
HOW'VE YOU BEEN?
I'm always in tip-top shape!
I mean it!
WHAT DID YOU MEAN...
...IT ISN'T UNRELATED?
Kodaira-sensei was sayin'...
..."I can hardly wait to see what those dears draw."

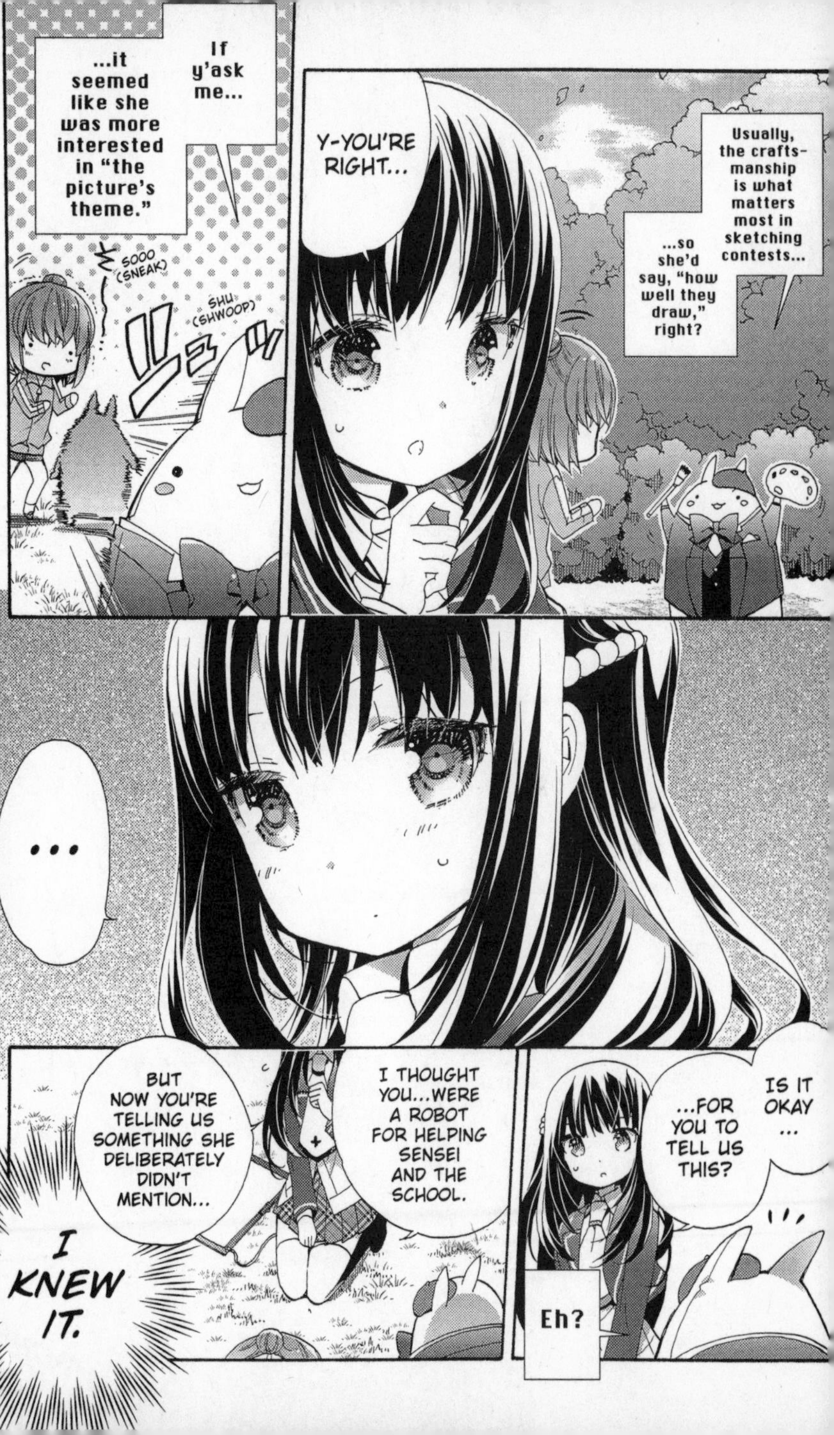

Usually, the craftsmanship is what matters most in sketching contests...
...so she'd say, "how well they draw," right?
Y-YOU'RE RIGHT...
If y'ask me...
...it seemed like she was more interested in "the picture's theme."
SOOO (SNEAK)
SHU (SHWOOP)
...
IS IT OKAY...
...FOR YOU TO TELL US THIS?
Eh?
I THOUGHT YOU...WERE A ROBOT FOR HELPING SENSEI AND THE SCHOOL.
BUT NOW YOU'RE TELLING US SOMETHING SHE DELIBERATELY DIDN'T MENTION...
I KNEW IT.

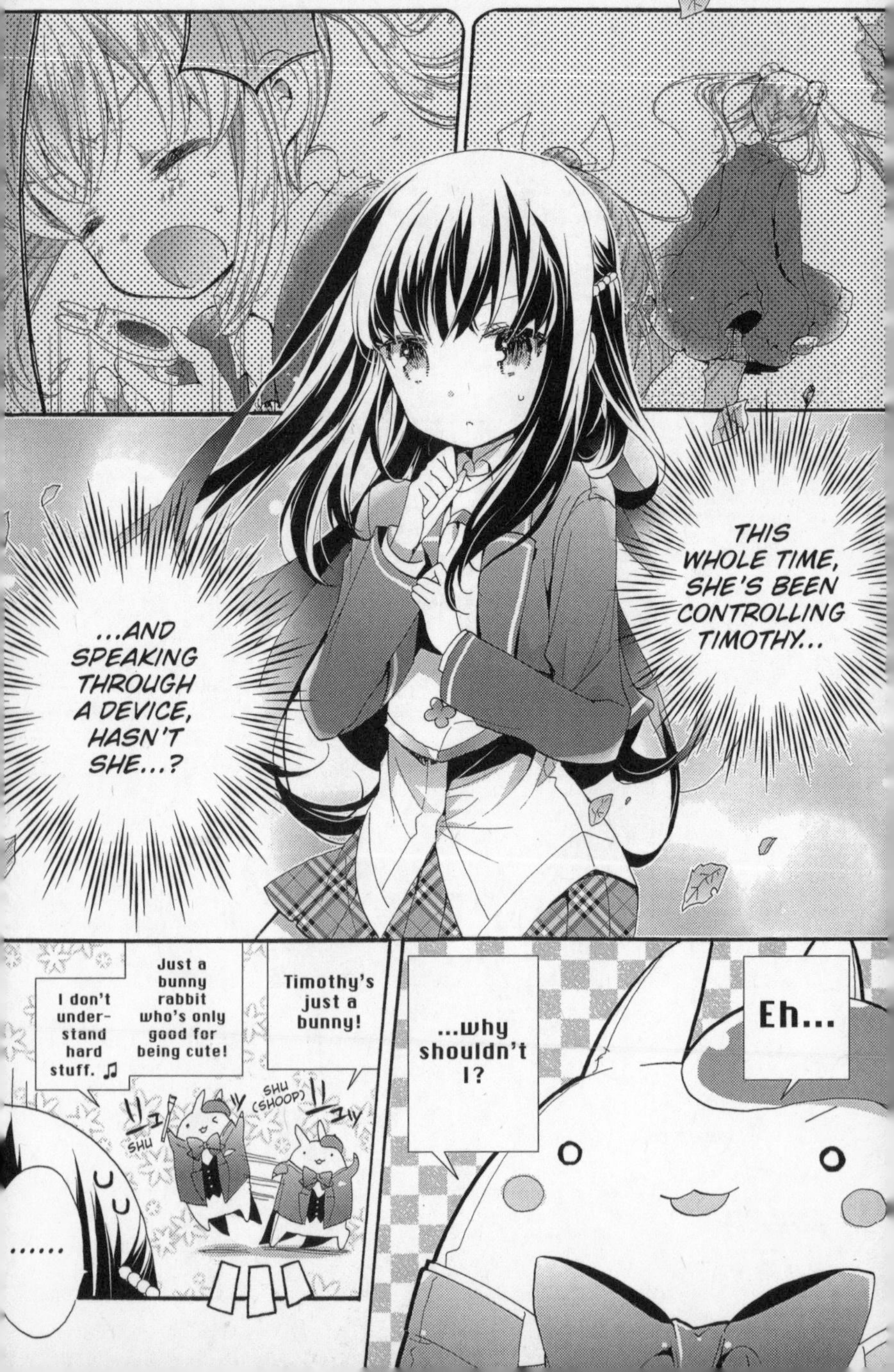
THIS WHOLE TIME, SHE'S BEEN CONTROLLING TIMOTHY...
...AND SPEAKING THROUGH A DEVICE, HASN'T SHE...?
Eh...
...why shouldn't I?
Timothy's just a bunny!
Just a bunny rabbit who's only good for being cute!
I don't under-stand hard stuff. ♫
SHU (SHOOP)
SHU
......

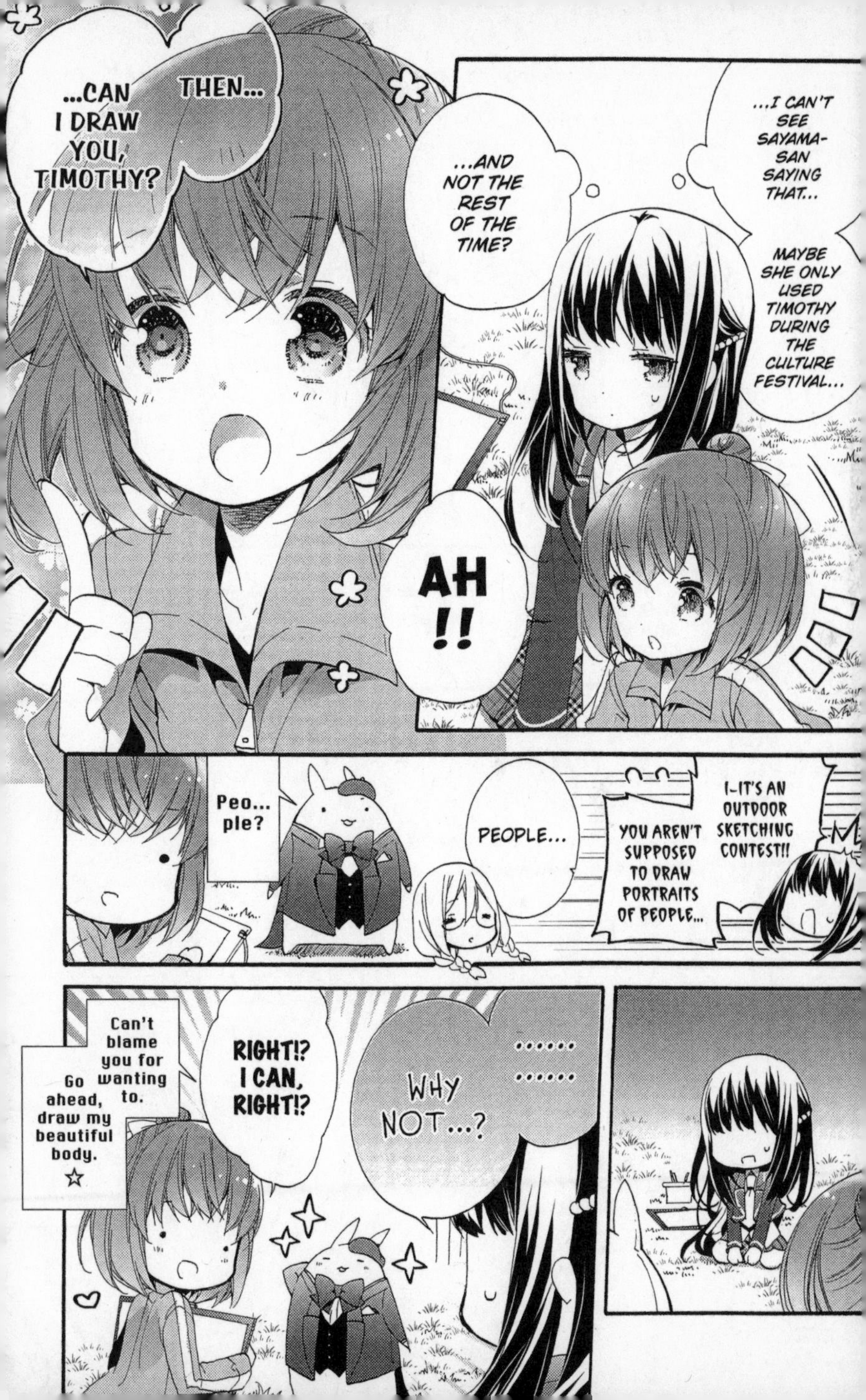
...I CAN'T SEE SAYAMA-SAN SAYING THAT...
MAYBE SHE ONLY USED TIMOTHY DURING THE CULTURE FESTIVAL...
...AND NOT THE REST OF THE TIME?
AH !!
THEN...
...CAN I DRAW YOU, TIMOTHY?
I-IT'S AN OUTDOOR SKETCHING CONTEST!!
YOU AREN'T SUPPOSED TO DRAW PORTRAITS OF PEOPLE...
PEOPLE...
Peo... ple?
......
......
WHY NOT...?
RIGHT!? I CAN, RIGHT!?
Can't blame you for wanting to.
Go ahead, draw my beautiful body. ☆

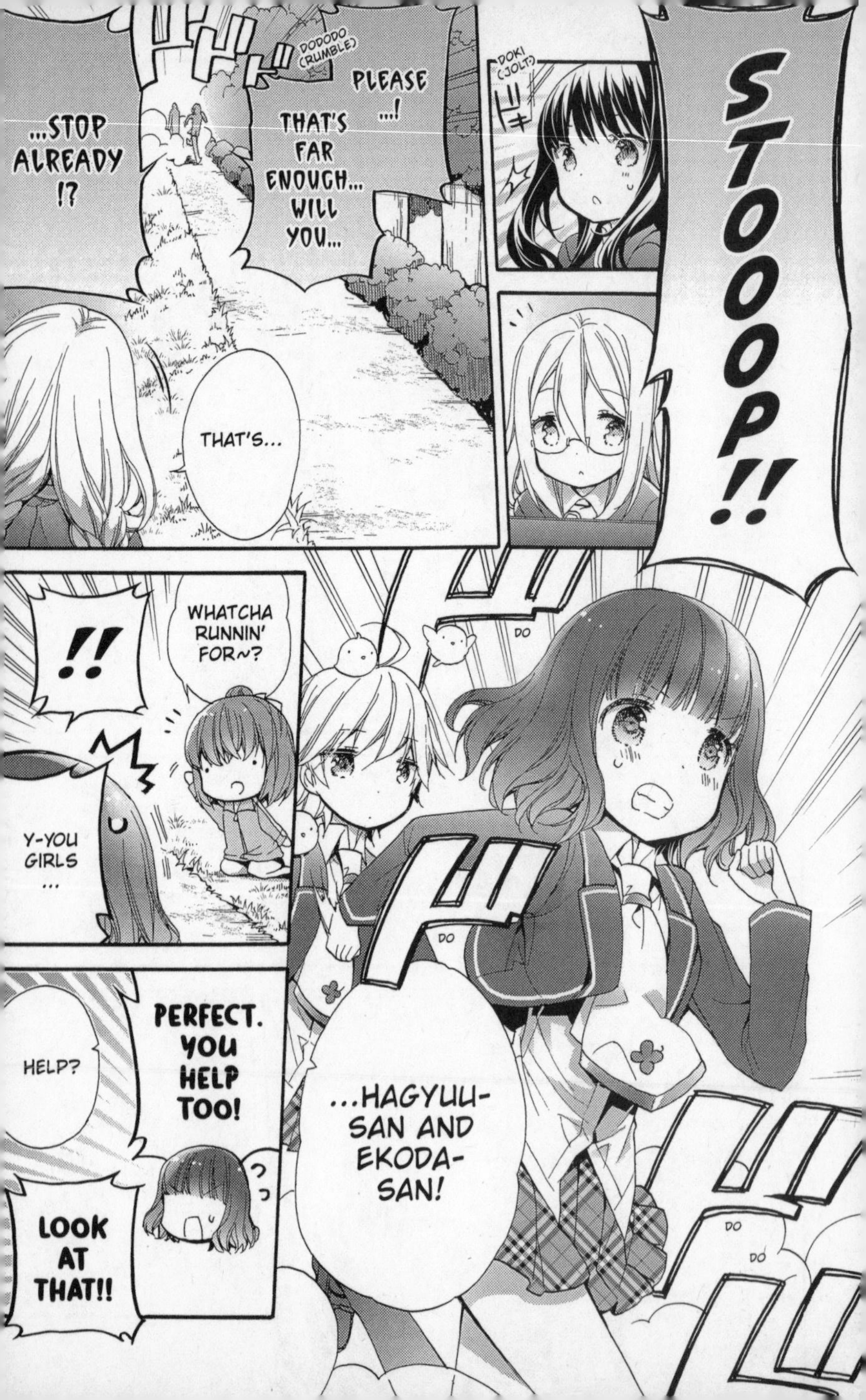
DOKI (JOLT)
STOOOP!!
DODODO (RUMBLE)
PLEASE ...!
THAT'S FAR ENOUGH... WILL YOU...
...STOP ALREADY !?
THAT'S...
DO
DO
DO
DO
...HAGYUU-SAN AND EKODA-SAN!
WHATCHA RUNNIN' FOR~?
!!
Y-YOU GIRLS ...
PERFECT. YOU HELP TOO!
HELP?
LOOK AT THAT!!

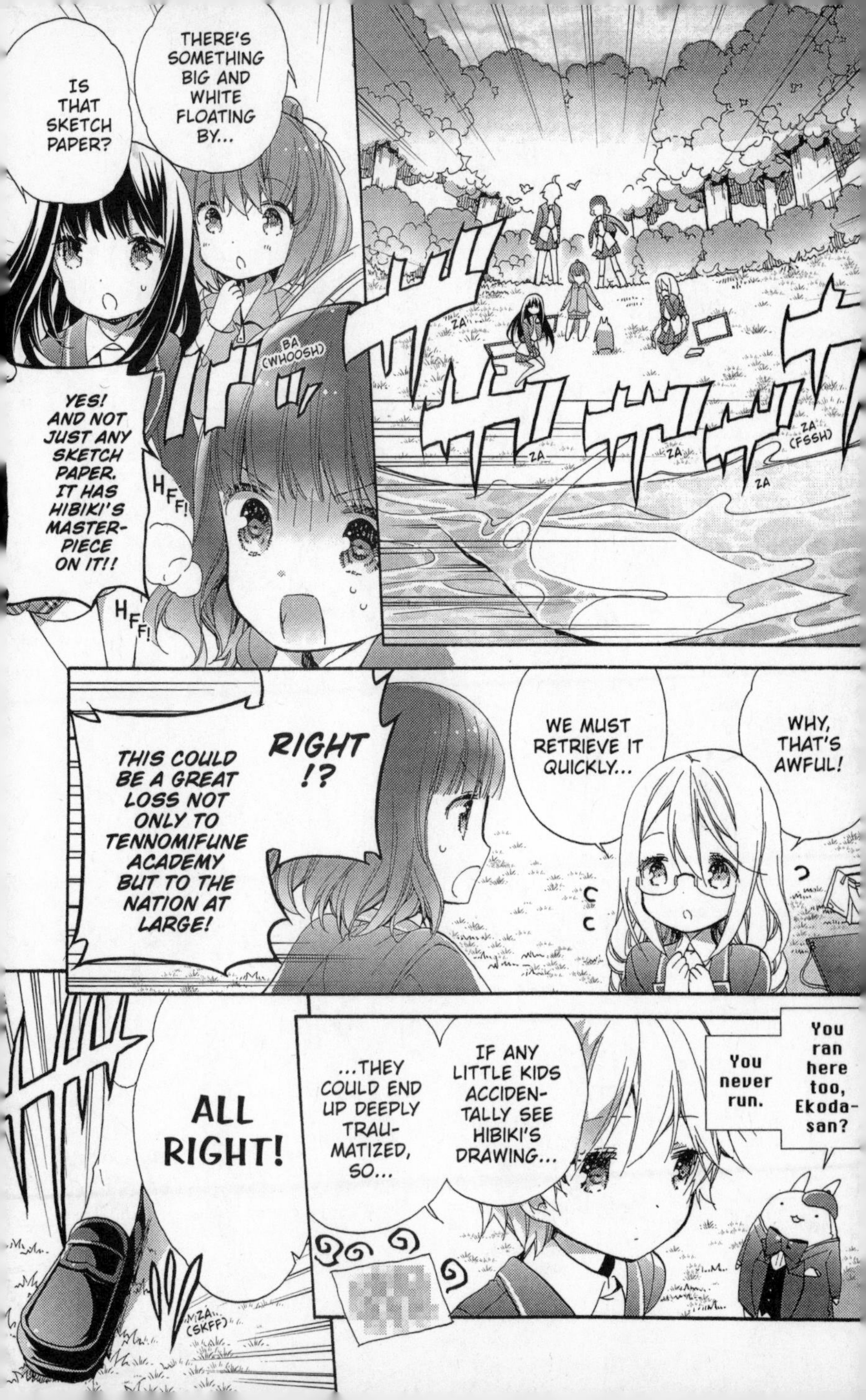
ZA
ZA
ZA (FSSH)
ZA
ZA
THERE'S SOMETHING BIG AND WHITE FLOATING BY...
IS THAT SKETCH PAPER?
BA (WHOOSH)
YES! AND NOT JUST ANY SKETCH PAPER. IT HAS HIBIKI'S MASTERPIECE ON IT!!
HFF!
HFF!
WHY, THAT'S AWFUL!
WE MUST RETRIEVE IT QUICKLY...
RIGHT!?
THIS COULD BE A GREAT LOSS NOT ONLY TO TENNOMIFUNE ACADEMY BUT TO THE NATION AT LARGE!
You ran here too, Ekoda-san?
You never run.
IF ANY LITTLE KIDS ACCIDENTALLY SEE HIBIKI'S DRAWING...
...THEY COULD END UP DEEPLY TRAUMATIZED, SO...
ALL RIGHT!
ZA (SKFF)

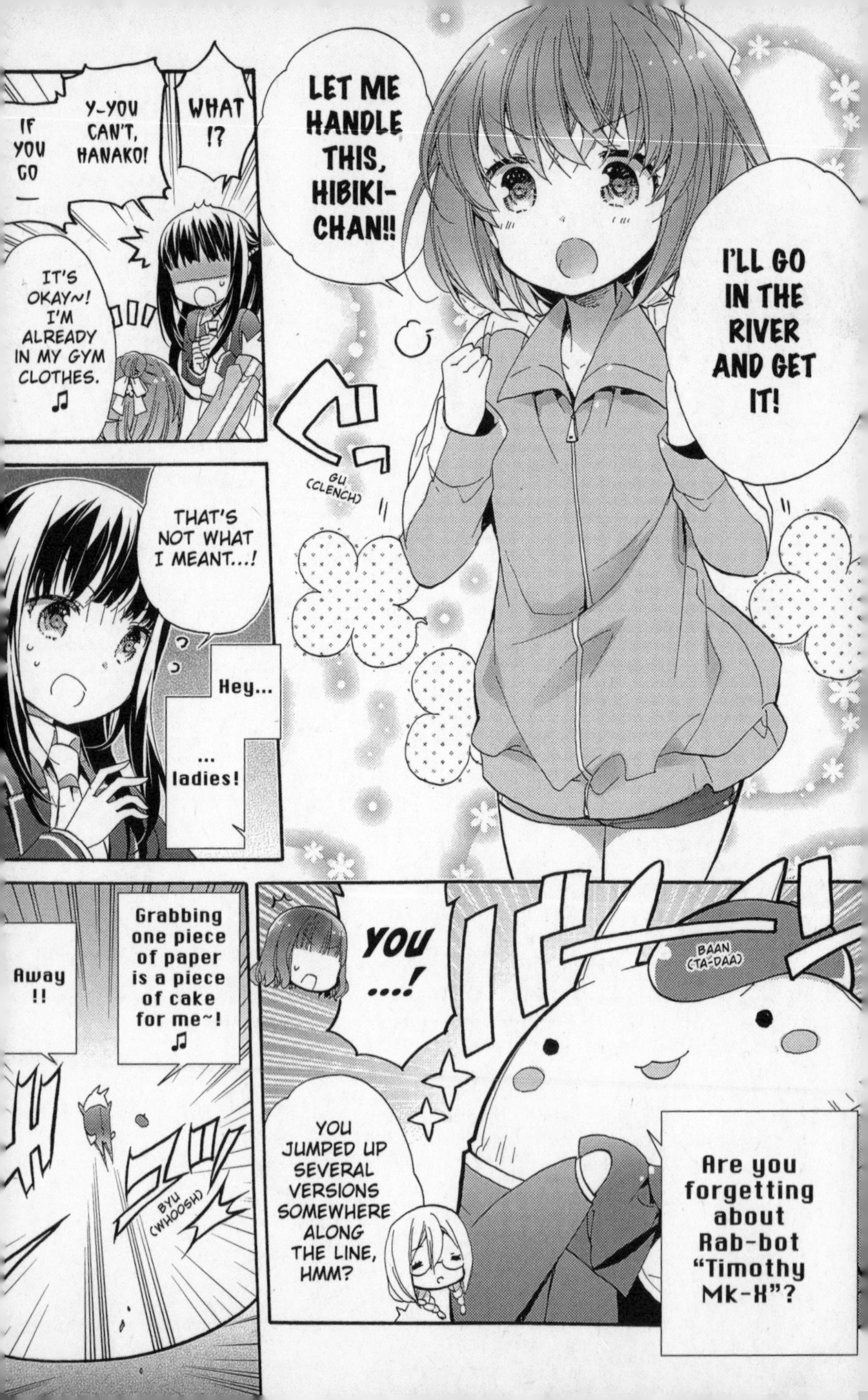
LET ME HANDLE THIS, HIBIKI-CHAN!!
I'LL GO IN THE RIVER AND GET IT!
GU (CLENCH)
WHAT !?
Y-YOU CAN'T, HANAKO!
IF YOU GO —
IT'S OKAY~! I'M ALREADY IN MY GYM CLOTHES. ♫
THAT'S NOT WHAT I MEANT...!
Hey...
... ladies!
YOU ...!
BAAN (TA-DAA)
Are you forgetting about Rab-bot "Timothy Mk-X"?
YOU JUMPED UP SEVERAL VERSIONS SOMEWHERE ALONG THE LINE, HMM?
Grabbing one piece of paper is a piece of cake for me~! ♫
Away !!
BYU (WHOOSH)

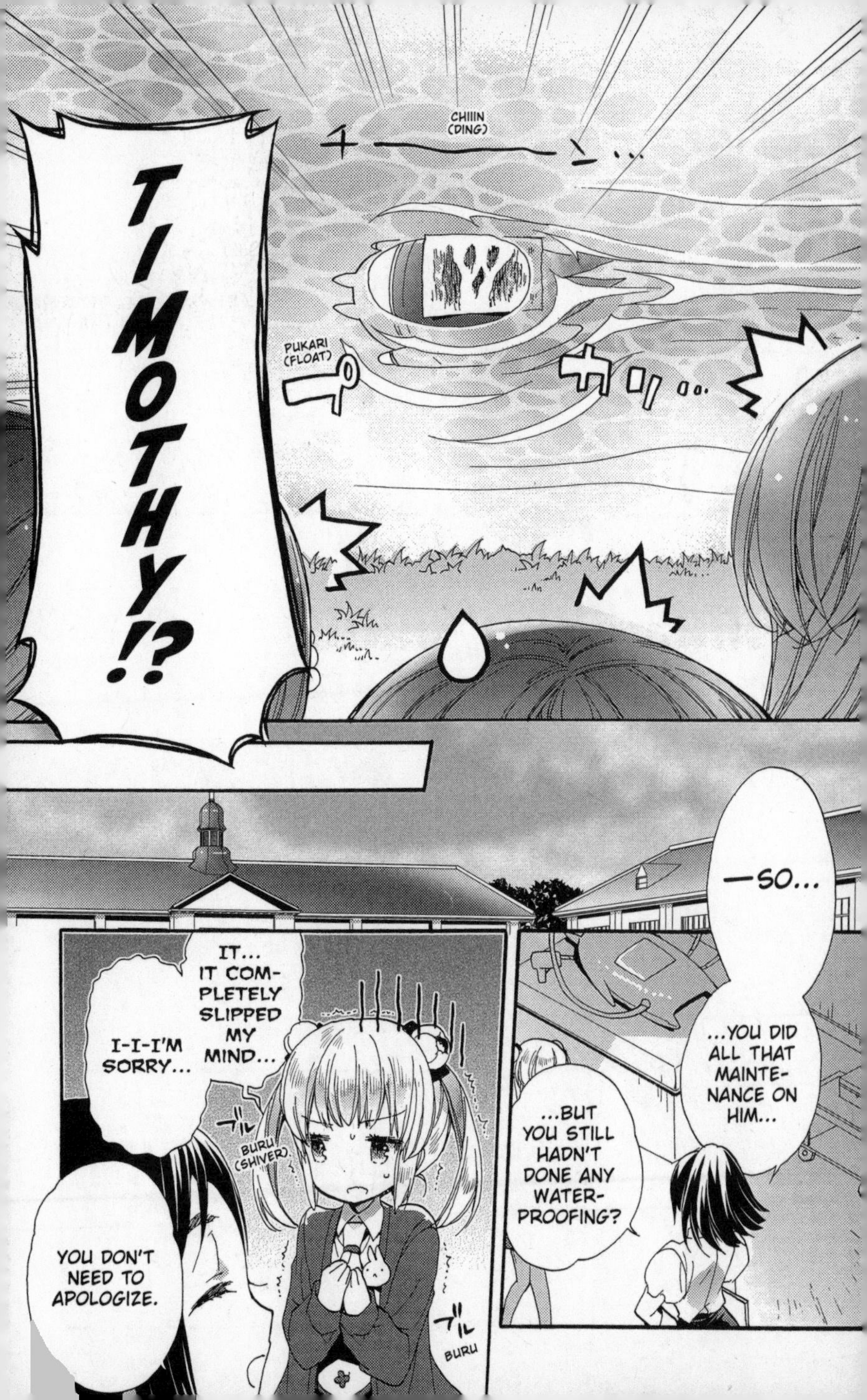
CHIIIN (DING)
PUKARI (FLOAT)
TIMOTHY!?
—SO...
...YOU DID ALL THAT MAINTE-NANCE ON HIM...
...BUT YOU STILL HADN'T DONE ANY WATER-PROOFING?
IT... IT COM-PLETELY SLIPPED MY MIND...
I-I-I'M SORRY...
BURU (SHIVER)
BURU
YOU DON'T NEED TO APOLOGIZE.

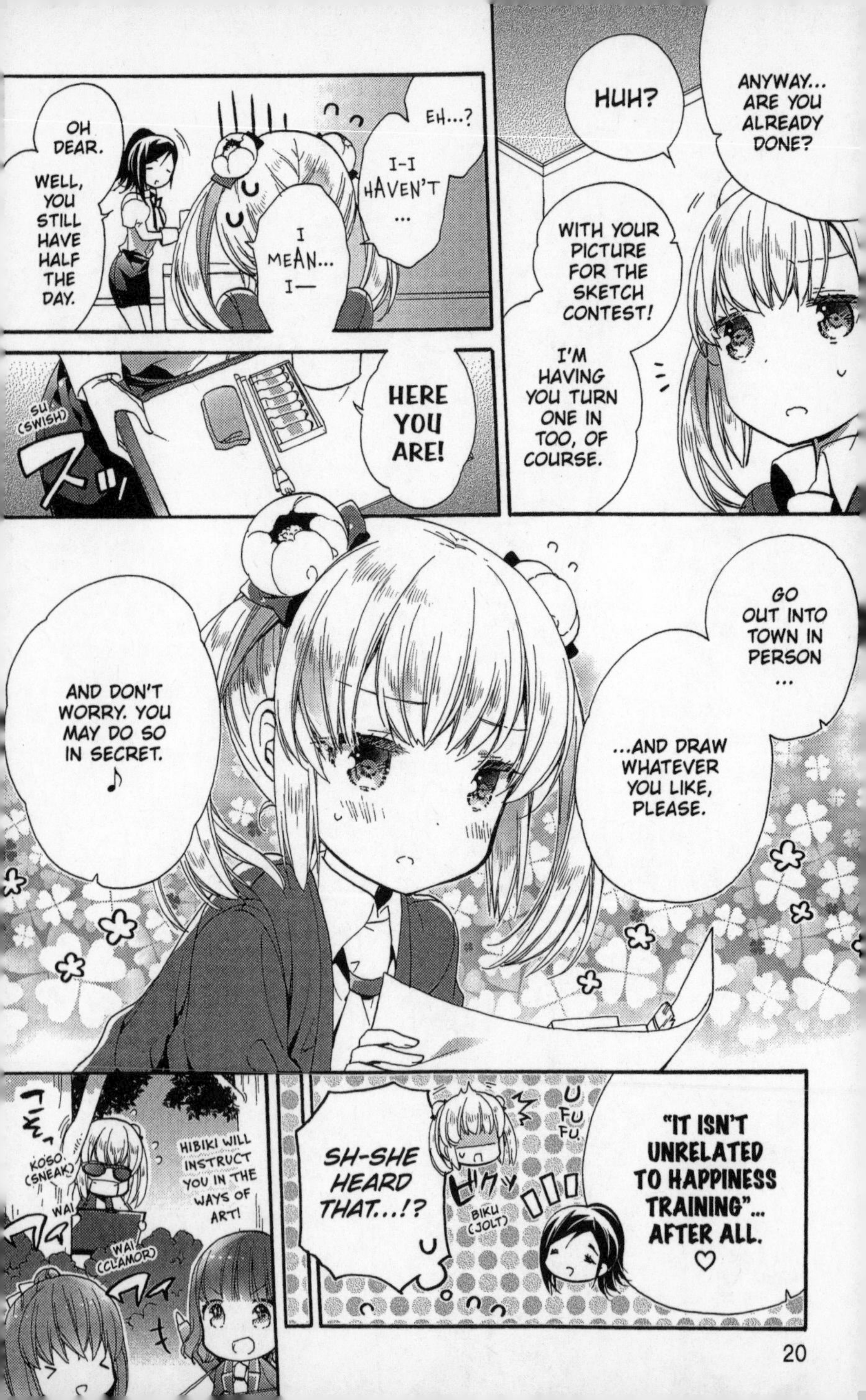
HUH?
ANYWAY... ARE YOU ALREADY DONE?
WITH YOUR PICTURE FOR THE SKETCH CONTEST!
I'M HAVING YOU TURN ONE IN TOO, OF COURSE.
EH...?
I-I HAVEN'T ...
I MEAN... I—
OH DEAR.
WELL, YOU STILL HAVE HALF THE DAY.
HERE YOU ARE!
SU (SWISH)
GO OUT INTO TOWN IN PERSON ...
...AND DRAW WHATEVER YOU LIKE, PLEASE.
AND DON'T WORRY. YOU MAY DO SO IN SECRET. ♪
UFUFU
"IT ISN'T UNRELATED TO HAPPINESS TRAINING"... AFTER ALL. ♡
BIKU (JOLT)
SH-SHE HEARD THAT...!?
HIBIKI WILL INSTRUCT YOU IN THE WAYS OF ART!
KOSO (SNEAK)
WAI
WAI (CLAMOR)

Anne Happy

unhappy go lucky!

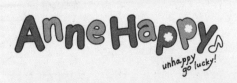

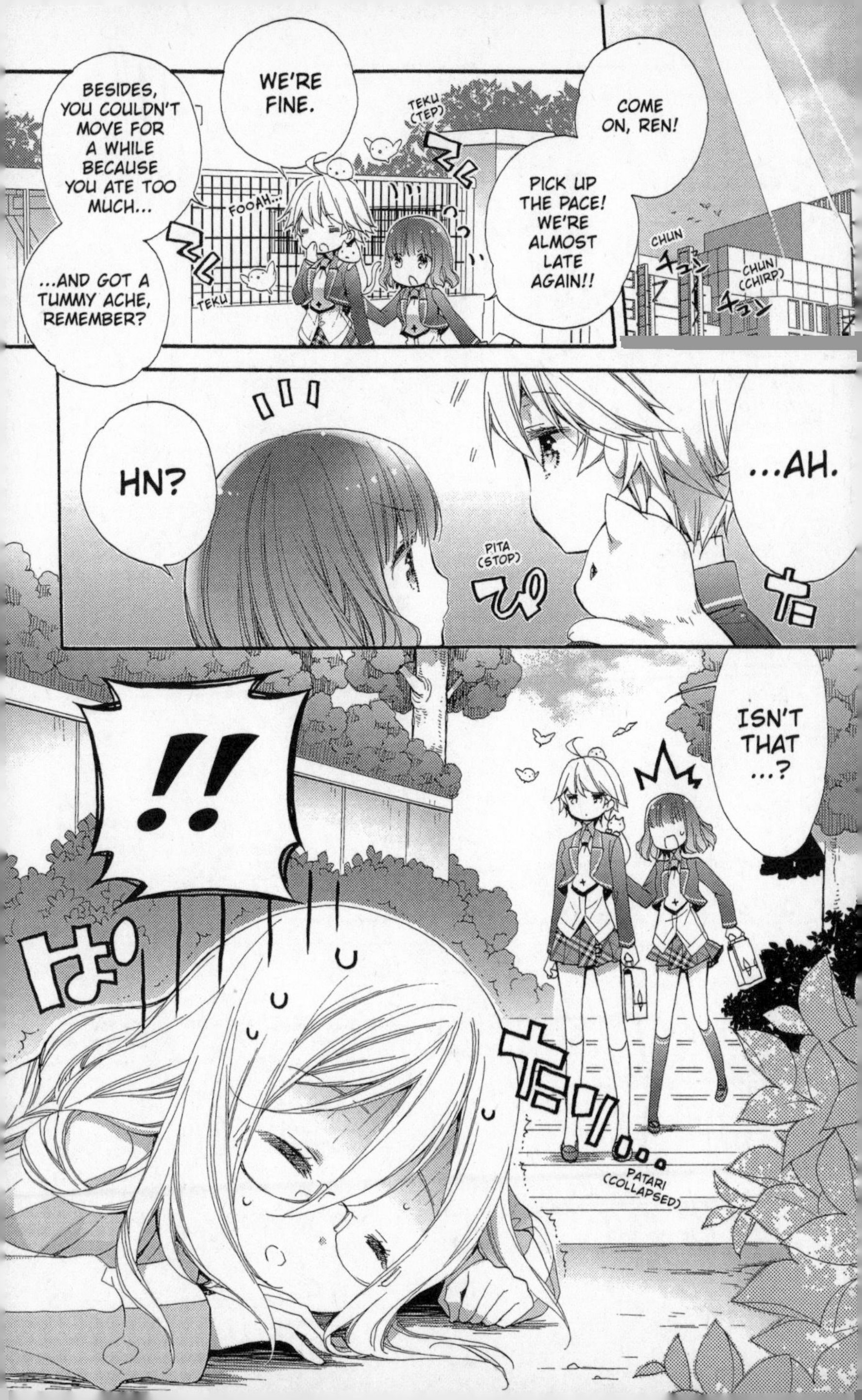
COME ON, REN!
PICK UP THE PACE! WE'RE ALMOST LATE AGAIN!!
CHUN
CHUN (CHIRP)
TEKU (TEP)
WE'RE FINE.
FOOAH...
BESIDES, YOU COULDN'T MOVE FOR A WHILE BECAUSE YOU ATE TOO MUCH...
...AND GOT A TUMMY ACHE, REMEMBER?
TEKU
...AH.
PITA (STOP)
HN?
ISN'T THAT ...?
PATARI (COLLAPSED)
!!

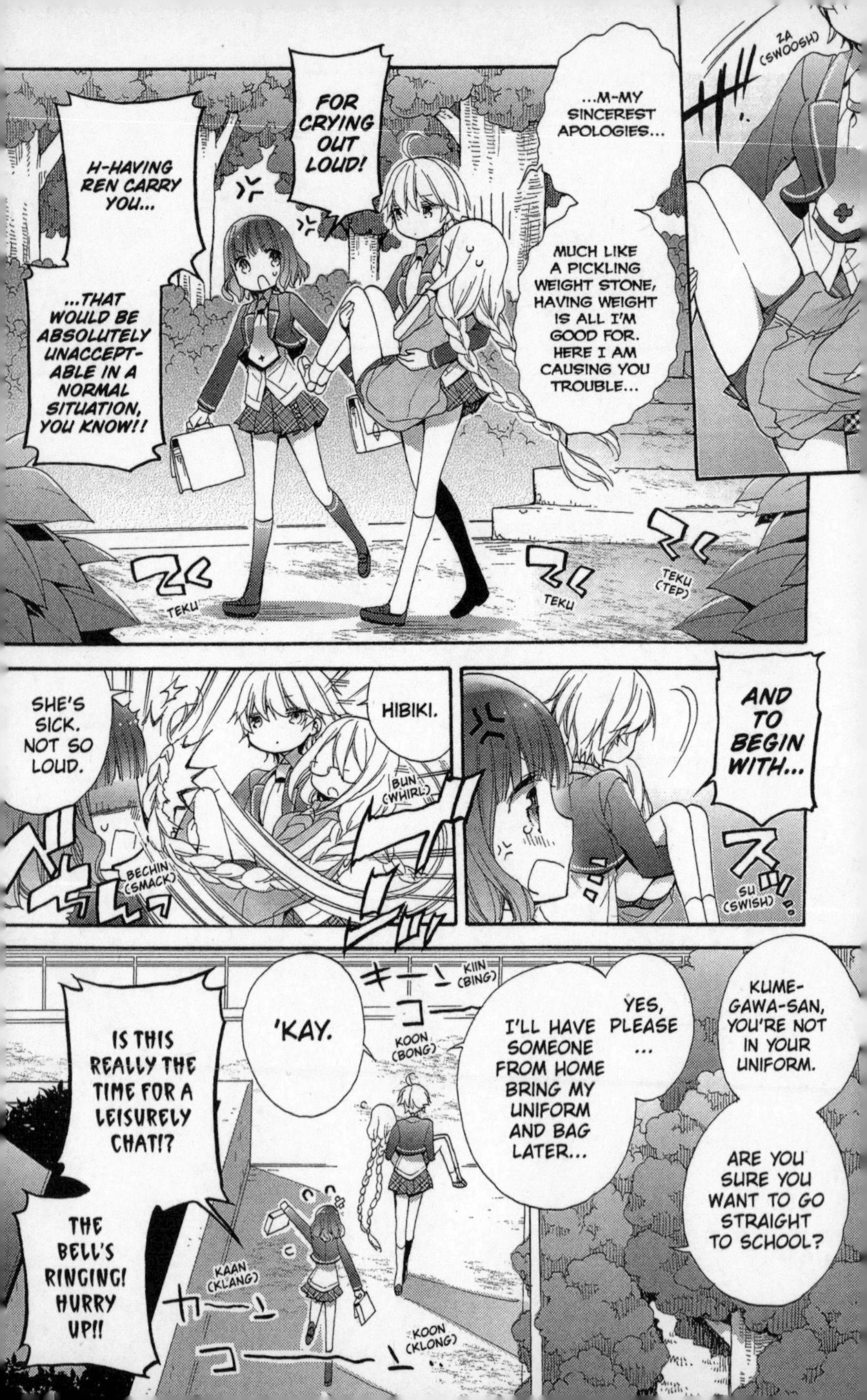
ZA (SWOOSH)
...M-MY SINCEREST APOLOGIES...
MUCH LIKE A PICKLING WEIGHT STONE, HAVING WEIGHT IS ALL I'M GOOD FOR. HERE I AM CAUSING YOU TROUBLE...
FOR CRYING OUT LOUD!
H-HAVING REN CARRY YOU...
...THAT WOULD BE ABSOLUTELY UNACCEPTABLE IN A NORMAL SITUATION, YOU KNOW!!
TEKU (TEP)
TEKU
TEKU
AND TO BEGIN WITH...
SU (SWISH)
HIBIKI.
BUN (WHIRL)
SHE'S SICK. NOT SO LOUD.
BECHIN (SMACK)
KUME-GAWA-SAN, YOU'RE NOT IN YOUR UNIFORM.
ARE YOU SURE YOU WANT TO GO STRAIGHT TO SCHOOL?
YES, PLEASE ...
I'LL HAVE SOMEONE FROM HOME BRING MY UNIFORM AND BAG LATER...
KIIN (BING)
'KAY.
KOON (BONG)
IS THIS REALLY THE TIME FOR A LEISURELY CHAT!?
THE BELL'S RINGING! HURRY UP!!
KAAN (KLANG)
KOON (KLONG)

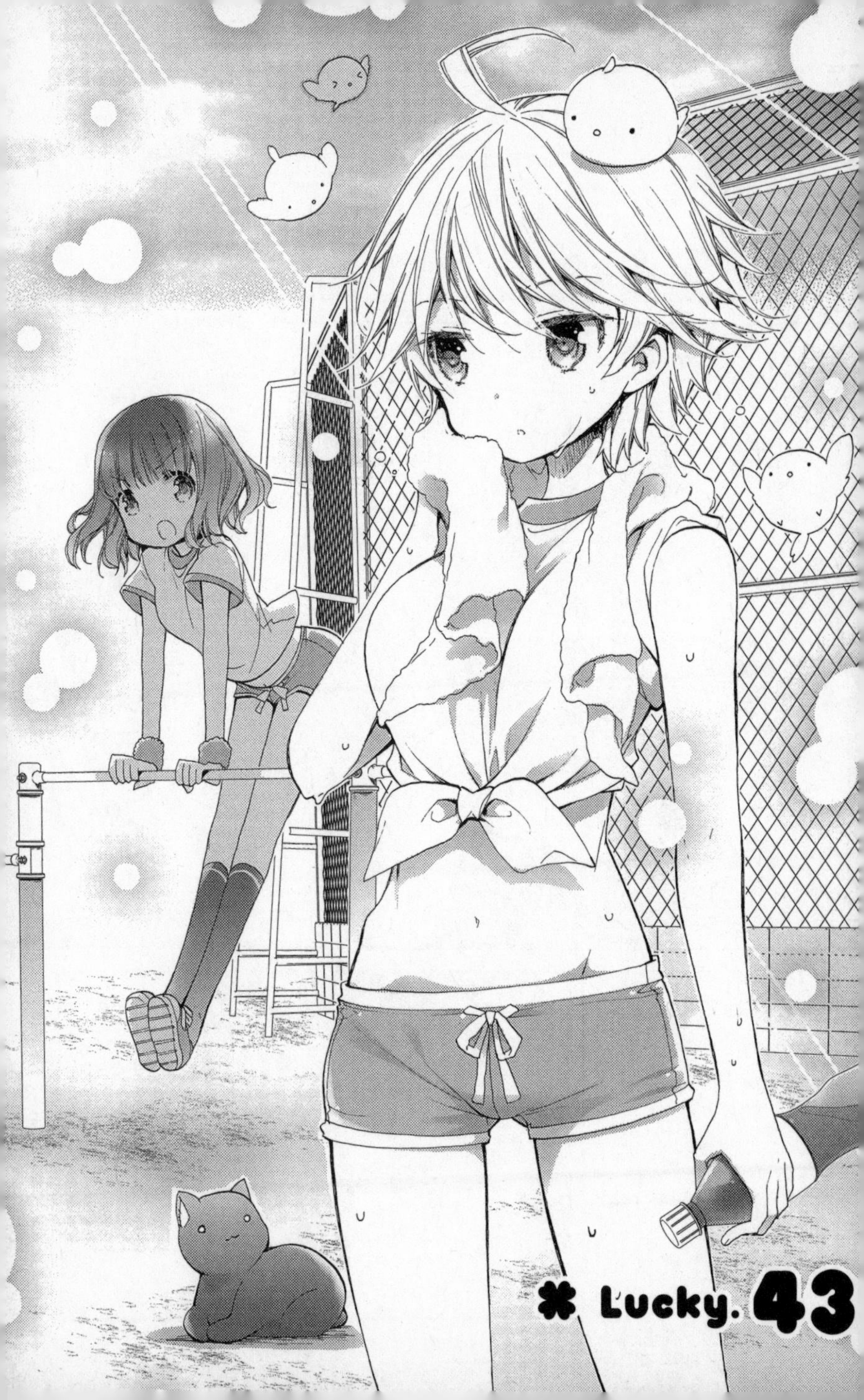
Lucky. 43

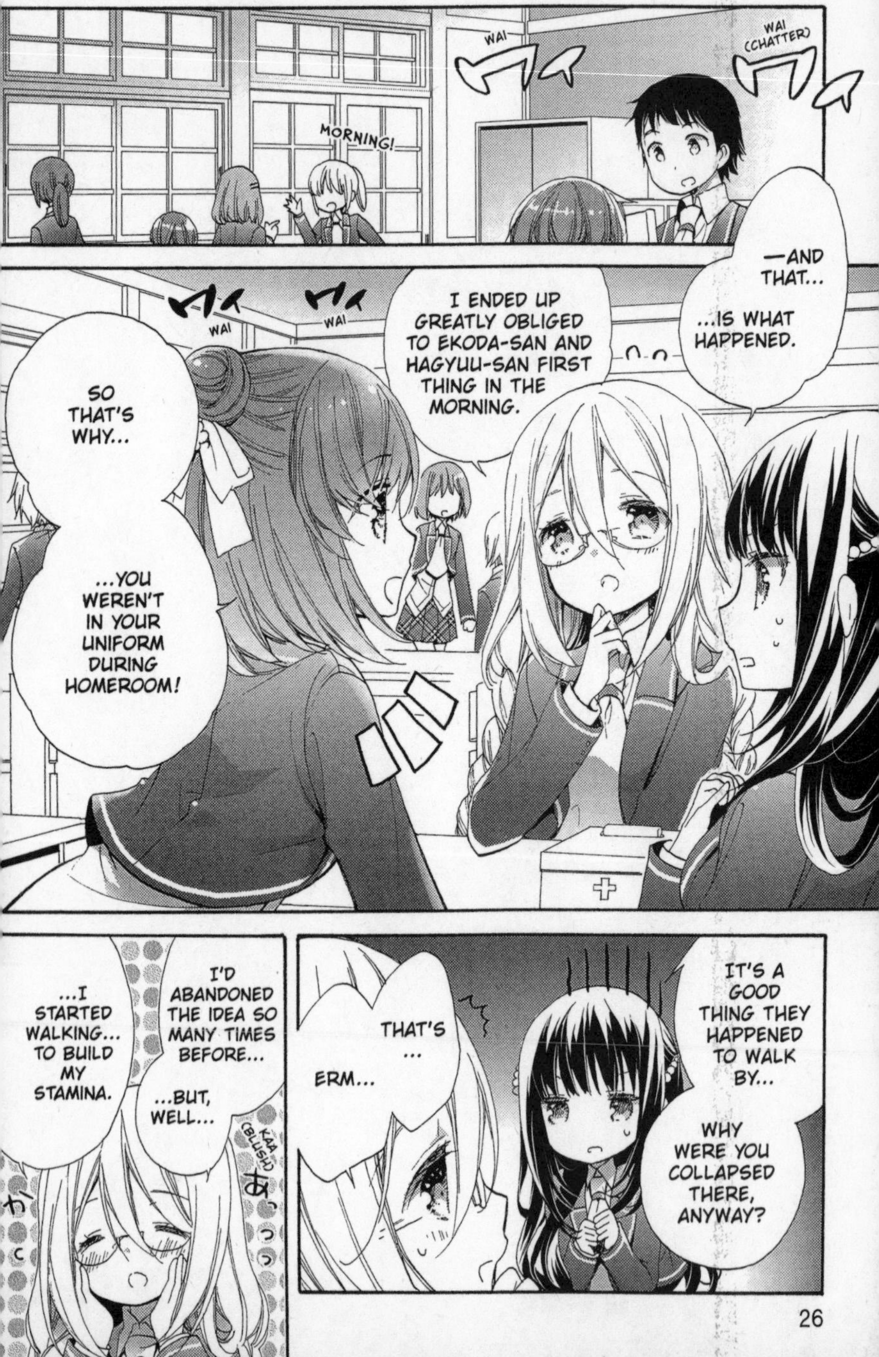
WAI (CHATTER)
WAI
MORNING!
—AND THAT...
...IS WHAT HAPPENED.
I ENDED UP GREATLY OBLIGED TO EKODA-SAN AND HAGYUU-SAN FIRST THING IN THE MORNING.
WAI
WAI
SO THAT'S WHY...
...YOU WEREN'T IN YOUR UNIFORM DURING HOMEROOM!
IT'S A GOOD THING THEY HAPPENED TO WALK BY...
WHY WERE YOU COLLAPSED THERE, ANYWAY?
THAT'S ...
ERM...
I'D ABANDONED THE IDEA SO MANY TIMES BEFORE...
...BUT, WELL...
KAA (BLUSH)
...I STARTED WALKING... TO BUILD MY STAMINA.

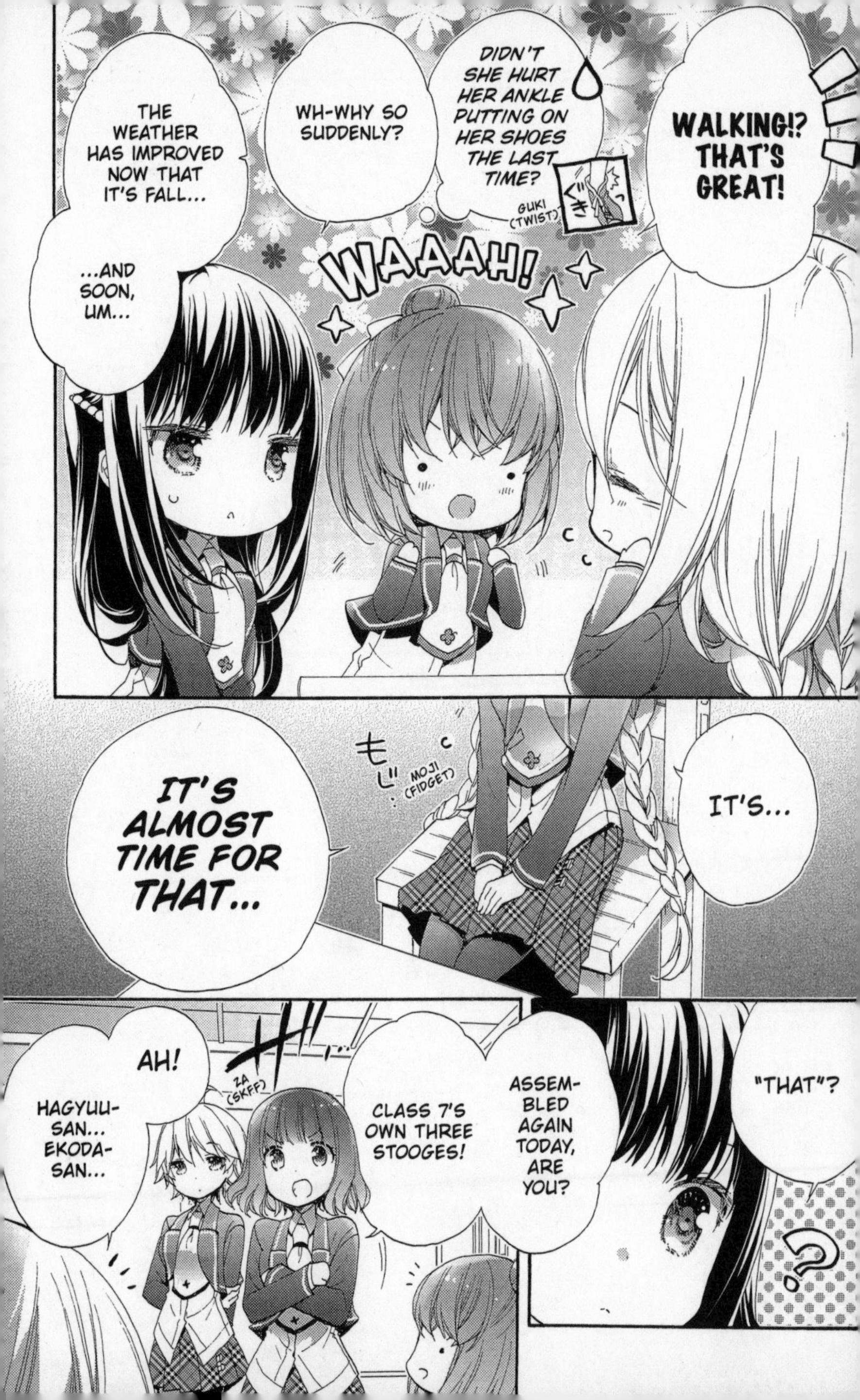
WALKING!? THAT'S GREAT!
DIDN'T SHE HURT HER ANKLE PUTTING ON HER SHOES THE LAST TIME?
GUKI (TWIST)
WH-WHY SO SUDDENLY?
THE WEATHER HAS IMPROVED NOW THAT IT'S FALL...
WAAAH!
...AND SOON, UM...
IT'S...
MOJI (FIDGET)
IT'S ALMOST TIME FOR THAT...
"THAT"?
ASSEM-BLED AGAIN TODAY, ARE YOU?
CLASS 7'S OWN THREE STOOGES!
ZA (SKFF)
AH!
HAGYUU-SAN... EKODA-SAN...

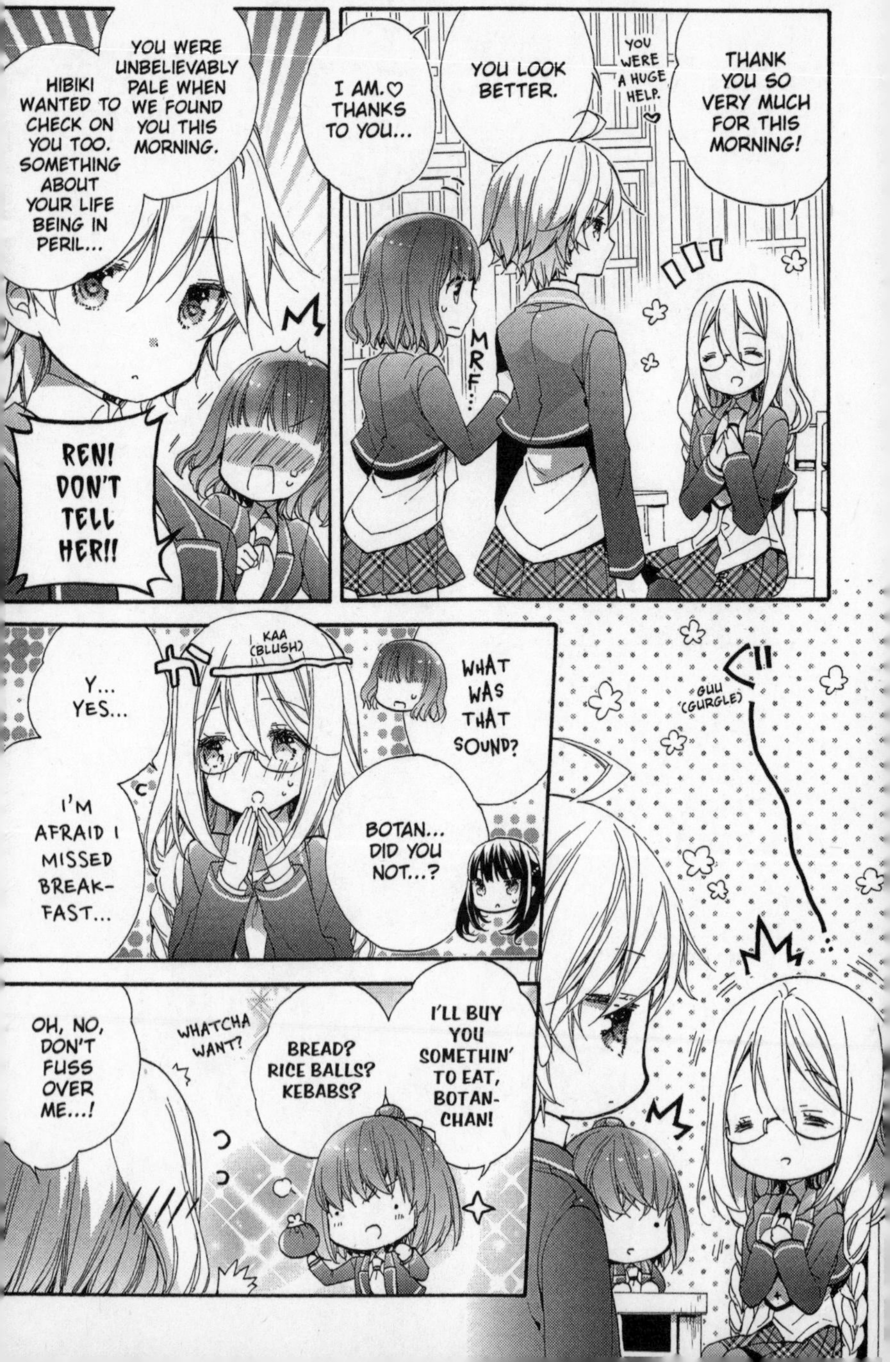
THANK YOU SO VERY MUCH FOR THIS MORNING!
YOU WERE A HUGE HELP. ♡
YOU LOOK BETTER.
I AM.♡ THANKS TO YOU...
MRF...
YOU WERE UNBELIEVABLY PALE WHEN WE FOUND YOU THIS MORNING.
HIBIKI WANTED TO CHECK ON YOU TOO. SOMETHING ABOUT YOUR LIFE BEING IN PERIL...
REN! DON'T TELL HER!!
GUU (GURGLE)
WHAT WAS THAT SOUND?
KAA (BLUSH)
BOTAN... DID YOU NOT...?
Y... YES...
I'M AFRAID I MISSED BREAKFAST...
I'LL BUY YOU SOMETHIN' TO EAT, BOTAN-CHAN!
BREAD? RICE BALLS? KEBABS?
WHATCHA WANT?
OH, NO, DON'T FUSS OVER ME...!

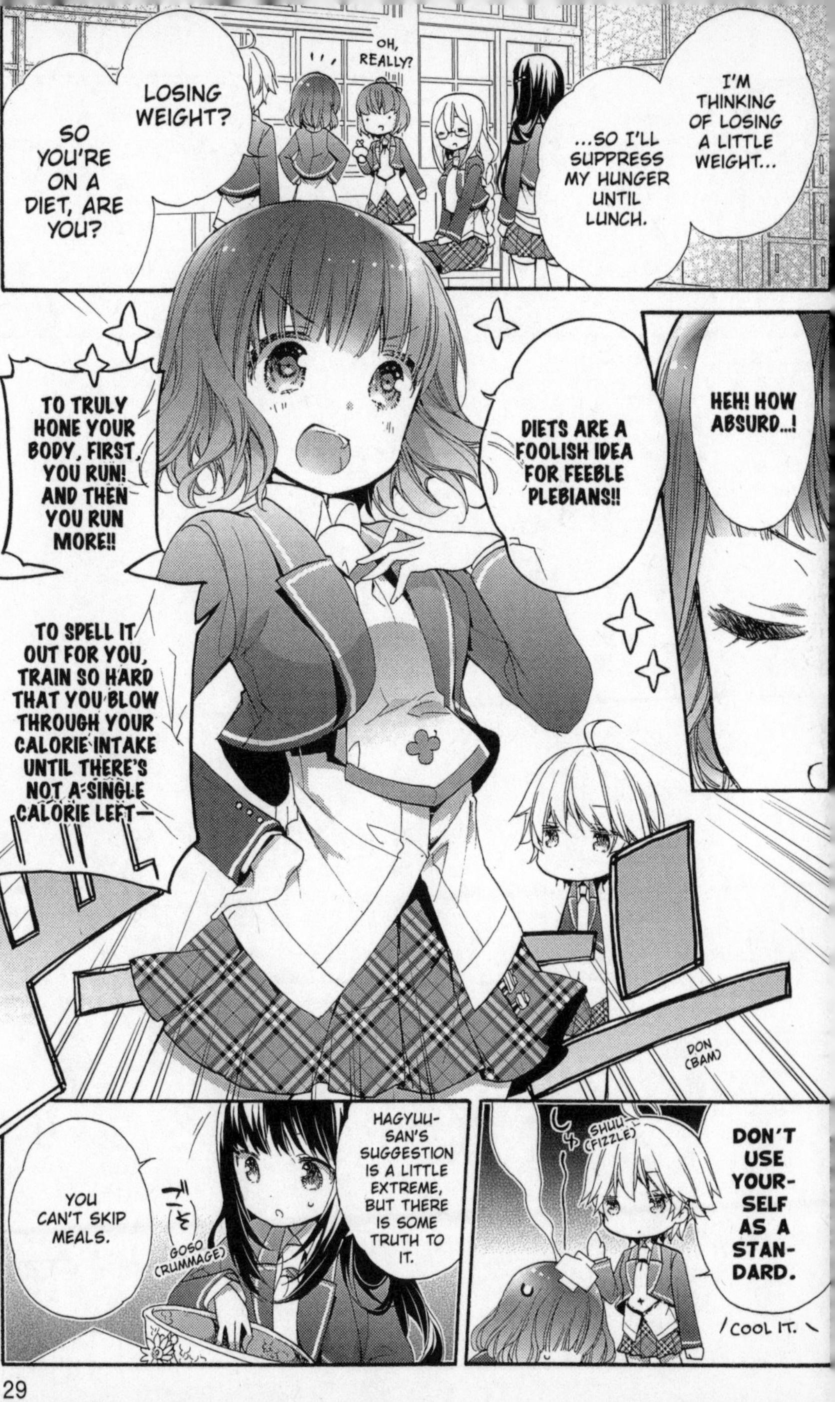
I'M THINKING OF LOSING A LITTLE WEIGHT...
...SO I'LL SUPPRESS MY HUNGER UNTIL LUNCH.
OH, REALLY?
LOSING WEIGHT?
SO YOU'RE ON A DIET, ARE YOU?
HEH! HOW ABSURD...!
DIETS ARE A FOOLISH IDEA FOR FEEBLE PLEBIANS!!
TO TRULY HONE YOUR BODY, FIRST, YOU RUN! AND THEN YOU RUN MORE!!
TO SPELL IT OUT FOR YOU, TRAIN SO HARD THAT YOU BLOW THROUGH YOUR CALORIE INTAKE UNTIL THERE'S NOT A SINGLE CALORIE LEFT—
DON (BAM)
SHUU (FIZZLE)
DON'T USE YOURSELF AS A STANDARD.
COOL IT.
HAGYUU-SAN'S SUGGESTION IS A LITTLE EXTREME, BUT THERE IS SOME TRUTH TO IT.
GOSO (RUMMAGE)
YOU CAN'T SKIP MEALS.

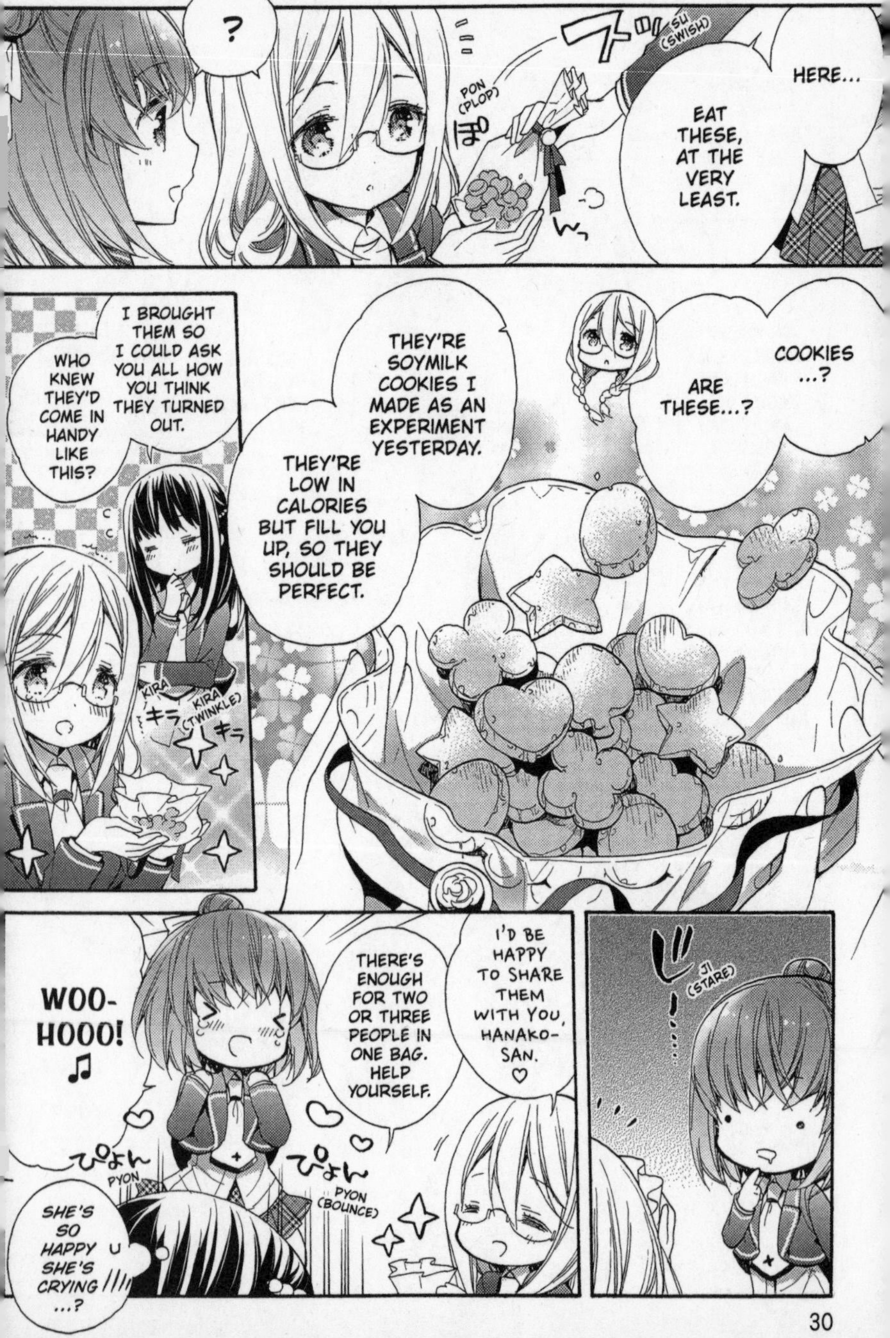

HERE...
EAT THESE, AT THE VERY LEAST.
SU (SWISH)
PON (PLOP)
?
ARE THESE...?
COOKIES ...?
THEY'RE SOYMILK COOKIES I MADE AS AN EXPERIMENT YESTERDAY.
THEY'RE LOW IN CALORIES BUT FILL YOU UP, SO THEY SHOULD BE PERFECT.
I BROUGHT THEM SO I COULD ASK YOU ALL HOW YOU THINK THEY TURNED OUT.
WHO KNEW THEY'D COME IN HANDY LIKE THIS?
KIRA KIRA (TWINKLE)
JI (STARE)
I'D BE HAPPY TO SHARE THEM WITH YOU, HANAKO-SAN. ♡
THERE'S ENOUGH FOR TWO OR THREE PEOPLE IN ONE BAG. HELP YOURSELF.
WOO-HOOO! ♫
PYON
PYON (BOUNCE)
SHE'S SO HAPPY SHE'S CRYING ...?

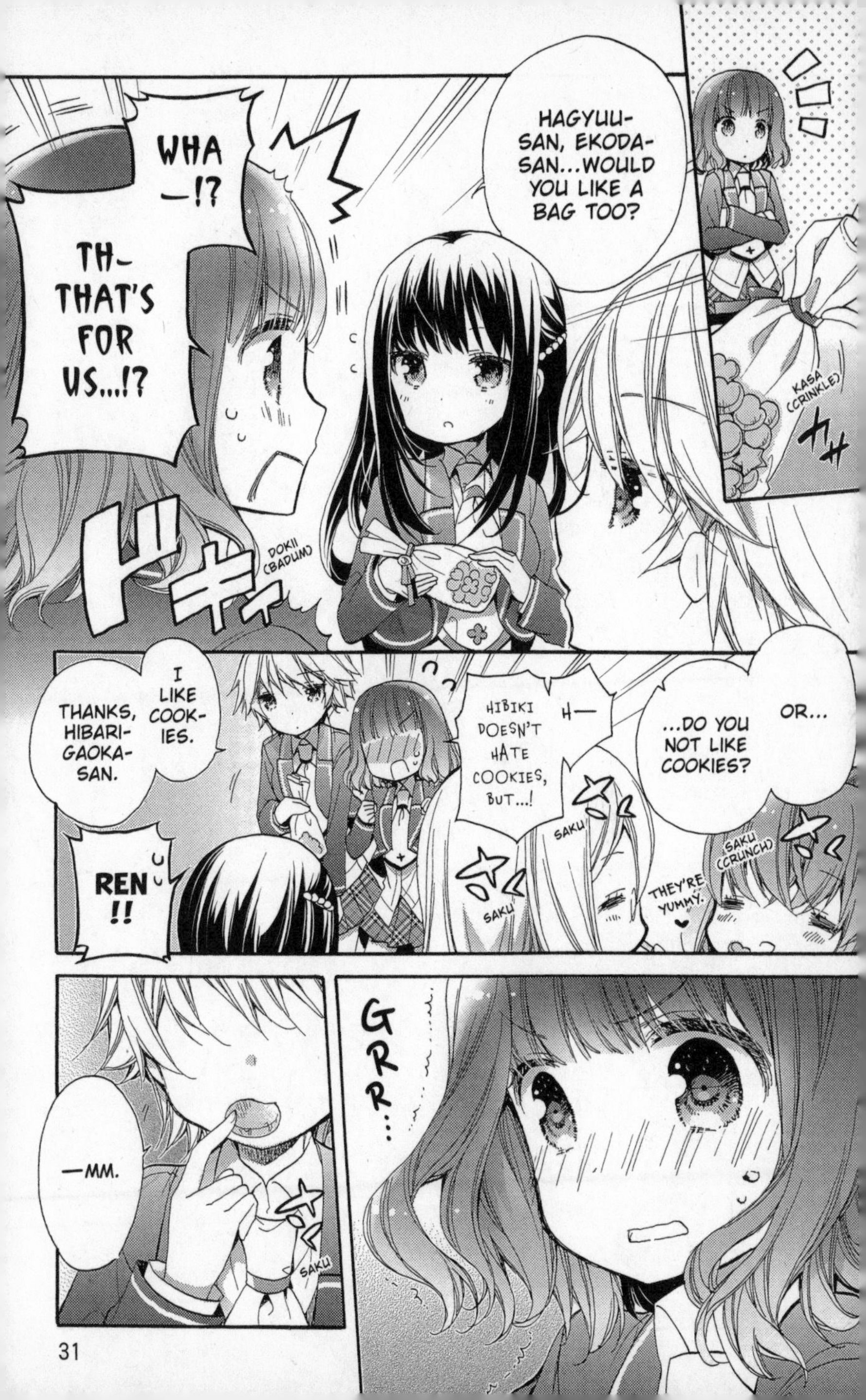
KASA (CRINKLE)
HAGYUU-SAN, EKODA-SAN...WOULD YOU LIKE A BAG TOO?
WHA—!?
TH-THAT'S FOR US...!?
DOKII (BADUM)
OR...
...DO YOU NOT LIKE COOKIES?
SAKU (CRUNCH)
THEY'RE YUMMY.
SAKU
H—
HIBIKI DOESN'T HATE COOKIES, BUT...!
SAKU
I LIKE COOKIES.
THANKS, HIBARIGAOKA-SAN.
REN!!
GRR...
—MM.
SAKU

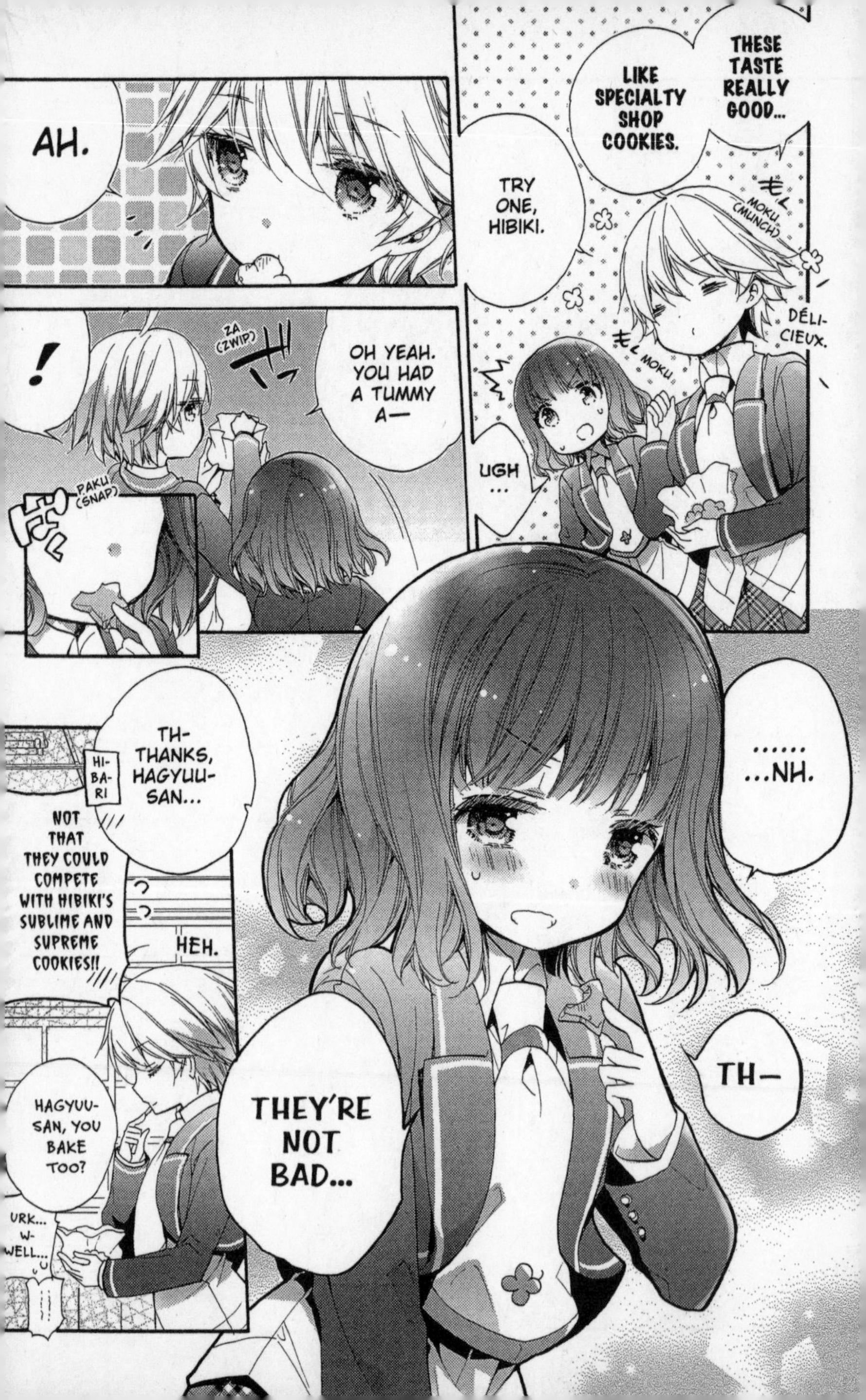

THESE TASTE REALLY GOOD...
LIKE SPECIALTY SHOP COOKIES.
TRY ONE, HIBIKI.
MOKU (MUNCH)
DÉLICIEUX.
MOKU
UGH...
AH.
OH YEAH. YOU HAD A TUMMY A—
ZA (ZWIP)
!
PAKU (SNAP)
......
...NH.
TH—
THEY'RE NOT BAD...
TH-THANKS, HAGYUU-SAN...
HI-BA-RI
NOT THAT THEY COULD COMPETE WITH HIBIKI'S SUBLIME AND SUPREME COOKIES!!
HEH.
HAGYUU-SAN, YOU BAKE TOO?
URK... W-WELL...

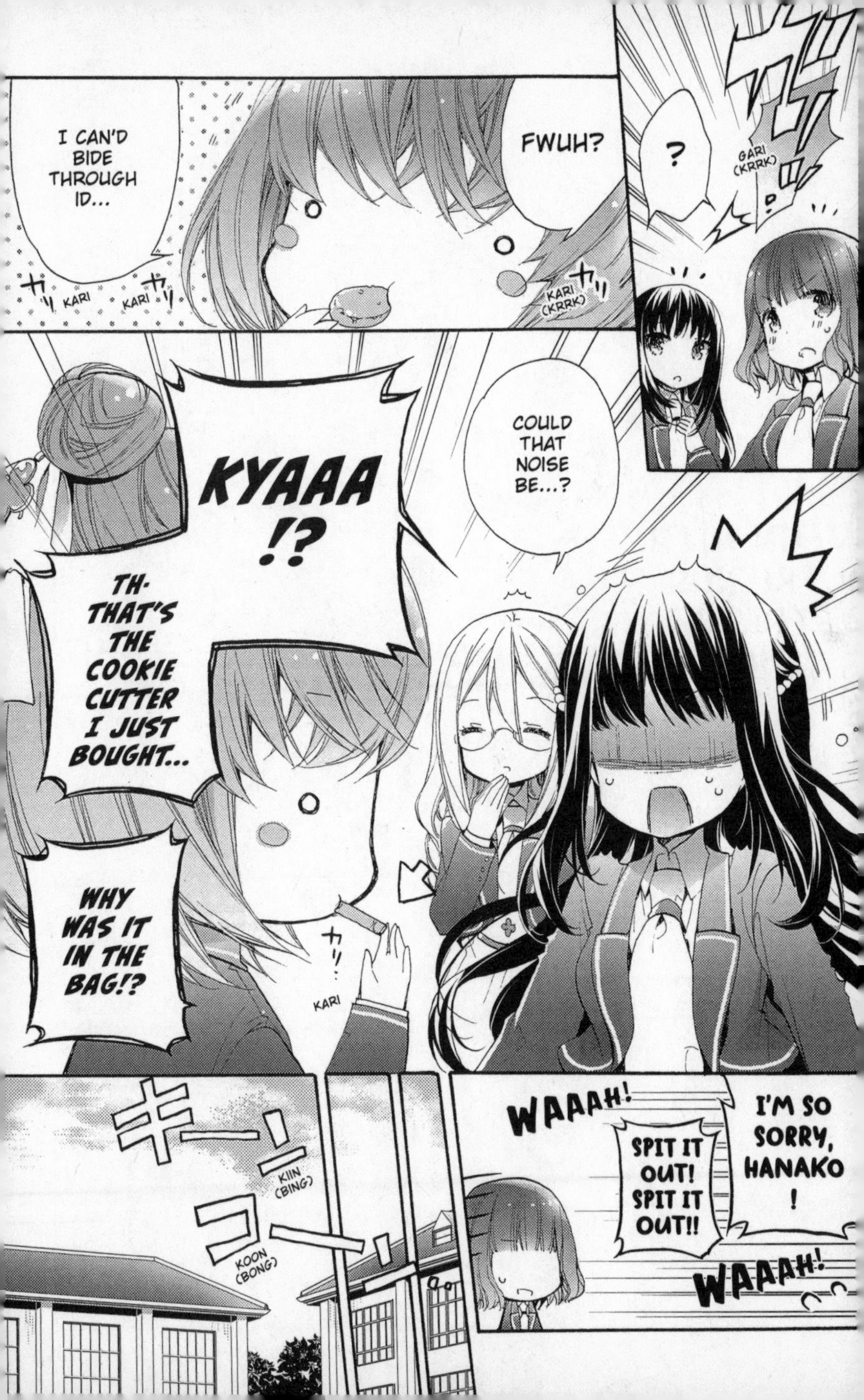
?
GARI (KRRK)
FWUH?
KARI (KRRK)
I CAN'D BIDE THROUGH ID...
KARI
KARI
COULD THAT NOISE BE...?
KYAAA!?
TH-THAT'S THE COOKIE CUTTER I JUST BOUGHT...
WHY WAS IT IN THE BAG!?
KARI
I'M SO SORRY, HANAKO!
WAAAH!
SPIT IT OUT! SPIT IT OUT!!
WAAAH!
KIIN (BING)
KOON (BONG)

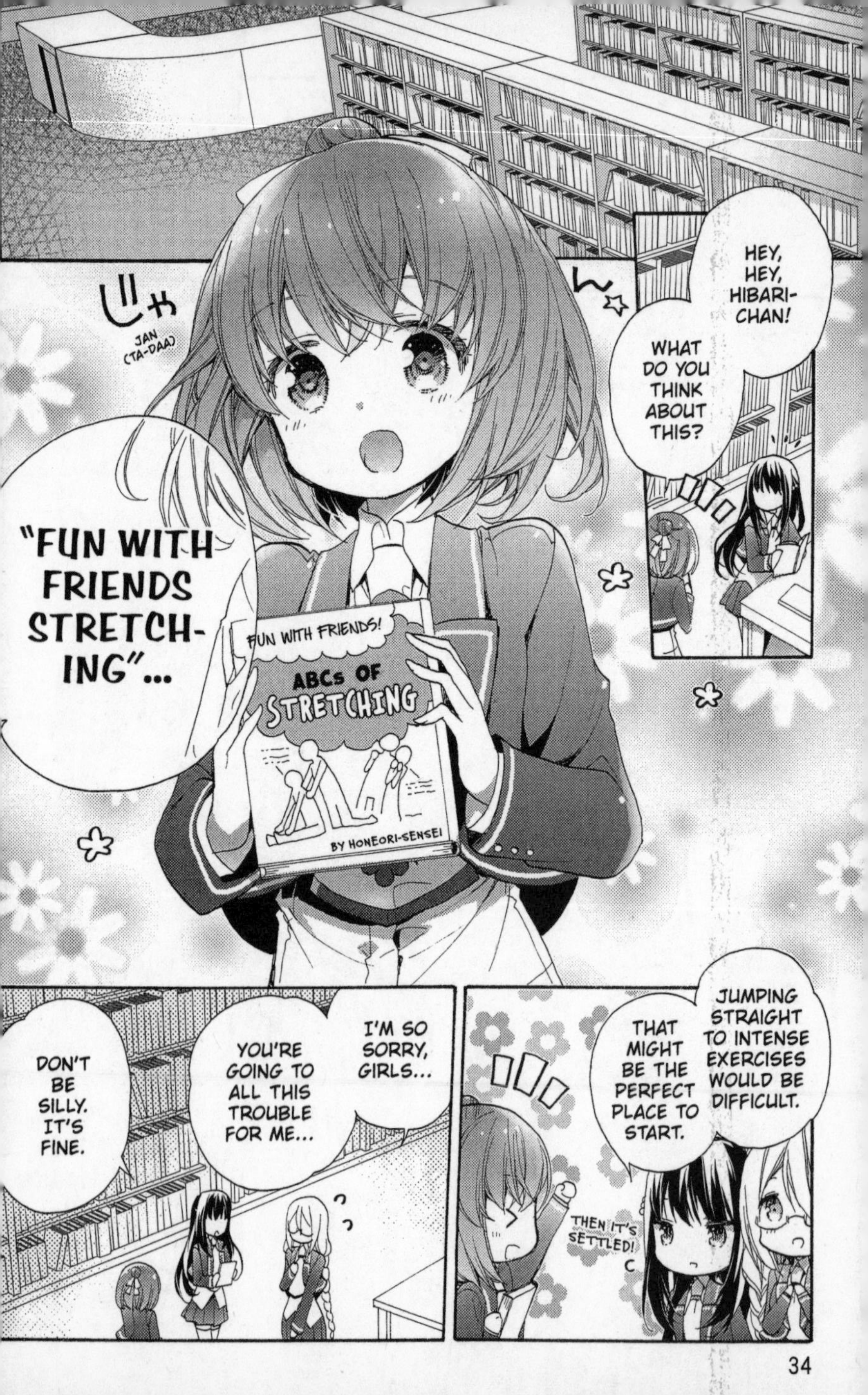
HEY, HEY, HIBARI-CHAN!
WHAT DO YOU THINK ABOUT THIS?
ん☆
じゃ
JAN (TA-DAA)
FUN WITH FRIENDS!
ABCs OF STRETCHING
BY HONEORI-SENSEI
"FUN WITH FRIENDS STRETCHING"...
JUMPING STRAIGHT TO INTENSE EXERCISES WOULD BE DIFFICULT.
THAT MIGHT BE THE PERFECT PLACE TO START.
THEN IT'S SETTLED!
I'M SO SORRY, GIRLS...
YOU'RE GOING TO ALL THIS TROUBLE FOR ME...
DON'T BE SILLY. IT'S FINE.

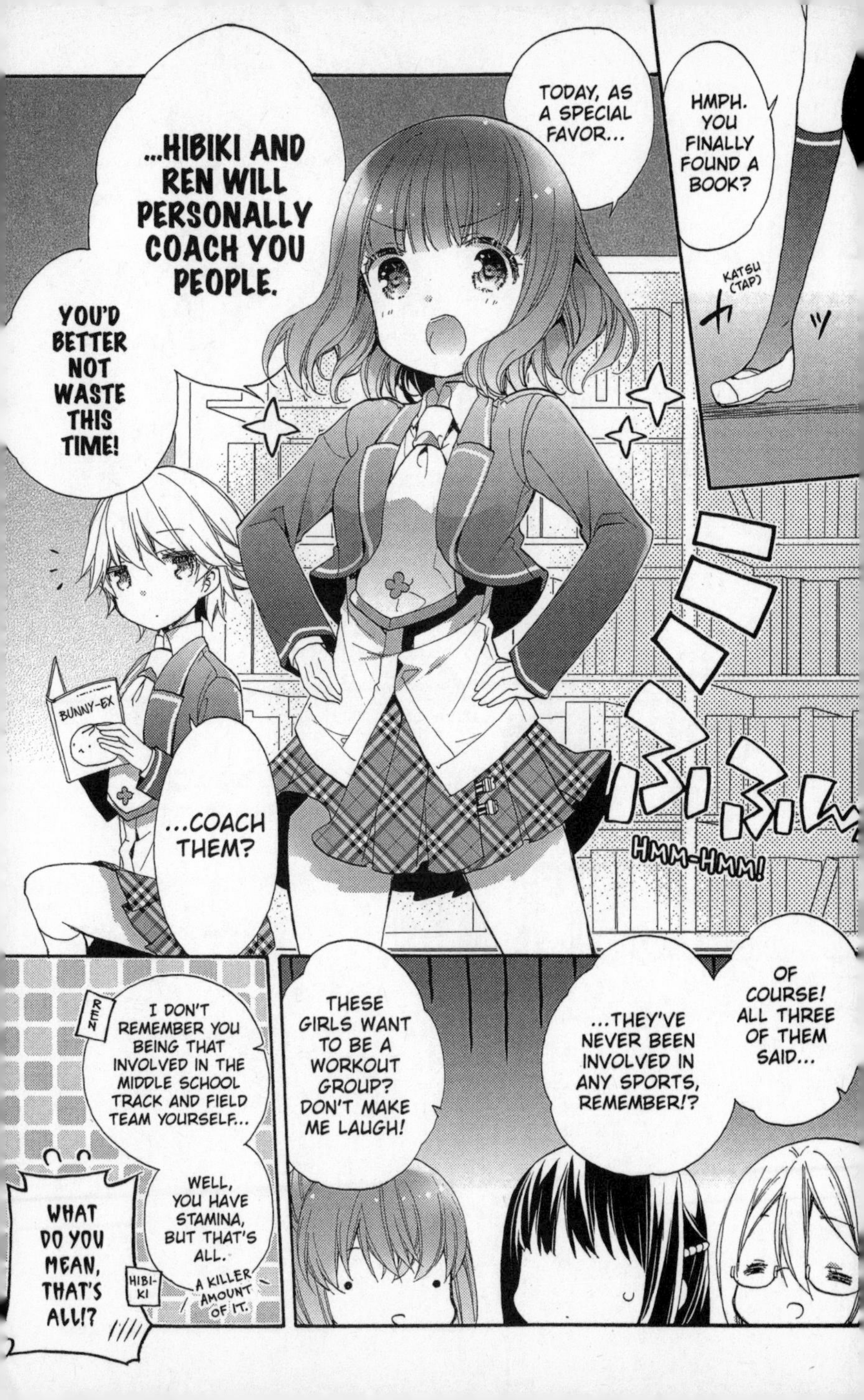
HMPH. YOU FINALLY FOUND A BOOK?
KATSU (TAP)
TODAY, AS A SPECIAL FAVOR...
...HIBIKI AND REN WILL PERSONALLY COACH YOU PEOPLE.
YOU'D BETTER NOT WASTE THIS TIME!
HMM-HMM!
...COACH THEM?
BUNNY-EX
OF COURSE! ALL THREE OF THEM SAID...
...THEY'VE NEVER BEEN INVOLVED IN ANY SPORTS, REMEMBER!?
THESE GIRLS WANT TO BE A WORKOUT GROUP? DON'T MAKE ME LAUGH!
REN
I DON'T REMEMBER YOU BEING THAT INVOLVED IN THE MIDDLE SCHOOL TRACK AND FIELD TEAM YOURSELF...
WELL, YOU HAVE STAMINA, BUT THAT'S ALL.
HIBIKI
A KILLER AMOUNT OF IT.
WHAT DO YOU MEAN, THAT'S ALL!?

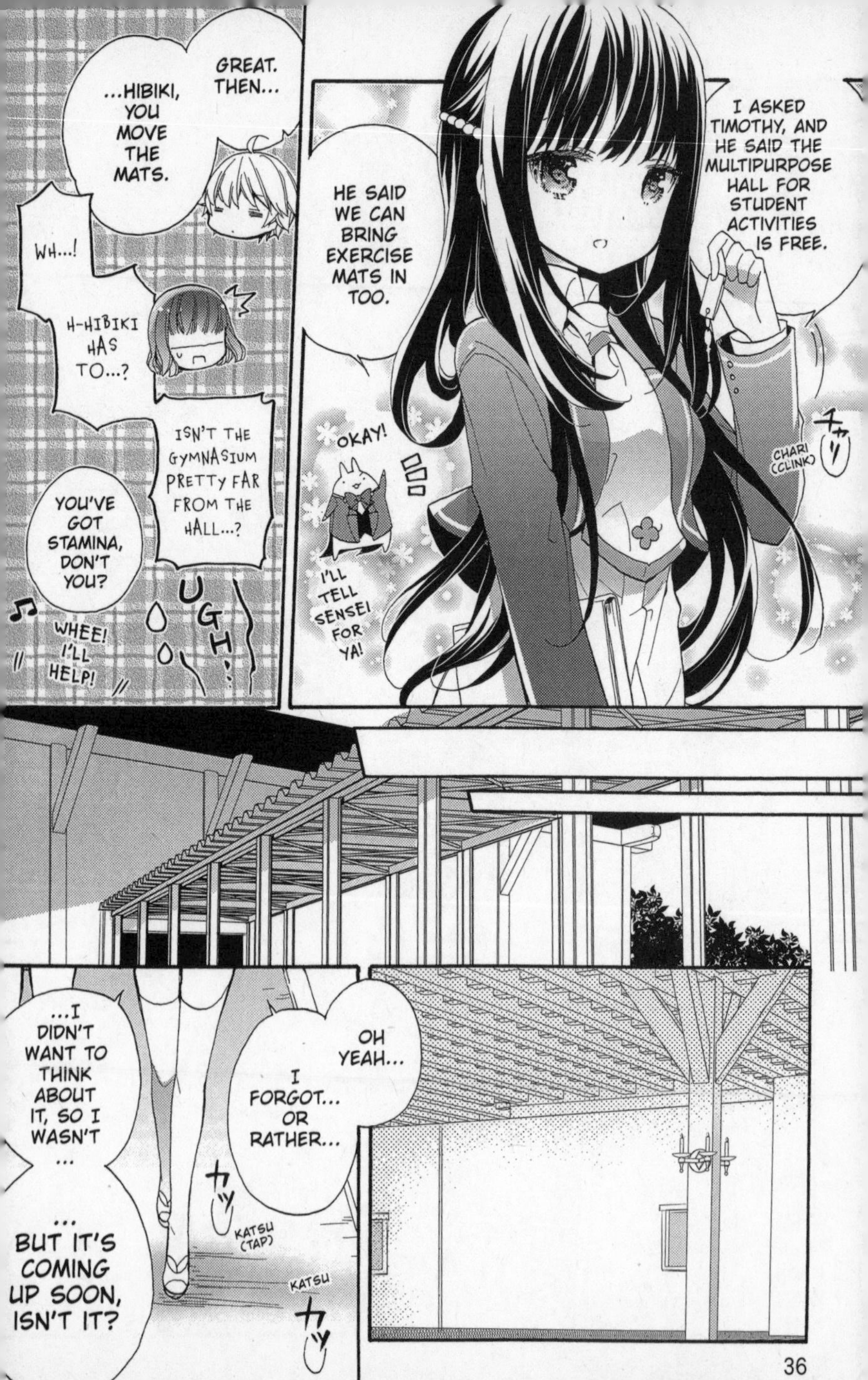
I ASKED TIMOTHY, AND HE SAID THE MULTIPURPOSE HALL FOR STUDENT ACTIVITIES IS FREE.
HE SAID WE CAN BRING EXERCISE MATS IN TOO.
CHARI (CLINK)
OKAY!
I'LL TELL SENSEI FOR YA!
GREAT. THEN...
...HIBIKI, YOU MOVE THE MATS.
WH...!
H-HIBIKI HAS TO...?
ISN'T THE GYMNASIUM PRETTY FAR FROM THE HALL...?
YOU'VE GOT STAMINA, DON'T YOU?
UGH
WHEE! I'LL HELP!
OH YEAH... I FORGOT... OR RATHER...
...I DIDN'T WANT TO THINK ABOUT IT, SO I WASN'T...
...BUT IT'S COMING UP SOON, ISN'T IT?
KATSU (TAP)
KATSU

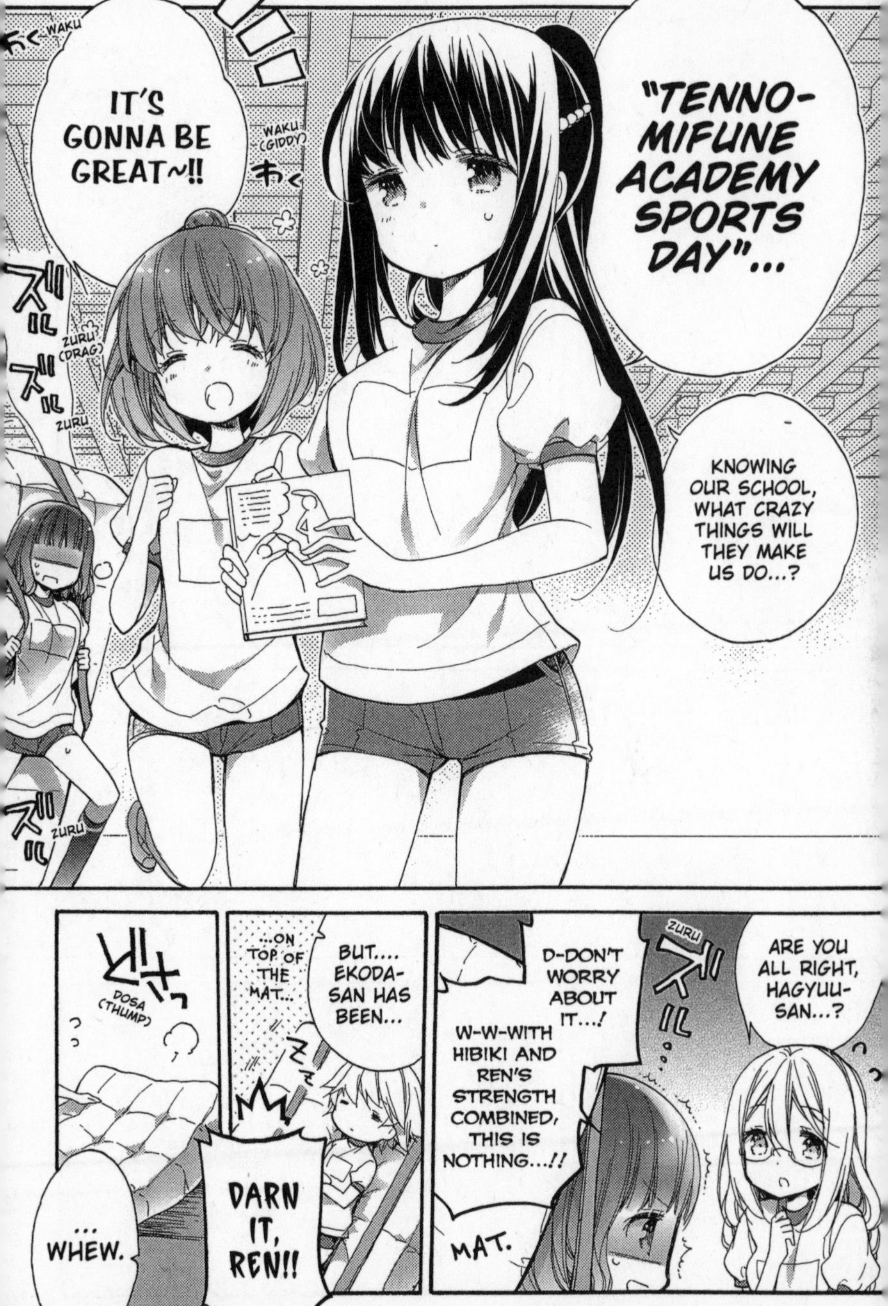
"TENNO-MIFUNE ACADEMY SPORTS DAY"...
WAKU
WAKU (GIDDY)
IT'S GONNA BE GREAT~!!
KNOWING OUR SCHOOL, WHAT CRAZY THINGS WILL THEY MAKE US DO...?
ZURU (DRAG)
ZURU
ZURU
ARE YOU ALL RIGHT, HAGYUU-SAN...?
ZURU
D-DON'T WORRY ABOUT IT...!
W-W-WITH HIBIKI AND REN'S STRENGTH COMBINED, THIS IS NOTHING...!!
MAT.
BUT.... EKODA-SAN HAS BEEN...
...ON TOP OF THE MAT...
DARN IT, REN!!
DOSA (THUMP)
... WHEW.

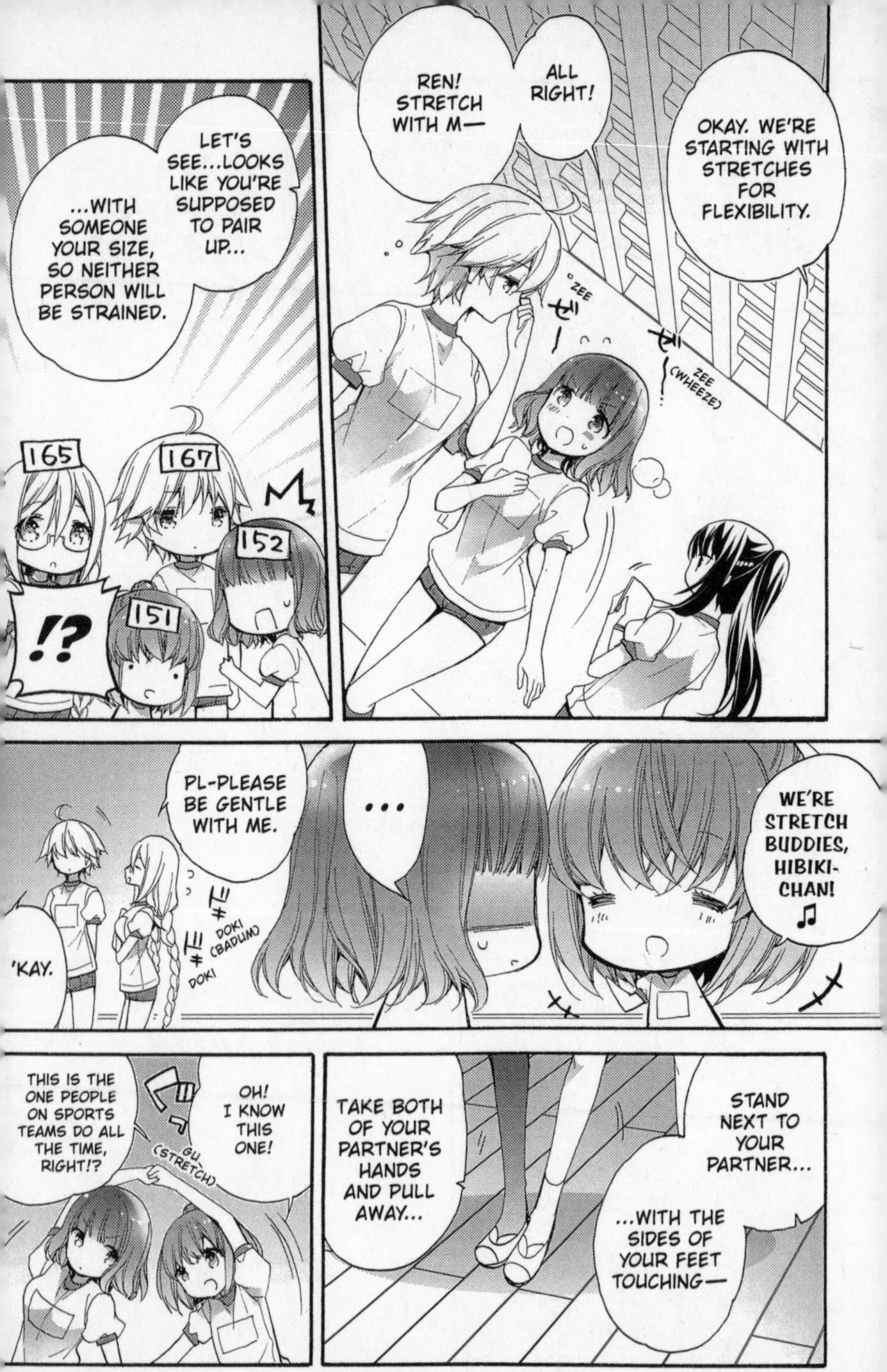
OKAY. WE'RE STARTING WITH STRETCHES FOR FLEXIBILITY.
ALL RIGHT!
REN! STRETCH WITH M—
ZEE
ZEE (WHEEZE)
LET'S SEE...LOOKS LIKE YOU'RE SUPPOSED TO PAIR UP...
...WITH SOMEONE YOUR SIZE, SO NEITHER PERSON WILL BE STRAINED.
167
165
152
151
!?
WE'RE STRETCH BUDDIES, HIBIKI-CHAN! ♫
...
PL-PLEASE BE GENTLE WITH ME.
DOKI (BADUM)
DOKI
'KAY.
STAND NEXT TO YOUR PARTNER...
...WITH THE SIDES OF YOUR FEET TOUCHING—
TAKE BOTH OF YOUR PARTNER'S HANDS AND PULL AWAY...
OH! I KNOW THIS ONE!
THIS IS THE ONE PEOPLE ON SPORTS TEAMS DO ALL THE TIME, RIGHT!?
GU (STRETCH)

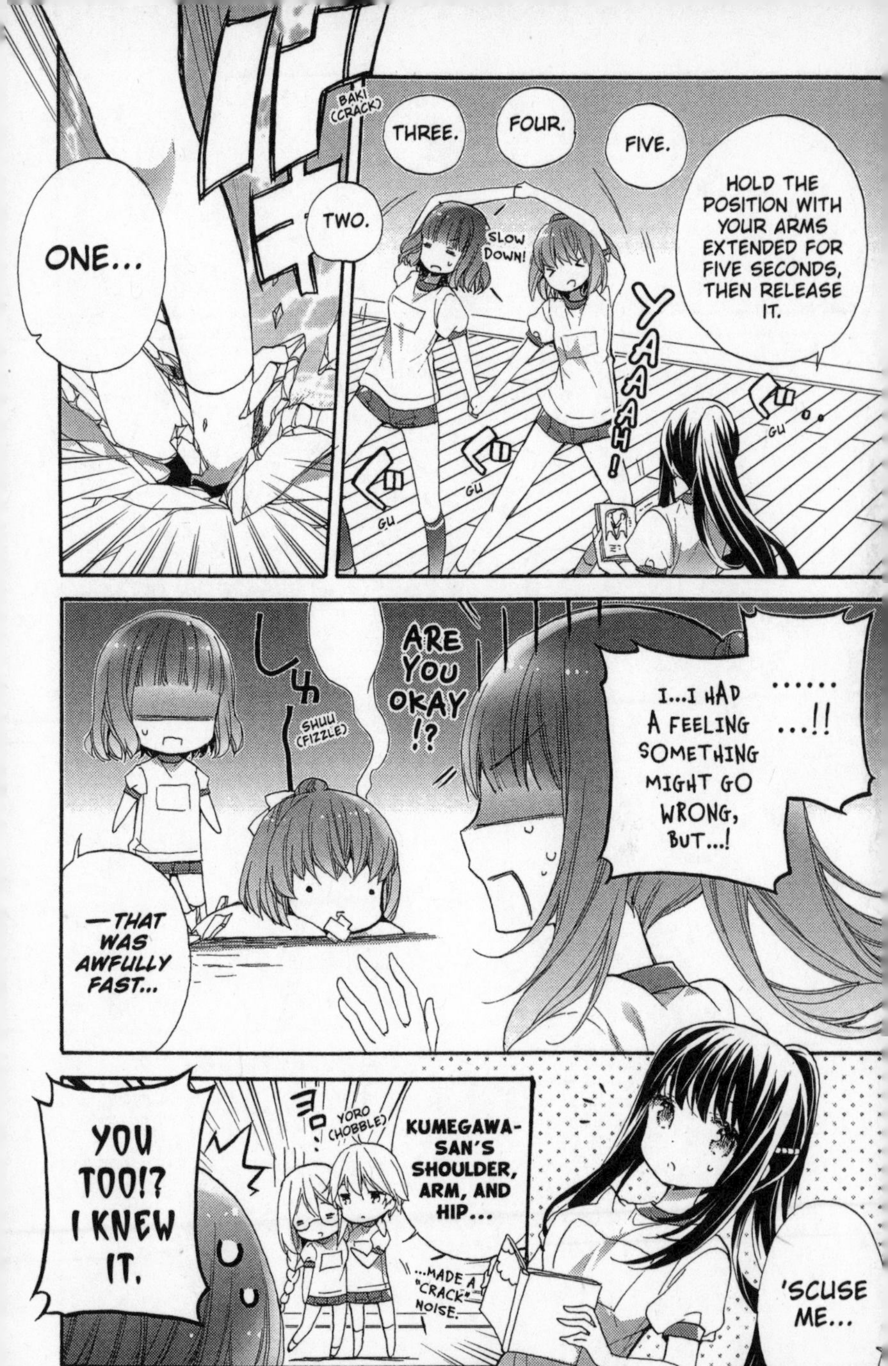
HOLD THE POSITION WITH YOUR ARMS EXTENDED FOR FIVE SECONDS, THEN RELEASE IT.
THREE.
FOUR.
FIVE.
YAAAAH!
SLOW DOWN!
GU
GU
GU
BAKI (CRACK)
TWO.
ONE...
......!!
I...I HAD A FEELING SOMETHING MIGHT GO WRONG, BUT...!
ARE YOU OKAY!?
SHUU (FIZZLE)
—THAT WAS AWFULLY FAST...
'SCUSE ME...
KUMEGAWA-SAN'S SHOULDER, ARM, AND HIP...
...MADE A "CRACK" NOISE.
YORO (HOBBLE)
YOU TOO!? I KNEW IT.

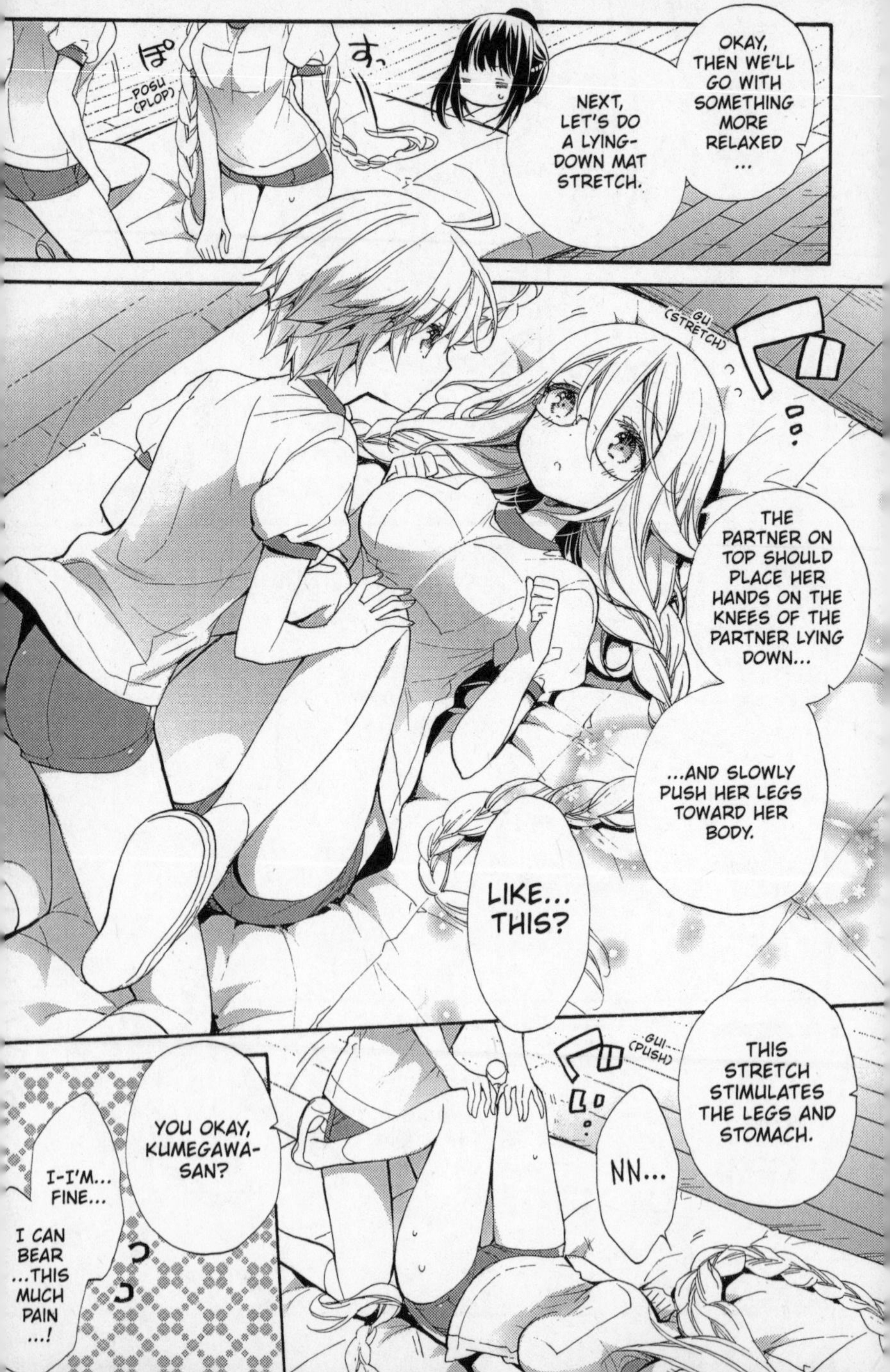
OKAY, THEN WE'LL GO WITH SOMETHING MORE RELAXED...
NEXT, LET'S DO A LYING-DOWN MAT STRETCH.
ぽすっ
POSU (PLOP)
GU (STRETCH)
THE PARTNER ON TOP SHOULD PLACE HER HANDS ON THE KNEES OF THE PARTNER LYING DOWN...
...AND SLOWLY PUSH HER LEGS TOWARD HER BODY.
LIKE... THIS?
GUI (PUSH)
THIS STRETCH STIMULATES THE LEGS AND STOMACH.
NN...
YOU OKAY, KUMEGAWA-SAN?
I-I'M... FINE...
I CAN BEAR ...THIS MUCH PAIN ...!

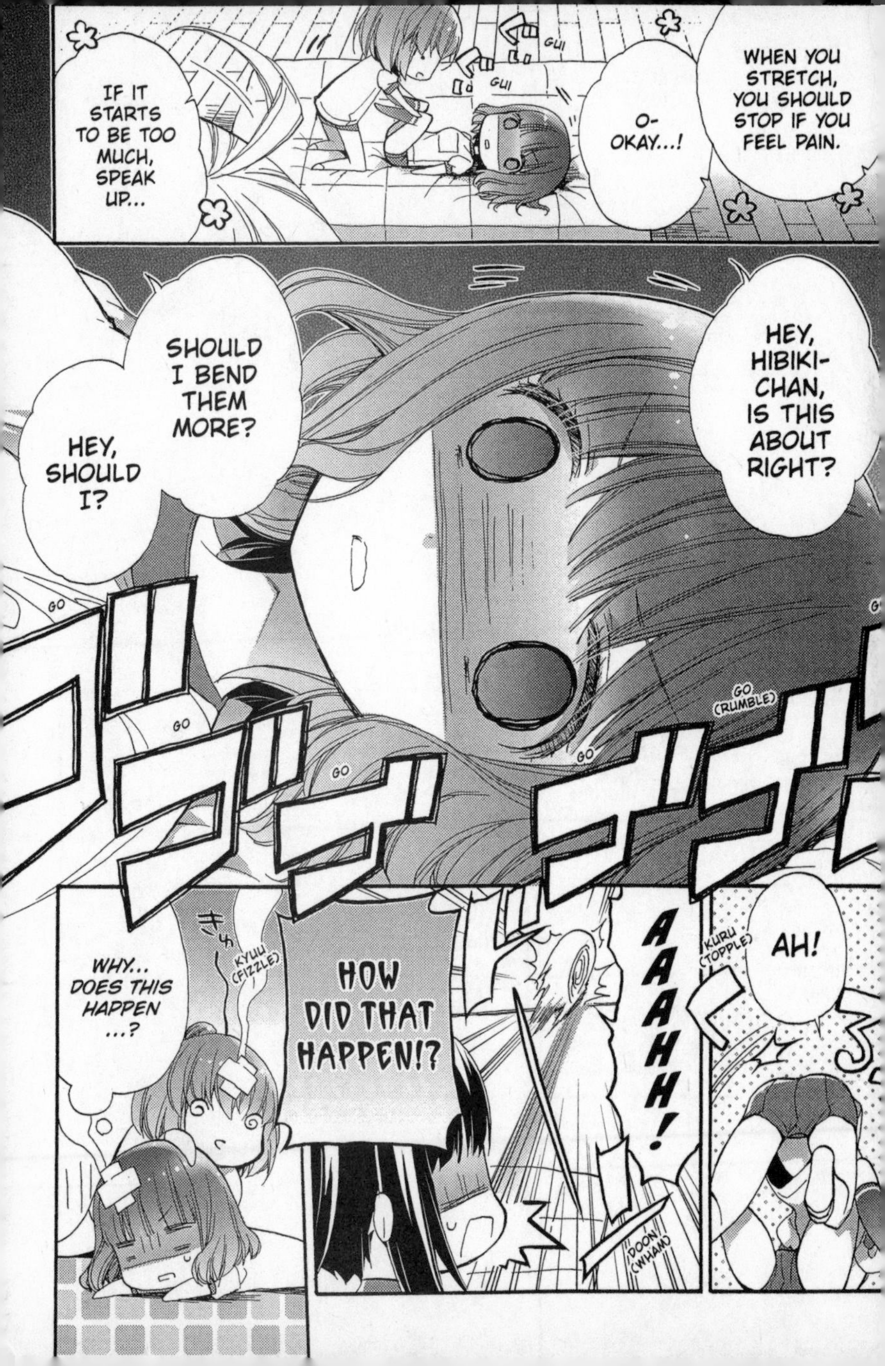
WHEN YOU STRETCH, YOU SHOULD STOP IF YOU FEEL PAIN.
O- OKAY...!
GUI
GUI
IF IT STARTS TO BE TOO MUCH, SPEAK UP...
HEY, HIBIKI-CHAN, IS THIS ABOUT RIGHT?
SHOULD I BEND THEM MORE?
HEY, SHOULD I?
GO (RUMBLE)
GO
GO
GO
GO
AH!
KURU (TOPPLE)
AAAAHH!
DOON (WHAM)
HOW DID THAT HAPPEN!?
KYUU (FIZZLE)
WHY... DOES THIS HAPPEN ...?

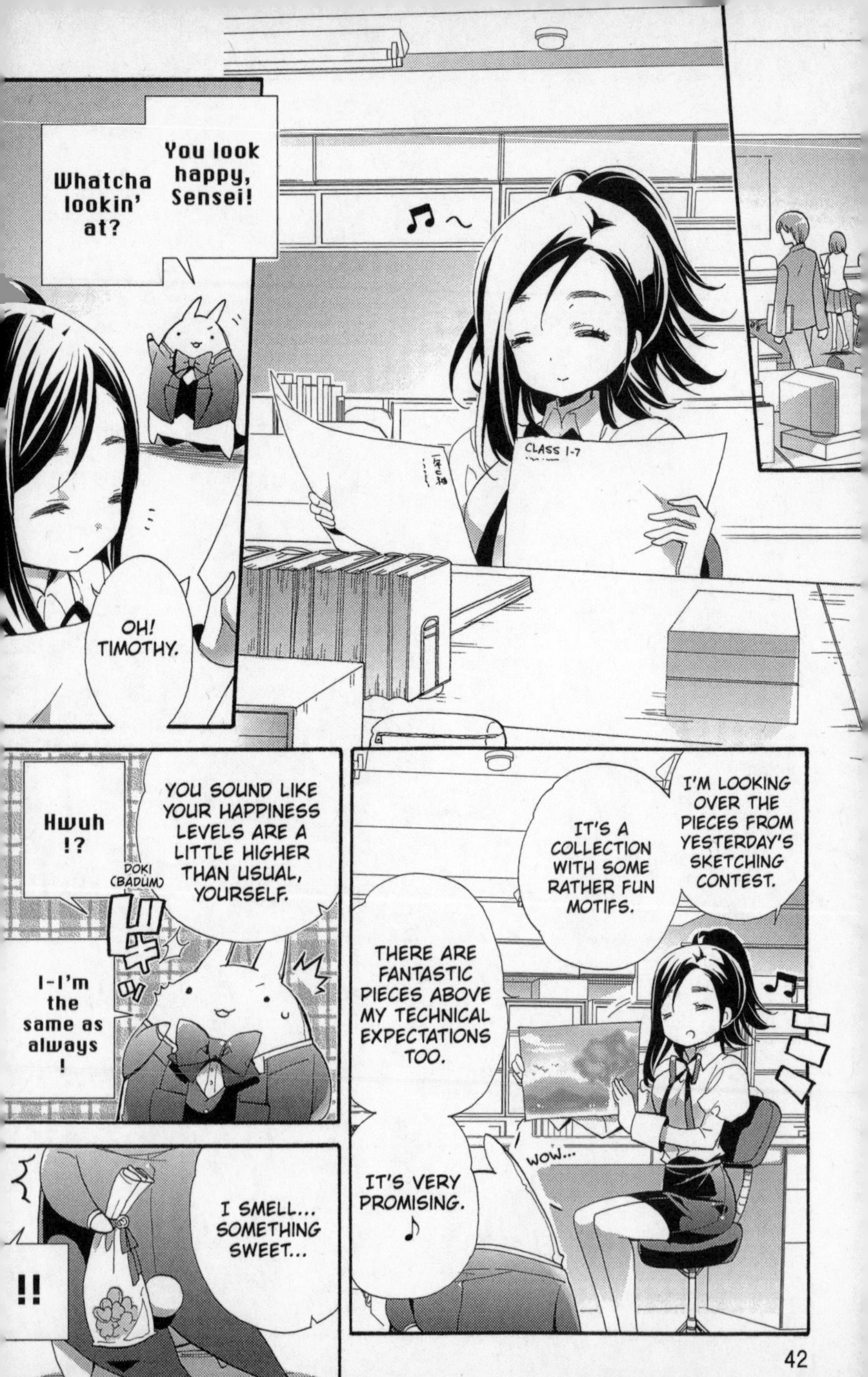
♪~
CLASS 1-7
You look happy, Sensei!
Whatcha lookin' at?
OH! TIMOTHY.
I'M LOOKING OVER THE PIECES FROM YESTERDAY'S SKETCHING CONTEST.
IT'S A COLLECTION WITH SOME RATHER FUN MOTIFS.
THERE ARE FANTASTIC PIECES ABOVE MY TECHNICAL EXPECTATIONS TOO.
WOW...
IT'S VERY PROMISING. ♪
YOU SOUND LIKE YOUR HAPPINESS LEVELS ARE A LITTLE HIGHER THAN USUAL, YOURSELF.
Hwuh!?
DOKI (BADUM)
I-I'm the same as always!
I SMELL... SOMETHING SWEET...
!!

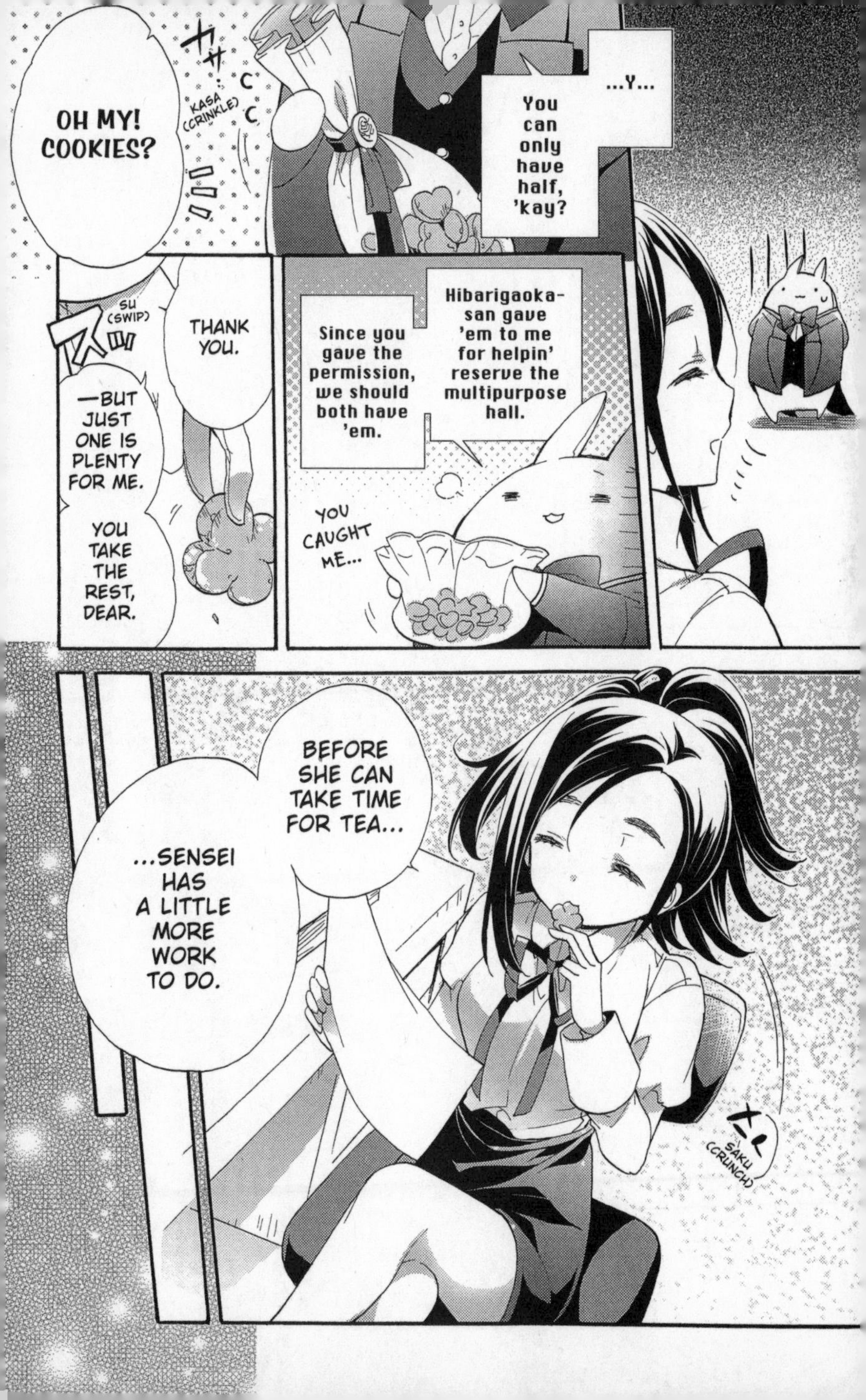
...Y...
You can only have half, 'kay?
KASA (CRINKLE)
OH MY! COOKIES?
Hibarigaoka-san gave 'em to me for helpin' reserve the multipurpose hall.
Since you gave the permission, we should both have 'em.
YOU CAUGHT ME...
SU (SWIP)
THANK YOU.
—BUT JUST ONE IS PLENTY FOR ME.
YOU TAKE THE REST, DEAR.
BEFORE SHE CAN TAKE TIME FOR TEA...
...SENSEI HAS A LITTLE MORE WORK TO DO.
SAKU (CRUNCH)

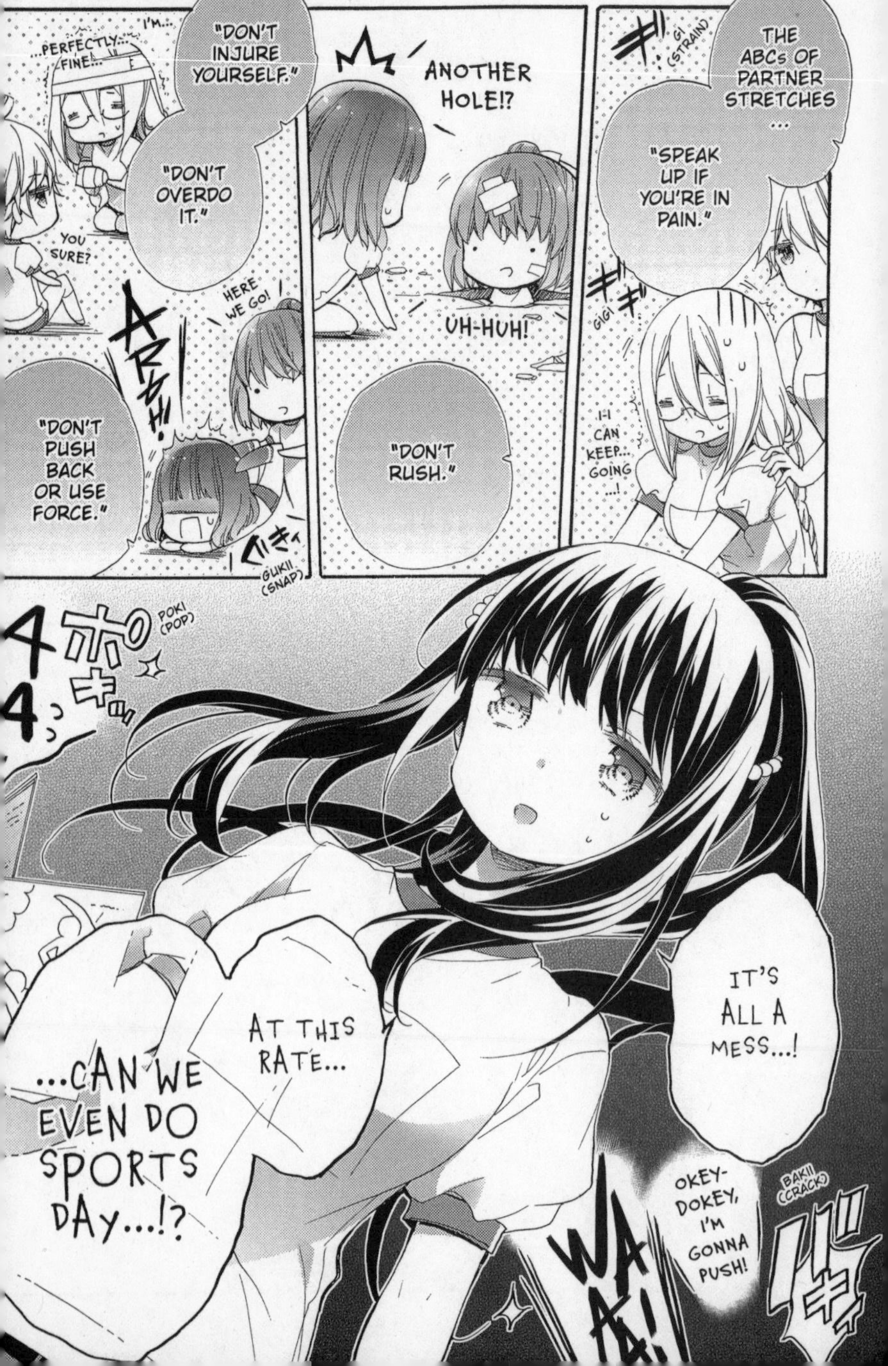
THE ABCs OF PARTNER STRETCHES...
"SPEAK UP IF YOU'RE IN PAIN."
GI (STRAIN)
GIGI
I-I CAN KEEP... GOING...!
ANOTHER HOLE!?
UH-HUH!
"DON'T RUSH."
"DON'T INJURE YOURSELF."
I'M...
...PERFECTLY... FINE...
"DON'T OVERDO IT."
YOU SURE?
HERE WE GO!
ARGH!!
"DON'T PUSH BACK OR USE FORCE."
GUKII (SNAP)
IT'S ALL A MESS...!
AT THIS RATE...
...CAN WE EVEN DO SPORTS DAY...!?
POKI (POP)
BAKII (CRACK)
OKEY-DOKEY, I'M GONNA PUSH!
WAAA!

Anne Happy

unhappy go lucky!

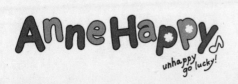

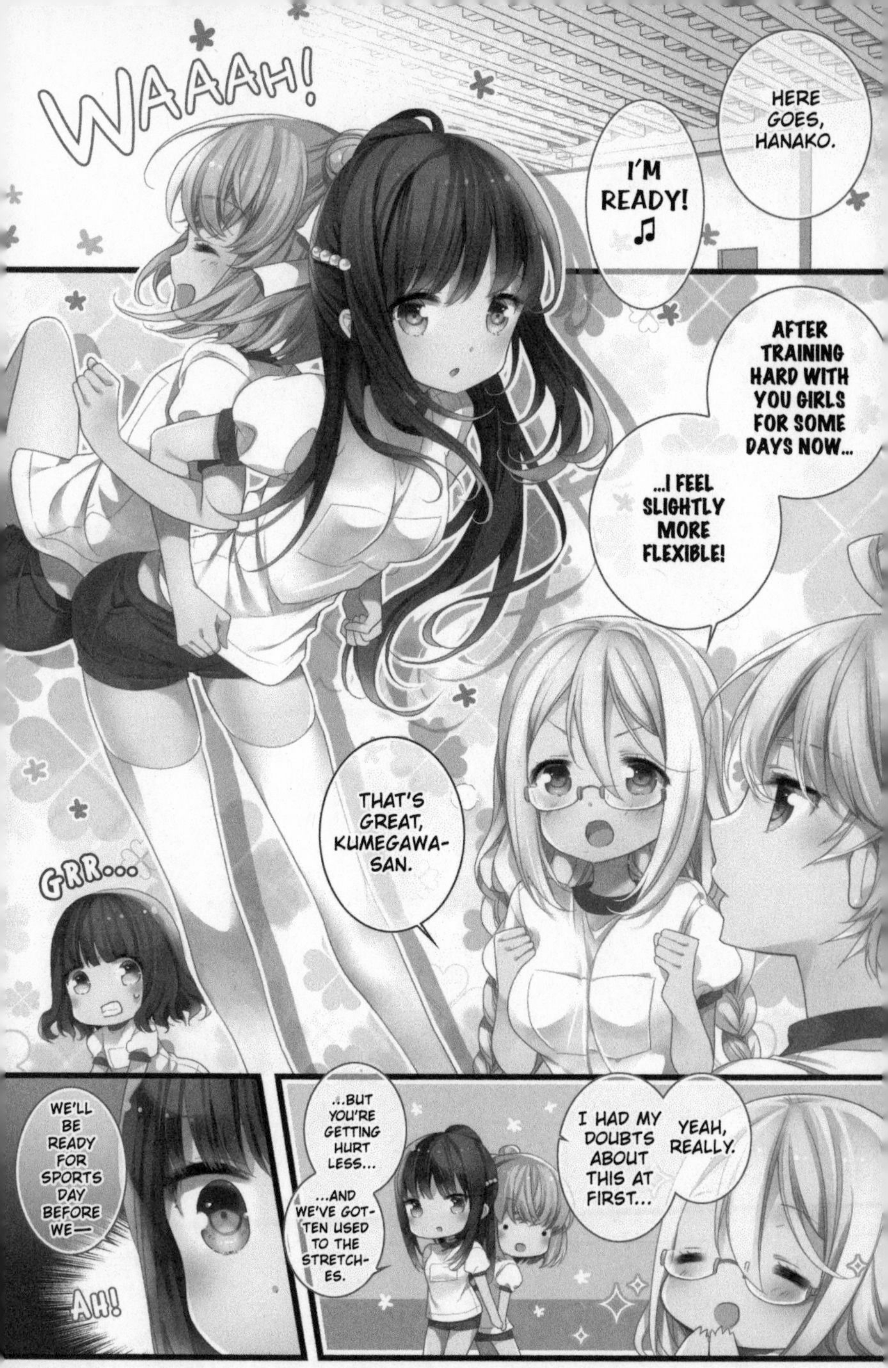
HERE GOES, HANAKO.
I'M READY! ♫
WAAAH!
AFTER TRAINING HARD WITH YOU GIRLS FOR SOME DAYS NOW...
...I FEEL SLIGHTLY MORE FLEXIBLE!
THAT'S GREAT, KUMEGAWA-SAN.
GRR...
YEAH, REALLY.
I HAD MY DOUBTS ABOUT THIS AT FIRST...
...BUT YOU'RE GETTING HURT LESS...
...AND WE'VE GOTTEN USED TO THE STRETCHES.
WE'LL BE READY FOR SPORTS DAY BEFORE WE—
AH!

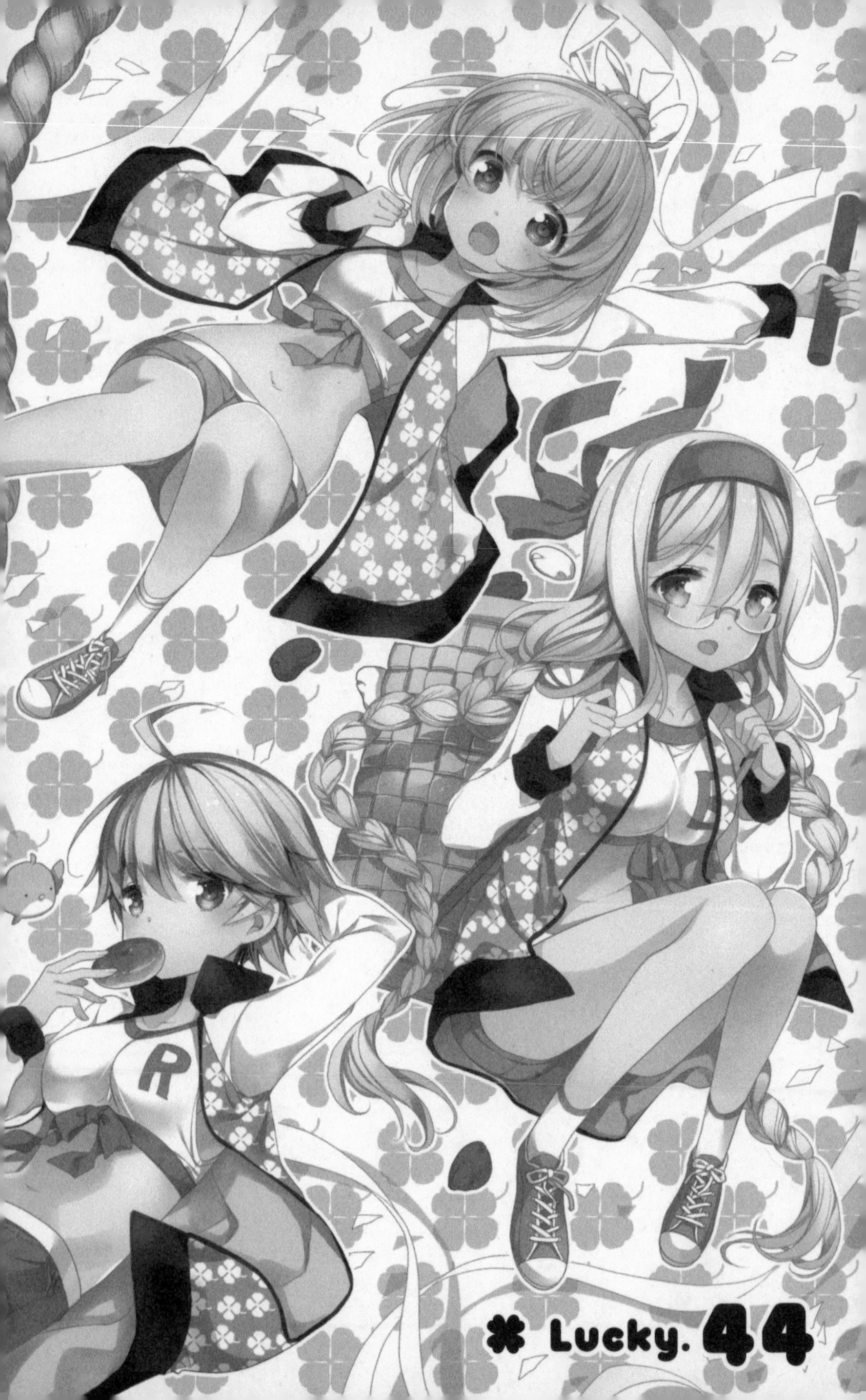
Lucky. 44

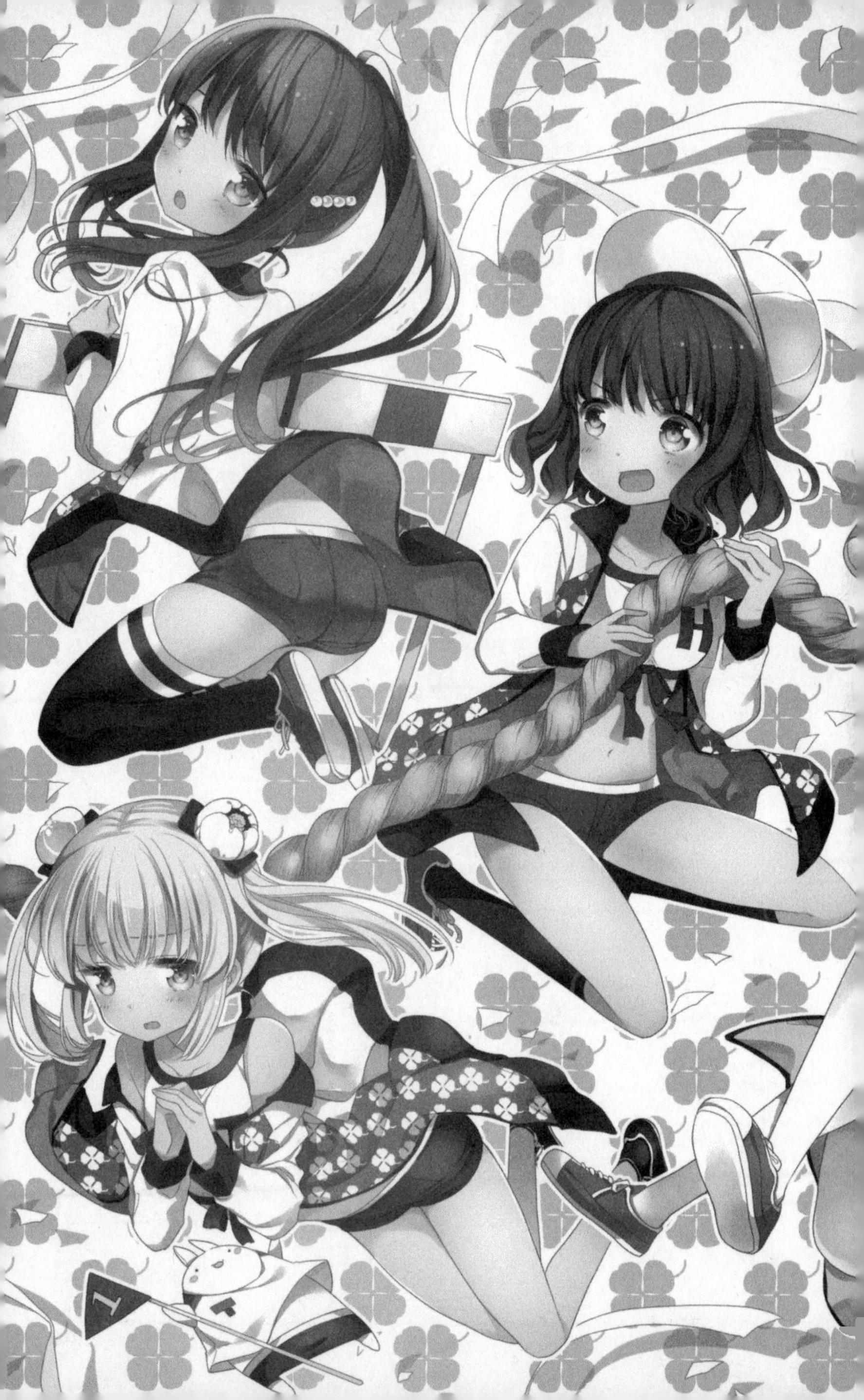

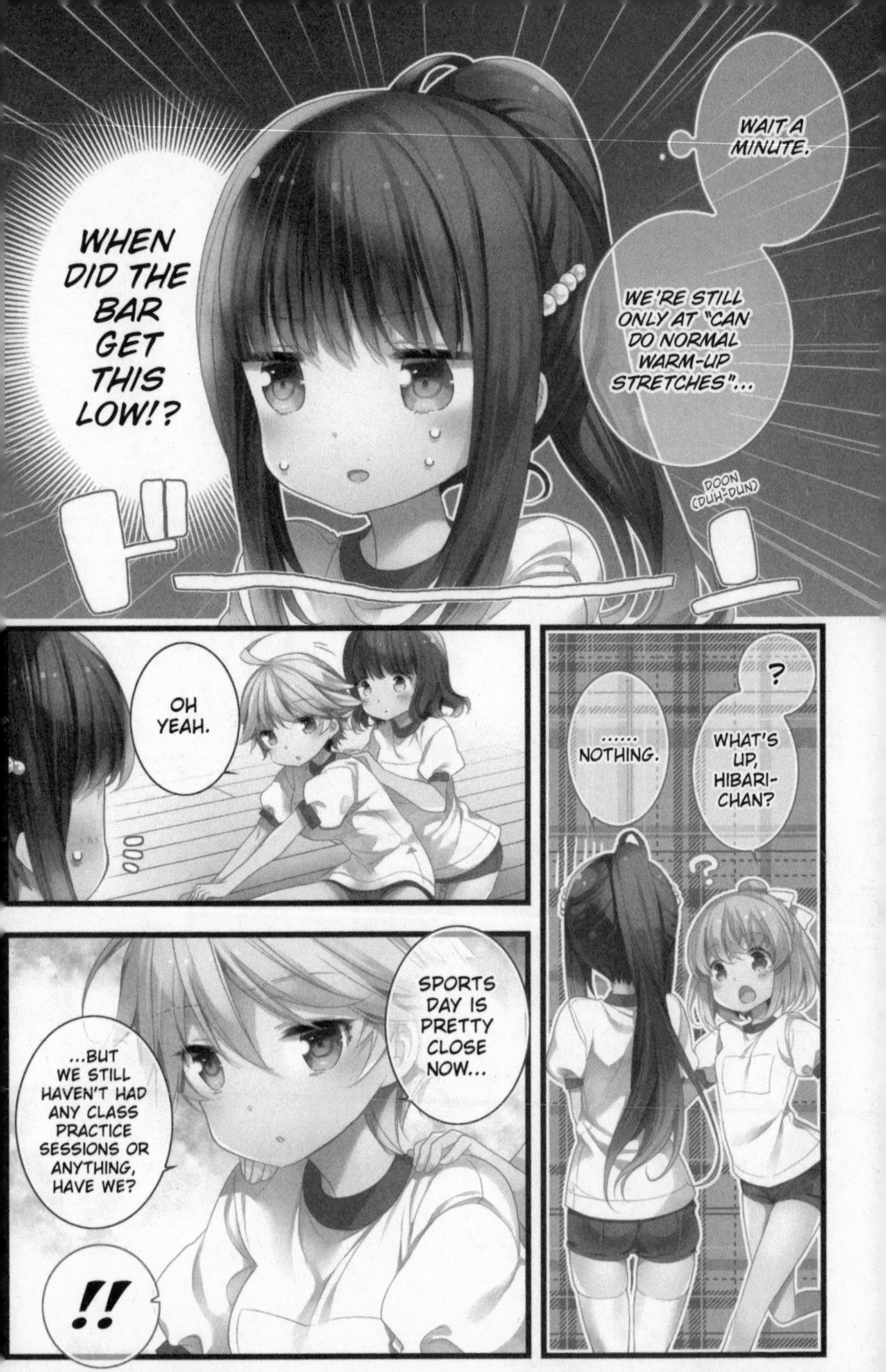
WAIT A MINUTE.
WE'RE STILL ONLY AT "CAN DO NORMAL WARM-UP STRETCHES"...
WHEN DID THE BAR GET THIS LOW!?
DOON (DUH-DUN)
?
WHAT'S UP, HIBARI-CHAN?
...... NOTHING.
OH YEAH.
SPORTS DAY IS PRETTY CLOSE NOW...
...BUT WE STILL HAVEN'T HAD ANY CLASS PRACTICE SESSIONS OR ANYTHING, HAVE WE?
!!

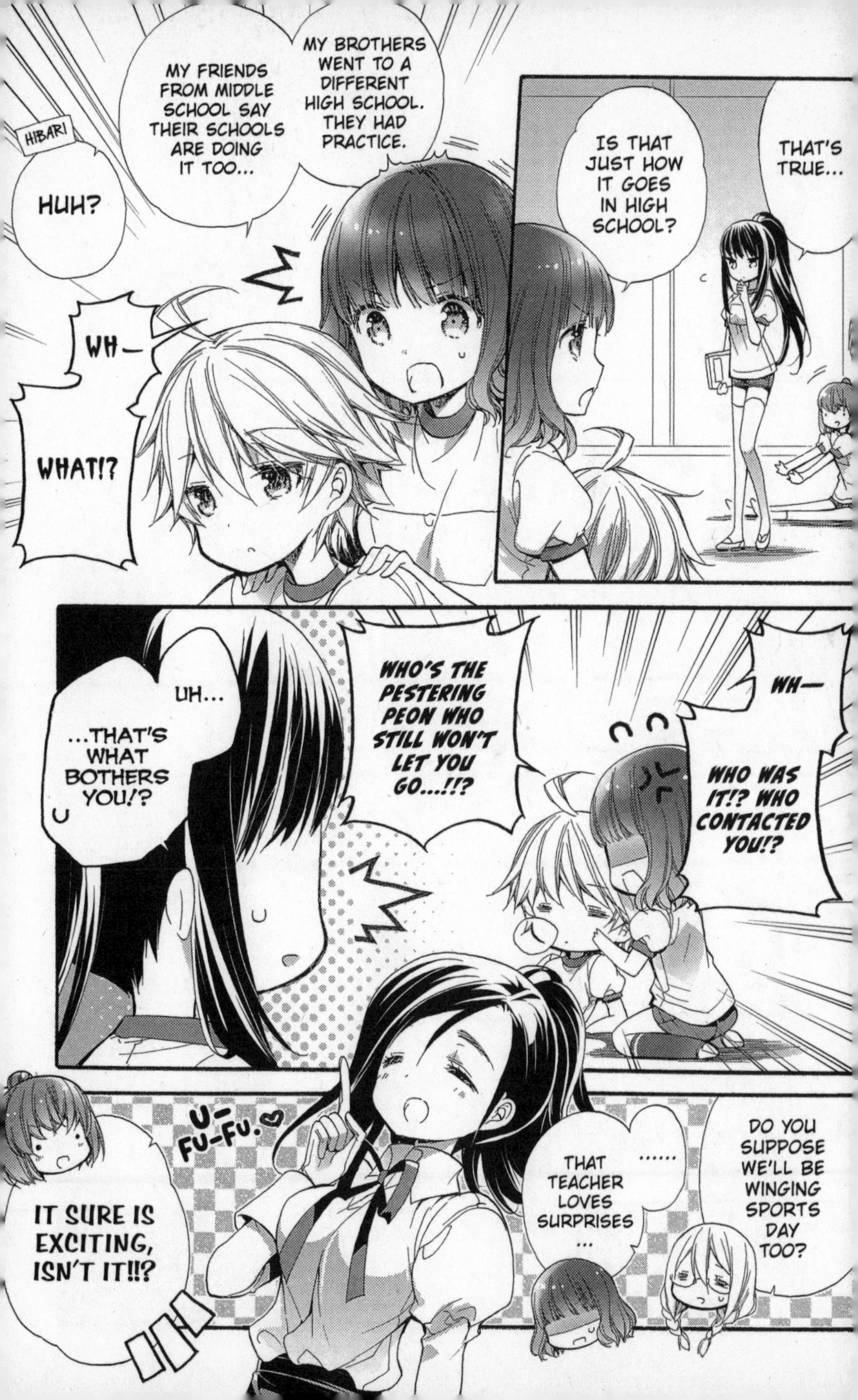
THAT'S TRUE...
IS THAT JUST HOW IT GOES IN HIGH SCHOOL?
MY BROTHERS WENT TO A DIFFERENT HIGH SCHOOL. THEY HAD PRACTICE.
MY FRIENDS FROM MIDDLE SCHOOL SAY THEIR SCHOOLS ARE DOING IT TOO...
HIBARI
HUH?
WH—
WHAT!?
WH—
WHO WAS IT!? WHO CONTACTED YOU!?
WHO'S THE PESTERING PEON WHO STILL WON'T LET YOU GO...!!?
UH...
...THAT'S WHAT BOTHERS YOU!?
DO YOU SUPPOSE WE'LL BE WINGING SPORTS DAY TOO?
......
THAT TEACHER LOVES SURPRISES ...
U-FU-FU.
IT SURE IS EXCITING, ISN'T IT!!?

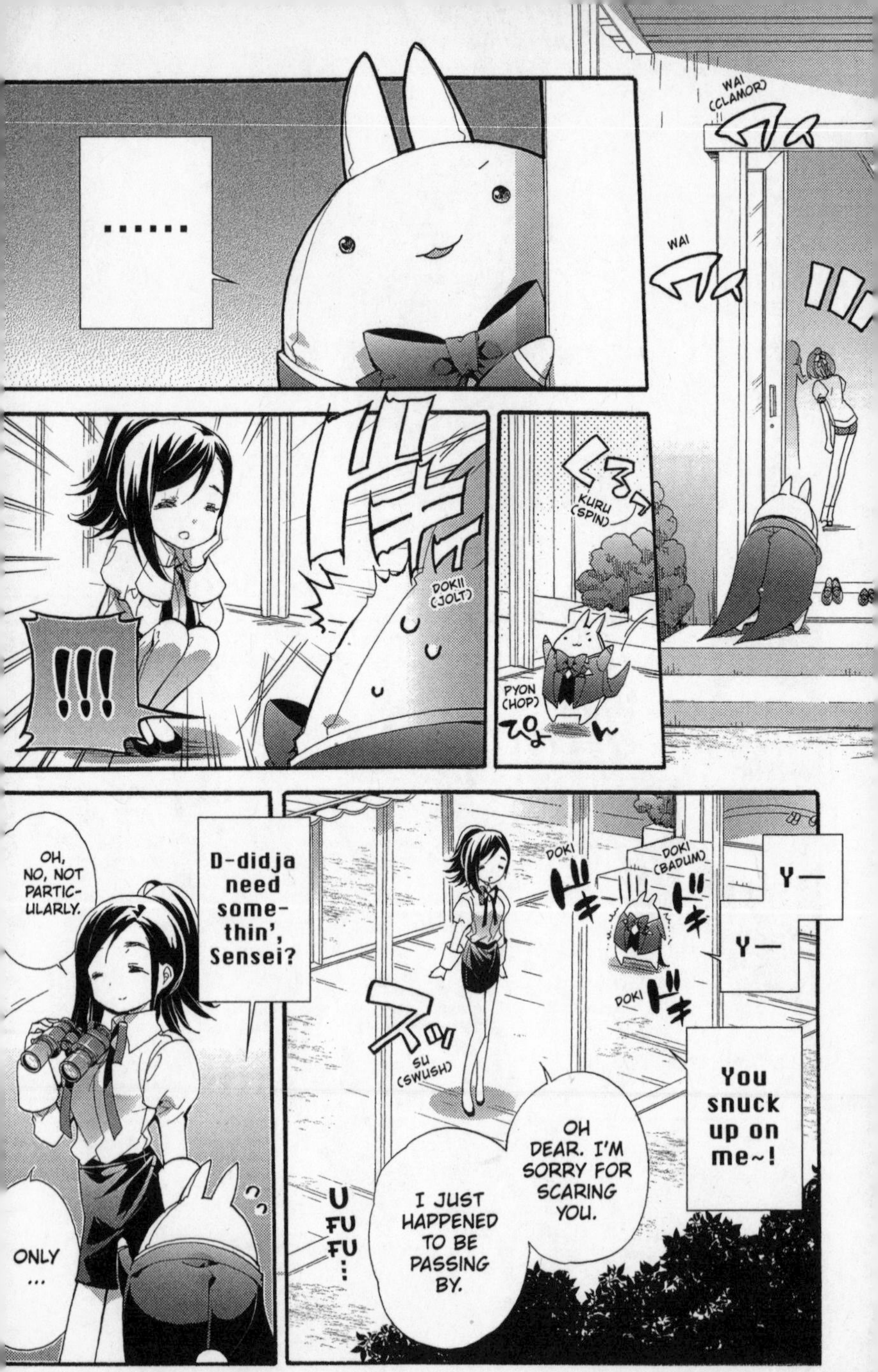
WAI (CLAMOR)
WAI
......
KURU (SPIN)
PYON (HOP)
DOKII (JOLT)
!!!
Y—
Y—
DOKI (BADUM)
DOKI
DOKI
You snuck up on me~!
OH DEAR. I'M SORRY FOR SCARING YOU.
I JUST HAPPENED TO BE PASSING BY.
UFUFU...
SU (SWUSH)
D-didja need somethin', Sensei?
OH, NO, NOT PARTICULARLY.
ONLY ...

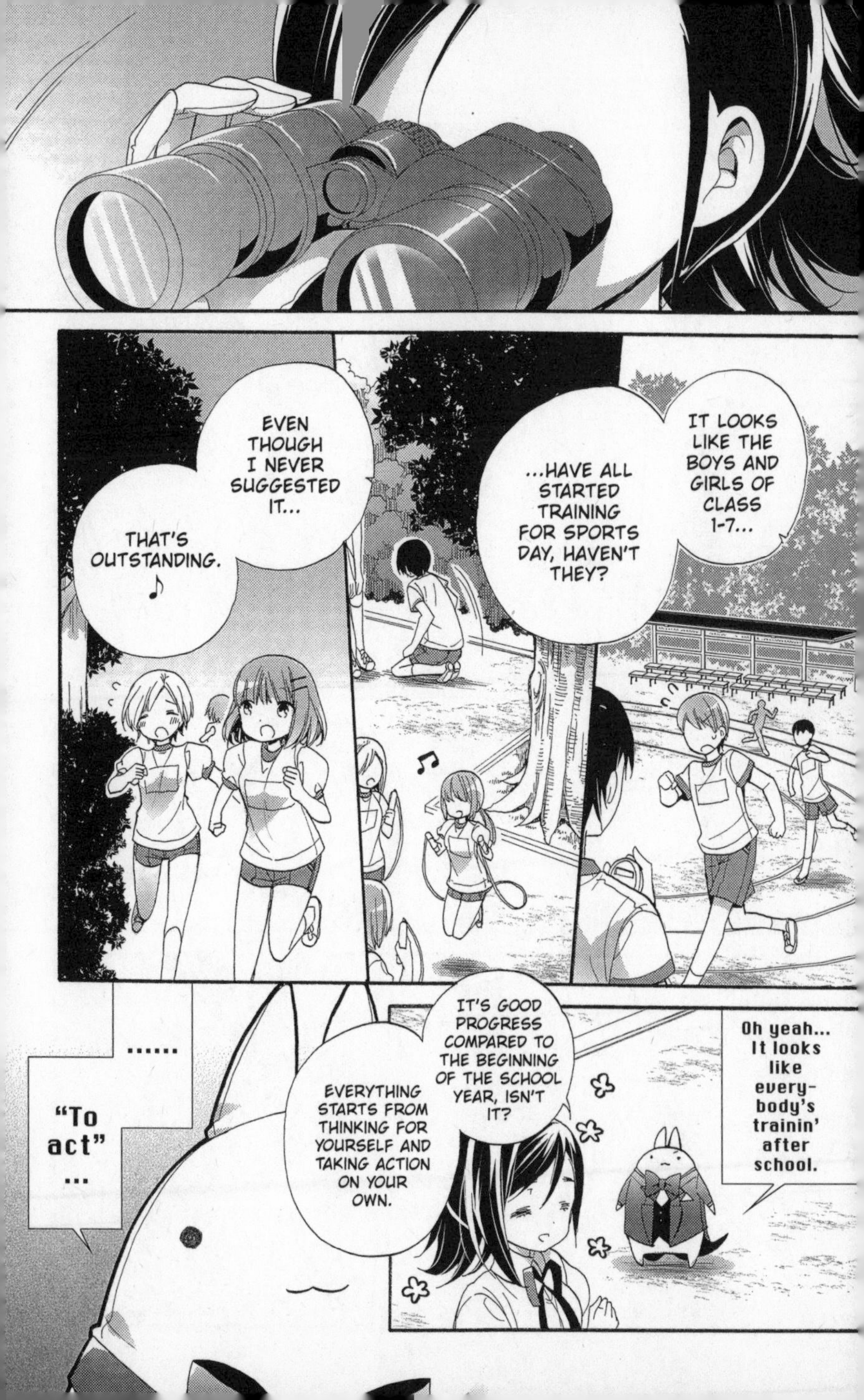
IT LOOKS LIKE THE BOYS AND GIRLS OF CLASS 1-7...
...HAVE ALL STARTED TRAINING FOR SPORTS DAY, HAVEN'T THEY?
EVEN THOUGH I NEVER SUGGESTED IT...
THAT'S OUTSTANDING. ♪
Oh yeah... It looks like every-body's trainin' after school.
IT'S GOOD PROGRESS COMPARED TO THE BEGINNING OF THE SCHOOL YEAR, ISN'T IT?
EVERYTHING STARTS FROM THINKING FOR YOURSELF AND TAKING ACTION ON YOUR OWN.
......
“To act” ...

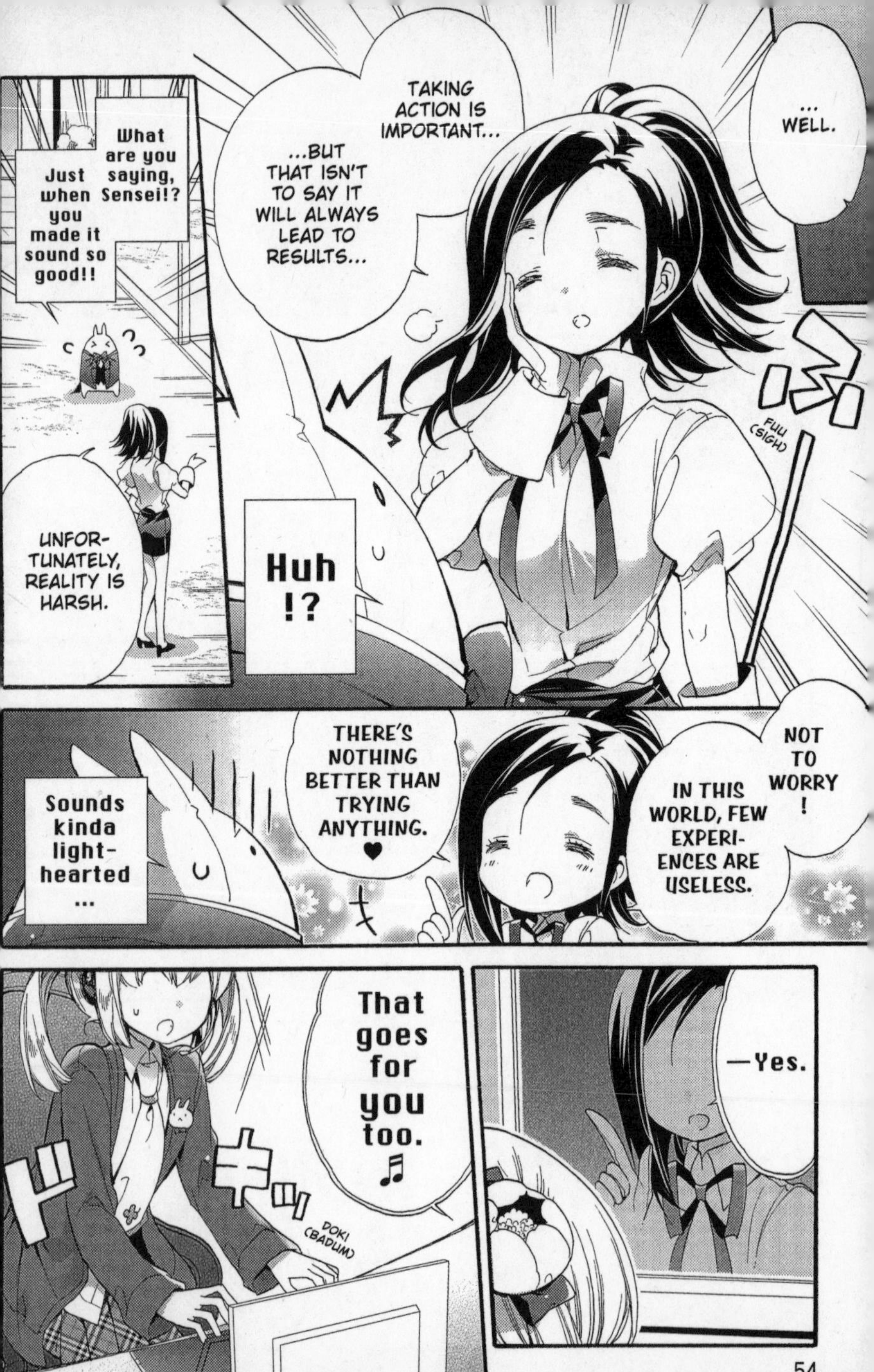
...WELL.
TAKING ACTION IS IMPORTANT...
...BUT THAT ISN'T TO SAY IT WILL ALWAYS LEAD TO RESULTS...
FUU (SIGH)
Huh!?
What are you saying, Sensei!?
Just when you made it sound so good!!
UNFOR-TUNATELY, REALITY IS HARSH.
NOT TO WORRY!
IN THIS WORLD, FEW EXPERI-ENCES ARE USELESS.
THERE'S NOTHING BETTER THAN TRYING ANYTHING. ♥
Sounds kinda light-hearted...
—Yes.
That goes for you too. ♬
DOKI (BADUM)

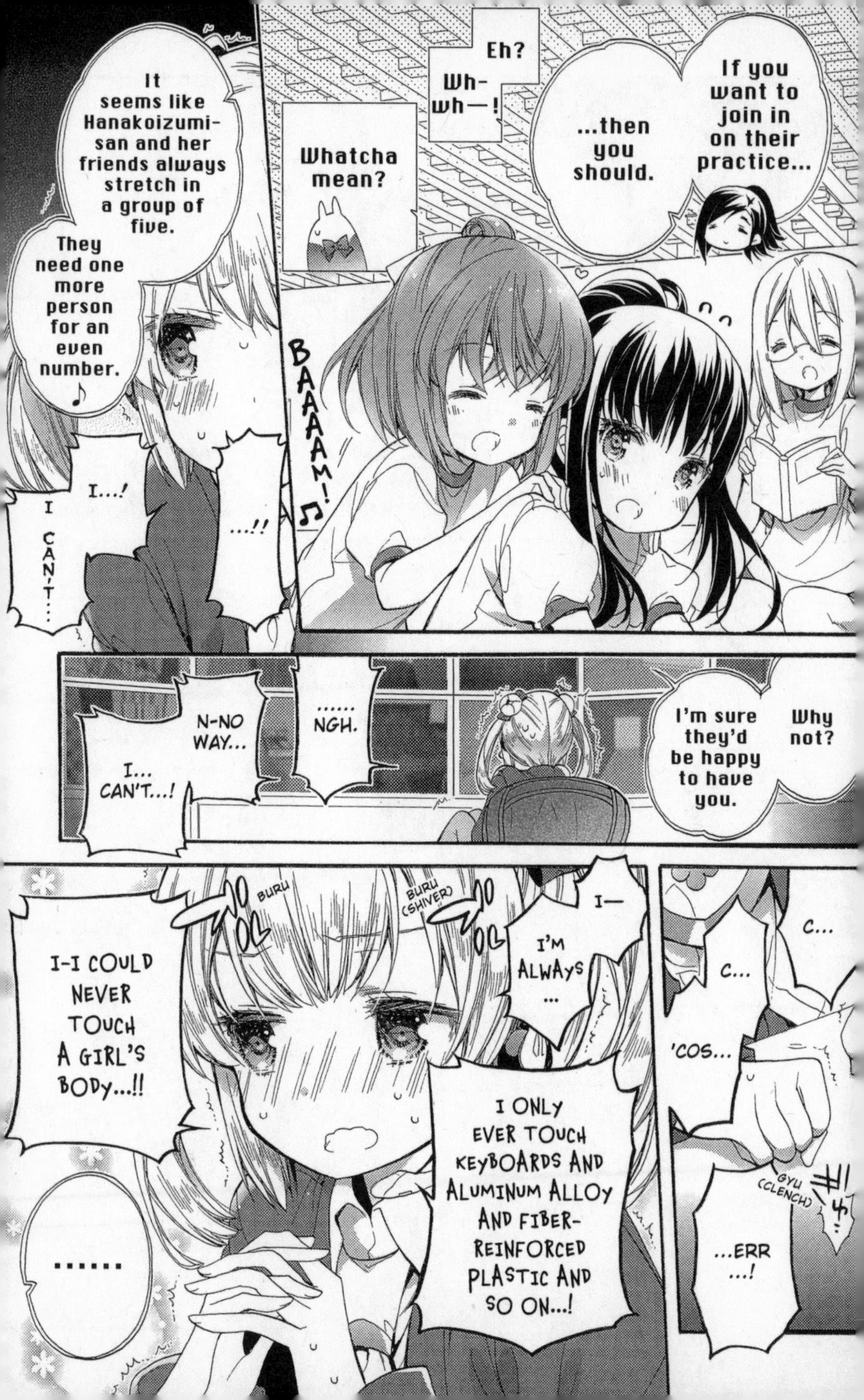
If you want to join in on their practice...
...then you should.
Eh?
Wh-wh—!
Whatcha mean?
BAAAAAM! ♫
It seems like Hanakoizumi-san and her friends always stretch in a group of five.
They need one more person for an even number. ♪
I...!
...!!
I CAN'T...
Why not?
I'm sure they'd be happy to have you.
...... NGH.
N-NO WAY...
I... CAN'T...!
C...
C...
'COS...
GYU (CLENCH)
...ERR ...!
I—
I'M ALWAYS ...
BURU (SHIVER)
BURU
I ONLY EVER TOUCH KEYBOARDS AND ALUMINUM ALLOY AND FIBER-REINFORCED PLASTIC AND SO ON...!
I-I COULD NEVER TOUCH A GIRL'S BODY...!!
......

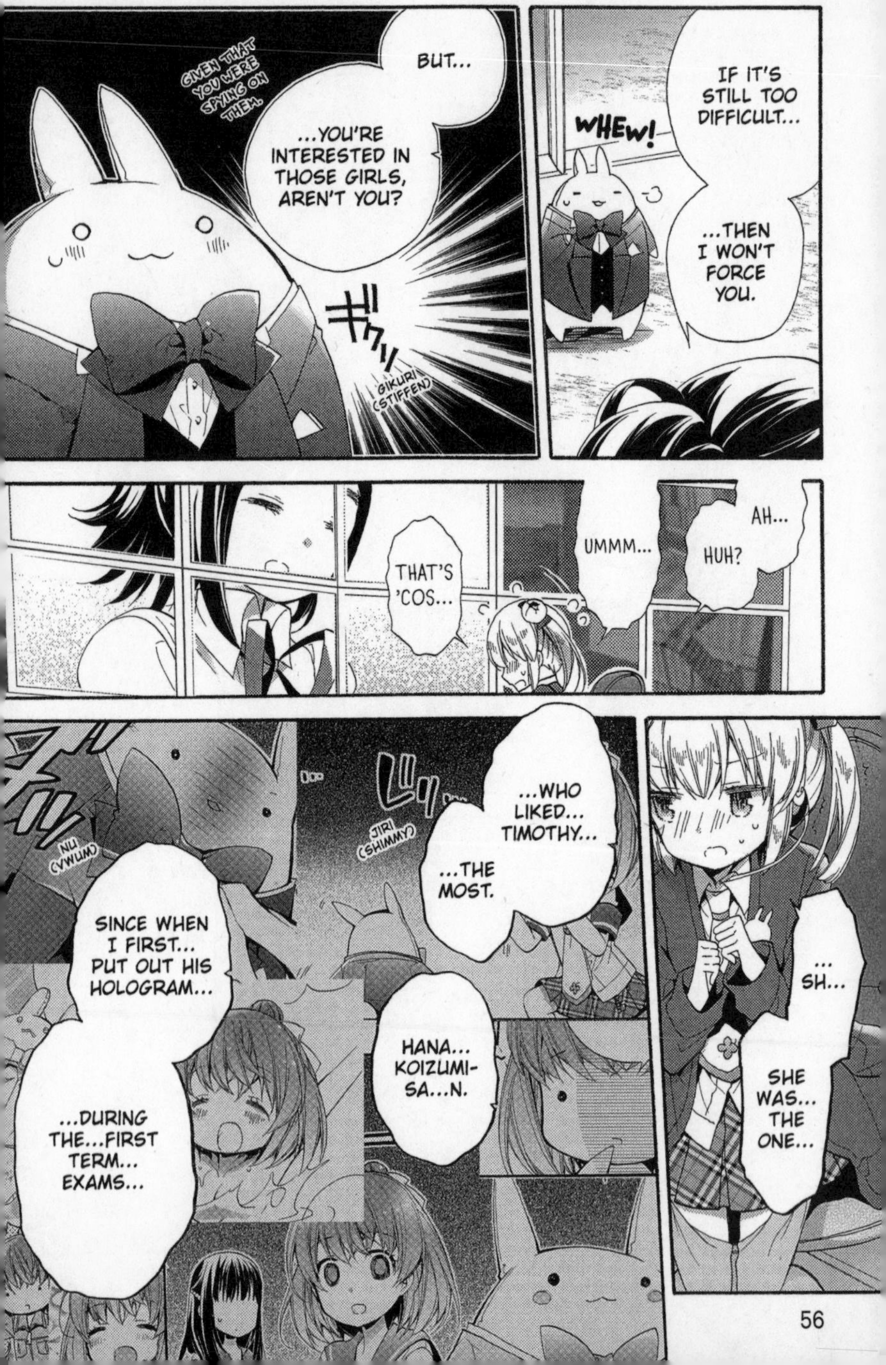
IF IT'S STILL TOO DIFFICULT...
WHEW!
...THEN I WON'T FORCE YOU.
BUT...
...YOU'RE INTERESTED IN THOSE GIRLS, AREN'T YOU?
GIVEN THAT YOU WERE SPYING ON THEM.
GIKURI (STIFFEN)
AH...
HUH?
UMMM...
THAT'S 'COS...
... SH...
SHE WAS... THE ONE...
...WHO LIKED... TIMOTHY...
...THE MOST.
JIRI (SHIMMY)
NU (VWUM)
HANA... KOIZUMI-SA...N.
SINCE WHEN I FIRST... PUT OUT HIS HOLOGRAM...
...DURING THE...FIRST TERM... EXAMS...

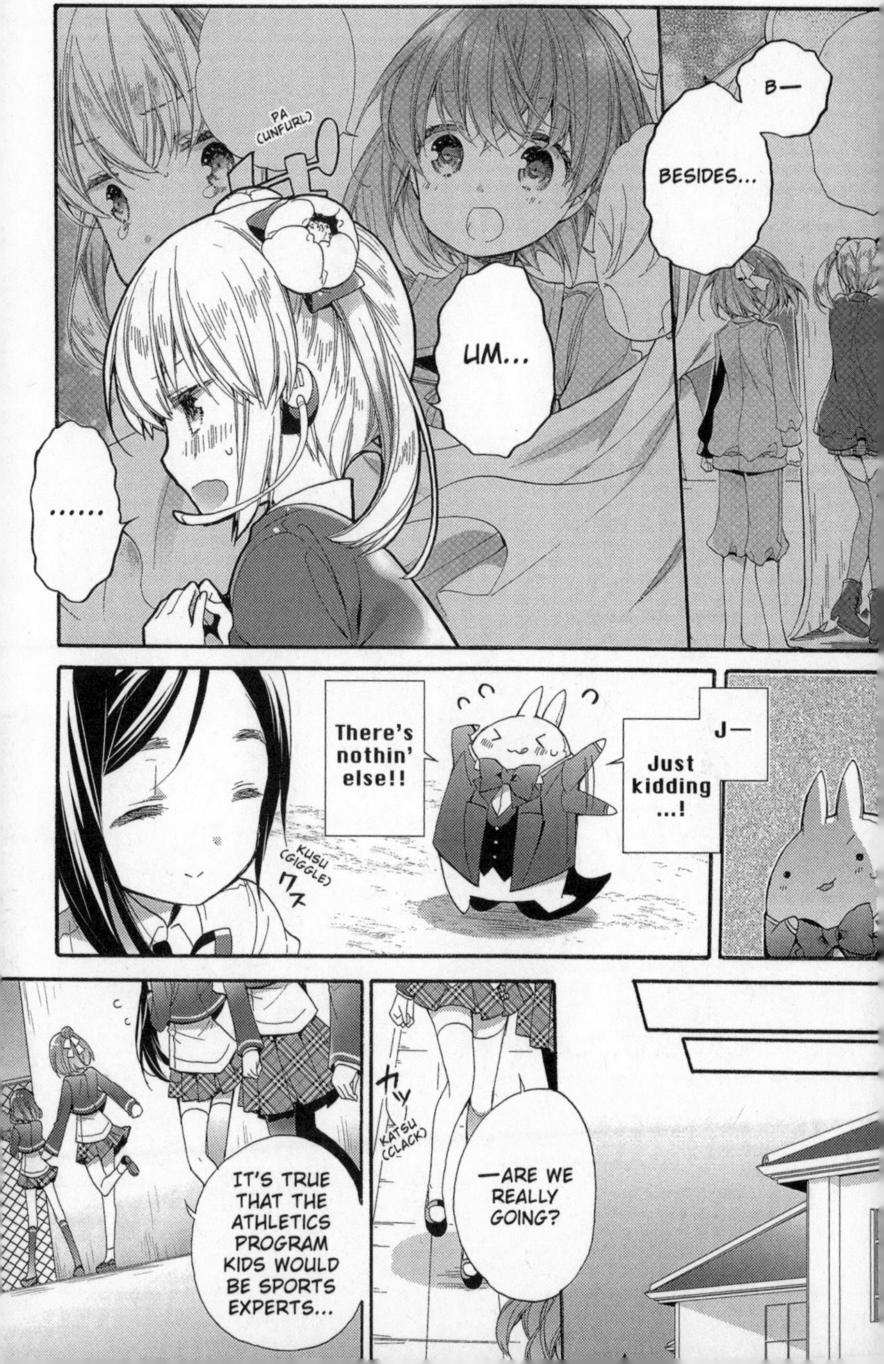
B—
BESIDES…
PA (UNFURL)
UM…
……
J—
Just kidding …!
There's nothin' else!!
KUSU (GIGGLE)
KATSU (CLACK)
—ARE WE REALLY GOING?
IT'S TRUE THAT THE ATHLETICS PROGRAM KIDS WOULD BE SPORTS EXPERTS…

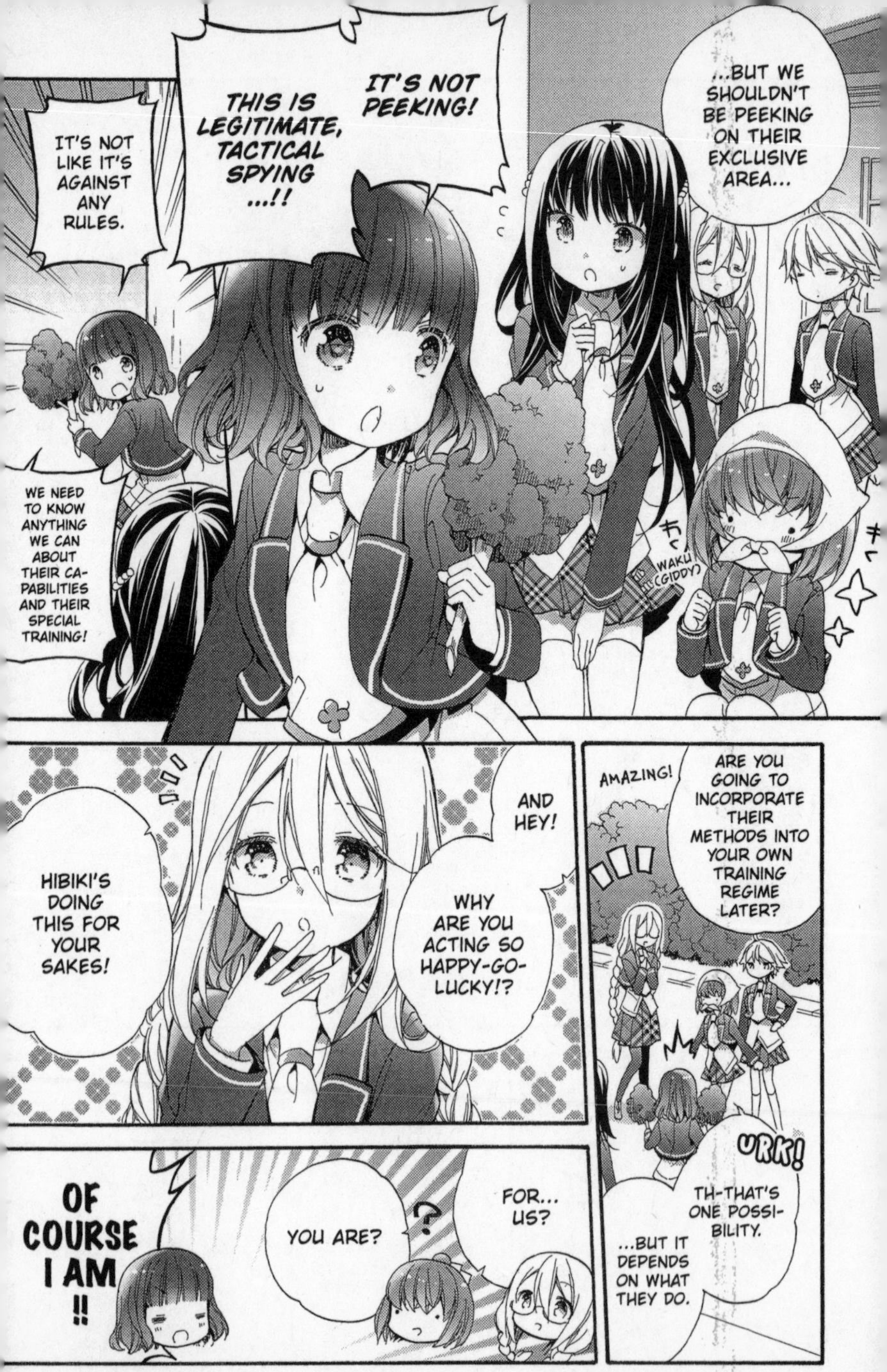
...BUT WE SHOULDN'T BE PEEKING ON THEIR EXCLUSIVE AREA...
IT'S NOT PEEKING!
THIS IS LEGITIMATE, TACTICAL SPYING ...!!
IT'S NOT LIKE IT'S AGAINST ANY RULES.
WAKU (GIDDY)
WE NEED TO KNOW ANYTHING WE CAN ABOUT THEIR CAPABILITIES AND THEIR SPECIAL TRAINING!
ARE YOU GOING TO INCORPORATE THEIR METHODS INTO YOUR OWN TRAINING REGIME LATER?
AMAZING!
URK!
TH-THAT'S ONE POSSIBILITY.
...BUT IT DEPENDS ON WHAT THEY DO.
AND HEY!
WHY ARE YOU ACTING SO HAPPY-GO-LUCKY!?
HIBIKI'S DOING THIS FOR YOUR SAKES!
FOR... US?
YOU ARE?
OF COURSE I AM!!

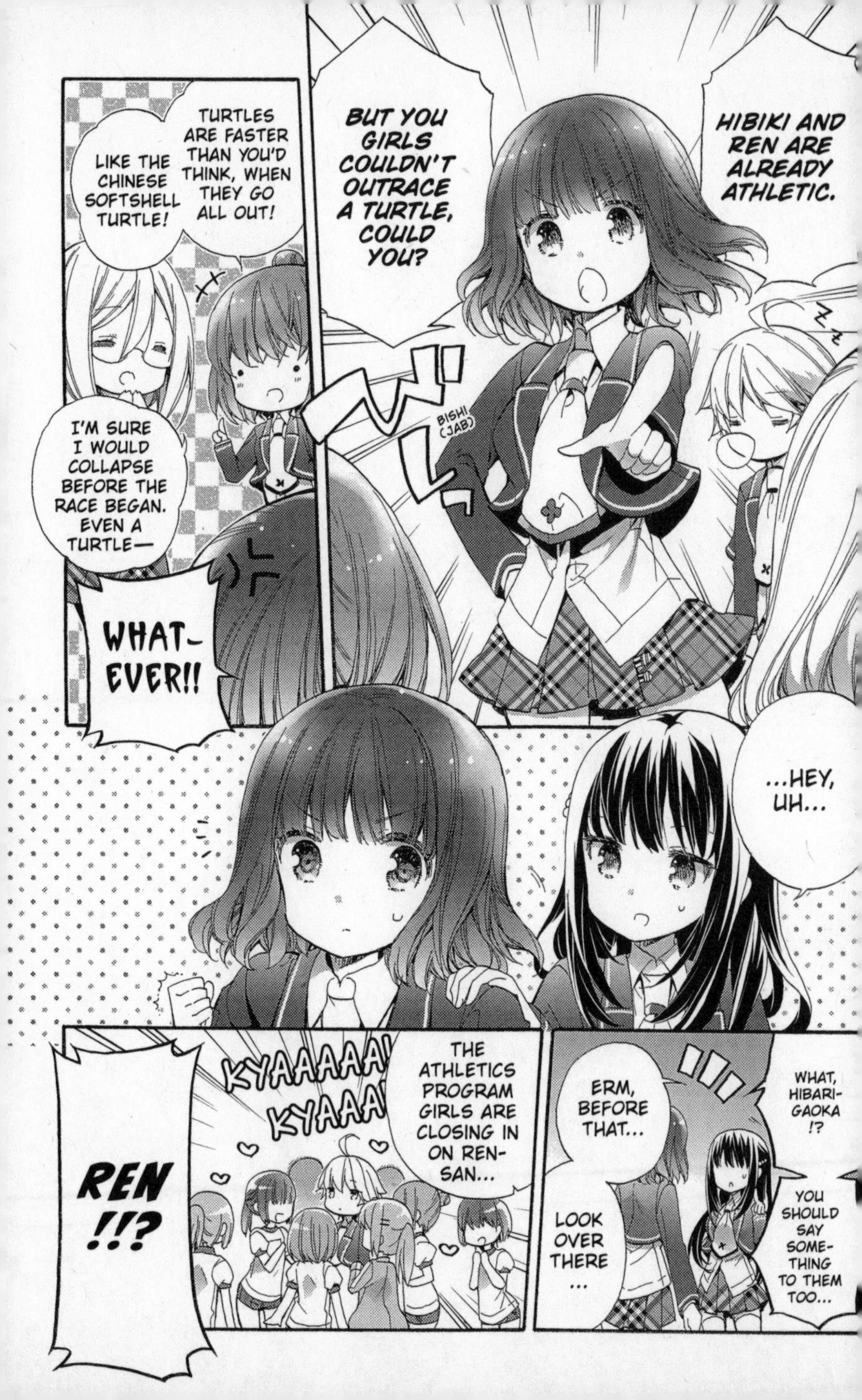
HIBIKI AND REN ARE ALREADY ATHLETIC.
BUT YOU GIRLS COULDN'T OUTRACE A TURTLE, COULD YOU?
BISHI (JAB)
TURTLES ARE FASTER THAN YOU'D THINK, WHEN THEY GO ALL OUT!
LIKE THE CHINESE SOFTSHELL TURTLE!
I'M SURE I WOULD COLLAPSE BEFORE THE RACE BEGAN. EVEN A TURTLE—
WHAT-EVER!!
...HEY, UH...
WHAT, HIBARI-GAOKA!?
ERM, BEFORE THAT...
YOU SHOULD SAY SOME-THING TO THEM TOO...
LOOK OVER THERE...
THE ATHLETICS PROGRAM GIRLS ARE CLOSING IN ON REN-SAN...
KYAAAAA!
KYAAA
REN!!?

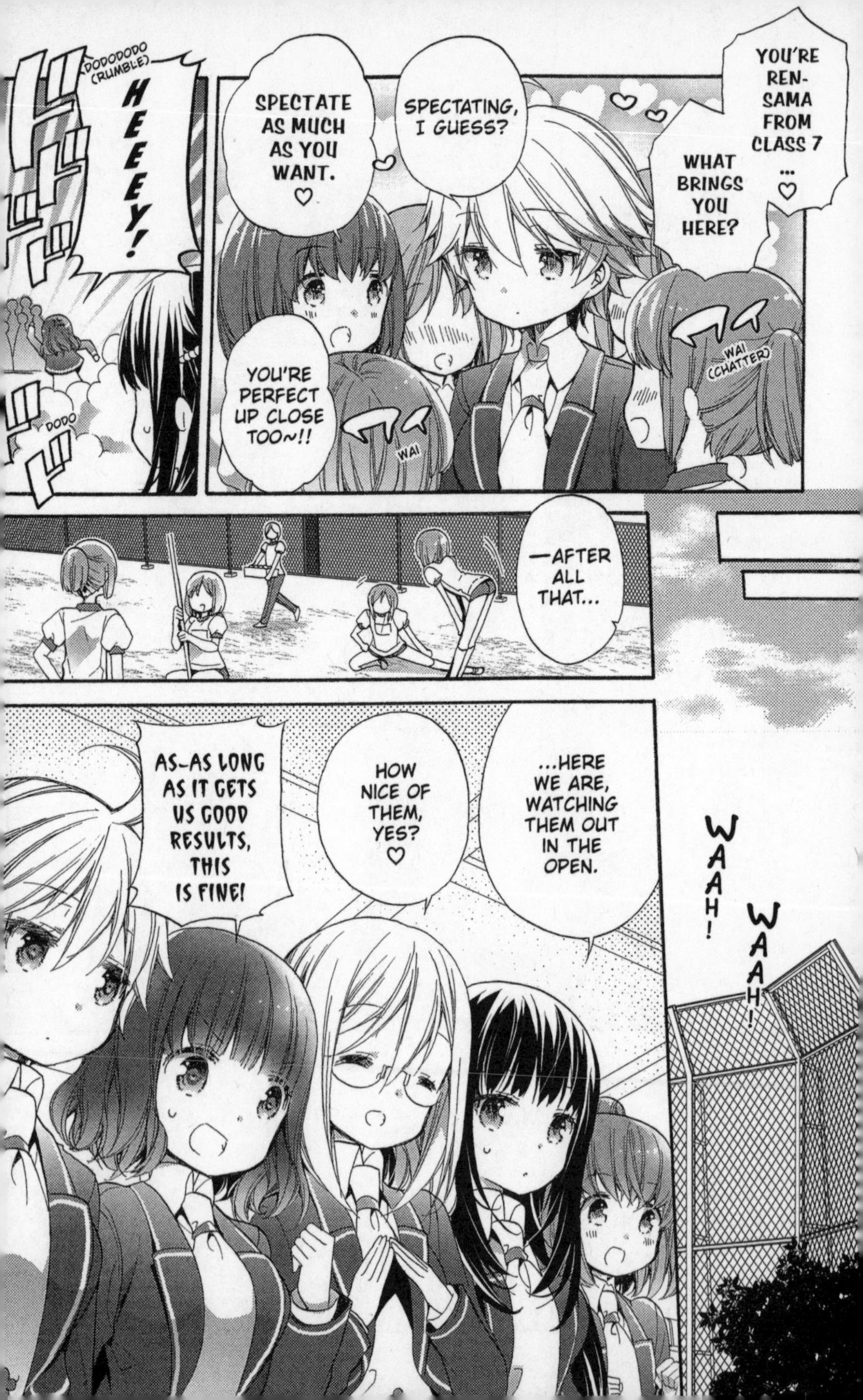
YOU'RE REN-SAMA FROM CLASS 7 ... ♡
WHAT BRINGS YOU HERE?
SPECTATING, I GUESS?
SPECTATE AS MUCH AS YOU WANT. ♡
WAI (CHATTER)
YOU'RE PERFECT UP CLOSE TOO~!!
WAI
DODODODO (RUMBLE)
HEEEEY!
DODO
—AFTER ALL THAT...
WAAAH! WAAAH!
...HERE WE ARE, WATCHING THEM OUT IN THE OPEN.
HOW NICE OF THEM, YES? ♡
AS-AS LONG AS IT GETS US GOOD RESULTS, THIS IS FINE!

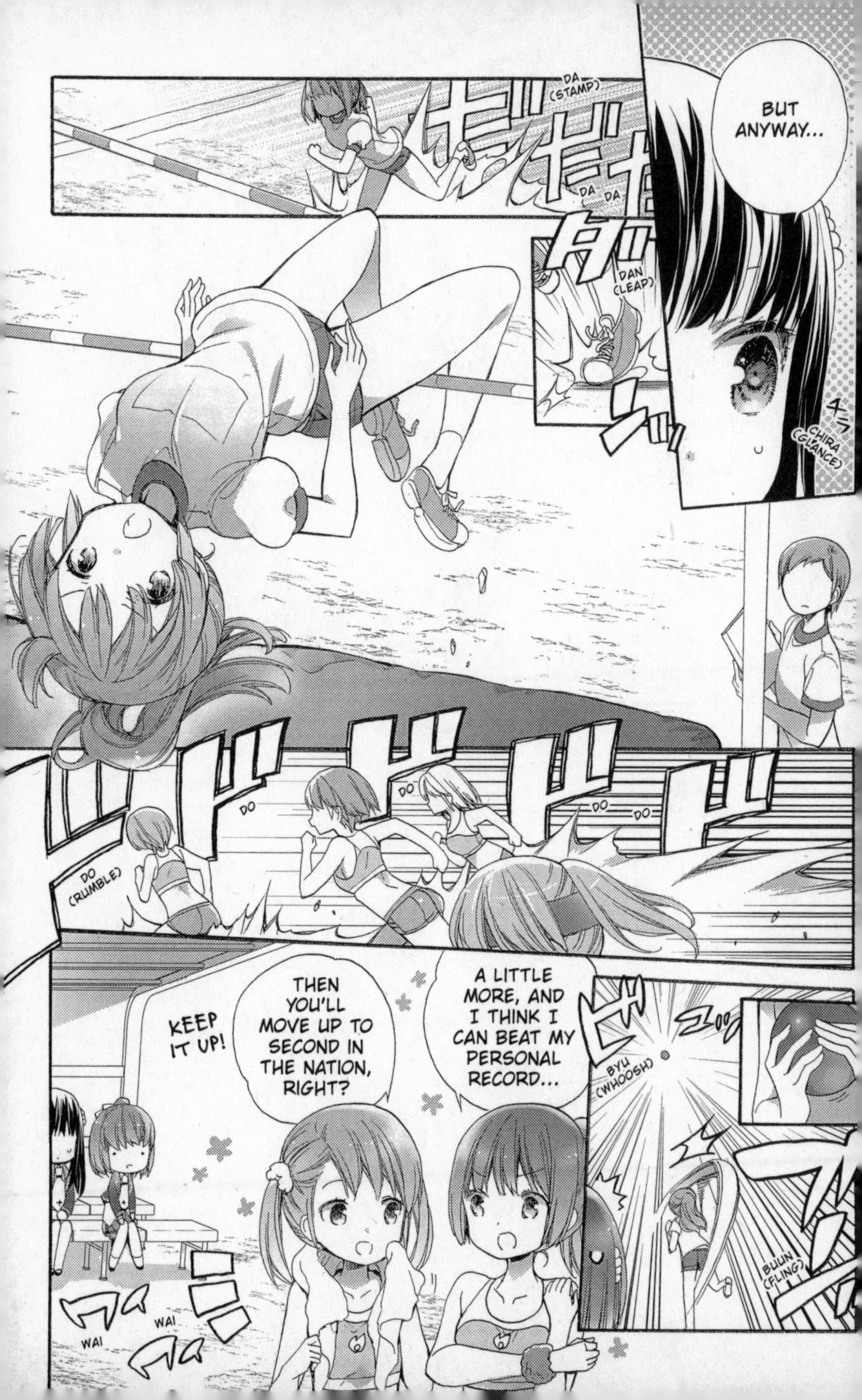
BUT ANYWAY...
CHIRA (GLANCE)
DA (STAMP)
DA DA
DAN (LEAP)
DO DO
DO
DO
DO (RUMBLE)
BYU (WHOOSH)
BUUN (FLING)
A LITTLE MORE, AND I THINK I CAN BEAT MY PERSONAL RECORD...
THEN YOU'LL MOVE UP TO SECOND IN THE NATION, RIGHT?
KEEP IT UP!
WAI
WAI

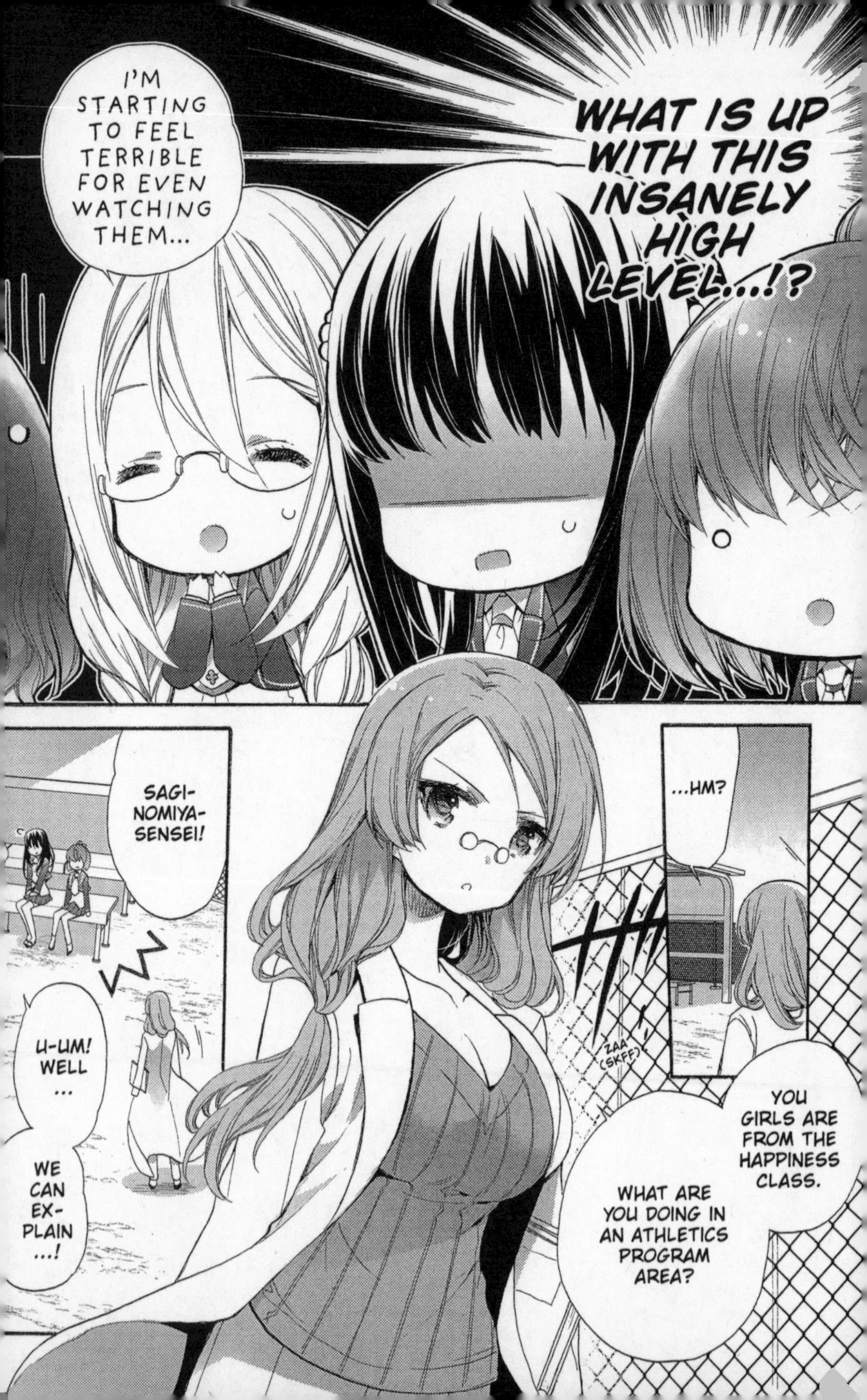
WHAT IS UP WITH THIS INSANELY HIGH LEVEL...!?
I'M STARTING TO FEEL TERRIBLE FOR EVEN WATCHING THEM...
...HM?
ZAA (SKFF)
YOU GIRLS ARE FROM THE HAPPINESS CLASS.
WHAT ARE YOU DOING IN AN ATHLETICS PROGRAM AREA?
SAGI-NOMIYA-SENSEI!
U-UM! WELL...
WE CAN EX-PLAIN...!

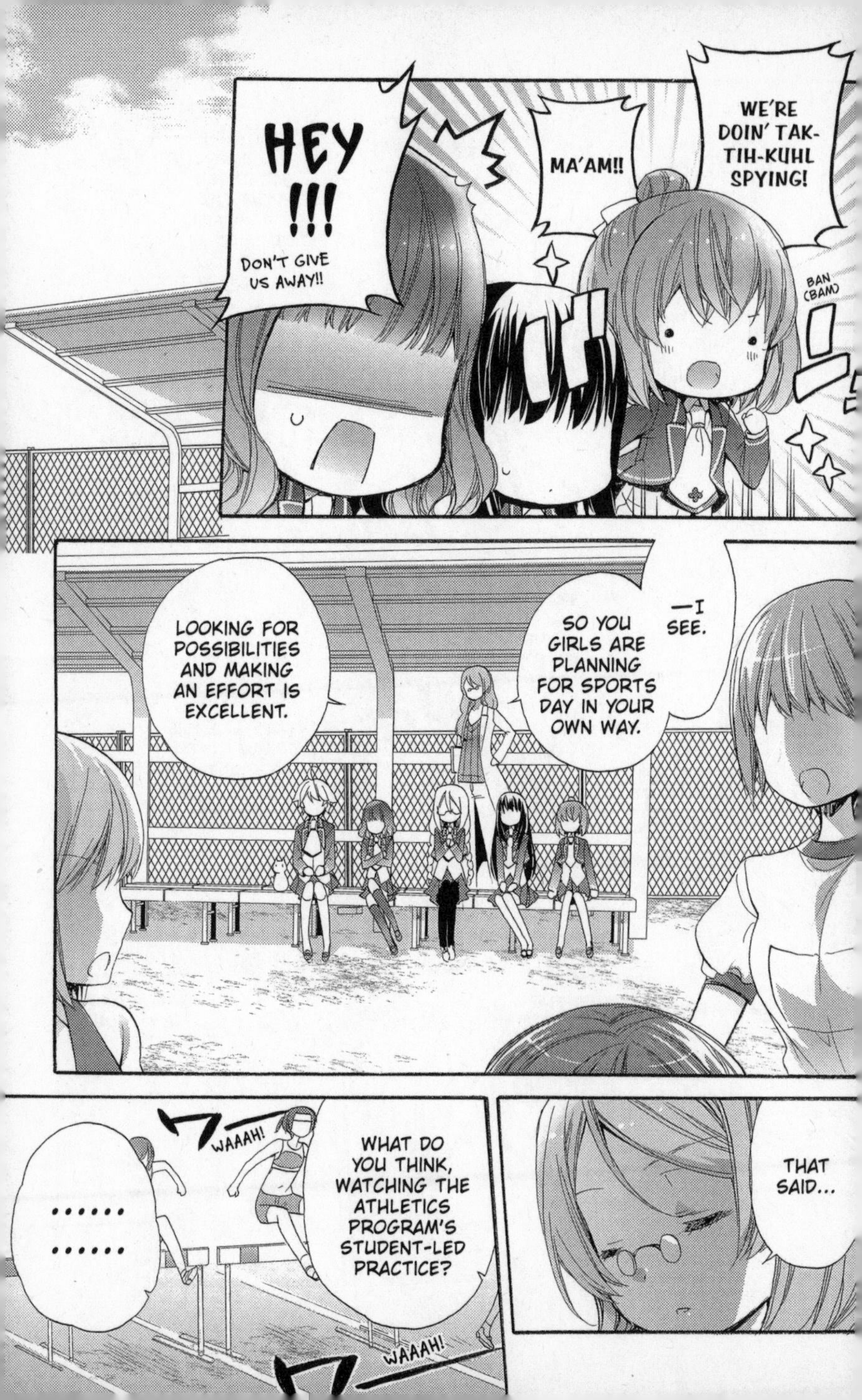
WE'RE DOIN' TAK-TIH-KUHL SPYING!
BAN (BAM)
MA'AM!!
HEY!!!
DON'T GIVE US AWAY!!
—I SEE.
SO YOU GIRLS ARE PLANNING FOR SPORTS DAY IN YOUR OWN WAY.
LOOKING FOR POSSIBILITIES AND MAKING AN EFFORT IS EXCELLENT.
THAT SAID...
WHAT DO YOU THINK, WATCHING THE ATHLETICS PROGRAM'S STUDENT-LED PRACTICE?
WAAAH!
WAAAH!
......
......

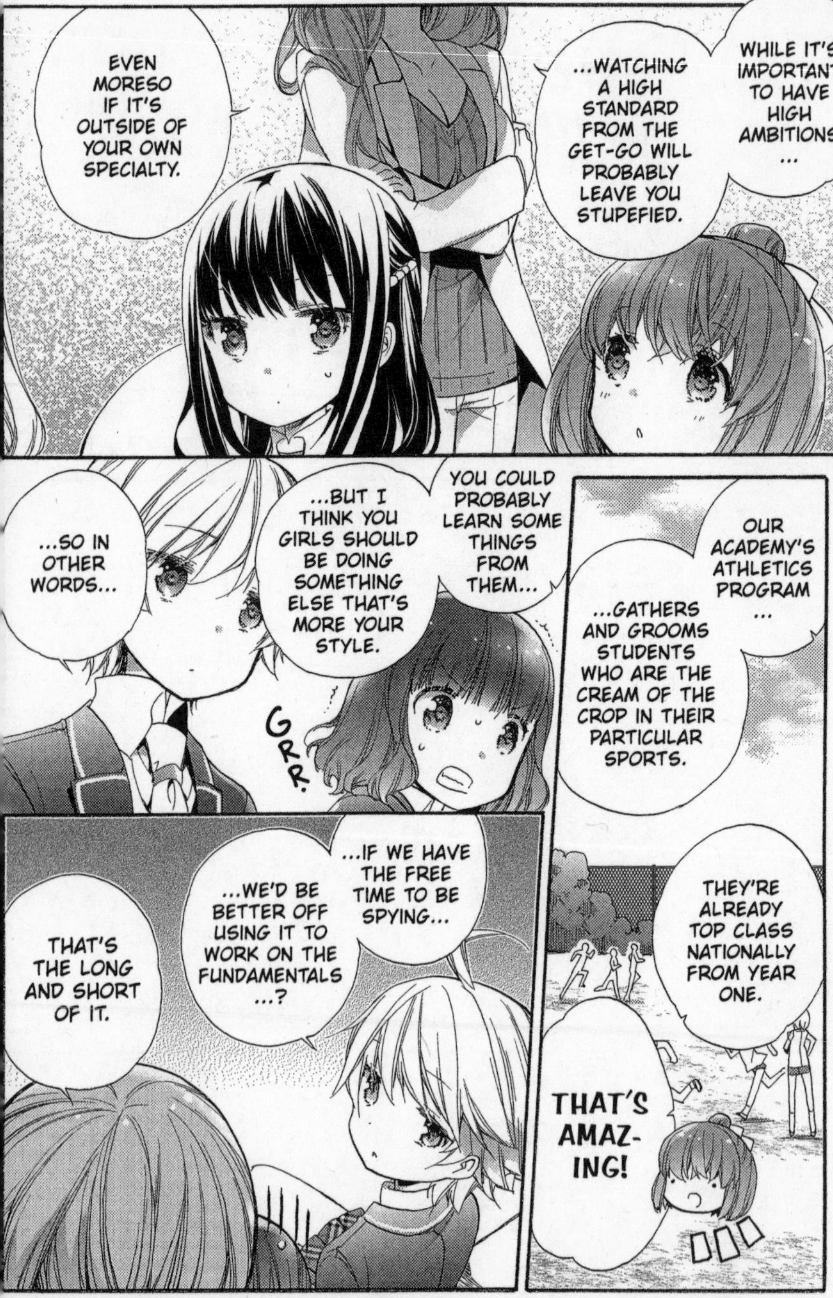
WHILE IT'S IMPORTANT TO HAVE HIGH AMBITIONS...
...WATCHING A HIGH STANDARD FROM THE GET-GO WILL PROBABLY LEAVE YOU STUPEFIED.
EVEN MORESO IF IT'S OUTSIDE OF YOUR OWN SPECIALTY.
OUR ACADEMY'S ATHLETICS PROGRAM...
...GATHERS AND GROOMS STUDENTS WHO ARE THE CREAM OF THE CROP IN THEIR PARTICULAR SPORTS.
THEY'RE ALREADY TOP CLASS NATIONALLY FROM YEAR ONE.
THAT'S AMAZ-ING!
YOU COULD PROBABLY LEARN SOME THINGS FROM THEM...
...BUT I THINK YOU GIRLS SHOULD BE DOING SOMETHING ELSE THAT'S MORE YOUR STYLE.
...SO IN OTHER WORDS...
GRR.
...IF WE HAVE THE FREE TIME TO BE SPYING...
...WE'D BE BETTER OFF USING IT TO WORK ON THE FUNDAMENTALS...?
THAT'S THE LONG AND SHORT OF IT.

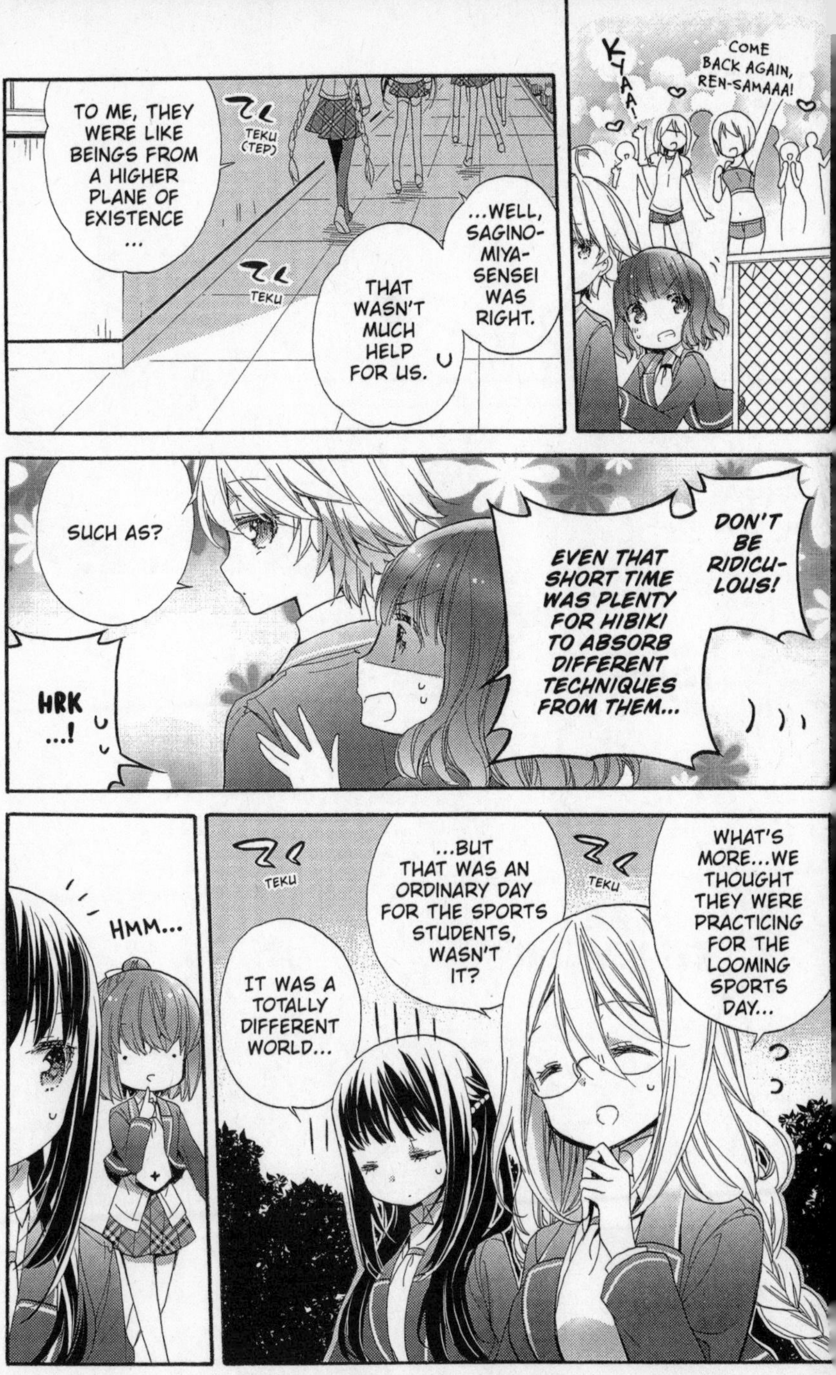
KYAA!
COME BACK AGAIN, REN-SAMAAA!
TEKU (TEP)
...WELL, SAGINOMIYA-SENSEI WAS RIGHT.
TEKU
THAT WASN'T MUCH HELP FOR US.
TO ME, THEY WERE LIKE BEINGS FROM A HIGHER PLANE OF EXISTENCE...
DON'T BE RIDICULOUS!
EVEN THAT SHORT TIME WAS PLENTY FOR HIBIKI TO ABSORB DIFFERENT TECHNIQUES FROM THEM...
SUCH AS?
HRK ...!
WHAT'S MORE...WE THOUGHT THEY WERE PRACTICING FOR THE LOOMING SPORTS DAY...
TEKU
...BUT THAT WAS AN ORDINARY DAY FOR THE SPORTS STUDENTS, WASN'T IT?
TEKU
IT WAS A TOTALLY DIFFERENT WORLD...
HMM...

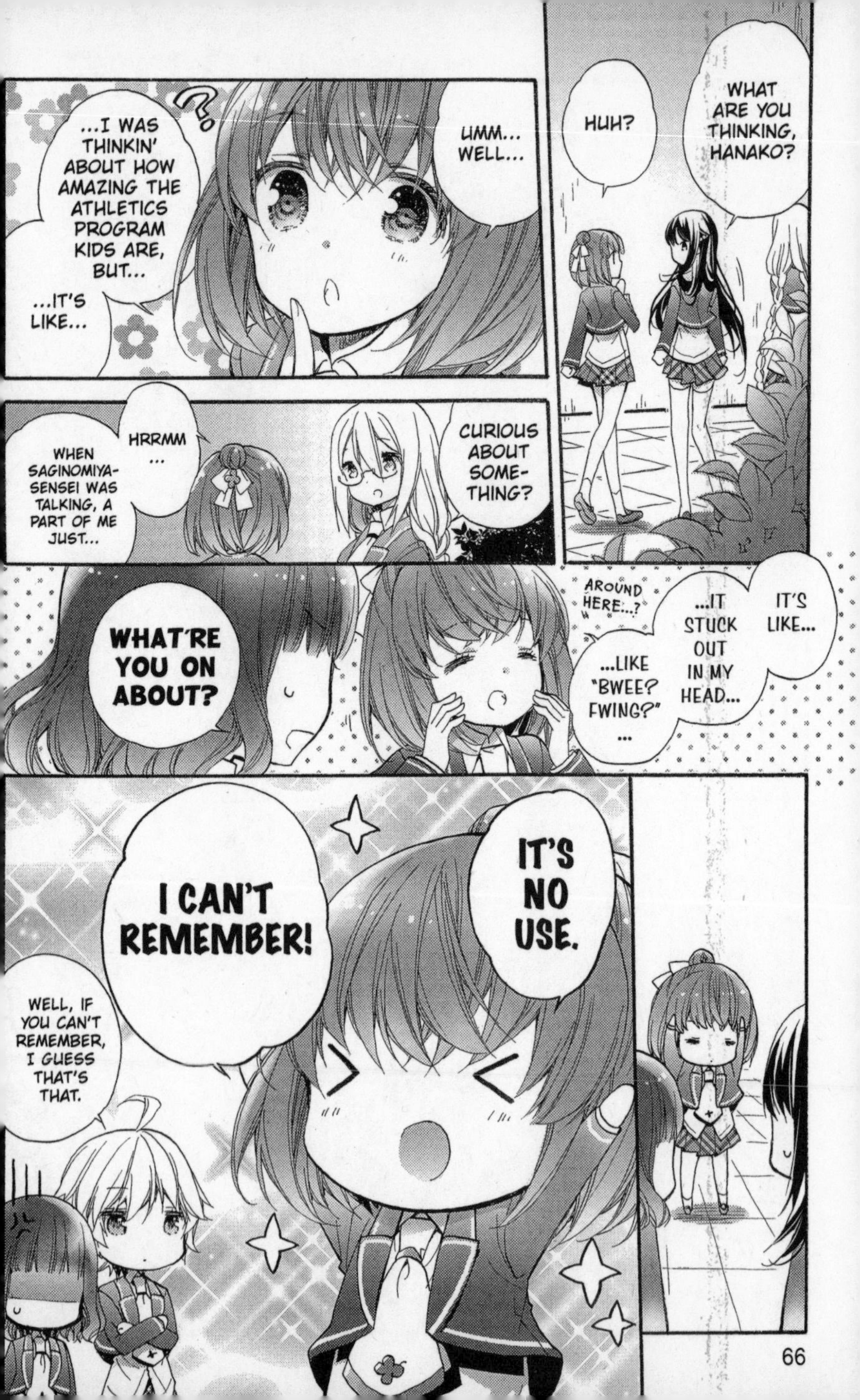
WHAT ARE YOU THINKING, HANAKO?
HUH?
UMM... WELL...
...I WAS THINKIN' ABOUT HOW AMAZING THE ATHLETICS PROGRAM KIDS ARE, BUT...
...IT'S LIKE...
CURIOUS ABOUT SOME-THING?
HRRMM ...
WHEN SAGINOMIYA-SENSEI WAS TALKING, A PART OF ME JUST...
IT'S LIKE...
...IT STUCK OUT IN MY HEAD...
AROUND HERE...?
...LIKE "BWEE? FWING?" ...
WHAT'RE YOU ON ABOUT?
IT'S NO USE.
I CAN'T REMEMBER!
WELL, IF YOU CAN'T REMEMBER, I GUESS THAT'S THAT.

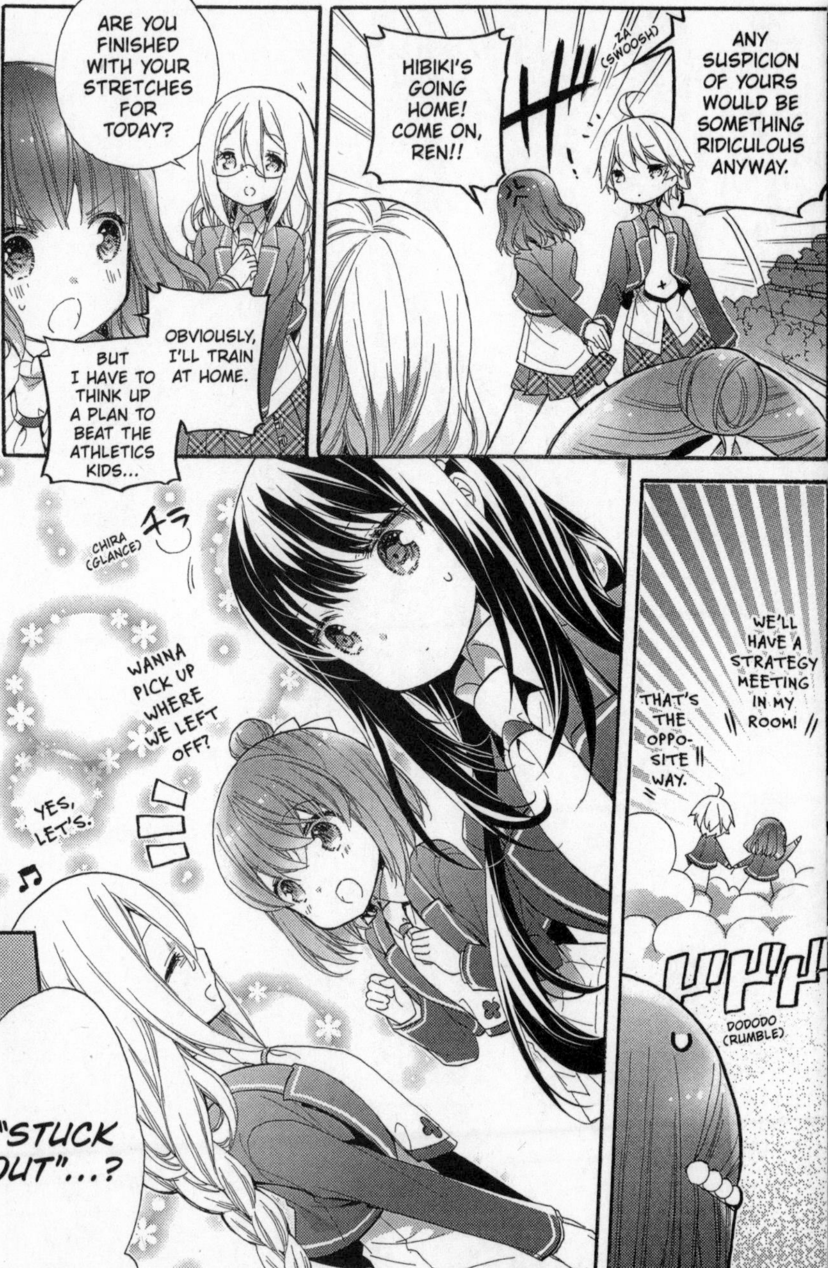
ANY SUSPICION OF YOURS WOULD BE SOMETHING RIDICULOUS ANYWAY.
ZA (SWOOSH)
HIBIKI'S GOING HOME! COME ON, REN!!
ARE YOU FINISHED WITH YOUR STRETCHES FOR TODAY?
OBVIOUSLY, I'LL TRAIN AT HOME.
BUT I HAVE TO THINK UP A PLAN TO BEAT THE ATHLETICS KIDS...
WE'LL HAVE A STRATEGY MEETING IN MY ROOM!
THAT'S THE OPPO-SITE WAY.
DODODO (RUMBLE)
チラ
CHIRA (GLANCE)
WANNA PICK UP WHERE WE LEFT OFF?
YES, LET'S.
♪
"STUCK OUT"...?

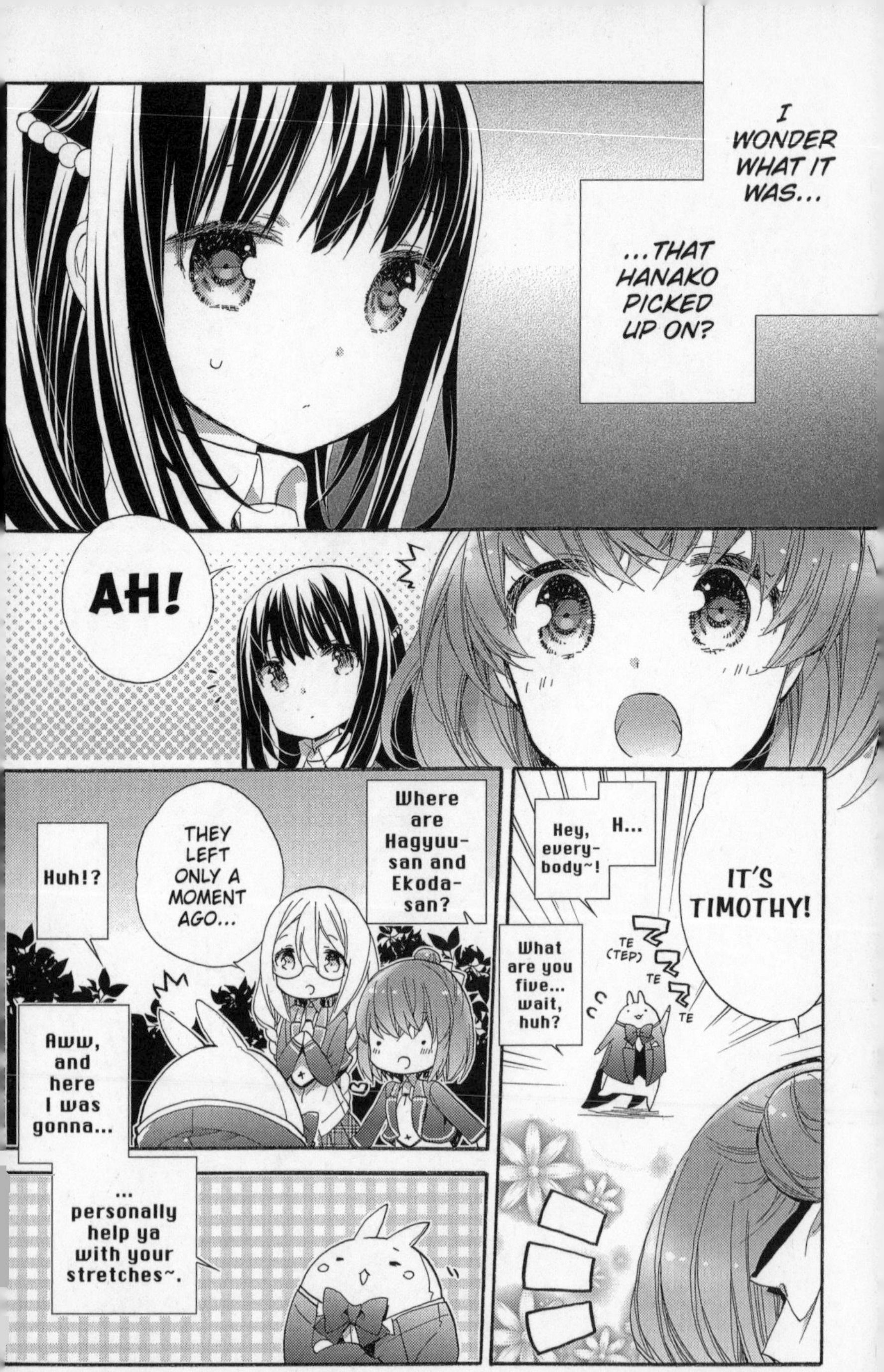
I WONDER WHAT IT WAS...
...THAT HANAKO PICKED UP ON?
AH!
H...
IT'S TIMOTHY!
Hey, everybody~!
TE (TEP) TE TE
What are you five... wait, huh?
Where are Hagyuu-san and Ekoda-san?
THEY LEFT ONLY A MOMENT AGO...
Huh!?
Aww, and here I was gonna...
...personally help ya with your stretches~.

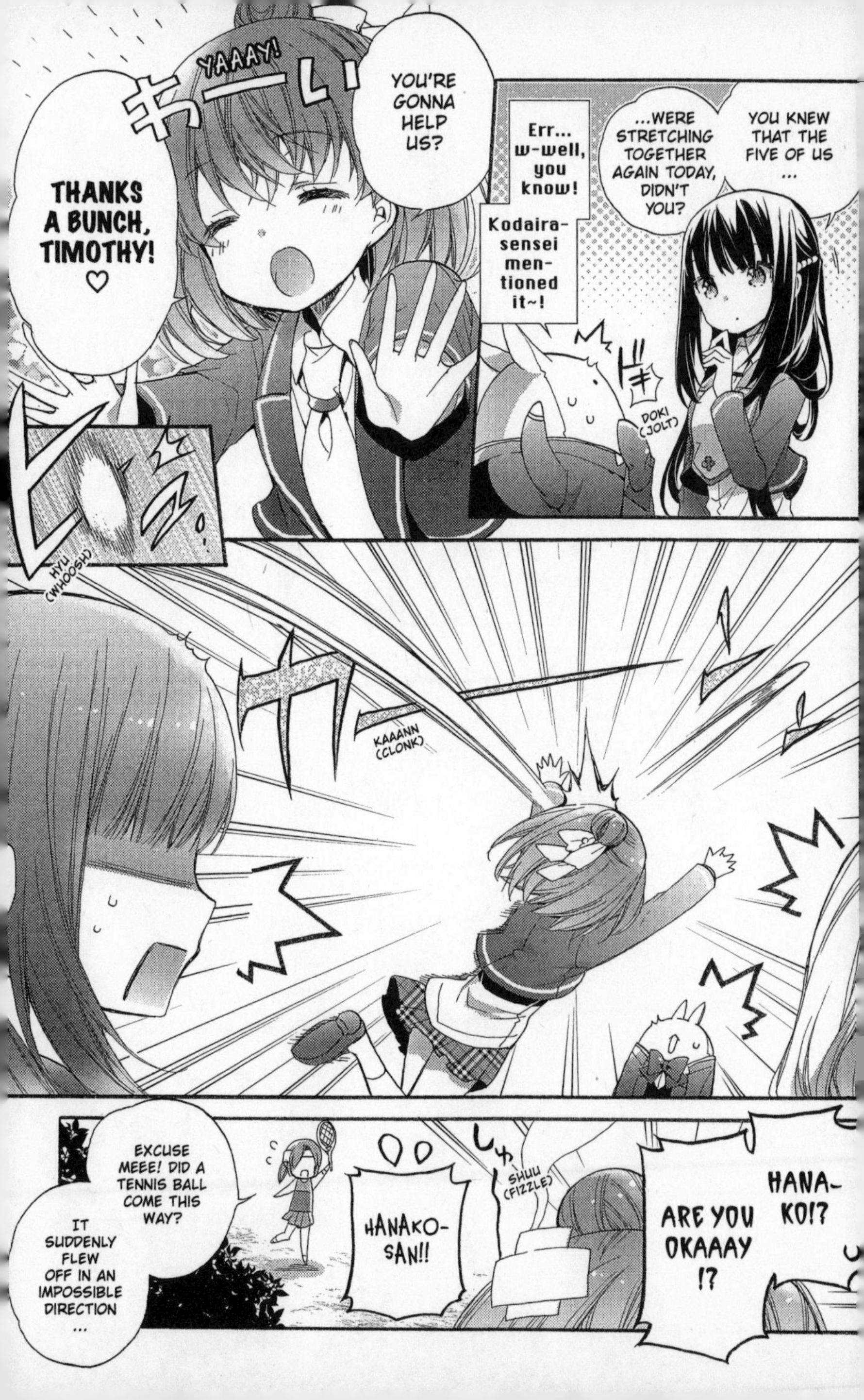
YOU KNEW THAT THE FIVE OF US ...
...WERE STRETCHING TOGETHER AGAIN TODAY, DIDN'T YOU?
Err... w-well, you know!
Kodaira-sensei men-tioned it~!
DOKI (JOLT)
YOU'RE GONNA HELP US?
YAAAY!
THANKS A BUNCH, TIMOTHY! ♡
HYU (WHOOSH)
KAAANN (CLONK)
HANA-KO!?
ARE YOU OKAAAY !?
SHUU (FIZZLE)
HANAKO-SAN!!
EXCUSE MEEE! DID A TENNIS BALL COME THIS WAY?
IT SUDDENLY FLEW OFF IN AN IMPOSSIBLE DIRECTION ...

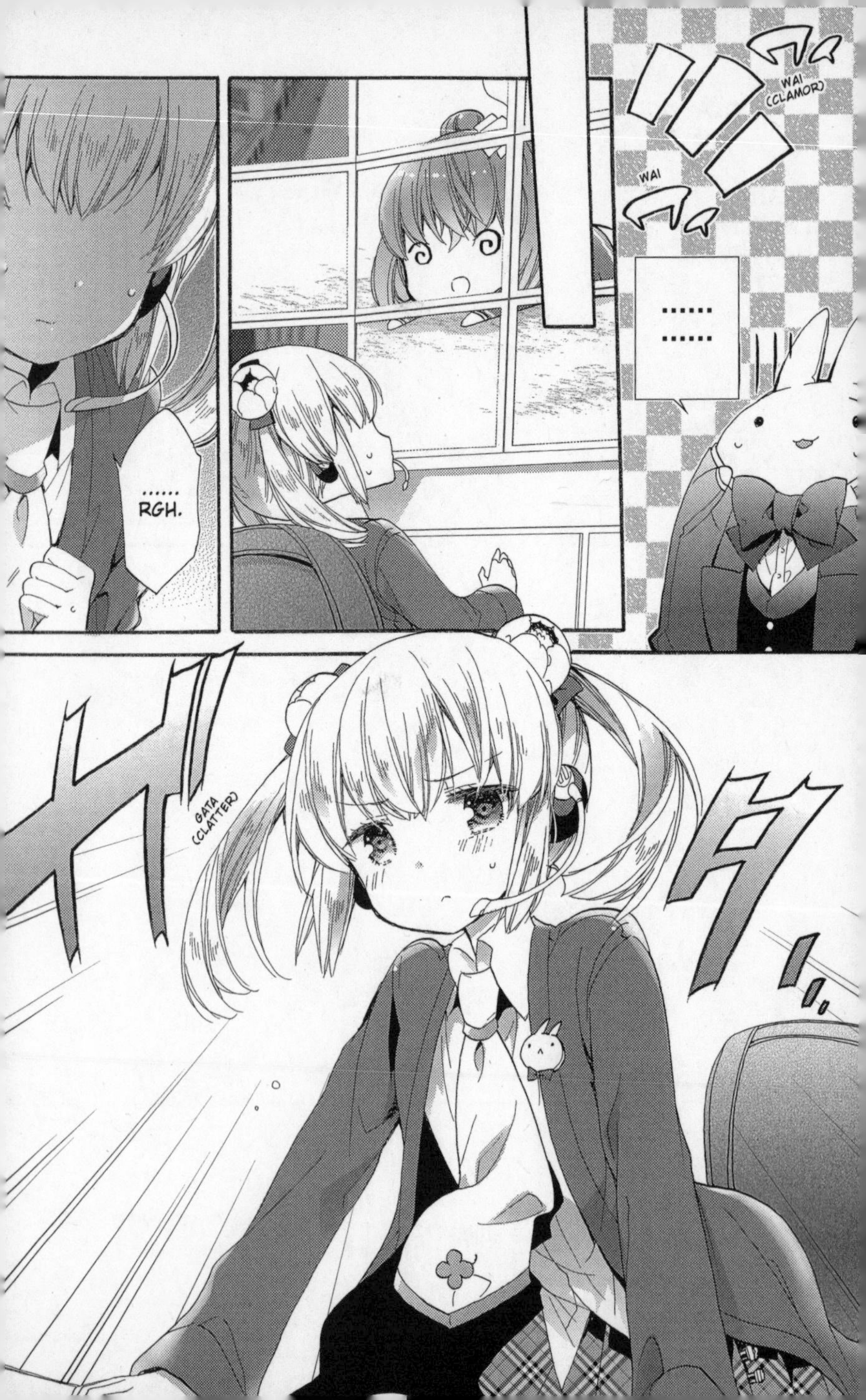
WAI (CLAMOR)
WAI
......
......
......
RGH.
GATA (CLATTER)

Anne Happy

unhappy go lucky!

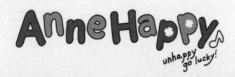

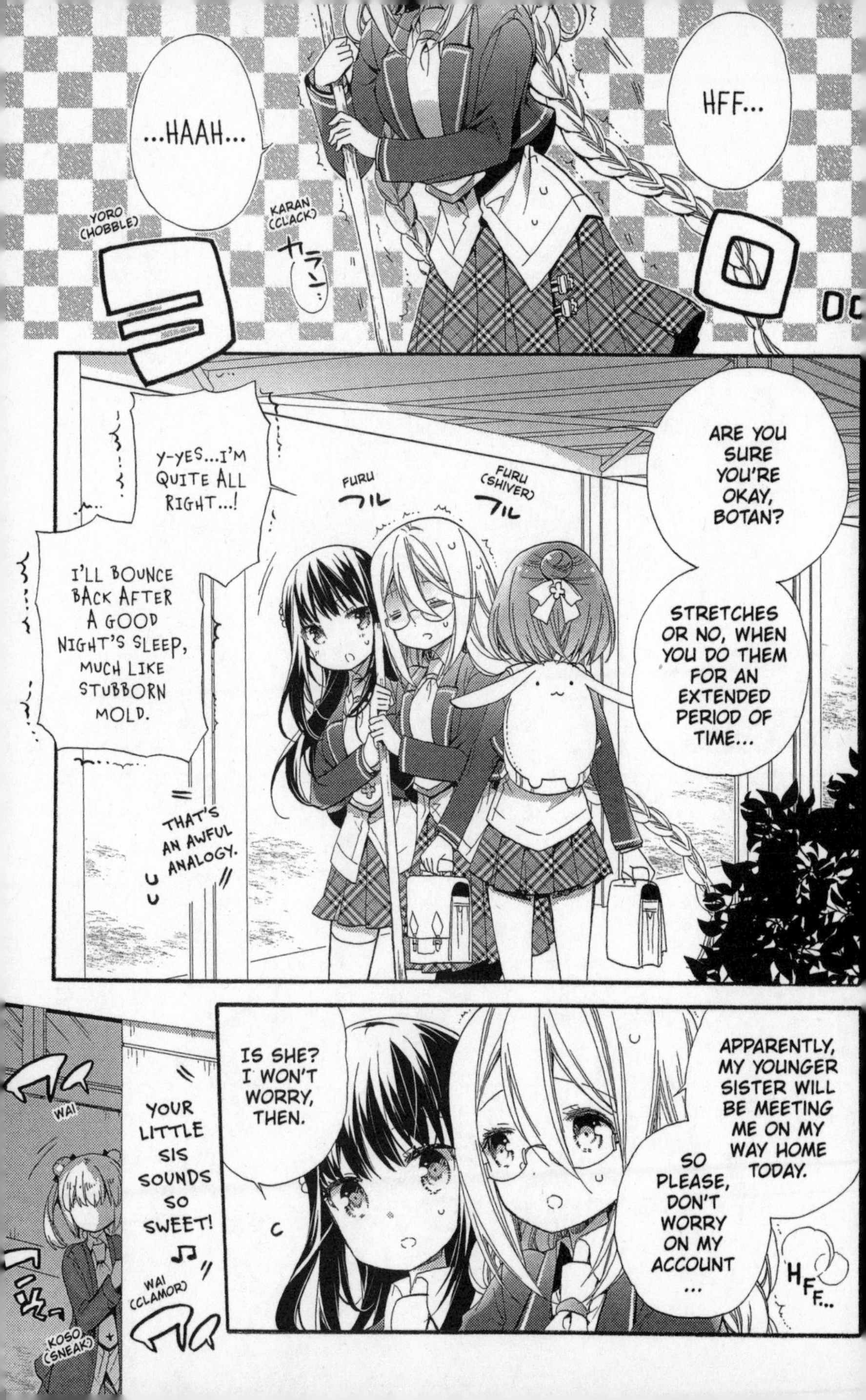
HFF...
...HAAH...
KARAN (CLACK)
YORO (HOBBLE)
ARE YOU SURE YOU'RE OKAY, BOTAN?
STRETCHES OR NO, WHEN YOU DO THEM FOR AN EXTENDED PERIOD OF TIME...
FURU (SHIVER)
FURU
Y-YES...I'M QUITE ALL RIGHT...!
I'LL BOUNCE BACK AFTER A GOOD NIGHT'S SLEEP, MUCH LIKE STUBBORN MOLD.
THAT'S AN AWFUL ANALOGY.
APPARENTLY, MY YOUNGER SISTER WILL BE MEETING ME ON MY WAY HOME TODAY.
SO PLEASE, DON'T WORRY ON MY ACCOUNT...
HFF...
IS SHE? I WON'T WORRY, THEN.
YOUR LITTLE SIS SOUNDS SO SWEET!
WAI
WAI (CLAMOR)
KOSO (SNEAK)

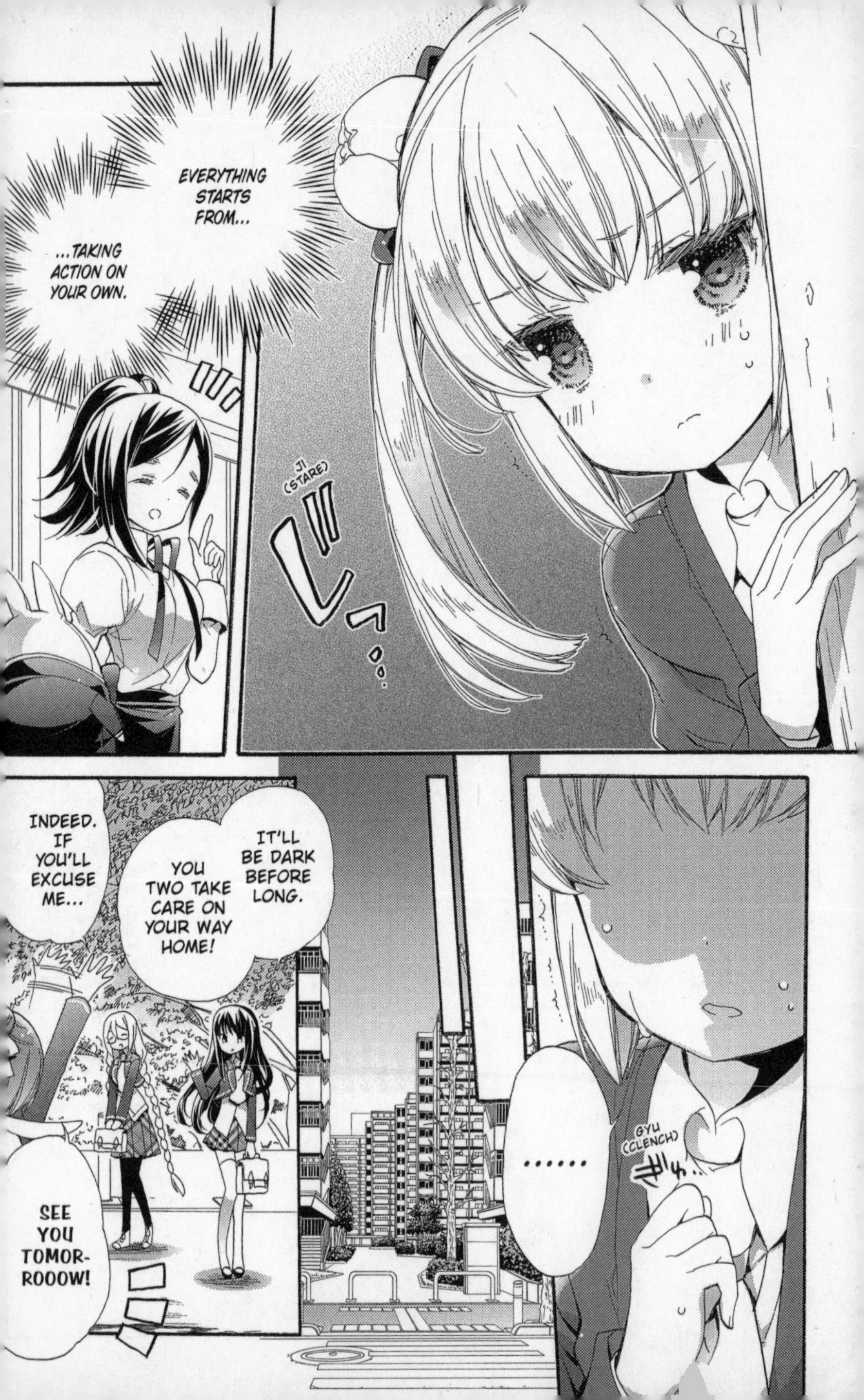
JI (STARE)
EVERYTHING STARTS FROM...
...TAKING ACTION ON YOUR OWN.
......
GYU (CLENCH)
IT'LL BE DARK BEFORE LONG.
YOU TWO TAKE CARE ON YOUR WAY HOME!
INDEED. IF YOU'LL EXCUSE ME...
SEE YOU TOMOR-ROOOW!

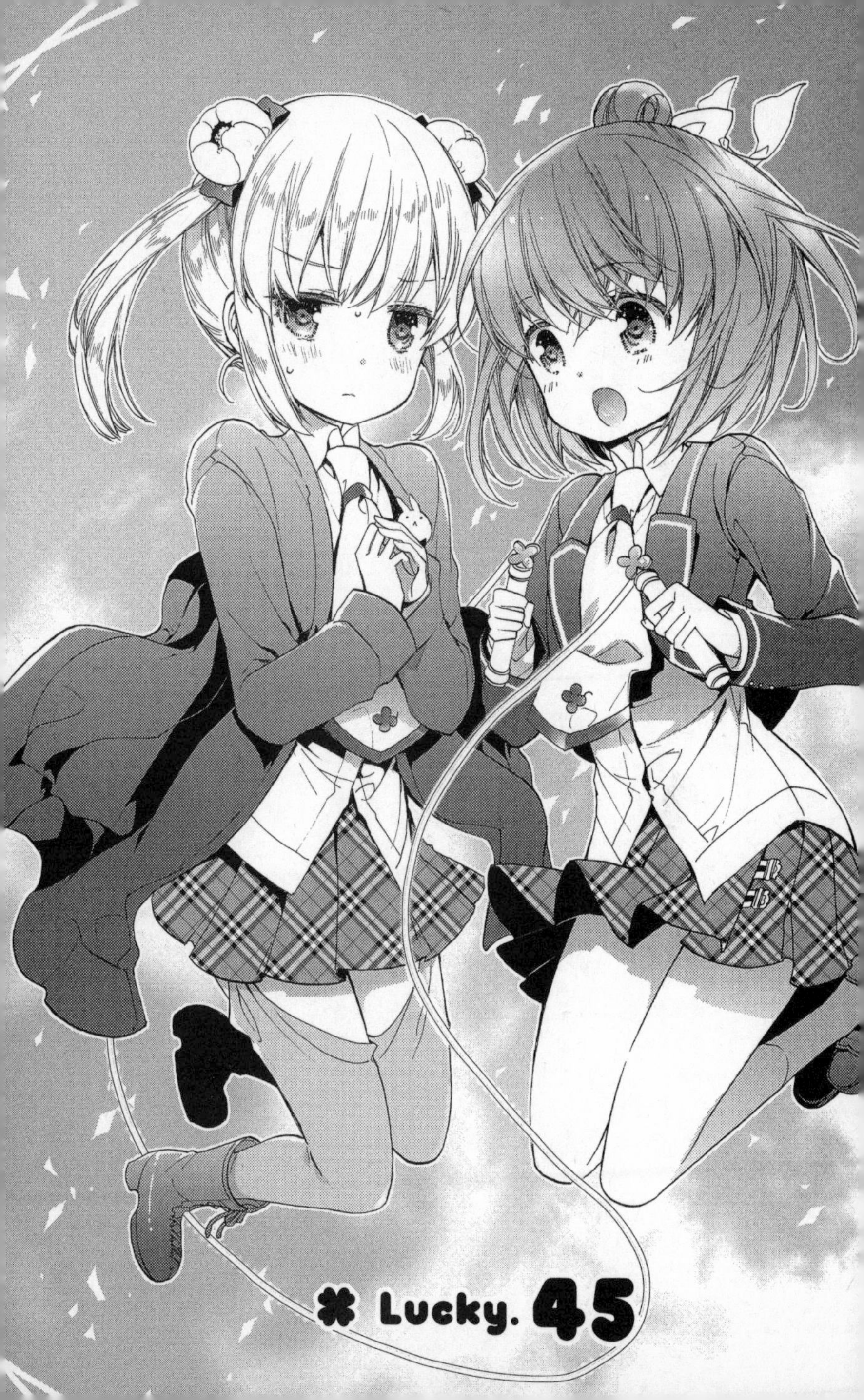
Lucky. 45

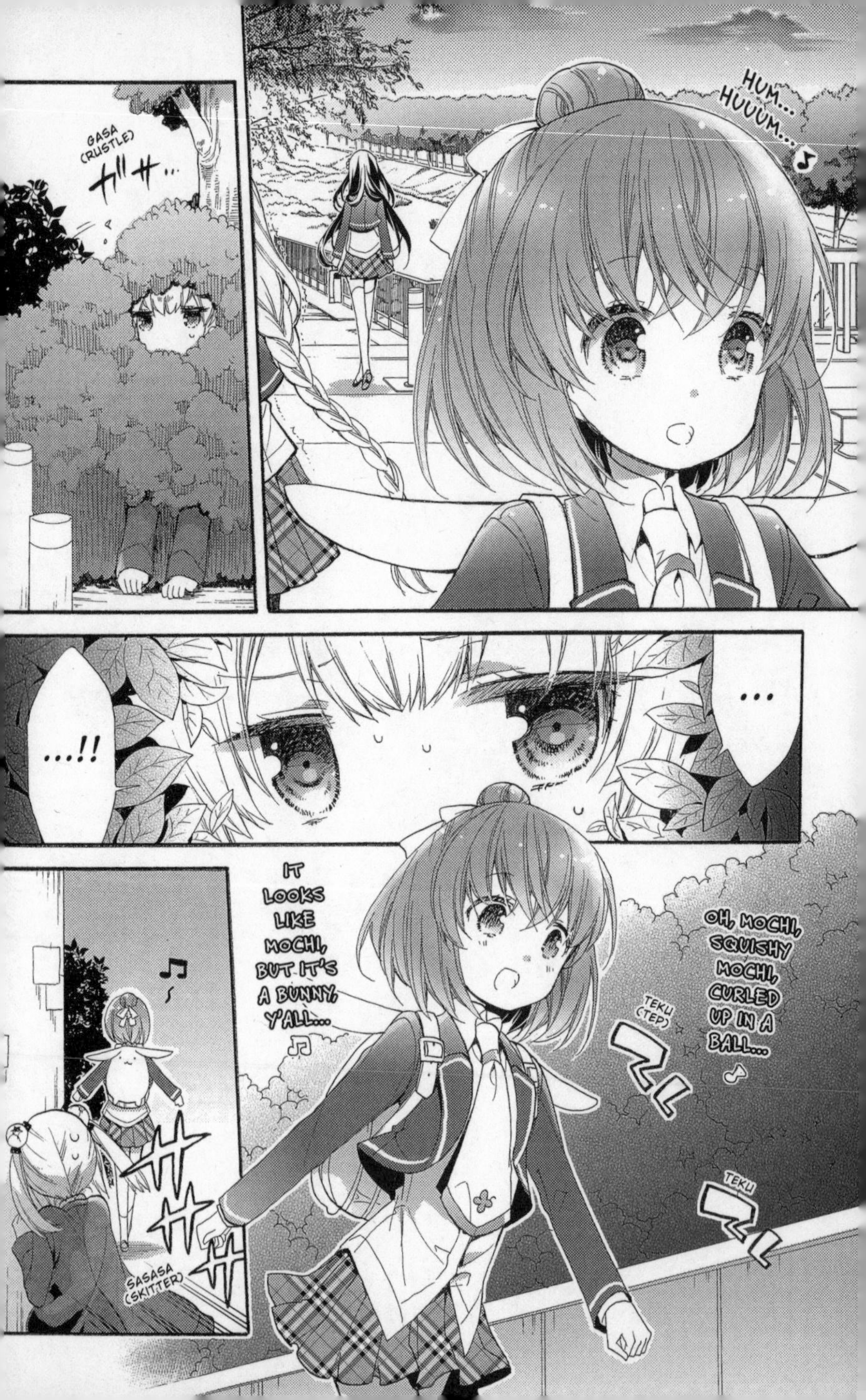
HUM... HUUUM...♪
GASA (RUSTLE)
ガサ…
...
...!!
OH, MOCHI, SQUISHY MOCHI, CURLED UP IN A BALL...♪
TEKU (TEP)
IT LOOKS LIKE MOCHI, BUT IT'S A BUNNY, Y'ALL...♪
TEKU
♪
SASASA (SKITTER)

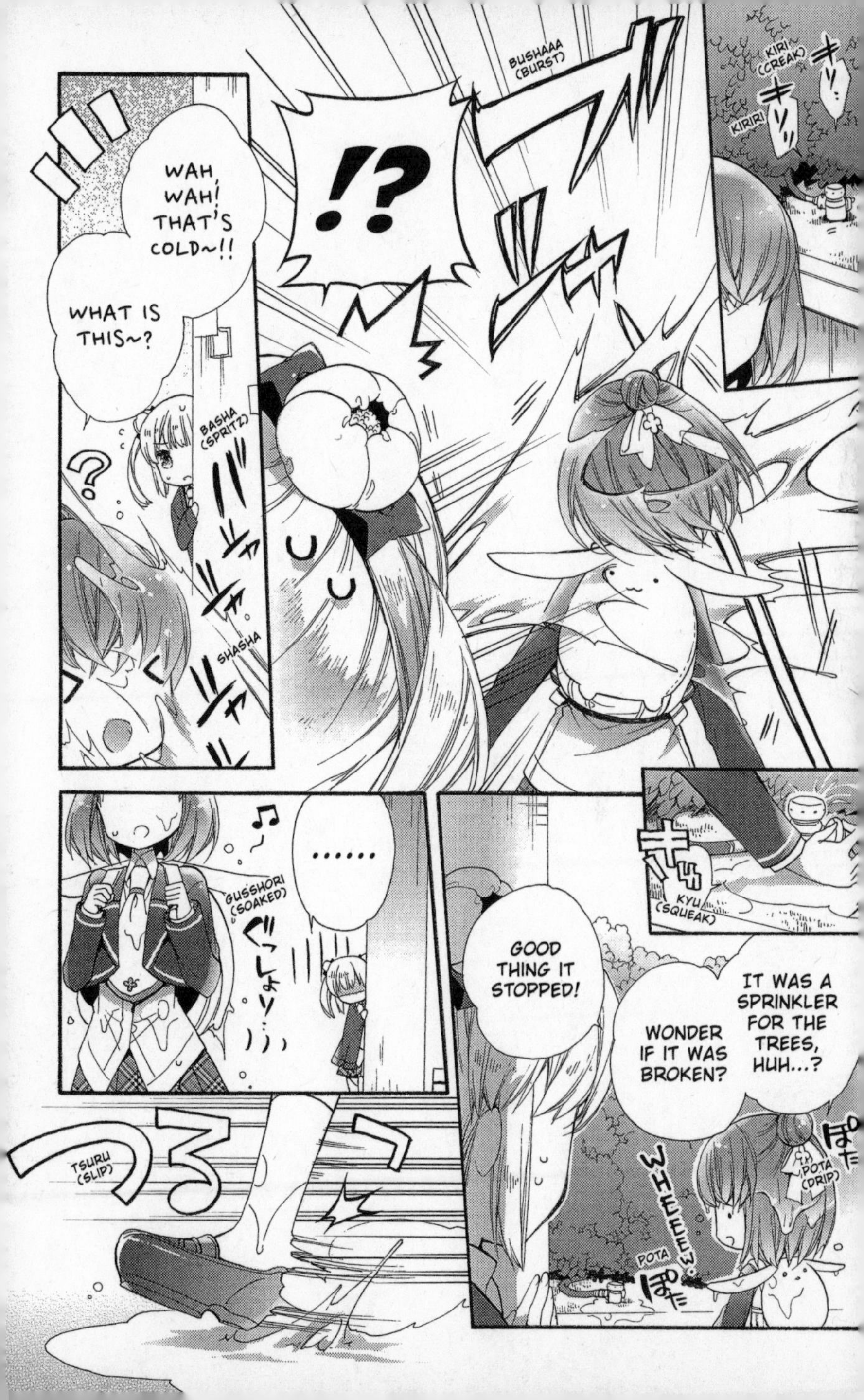

KIRI (CREAK)
KIRIRI
BUSHAAA (BURST)
!?
BASHA (SPRITZ)
SHASHA
WAH, WAH! THAT'S COLD~!!
WHAT IS THIS~?
KYU (SQUEAK)
IT WAS A SPRINKLER FOR THE TREES, HUH...?
GOOD THING IT STOPPED!
WONDER IF IT WAS BROKEN?
POTA (DRIP)
WHEEEW.
POTA
......
GUSSHORI (SOAKED)
TSURU (SLIP)

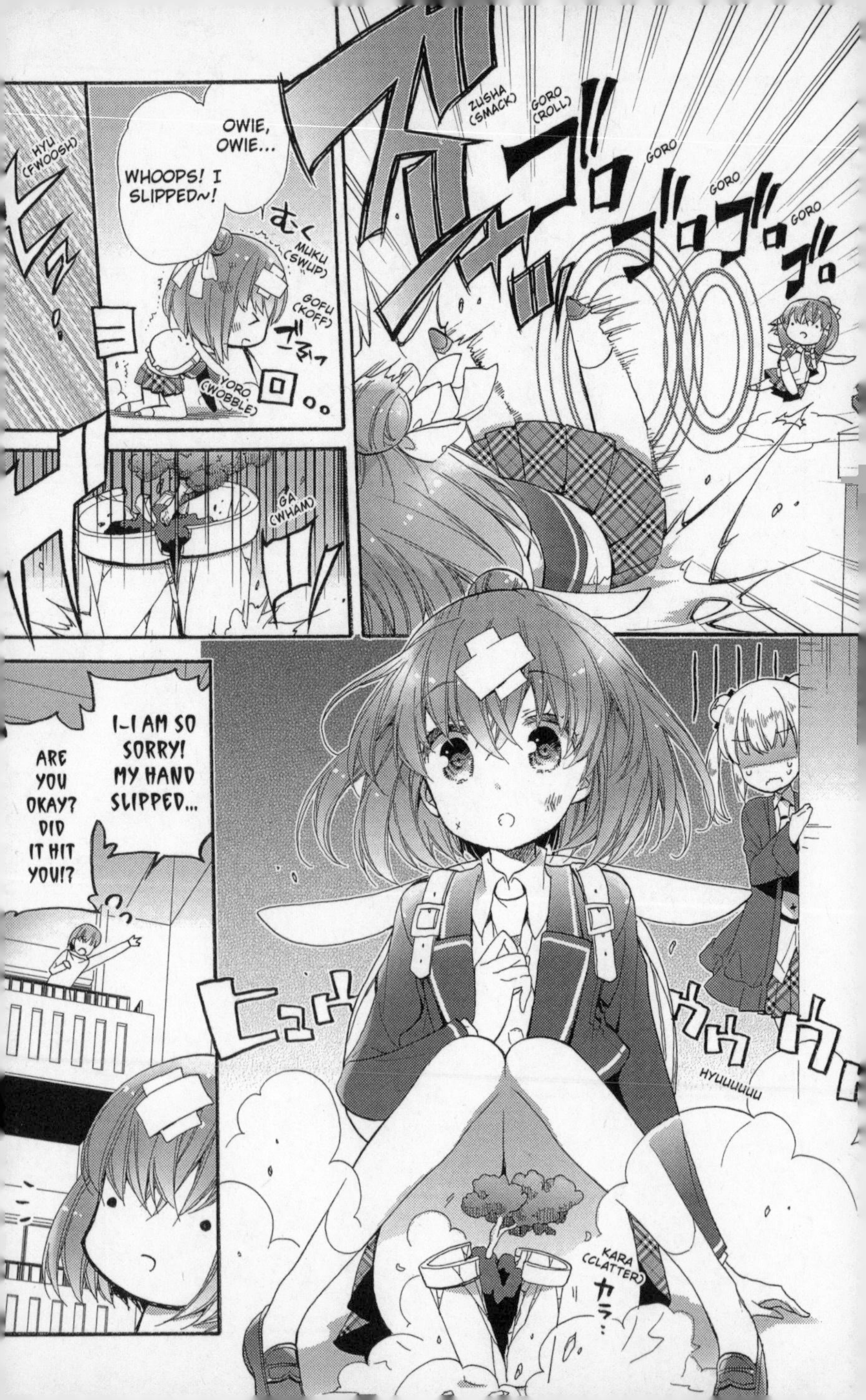

ZUSHA (SMACK)
GORO (ROLL)
GORO
GORO
GORO
OWIE, OWIE...
WHOOPS! I SLIPPED~!
MUKU (SWUP)
GOFU (KOFF)
YORO (WOBBLE)
HYU (FWOOSH)
GA (WHAM)
HYUUUUUU
KARA (CLATTER)
I-I AM SO SORRY! MY HAND SLIPPED...
ARE YOU OKAY? DID IT HIT YOU!?

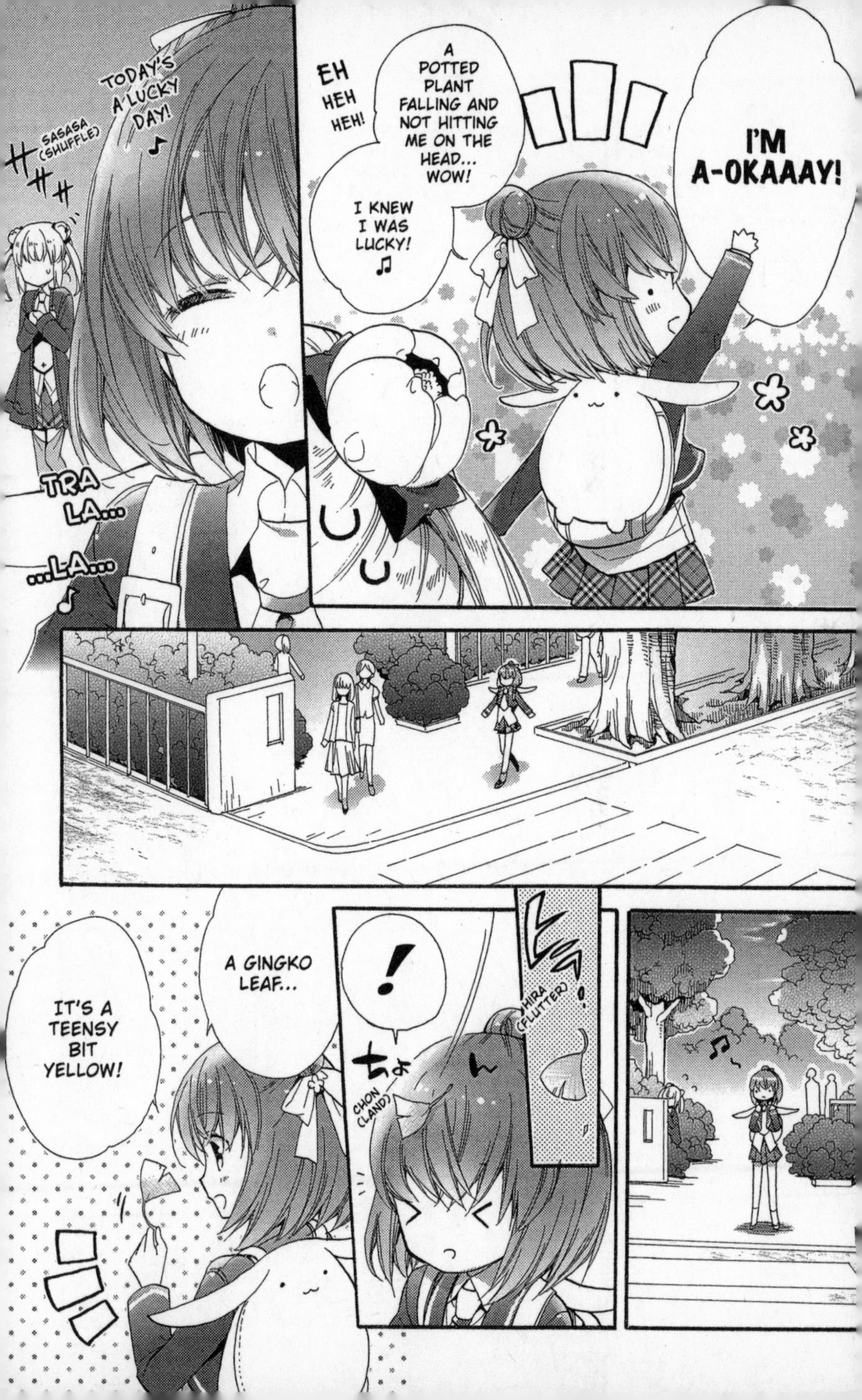

I'M A-OKAAAY!
A POTTED PLANT FALLING AND NOT HITTING ME ON THE HEAD... WOW!
EH HEH HEH!
I KNEW I WAS LUCKY! ♫
TODAY'S A LUCKY DAY! ♪
SASASA (SHUFFLE)
TRA LA...
...LA... ♪
♪
HIRA (FLUTTER)
!
ちょ
CHON (LAND)
A GINGKO LEAF...
IT'S A TEENSY BIT YELLOW!

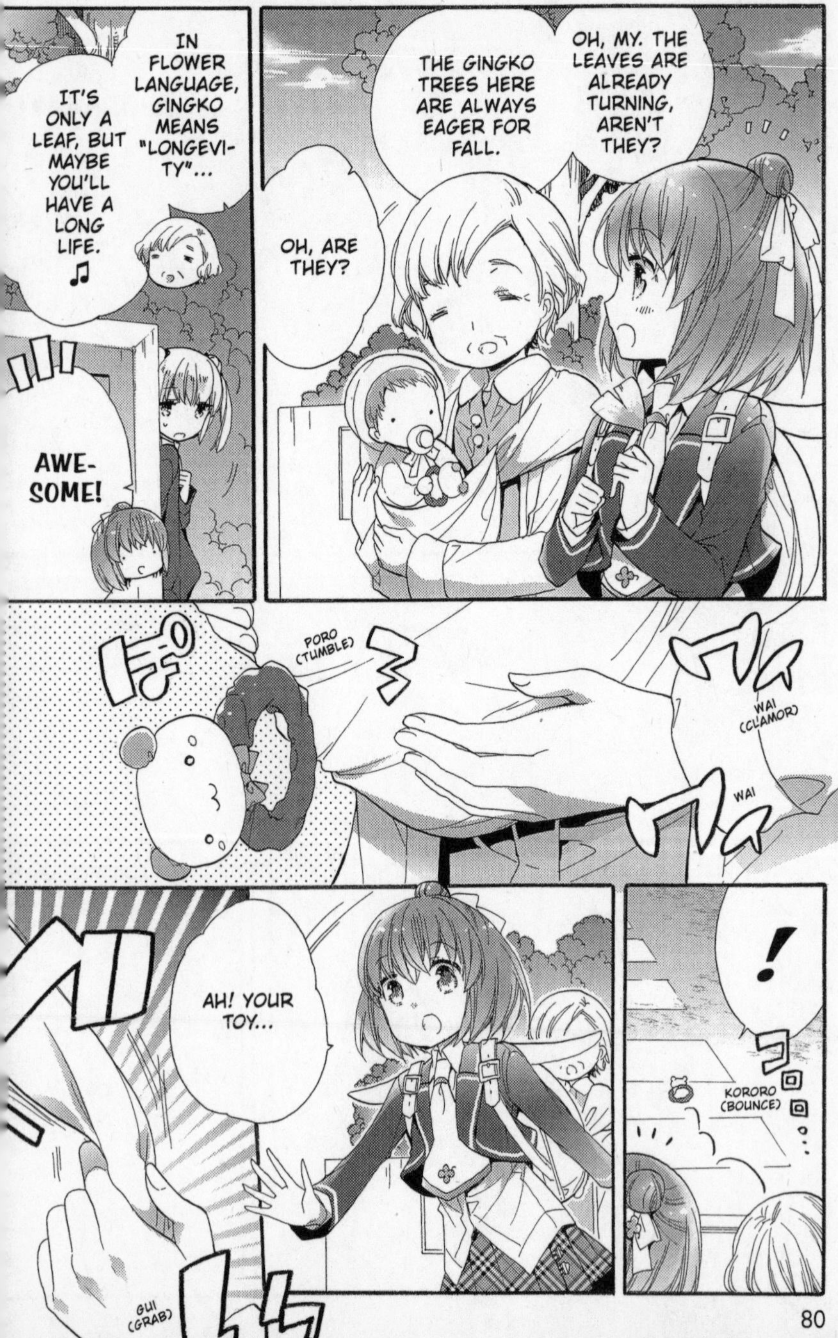
OH, MY. THE LEAVES ARE ALREADY TURNING, AREN'T THEY?
THE GINGKO TREES HERE ARE ALWAYS EAGER FOR FALL.
OH, ARE THEY?
IN FLOWER LANGUAGE, GINGKO MEANS "LONGEVI-TY"...
IT'S ONLY A LEAF, BUT MAYBE YOU'LL HAVE A LONG LIFE. ♫
AWE-SOME!
WAI (CLAMOR)
WAI
PORO (TUMBLE)
!
KORORO (BOUNCE)
AH! YOUR TOY...
GUI (GRAB)

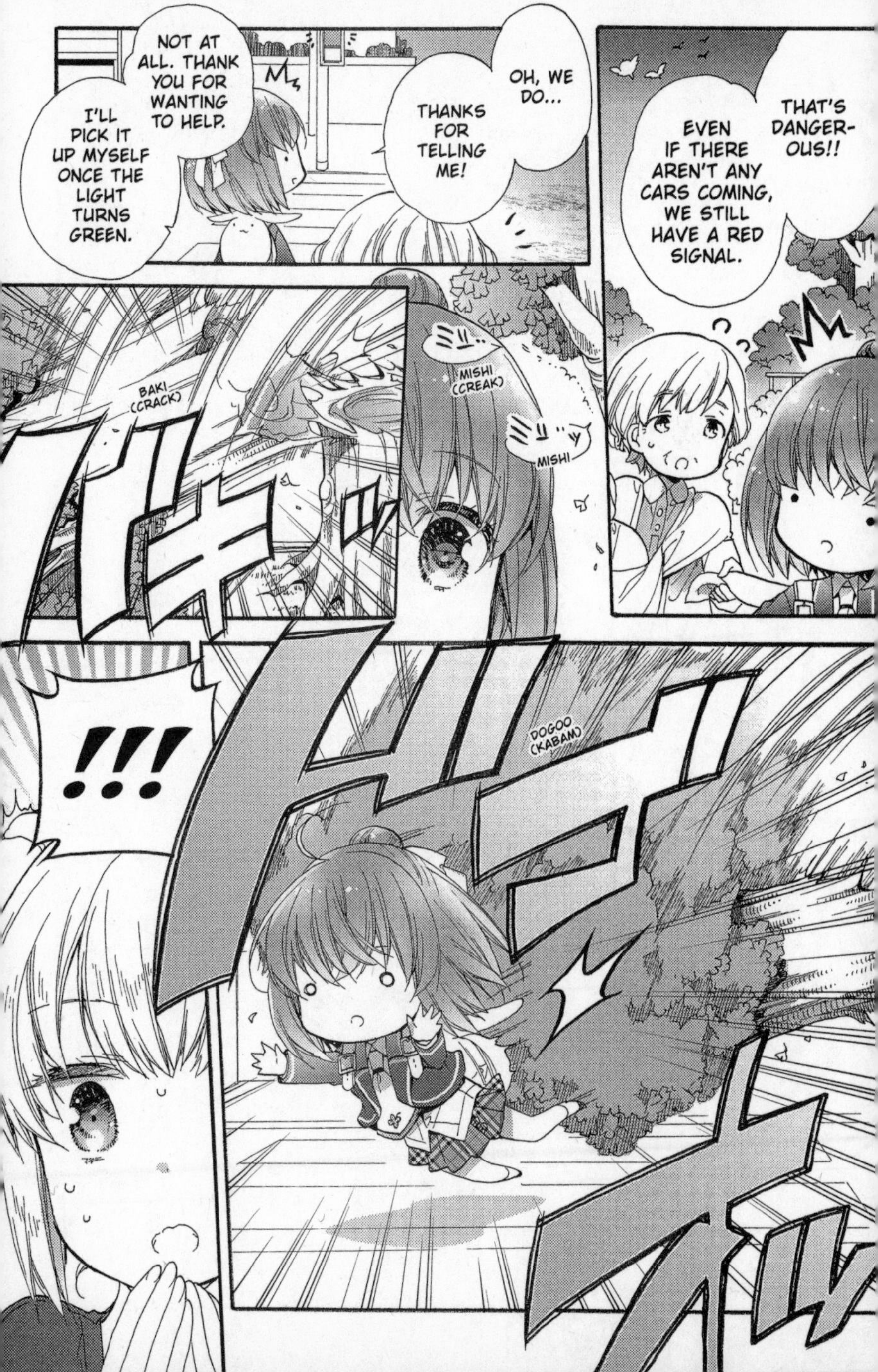
THAT'S DANGER-OUS!!
EVEN IF THERE AREN'T ANY CARS COMING, WE STILL HAVE A RED SIGNAL.
OH, WE DO...
THANKS FOR TELLING ME!
NOT AT ALL. THANK YOU FOR WANTING TO HELP.
I'LL PICK IT UP MYSELF ONCE THE LIGHT TURNS GREEN.
MISHI (CREAK)
MISHI
BAKI (CRACK)
DOGOO (KABAM)
!!!

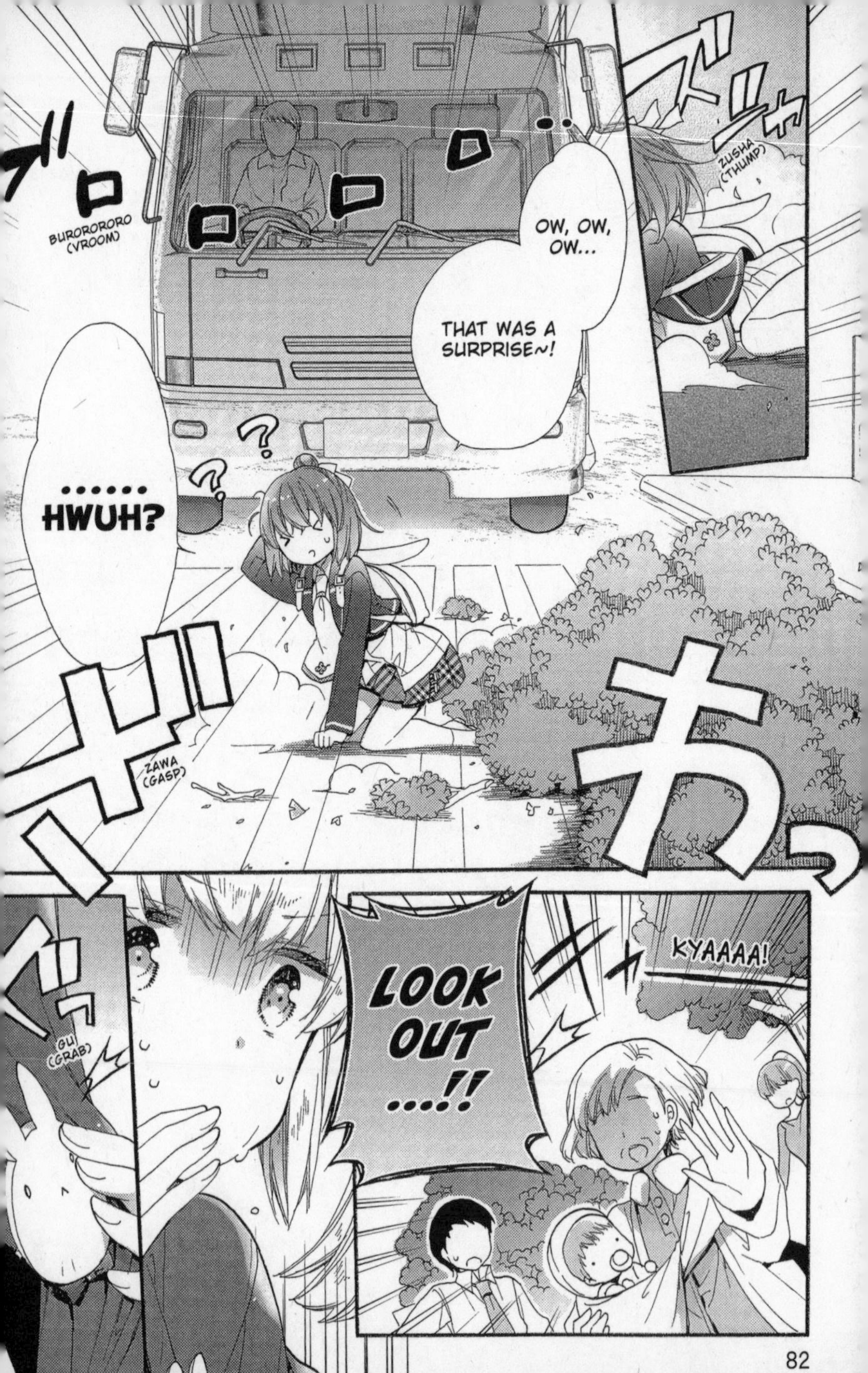
ZUSHA (THUMP)
OW, OW, OW...
THAT WAS A SURPRISE~!
BURORORORO (VROOM)
......HWUH?
ZAWA (GASP)
KYAAAA!
LOOK OUT ....!!
GU (GRAB)

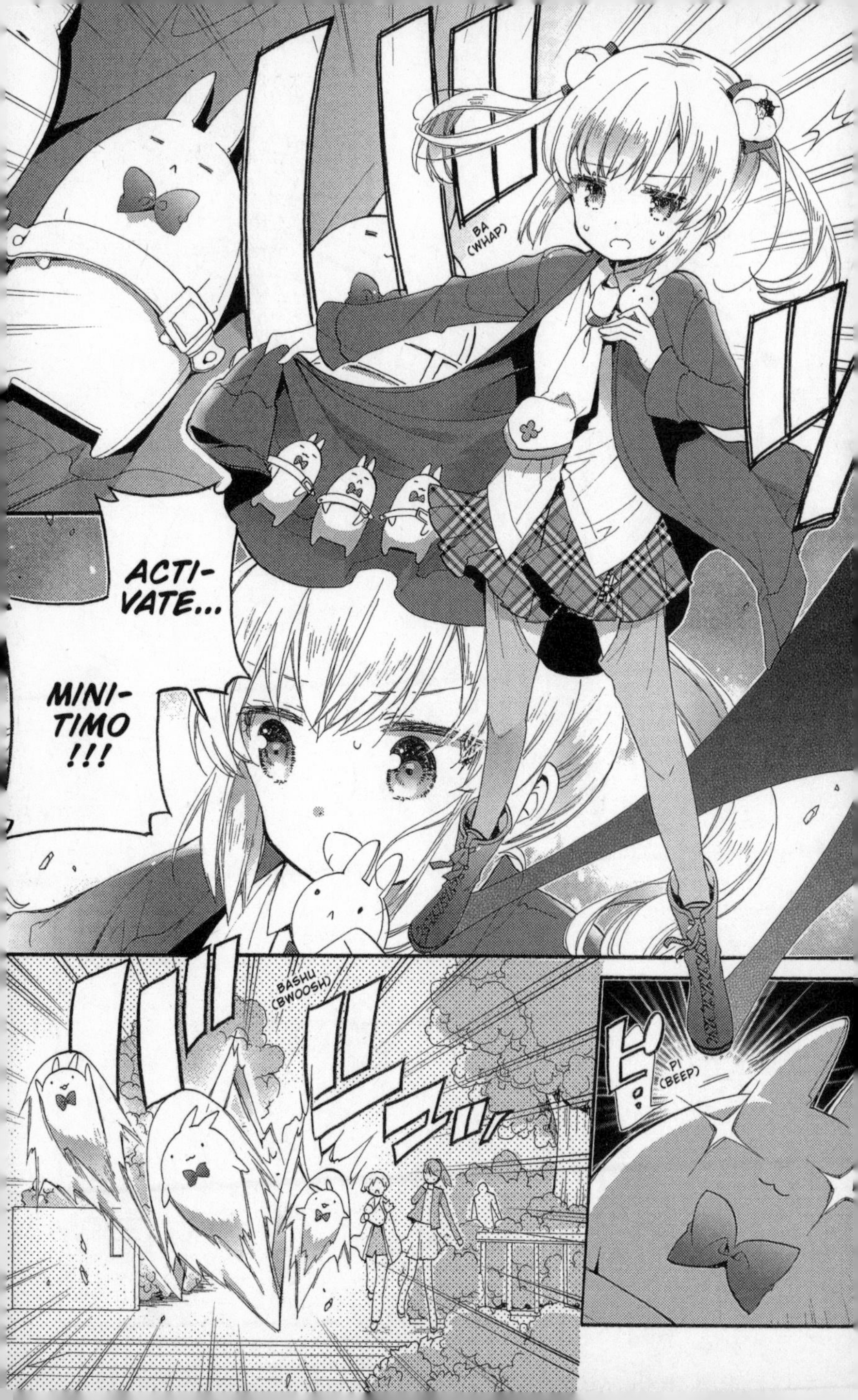
BA (WHAP)
ACTI-VATE...
MINI-TIMO !!!
PI (BEEP)
BASHU (BWOOSH)

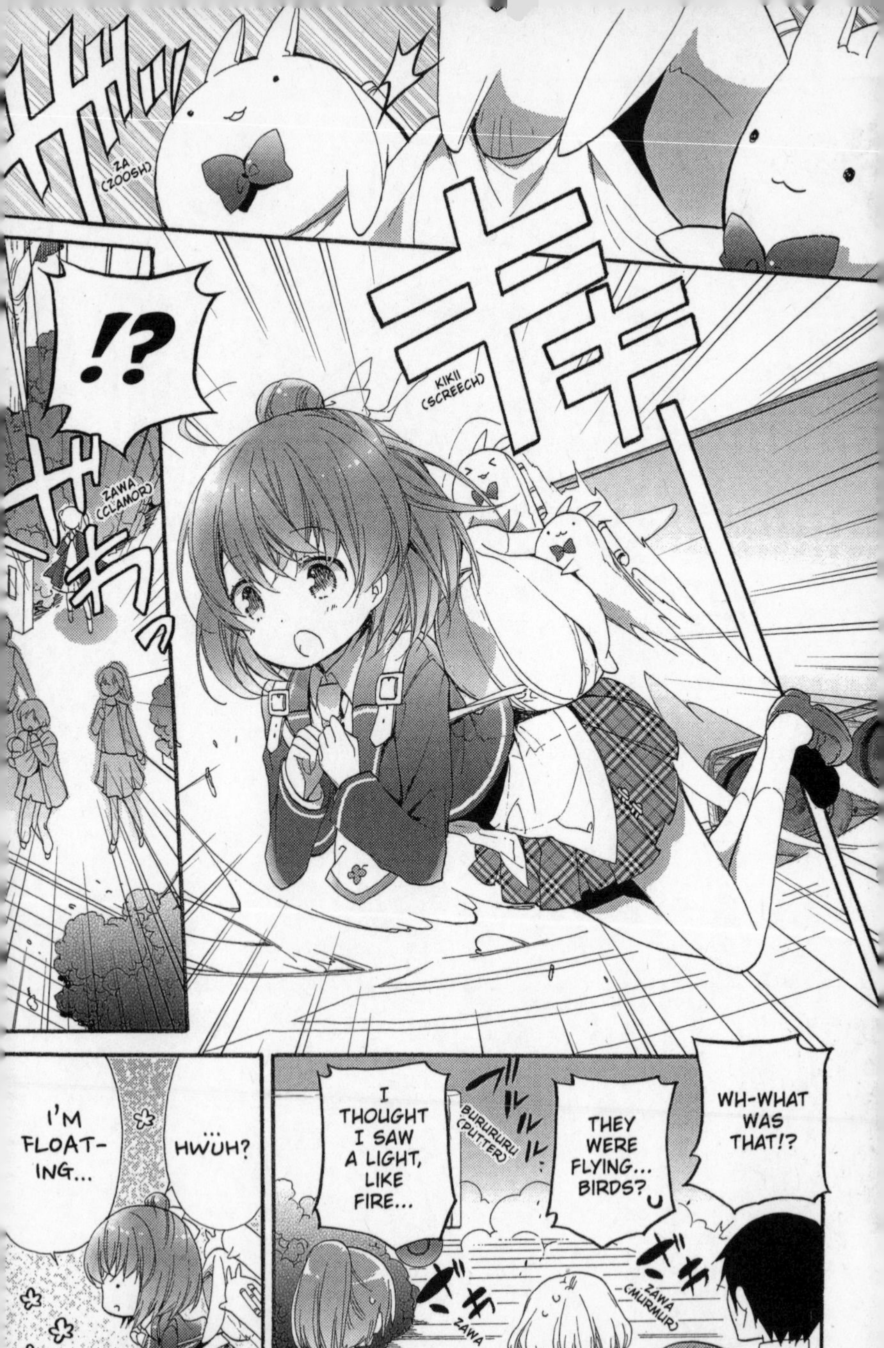
ZA (ZOOSH)
KIKII (SCREECH)
!?
ZAWA (CLAMOR)
WH-WHAT WAS THAT!?
THEY WERE FLYING... BIRDS?
BURURURU (PUTTER)
I THOUGHT I SAW A LIGHT, LIKE FIRE...
ZAWA (MURMUR)
ZAWA
...HWUH?
I'M FLOAT-ING...
GOO (WHOOSH)

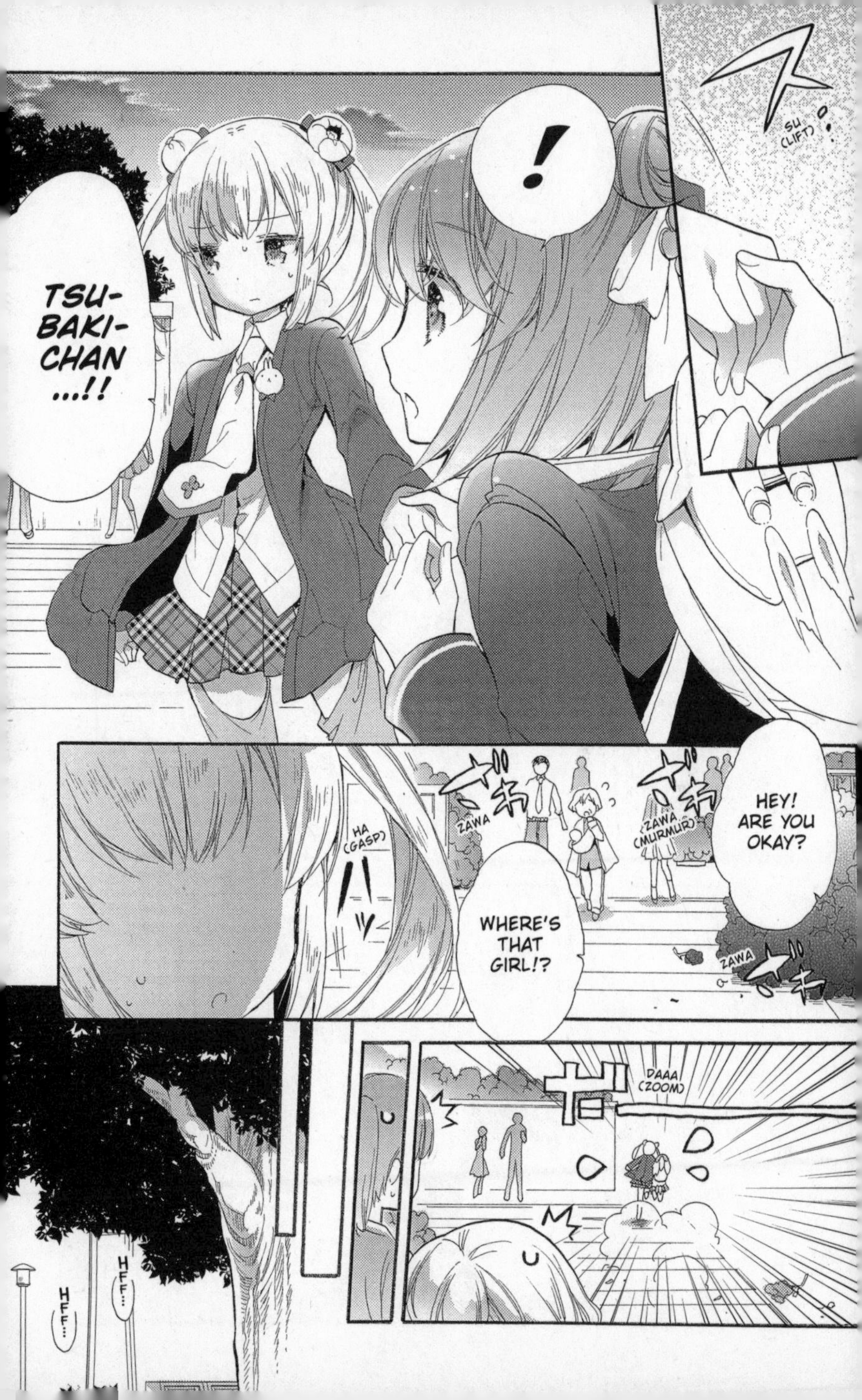
SU
(LIFT)
!
TSU-
BAKI-
CHAN
...!!
HEY!
ARE YOU
OKAY?
ZAWA
(MURMUR)
ZAWA
ZAWA
WHERE'S
THAT
GIRL!?
HA
(GASP)
DAAA
(ZOOM)
HFF...
HFF...

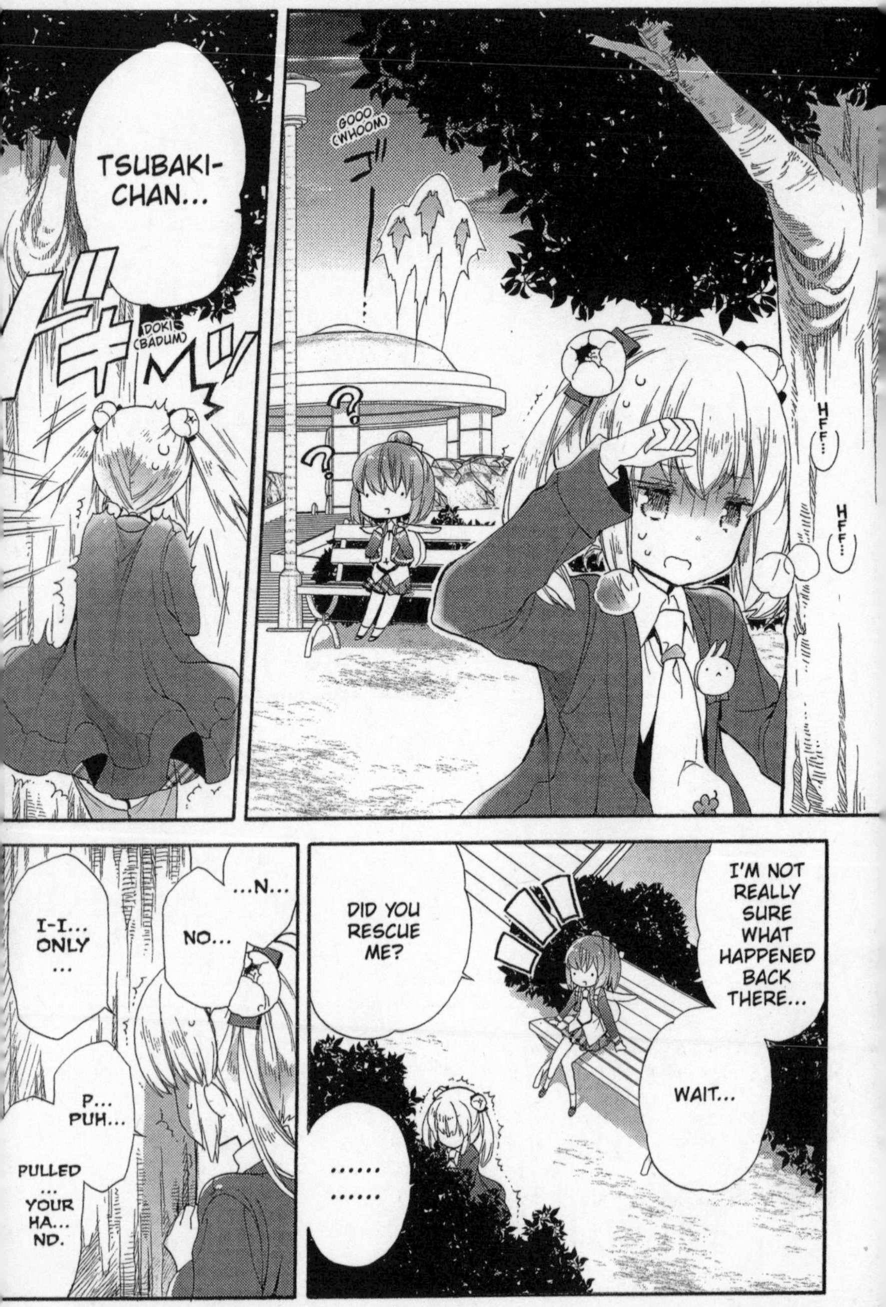
HFF...
HFF...
GOOO (WHOOM)
TSUBAKI-CHAN...
DOKI (BADUM)
I'M NOT REALLY SURE WHAT HAPPENED BACK THERE...
DID YOU RESCUE ME?
WAIT...
....
...N... NO...
I-I... ONLY ...
P... PUH...
PULLED ... YOUR HA... ND.

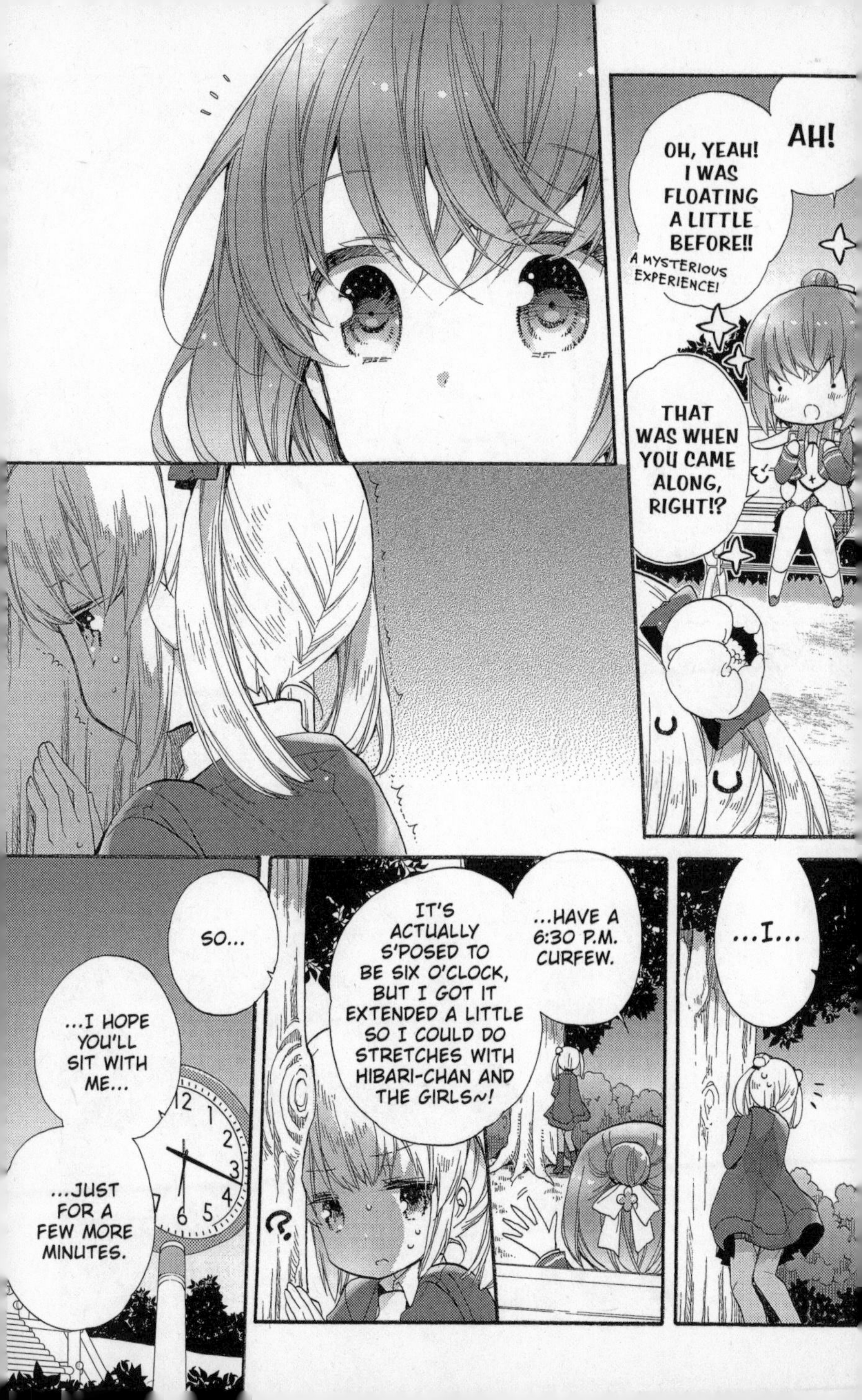
AH!
OH, YEAH! I WAS FLOATING A LITTLE BEFORE!!
A MYSTERIOUS EXPERIENCE!
THAT WAS WHEN YOU CAME ALONG, RIGHT!?
...I...
...HAVE A 6:30 P.M. CURFEW.
IT'S ACTUALLY S'POSED TO BE SIX O'CLOCK, BUT I GOT IT EXTENDED A LITTLE SO I COULD DO STRETCHES WITH HIBARI-CHAN AND THE GIRLS~!
SO...
...I HOPE YOU'LL SIT WITH ME...
...JUST FOR A FEW MORE MINUTES.

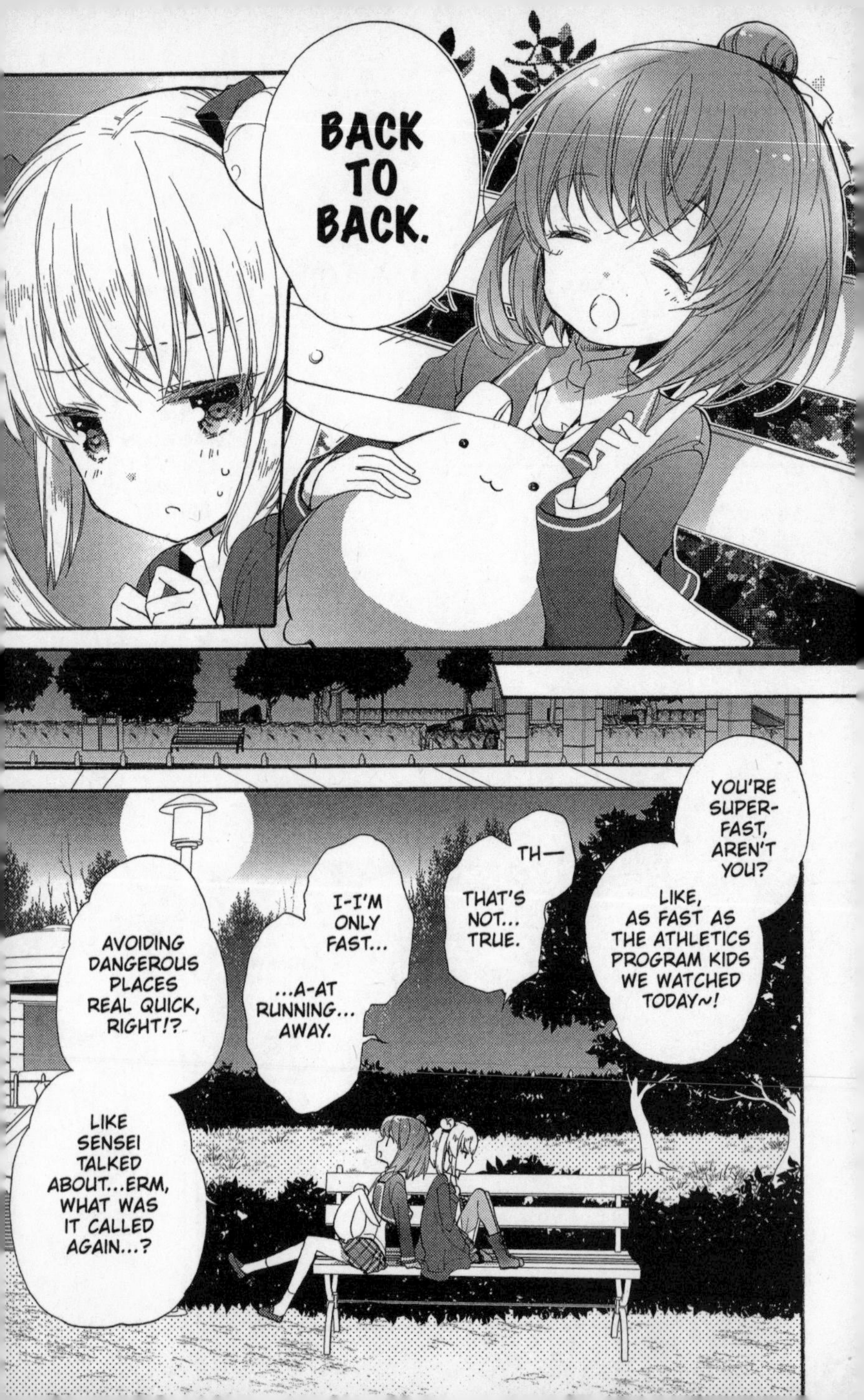

BACK TO BACK.
YOU'RE SUPER-FAST, AREN'T YOU?
LIKE, AS FAST AS THE ATHLETICS PROGRAM KIDS WE WATCHED TODAY~!
TH— THAT'S NOT... TRUE.
I-I'M ONLY FAST...
...A-AT RUNNING... AWAY.
AVOIDING DANGEROUS PLACES REAL QUICK, RIGHT!?
LIKE SENSEI TALKED ABOUT...ERM, WHAT WAS IT CALLED AGAIN...?

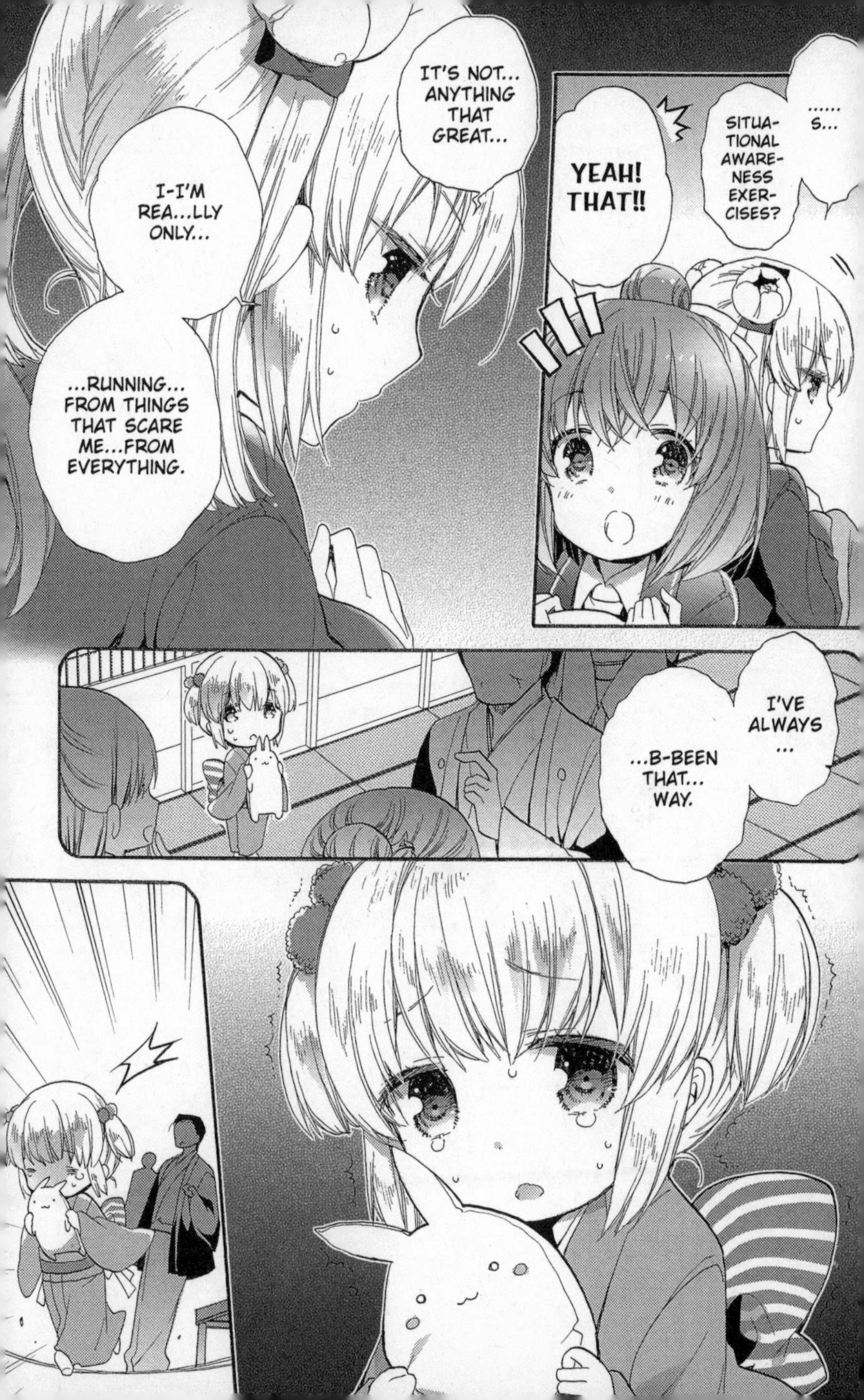
......S...
SITUA-TIONAL AWARE-NESS EXER-CISES?
YEAH! THAT!!
IT'S NOT... ANYTHING THAT GREAT...
I-I'M REA...LLY ONLY...
...RUNNING... FROM THINGS THAT SCARE ME...FROM EVERYTHING.
I'VE ALWAYS ...
...B-BEEN THAT... WAY.

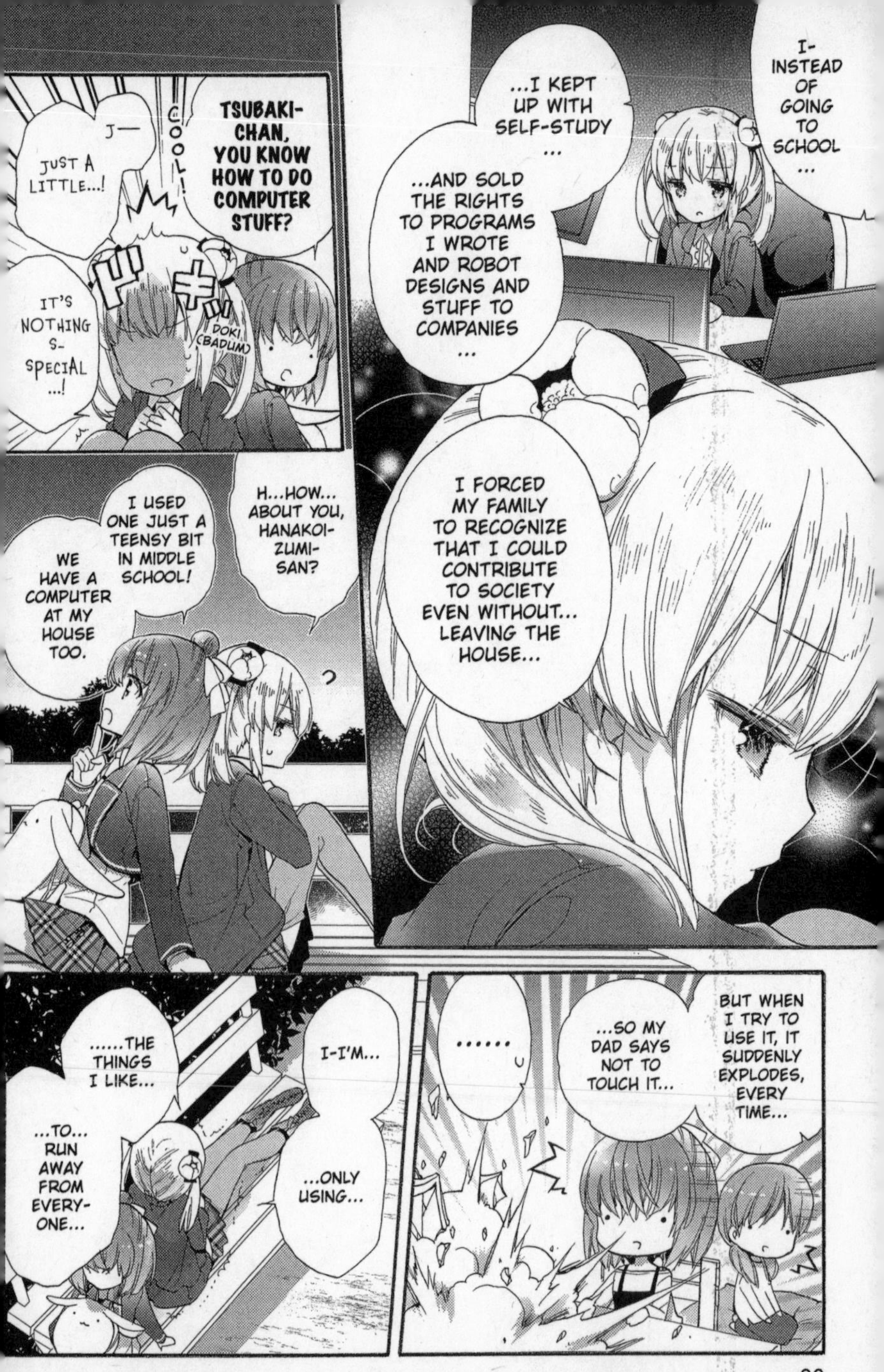
I- INSTEAD OF GOING TO SCHOOL...
...I KEPT UP WITH SELF-STUDY...
...AND SOLD THE RIGHTS TO PROGRAMS I WROTE AND ROBOT DESIGNS AND STUFF TO COMPANIES...
I FORCED MY FAMILY TO RECOGNIZE THAT I COULD CONTRIBUTE TO SOCIETY EVEN WITHOUT... LEAVING THE HOUSE...
TSUBAKI-CHAN, YOU KNOW HOW TO DO COMPUTER STUFF?
COOL!
J— JUST A LITTLE...!
DOKI (BADUM)
IT'S NOTHING S-SPECIAL...!
H...HOW... ABOUT YOU, HANAKOIZUMI-SAN?
I USED ONE JUST A TEENSY BIT IN MIDDLE SCHOOL!
WE HAVE A COMPUTER AT MY HOUSE TOO.
BUT WHEN I TRY TO USE IT, IT SUDDENLY EXPLODES, EVERY TIME...
...SO MY DAD SAYS NOT TO TOUCH IT...
......
I-I'M...
......THE THINGS I LIKE...
...ONLY USING...
...TO... RUN AWAY FROM EVERYONE...

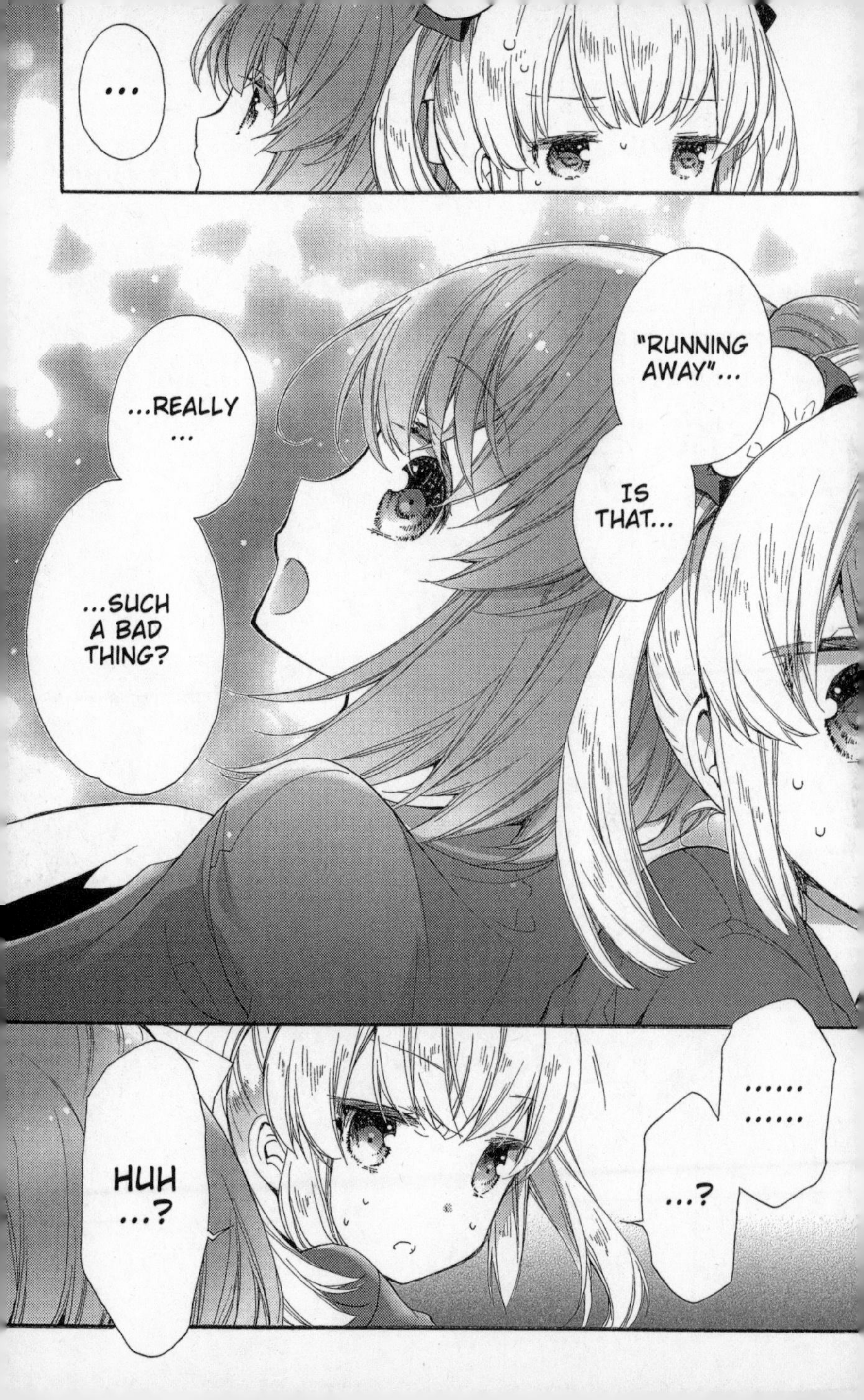
...
"RUNNING AWAY"...
IS THAT...
...REALLY ...
...SUCH A BAD THING?
....?
HUH ...?

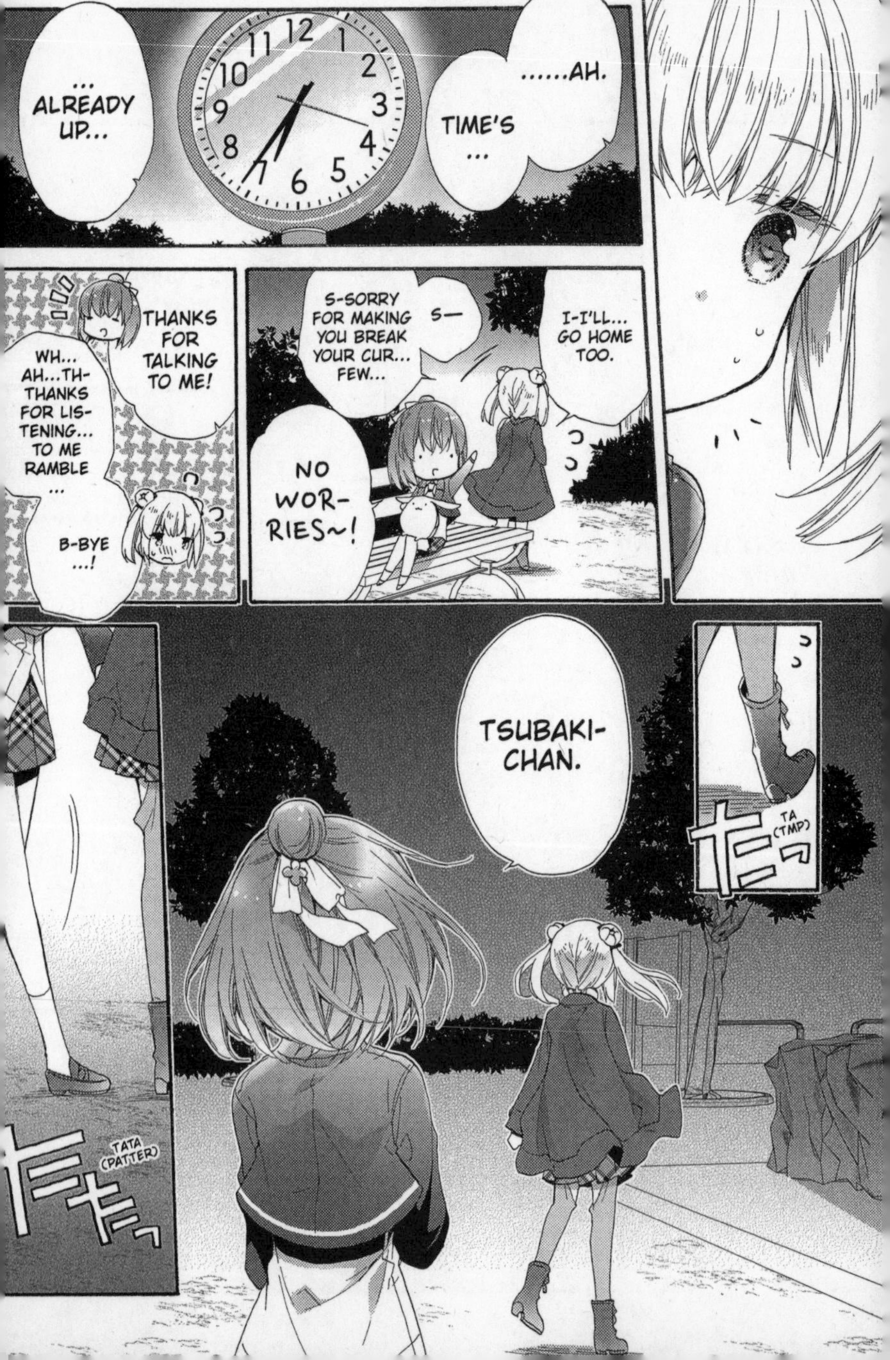
......AH.
TIME'S ...
... ALREADY UP...
I-I'LL... GO HOME TOO.
S—
S-SORRY FOR MAKING YOU BREAK YOUR CUR... FEW...
NO WOR-RIES~!
THANKS FOR TALKING TO ME!
WH... AH...TH-THANKS FOR LIS-TENING... TO ME RAMBLE ...
B-BYE ...!
TA (TMP)
TSUBAKI-CHAN.
TATA (PATTER)

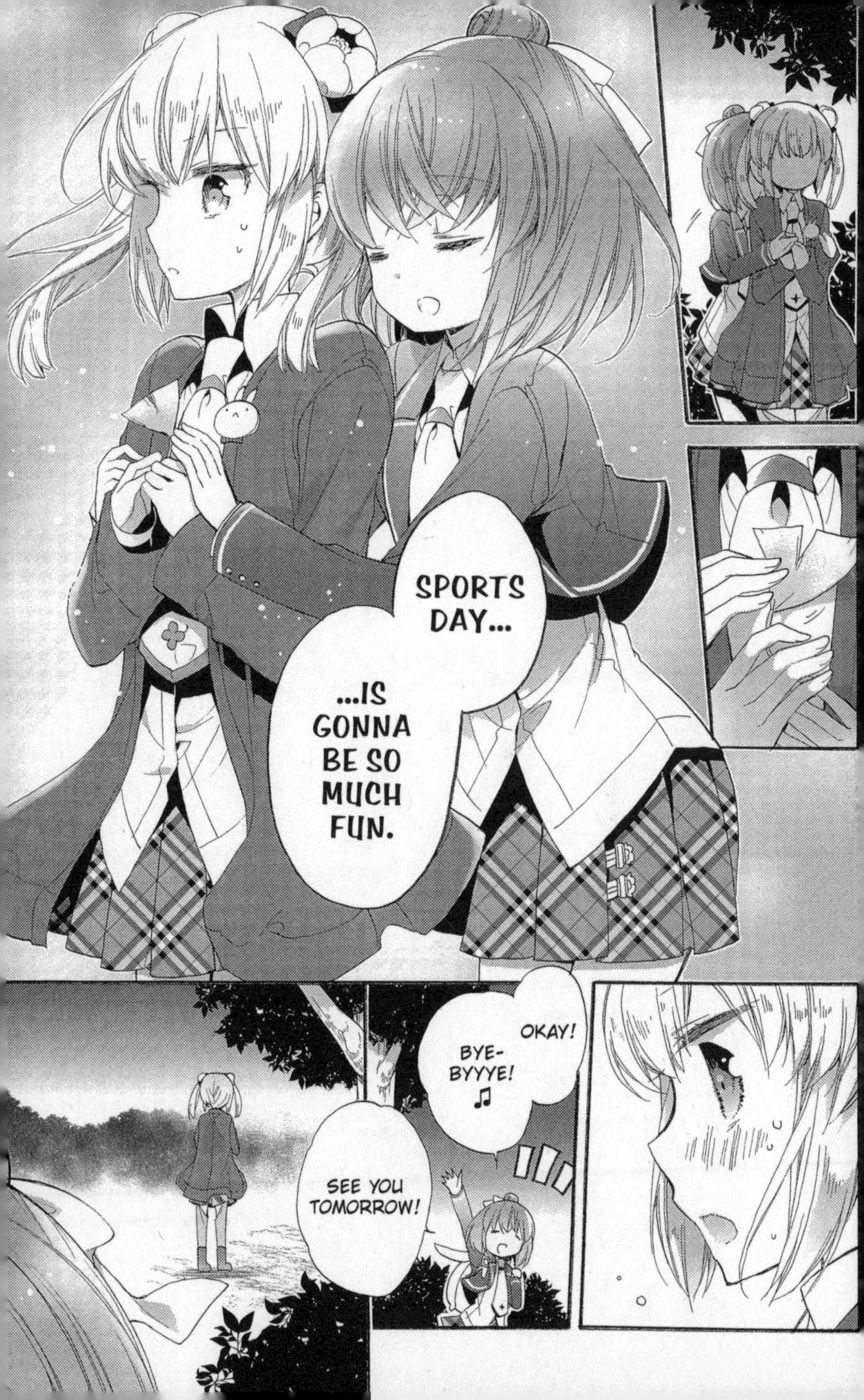
SPORTS DAY...
...IS GONNA BE SO MUCH FUN.
OKAY!
BYE-BYYYE! ♪
SEE YOU TOMORROW!

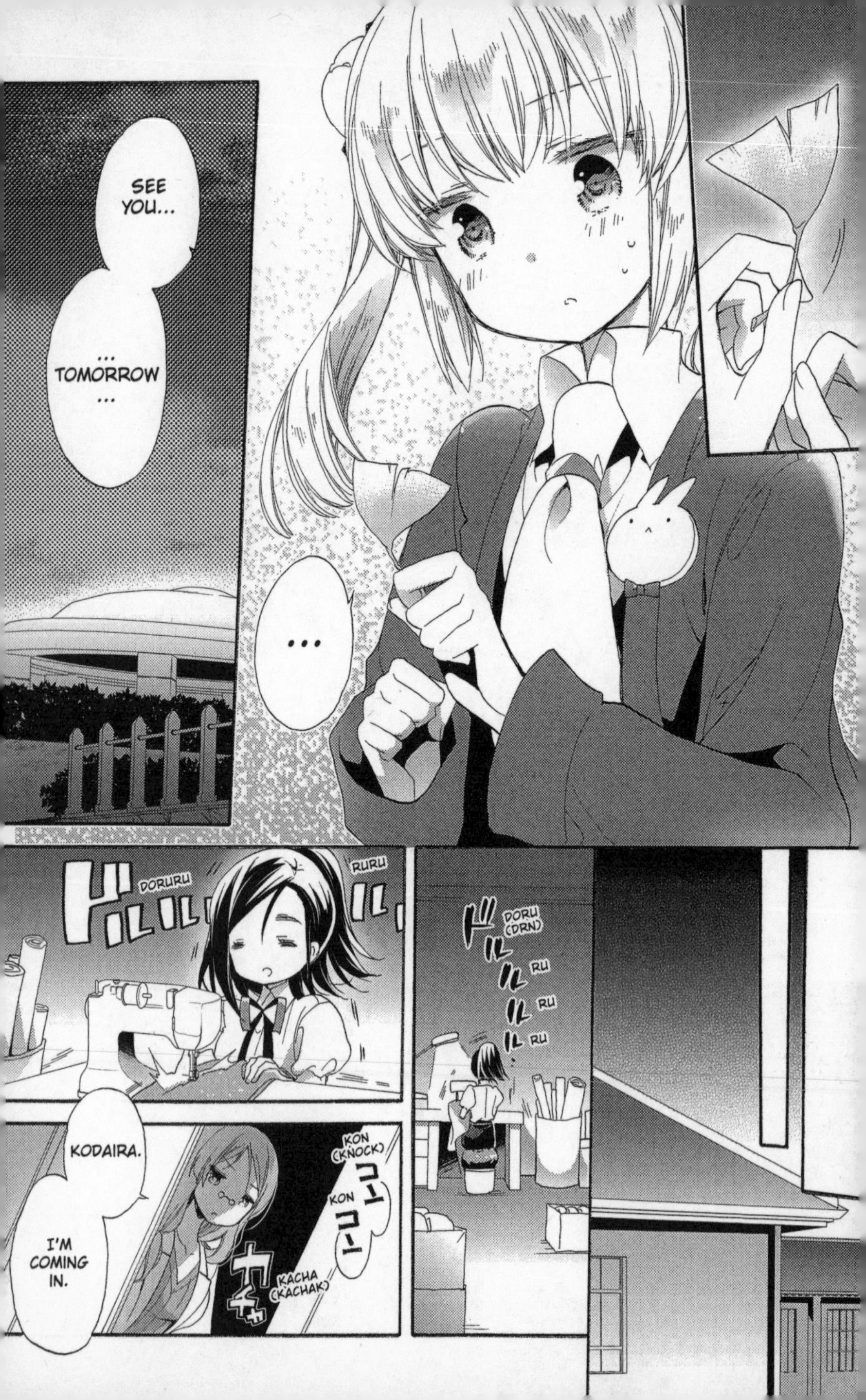
...
SEE YOU...
...TOMORROW...
DORU (DRN)
RU
RU
RU
DORURU
RURU
KON (KNOCK)
KON
KACHA (KACHAK)
KODAIRA.
I'M COMING IN.

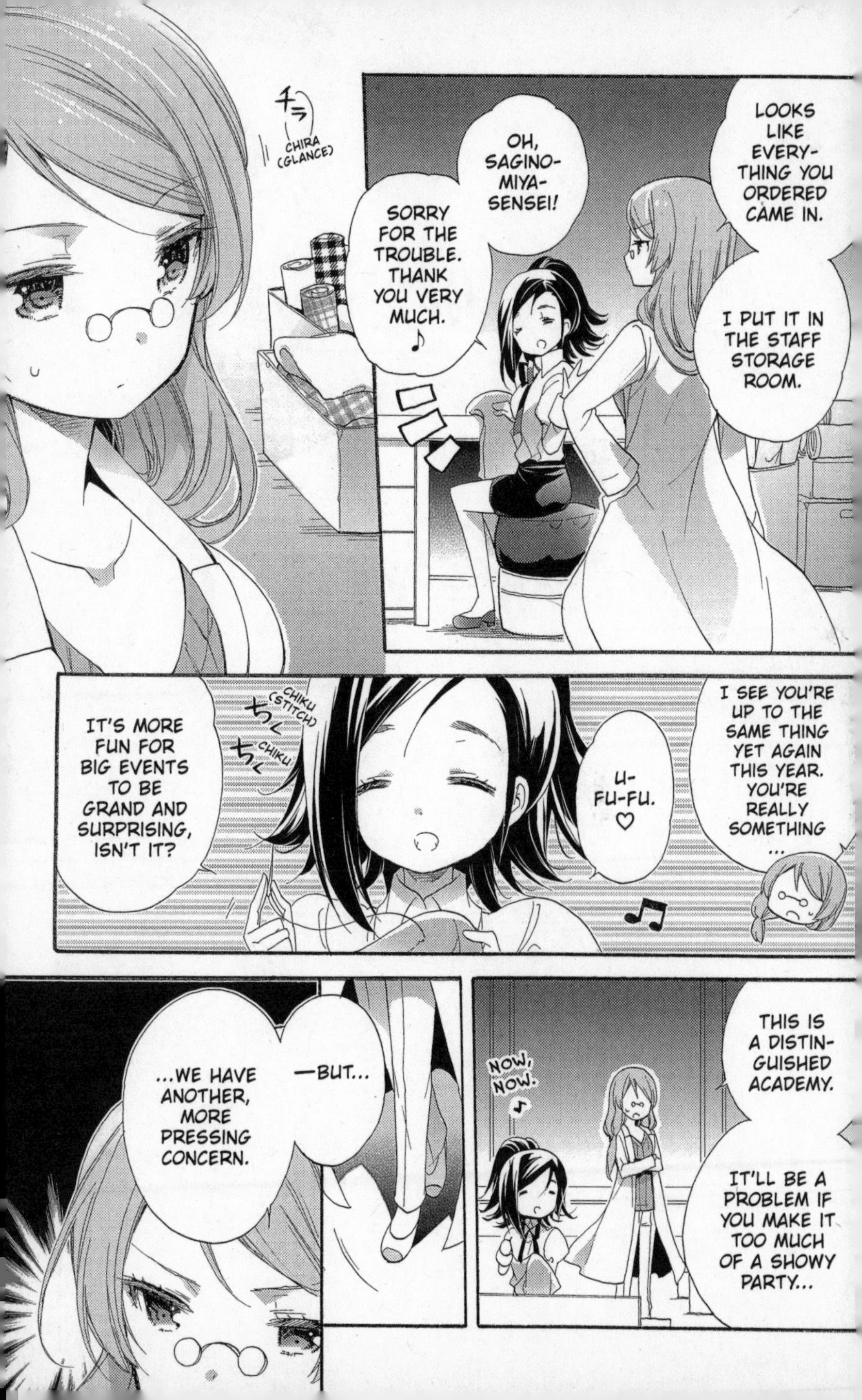
LOOKS LIKE EVERYTHING YOU ORDERED CAME IN.
I PUT IT IN THE STAFF STORAGE ROOM.
OH, SAGINOMIYA-SENSEI!
SORRY FOR THE TROUBLE. THANK YOU VERY MUCH. ♪
チラ
CHIRA (GLANCE)
I SEE YOU'RE UP TO THE SAME THING YET AGAIN THIS YEAR. YOU'RE REALLY SOMETHING...
U-FU-FU. ♡
ちく
CHIKU (STITCH)
ちく
CHIKU
IT'S MORE FUN FOR BIG EVENTS TO BE GRAND AND SURPRISING, ISN'T IT?
THIS IS A DISTINGUISHED ACADEMY.
IT'LL BE A PROBLEM IF YOU MAKE IT TOO MUCH OF A SHOWY PARTY...
NOW, NOW. ♪
—BUT...
...WE HAVE ANOTHER, MORE PRESSING CONCERN.

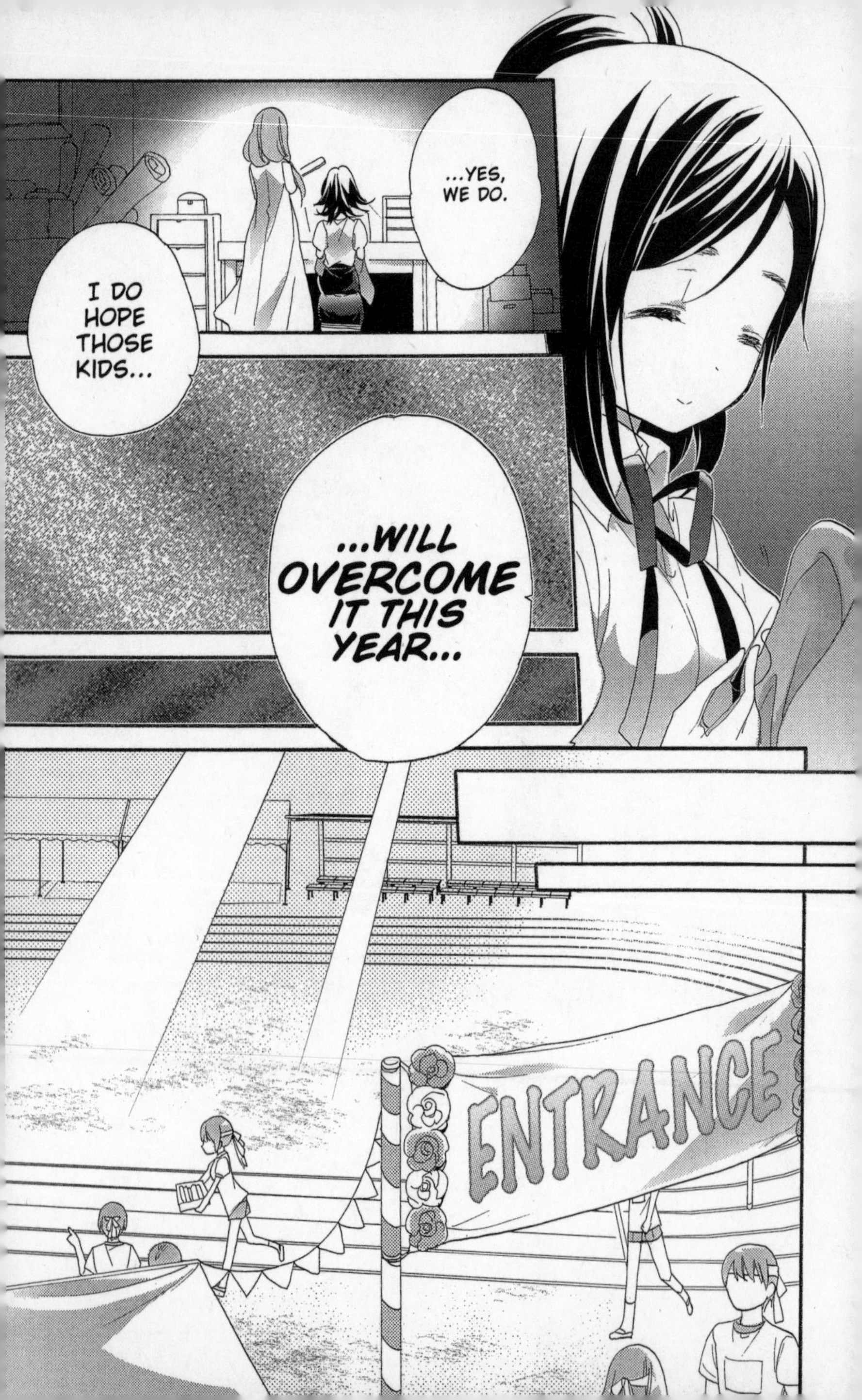
...YES, WE DO.
I DO HOPE THOSE KIDS...
...WILL OVERCOME IT THIS YEAR...
ENTRANCE

AnneHappy
unhappy
go lucky!

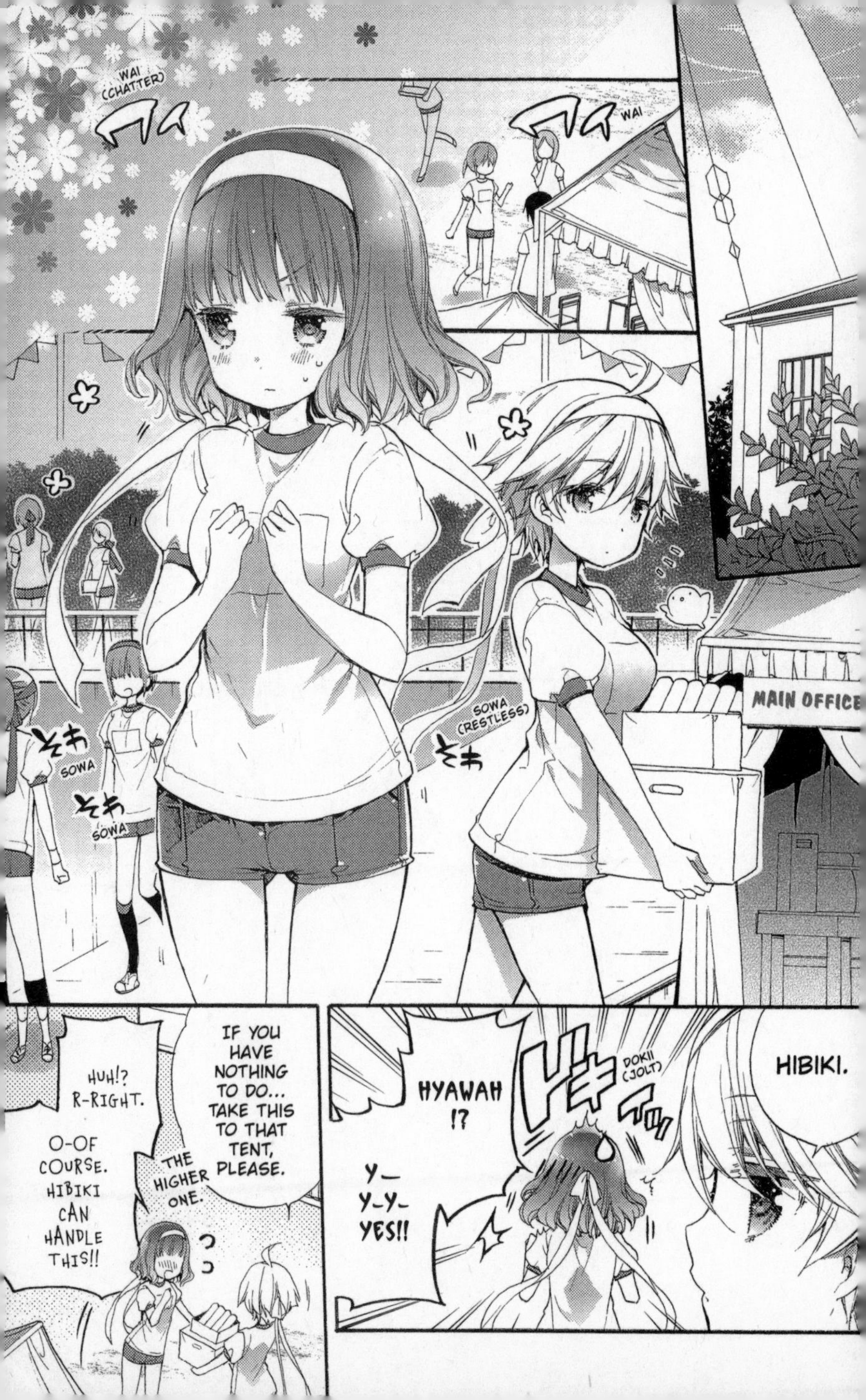
ワイ
WAI
ワイ
WAI (CHATTER)
MAIN OFFICE
そわ
SOWA (RESTLESS)
そわ
SOWA
そわ
SOWA
HIBIKI.
ドキッ
DOKII (JOLT)
HYAWAH !?
Y- Y-Y- YES!!
IF YOU HAVE NOTHING TO DO... TAKE THIS TO THAT TENT, PLEASE.
THE HIGHER ONE.
HUH!? R-RIGHT.
O-OF COURSE. HIBIKI CAN HANDLE THIS!!

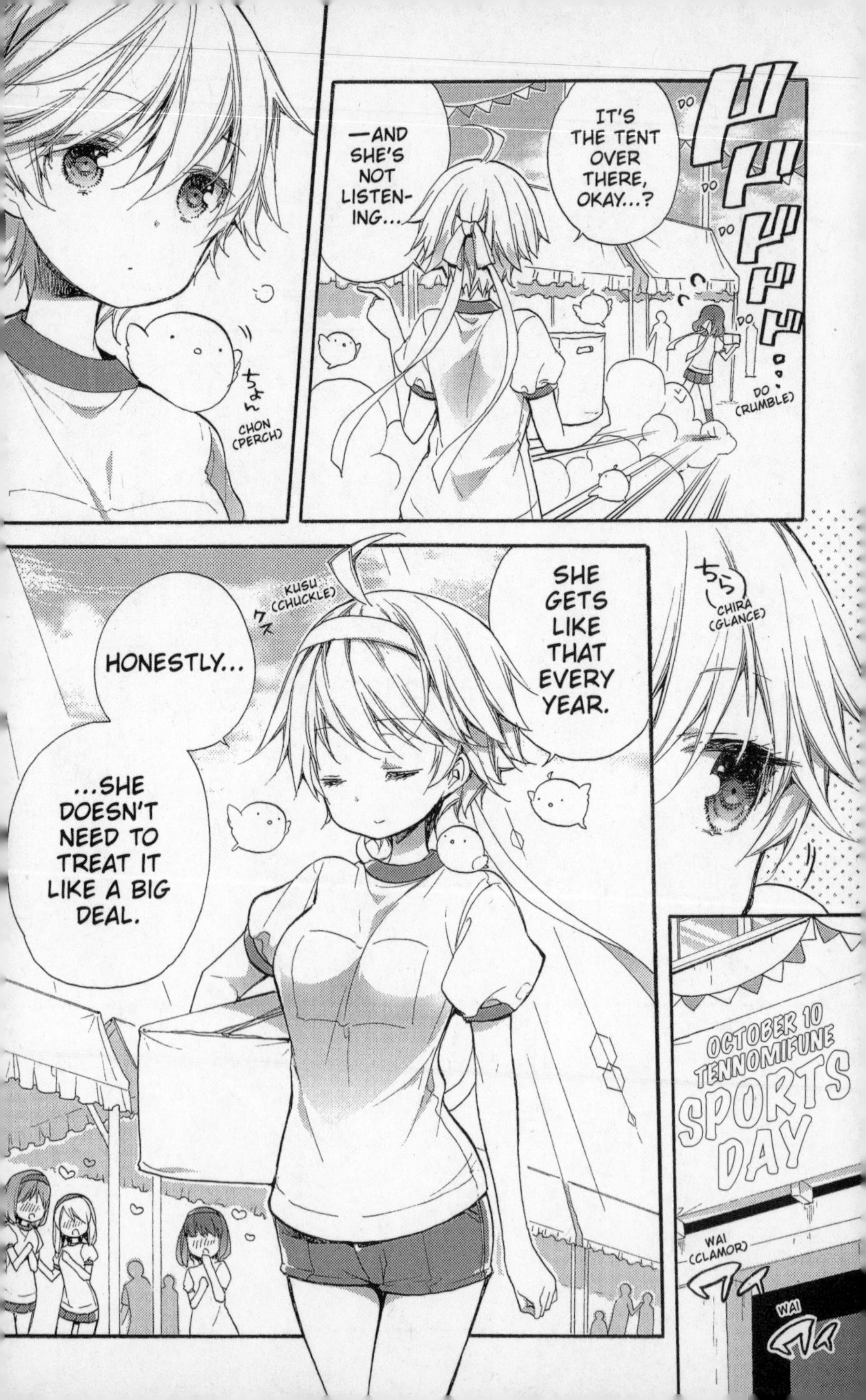
DO
DO
DO
DO
DO (RUMBLE)
IT'S THE TENT OVER THERE, OKAY...?
—AND SHE'S NOT LISTENING...
ちょん
CHON (PERCH)
ちら
CHIRA (GLANCE)
OCTOBER 10 TENNOMIFUNE SPORTS DAY
WAI (CLAMOR)
WAI
SHE GETS LIKE THAT EVERY YEAR.
クス
KUSU (CHUCKLE)
HONESTLY...
...SHE DOESN'T NEED TO TREAT IT LIKE A BIG DEAL.

� Lucky.46

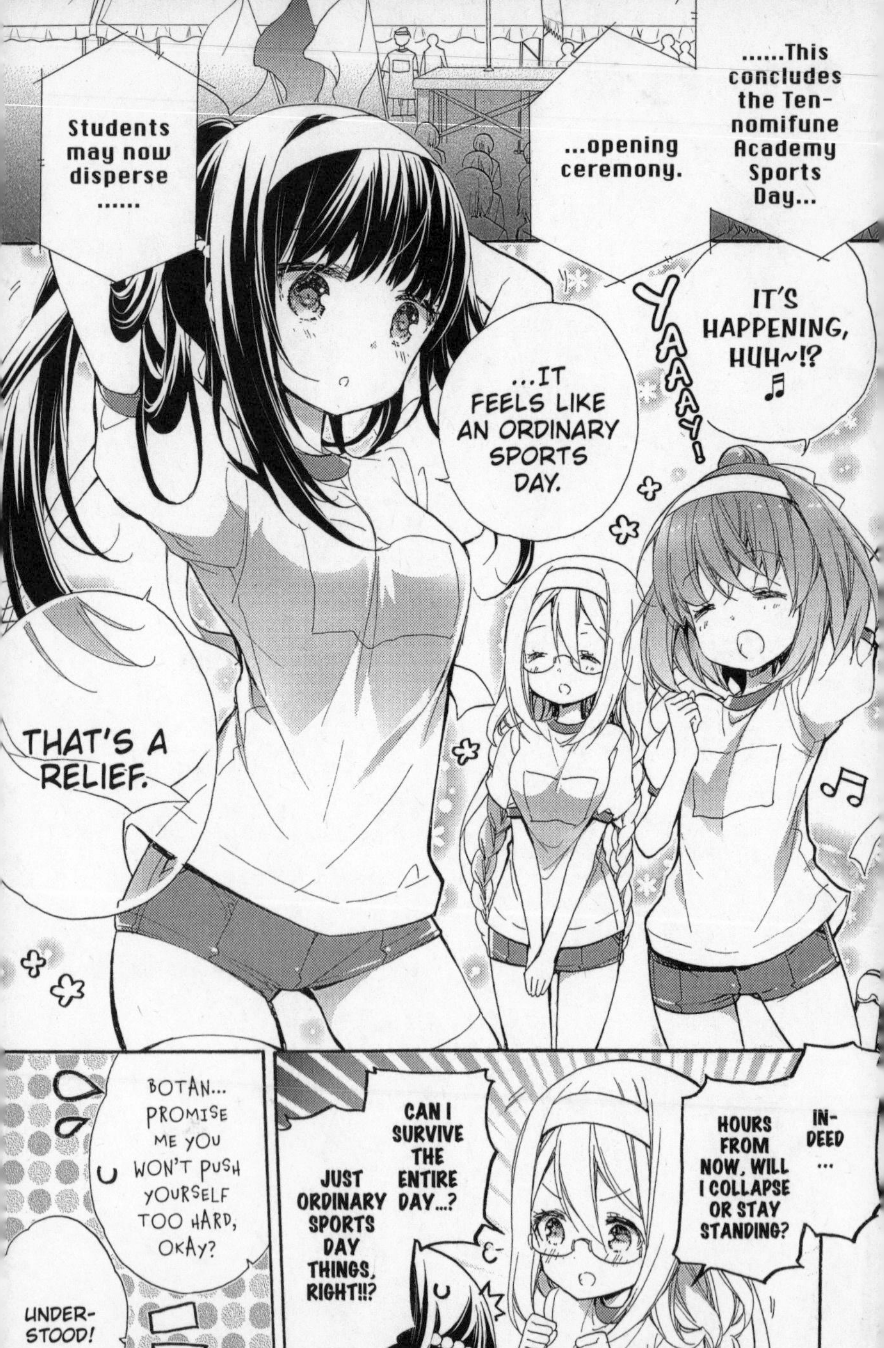

......This concludes the Ten-nomifune Academy Sports Day...
...opening ceremony.
Students may now disperse ......
IT'S HAPPENING, HUH~!? ♪
YAAAAY!
...IT FEELS LIKE AN ORDINARY SPORTS DAY.
THAT'S A RELIEF.
IN-DEED...
HOURS FROM NOW, WILL I COLLAPSE OR STAY STANDING?
CAN I SURVIVE THE ENTIRE DAY...?
JUST ORDINARY SPORTS DAY THINGS, RIGHT!!?
BOTAN... PROMISE ME YOU WON'T PUSH YOURSELF TOO HARD, OKAY?
UNDER-STOOD!

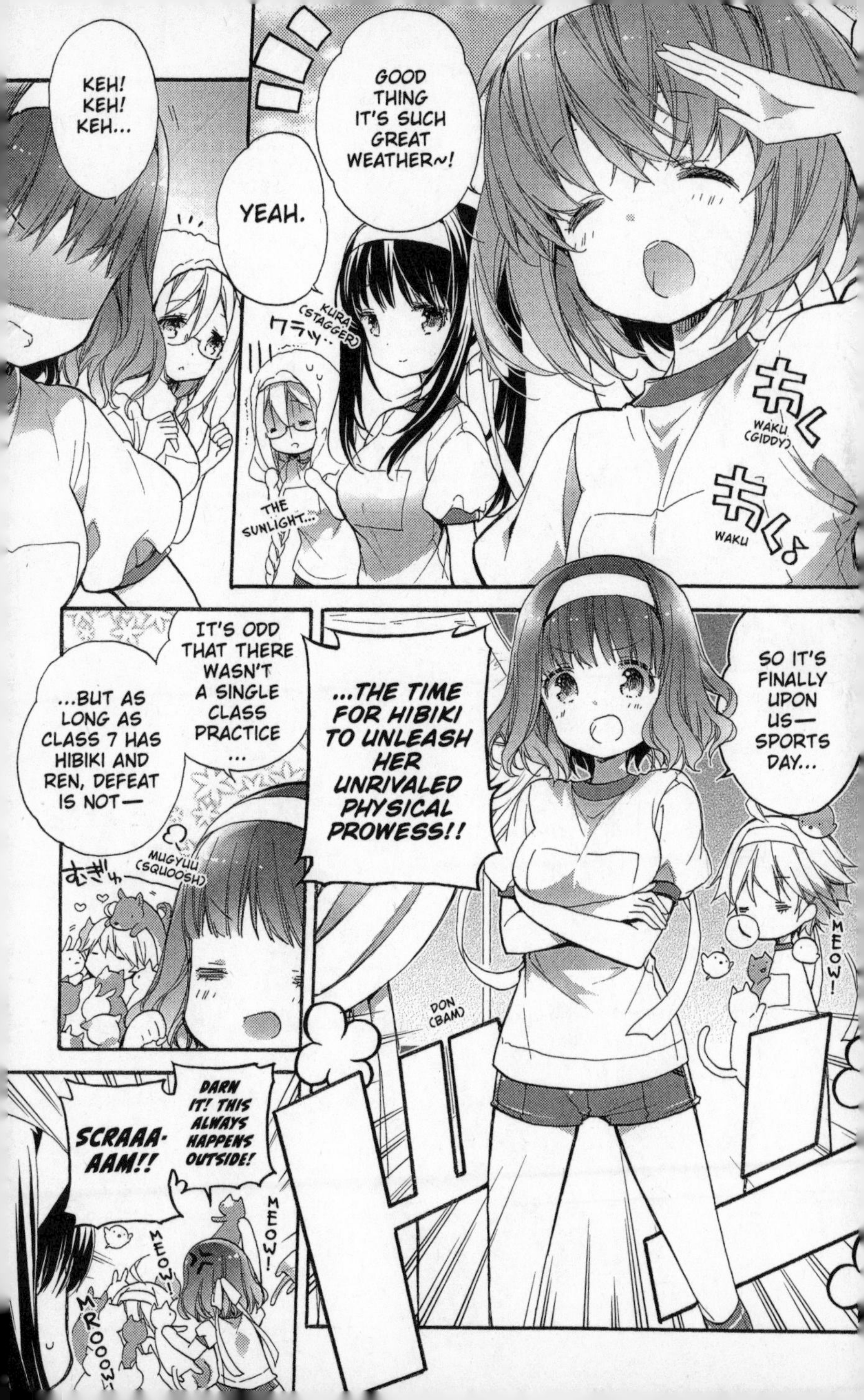
GOOD THING IT'S SUCH GREAT WEATHER~!
わく
WAKU (GIDDY)
わく♪
WAKU
YEAH.
KURA (STAGGER)
クラッ
THE SUNLIGHT...
KEH! KEH! KEH...
SO IT'S FINALLY UPON US— SPORTS DAY...
...THE TIME FOR HIBIKI TO UNLEASH HER UNRIVALED PHYSICAL PROWESS!!
DON (BAM)
MEOW!
IT'S ODD THAT THERE WASN'T A SINGLE CLASS PRACTICE...
...BUT AS LONG AS CLASS 7 HAS HIBIKI AND REN, DEFEAT IS NOT—
むぎゅ
MUGYUU (SQUOOSH)
DARN IT! THIS ALWAYS HAPPENS OUTSIDE!
SCRAAA-AAM!!
MEOW!
MEOW!
MROOOW

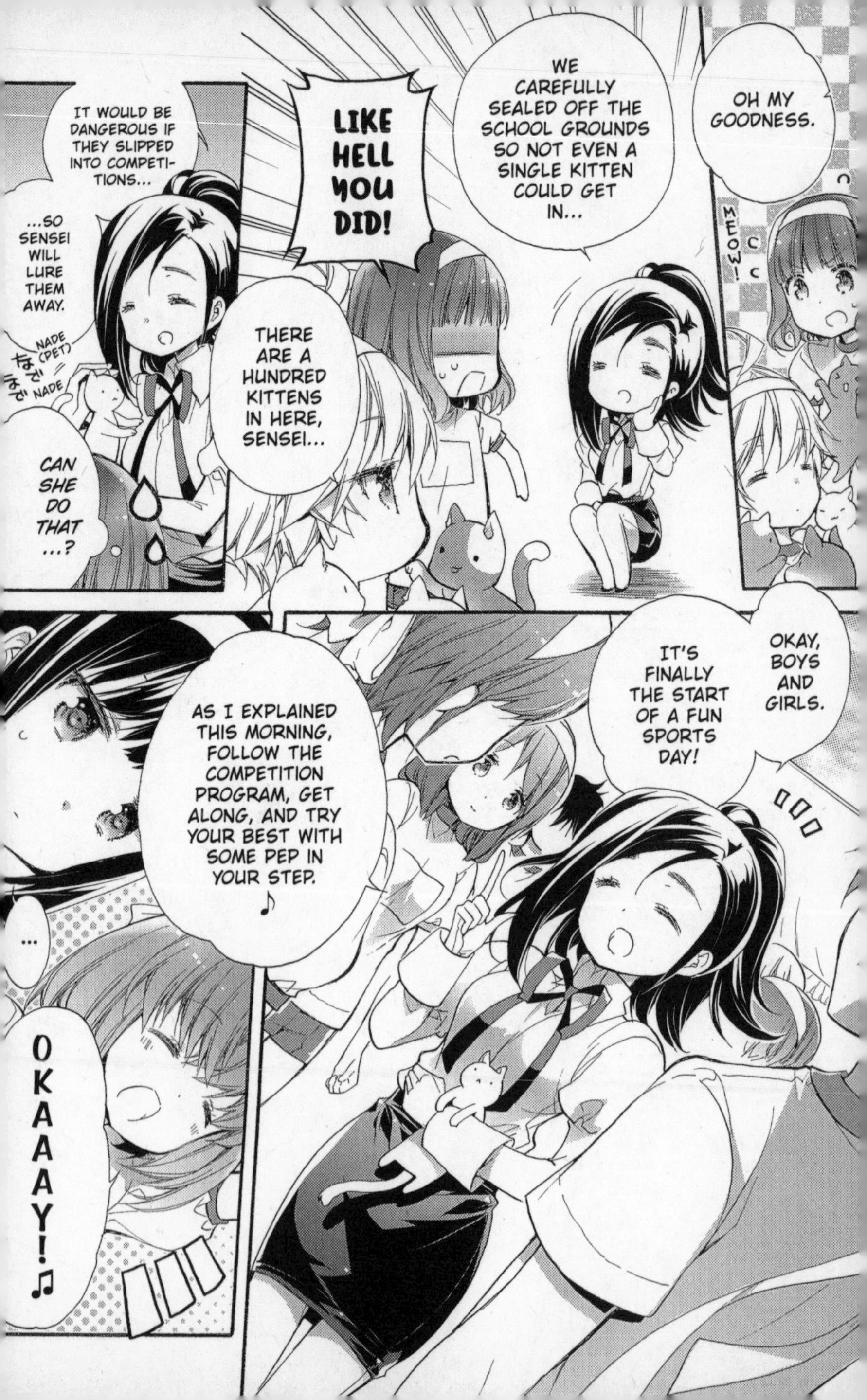
OH MY GOODNESS.
MEOW!
WE CAREFULLY SEALED OFF THE SCHOOL GROUNDS SO NOT EVEN A SINGLE KITTEN COULD GET IN...
LIKE HELL YOU DID!
THERE ARE A HUNDRED KITTENS IN HERE, SENSEI...
IT WOULD BE DANGEROUS IF THEY SLIPPED INTO COMPETITIONS...
...SO SENSEI WILL LURE THEM AWAY.
なでなで
NADE (PET) NADE
CAN SHE DO THAT...?
OKAY, BOYS AND GIRLS.
IT'S FINALLY THE START OF A FUN SPORTS DAY!
AS I EXPLAINED THIS MORNING, FOLLOW THE COMPETITION PROGRAM, GET ALONG, AND TRY YOUR BEST WITH SOME PEP IN YOUR STEP. ♪
...
OKAAAAY!♫

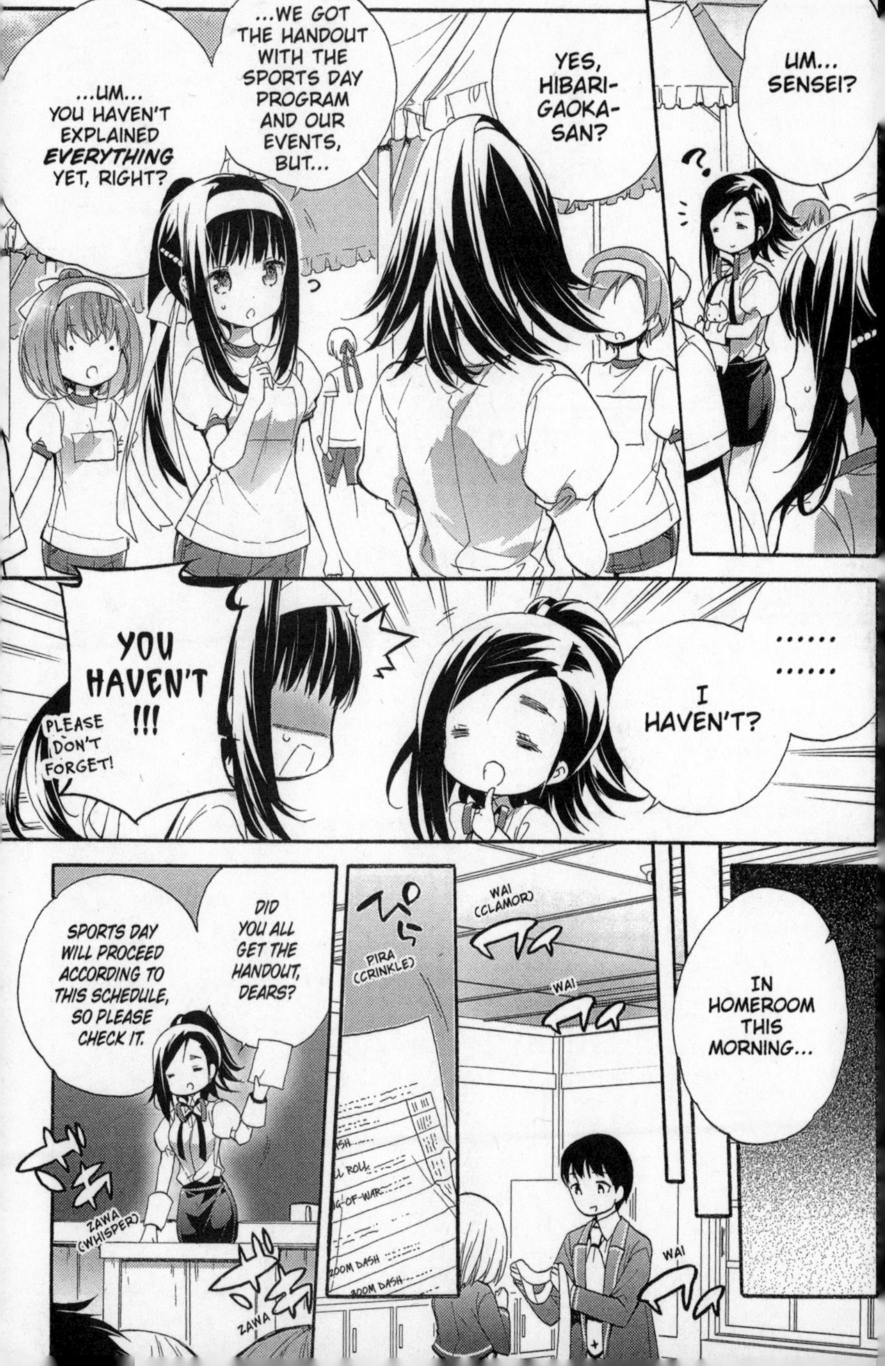
UM... SENSEI?
YES, HIBARI-GAOKA-SAN?
...WE GOT THE HANDOUT WITH THE SPORTS DAY PROGRAM AND OUR EVENTS, BUT...
...UM... YOU HAVEN'T EXPLAINED *EVERYTHING* YET, RIGHT?
....
I HAVEN'T?
YOU HAVEN'T!!!
PLEASE DON'T FORGET!
IN HOMEROOM THIS MORNING...
WAI (CLAMOR)
WAI
WAI
PIRA (CRINKLE)
DASH...
ZOOM DASH
ZOOM DASH
DID YOU ALL GET THE HANDOUT, DEARS?
SPORTS DAY WILL PROCEED ACCORDING TO THIS SCHEDULE, SO PLEASE CHECK IT.
ZAWA (WHISPER)
ZAWA

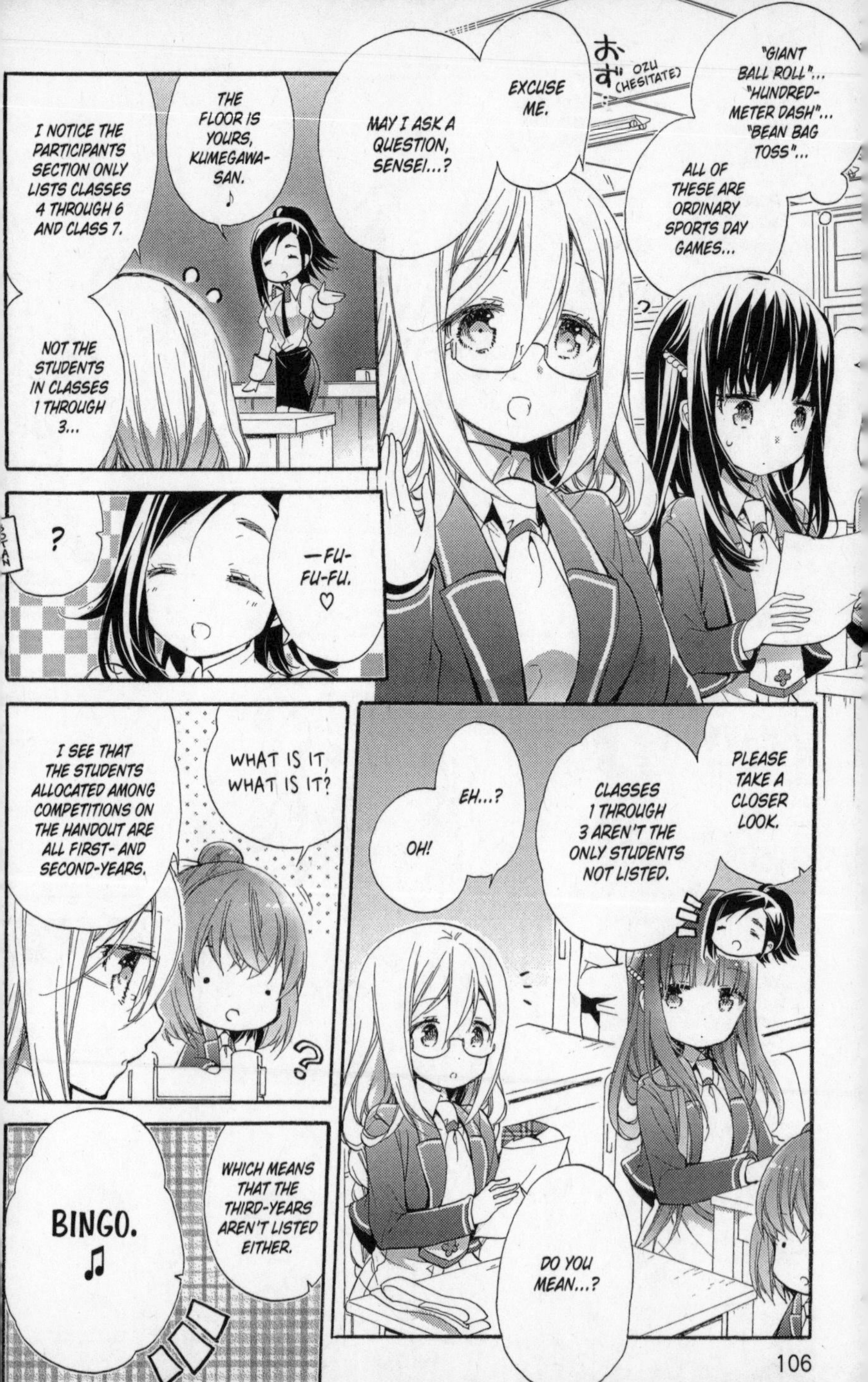
"GIANT BALL ROLL"... "HUNDRED-METER DASH"... "BEAN BAG TOSS"...
ALL OF THESE ARE ORDINARY SPORTS DAY GAMES...
おず OZU (HESITATE)
EXCUSE ME.
MAY I ASK A QUESTION, SENSEI...?
THE FLOOR IS YOURS, KUMEGAWA-SAN. ♪
I NOTICE THE PARTICIPANTS SECTION ONLY LISTS CLASSES 4 THROUGH 6 AND CLASS 7.
NOT THE STUDENTS IN CLASSES 1 THROUGH 3...
—FU-FU-FU. ♡
?
PLEASE TAKE A CLOSER LOOK.
CLASSES 1 THROUGH 3 AREN'T THE ONLY STUDENTS NOT LISTED.
EH...?
OH!
DO YOU MEAN...?
WHAT IS IT, WHAT IS IT?
I SEE THAT THE STUDENTS ALLOCATED AMONG COMPETITIONS ON THE HANDOUT ARE ALL FIRST- AND SECOND-YEARS.
WHICH MEANS THAT THE THIRD-YEARS AREN'T LISTED EITHER.
BINGO. ♫

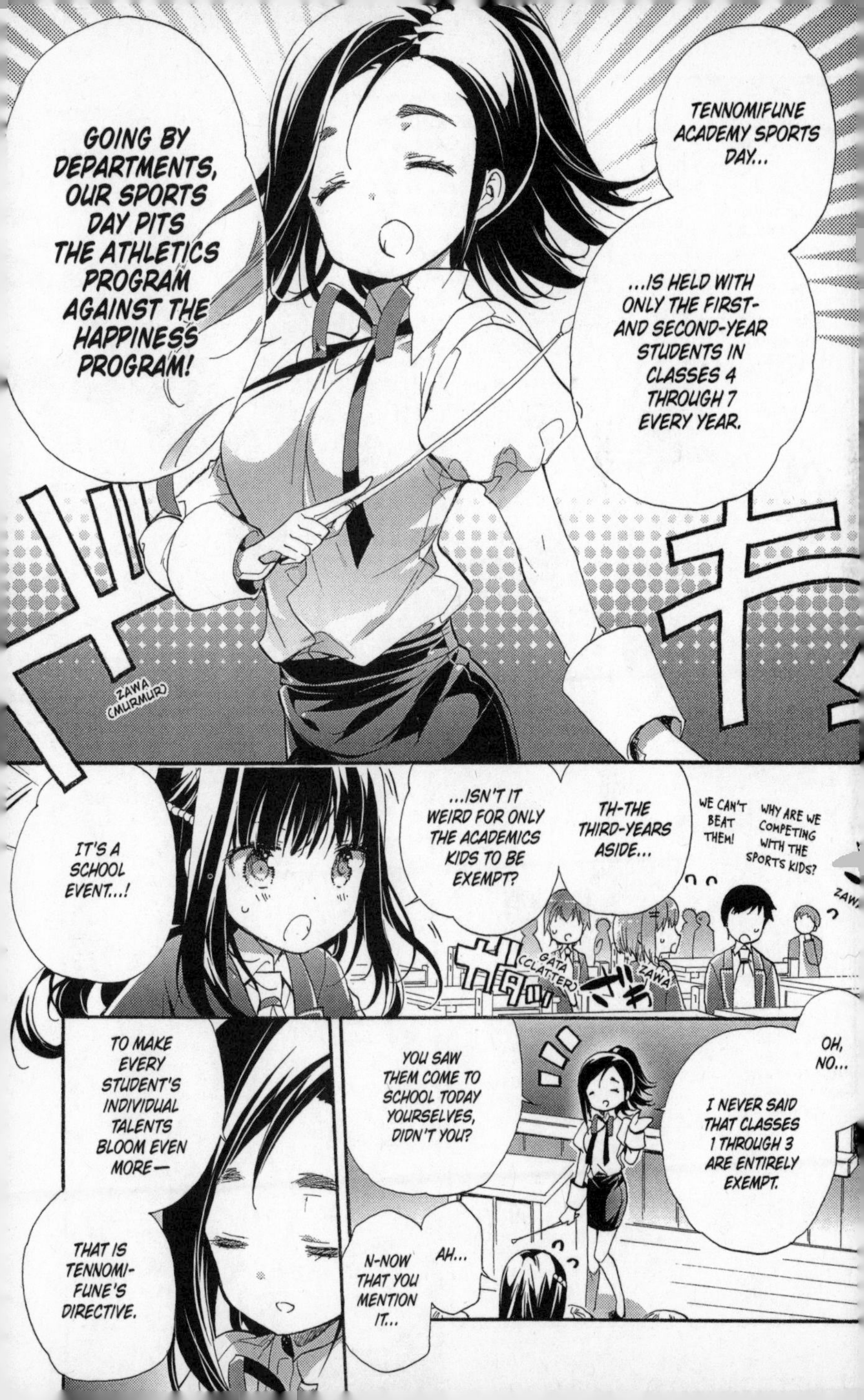
TENNOMIFUNE ACADEMY SPORTS DAY...
...IS HELD WITH ONLY THE FIRST- AND SECOND-YEAR STUDENTS IN CLASSES 4 THROUGH 7 EVERY YEAR.
GOING BY DEPARTMENTS, OUR SPORTS DAY PITS THE ATHLETICS PROGRAM AGAINST THE HAPPINESS PROGRAM!
ZAWA (MURMUR)
ZAWA
WHY ARE WE COMPETING WITH THE SPORTS KIDS?
WE CAN'T BEAT THEM!
TH-THE THIRD-YEARS ASIDE...
...ISN'T IT WEIRD FOR ONLY THE ACADEMICS KIDS TO BE EXEMPT?
ZAWA
GATA (CLATTER)
IT'S A SCHOOL EVENT...!
OH, NO...
I NEVER SAID THAT CLASSES 1 THROUGH 3 ARE ENTIRELY EXEMPT.
YOU SAW THEM COME TO SCHOOL TODAY YOURSELVES, DIDN'T YOU?
AH...
N-NOW THAT YOU MENTION IT...
TO MAKE EVERY STUDENT'S INDIVIDUAL TALENTS BLOOM EVEN MORE—
THAT IS TENNOMI-FUNE'S DIRECTIVE.

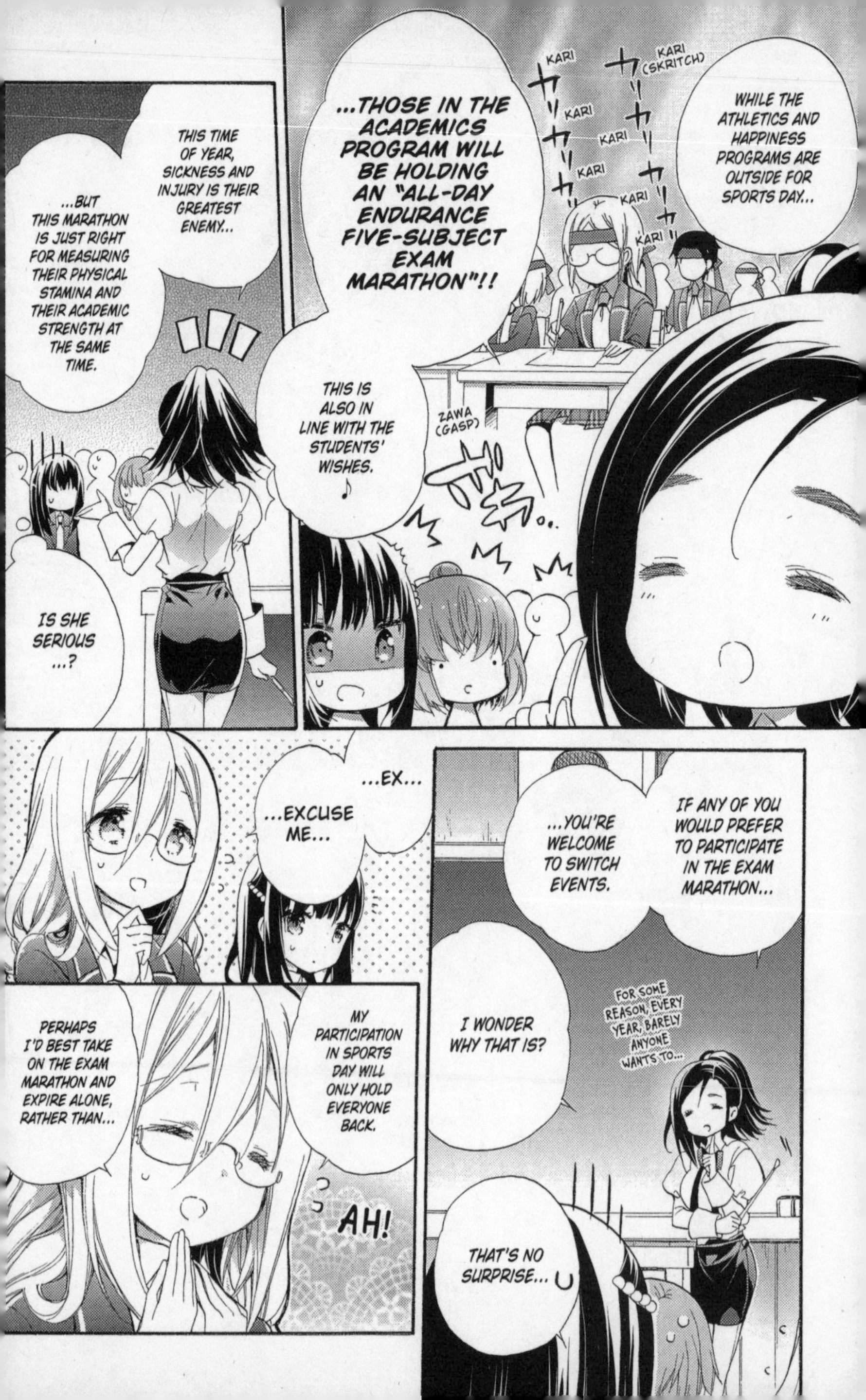
KARI (SKRITCH)
KARI
KARI
KARI
KARI
KARI
KARI
WHILE THE ATHLETICS AND HAPPINESS PROGRAMS ARE OUTSIDE FOR SPORTS DAY...
...THOSE IN THE ACADEMICS PROGRAM WILL BE HOLDING AN "ALL-DAY ENDURANCE FIVE-SUBJECT EXAM MARATHON"!!
THIS IS ALSO IN LINE WITH THE STUDENTS' WISHES. ♪
ZAWA (GASP)
THIS TIME OF YEAR, SICKNESS AND INJURY IS THEIR GREATEST ENEMY...
...BUT THIS MARATHON IS JUST RIGHT FOR MEASURING THEIR PHYSICAL STAMINA AND THEIR ACADEMIC STRENGTH AT THE SAME TIME.
IS SHE SERIOUS ...?
IF ANY OF YOU WOULD PREFER TO PARTICIPATE IN THE EXAM MARATHON...
...YOU'RE WELCOME TO SWITCH EVENTS.
I WONDER WHY THAT IS?
FOR SOME REASON, EVERY YEAR, BARELY ANYONE WANTS TO...
THAT'S NO SURPRISE...
...EX...
...EXCUSE ME...
MY PARTICIPATION IN SPORTS DAY WILL ONLY HOLD EVERYONE BACK.
PERHAPS I'D BEST TAKE ON THE EXAM MARATHON AND EXPIRE ALONE, RATHER THAN...
AH!

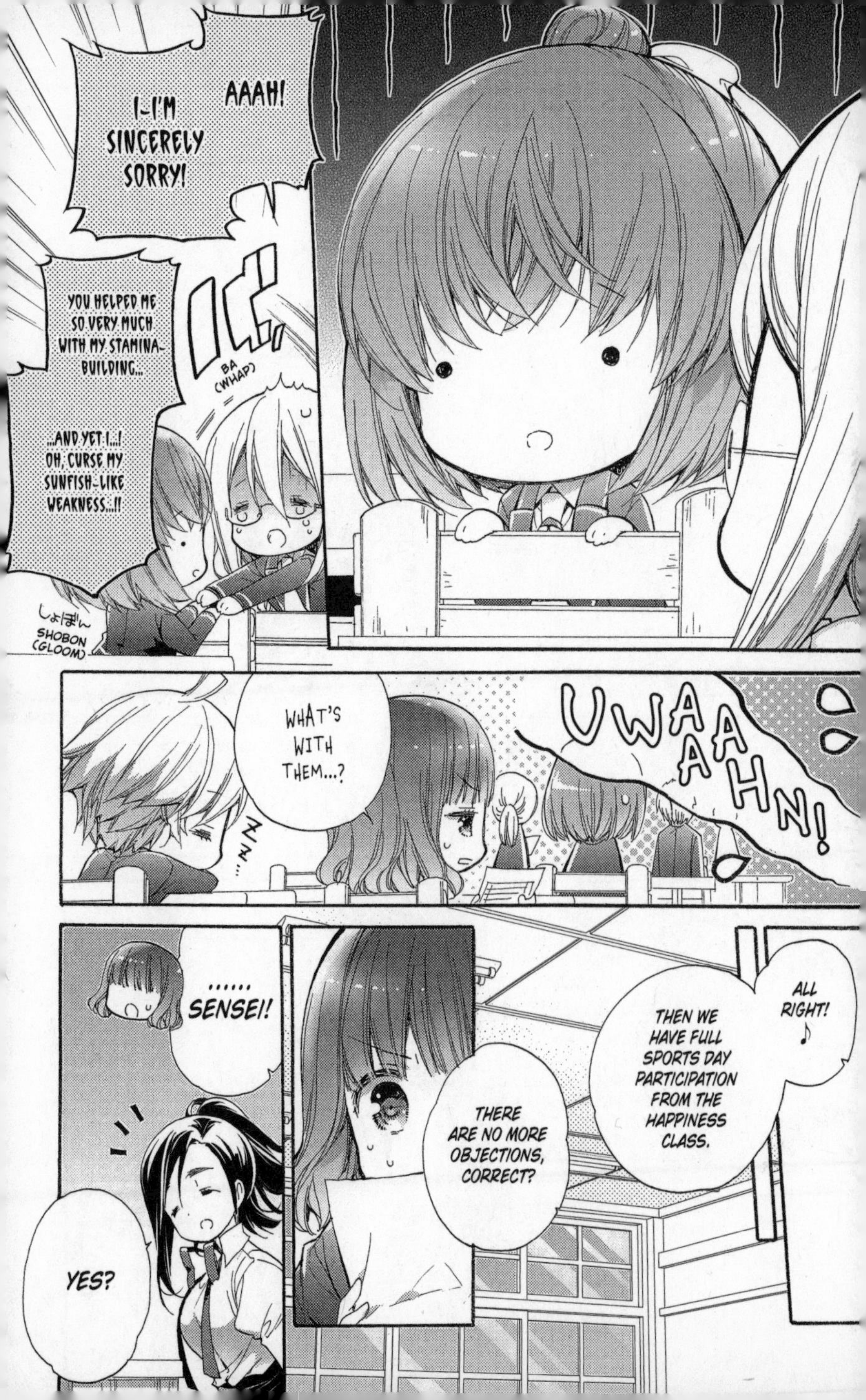
AAAH! I-I'M SINCERELY SORRY!
BA (WHAP)
YOU HELPED ME SO VERY MUCH WITH MY STAMINA-BUILDING...
...AND YET I...! OH, CURSE MY SUNFISH-LIKE WEAKNESS...!!
しょぼん SHOBON (GLOOM)
UWAAAAHN!
WHAT'S WITH THEM...?
ALL RIGHT! ♪
THEN WE HAVE FULL SPORTS DAY PARTICIPATION FROM THE HAPPINESS CLASS.
THERE ARE NO MORE OBJECTIONS, CORRECT?
...... SENSEI!
YES?

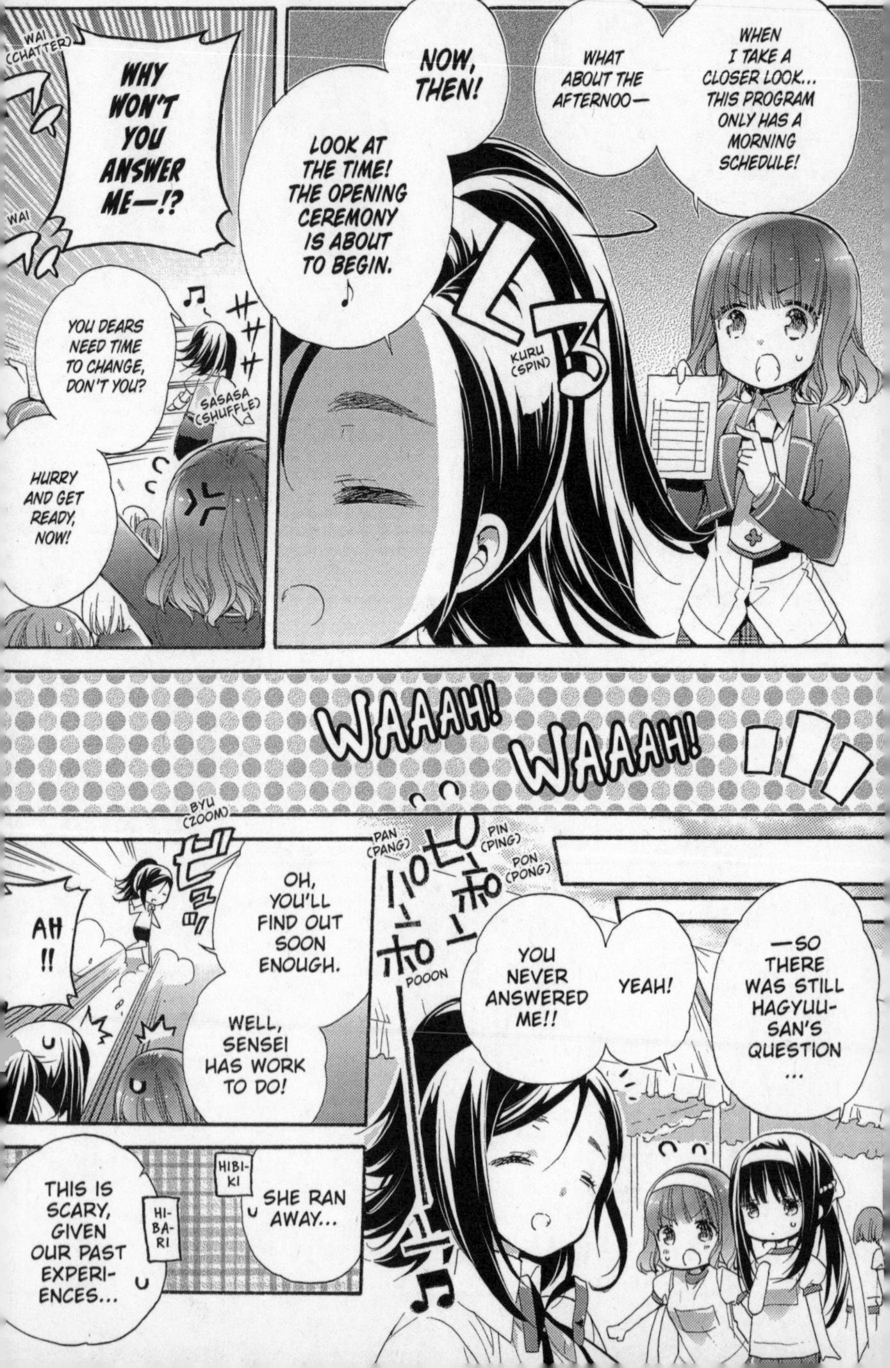
WHEN I TAKE A CLOSER LOOK... THIS PROGRAM ONLY HAS A MORNING SCHEDULE!
WHAT ABOUT THE AFTERNOO—
NOW, THEN!
LOOK AT THE TIME! THE OPENING CEREMONY IS ABOUT TO BEGIN. ♪
KURU (SPIN)
WAI (CHATTER)
WHY WON'T YOU ANSWER ME—!?
WAI
YOU DEARS NEED TIME TO CHANGE, DON'T YOU?
SASASA (SHUFFLE)
HURRY AND GET READY, NOW!
WAAAH!
WAAAH!
—SO THERE WAS STILL HAGYUU-SAN'S QUESTION...
YEAH!
YOU NEVER ANSWERED ME!!
PIN (PING)
PON (PONG)
PAN (PANG)
POOON
OH, YOU'LL FIND OUT SOON ENOUGH.
WELL, SENSEI HAS WORK TO DO!
BYU (ZOOM)
AH !!
HIBIKI
SHE RAN AWAY...
HIBARI
THIS IS SCARY, GIVEN OUR PAST EXPERIENCES...

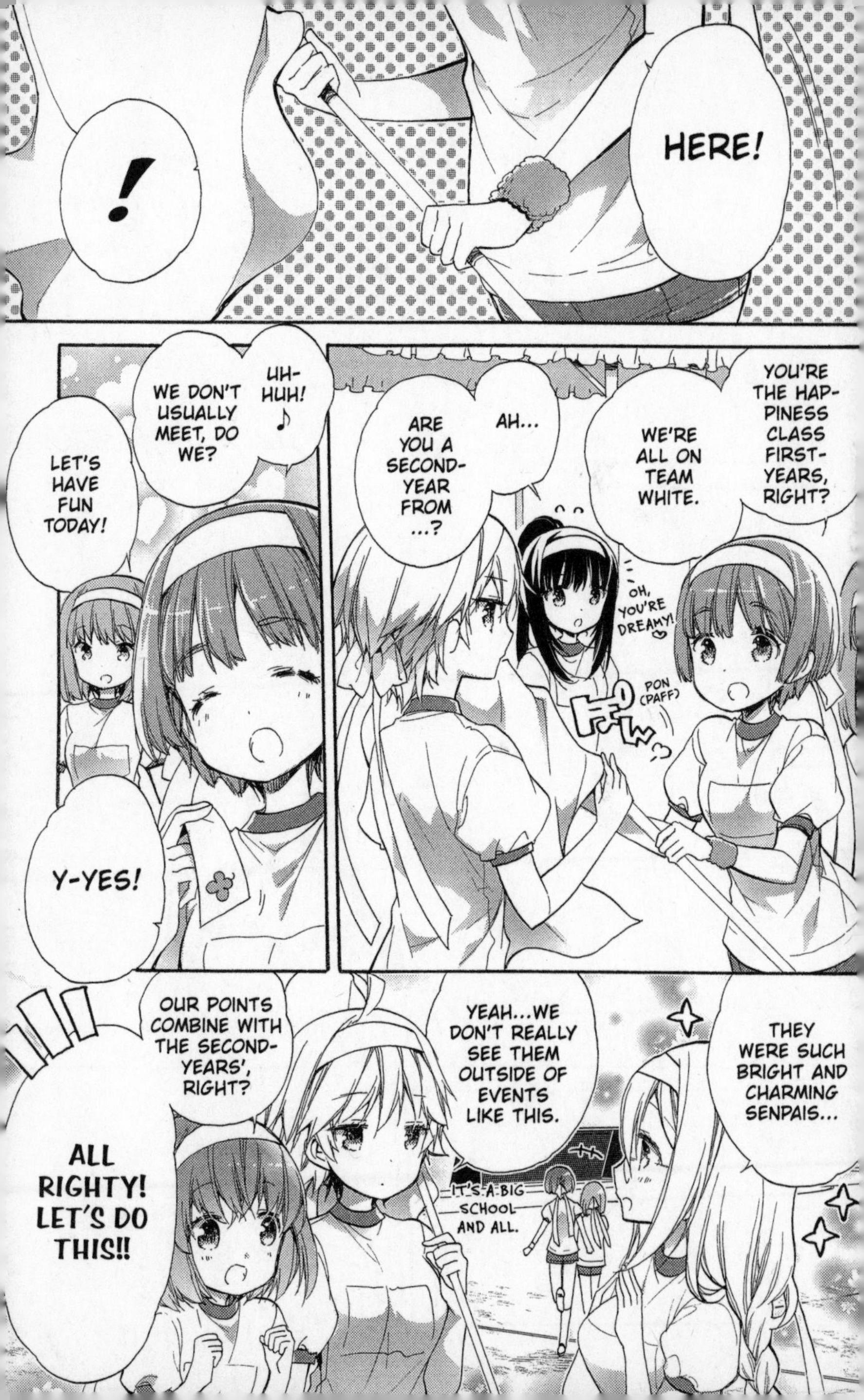
HERE!
!
YOU'RE THE HAPPINESS CLASS FIRST-YEARS, RIGHT?
WE'RE ALL ON TEAM WHITE.
OH, YOU'RE DREAMY!
PON (PAFF)
AH...
ARE YOU A SECOND-YEAR FROM ...?
UH-HUH! ♪
WE DON'T USUALLY MEET, DO WE?
LET'S HAVE FUN TODAY!
Y-YES!
THEY WERE SUCH BRIGHT AND CHARMING SENPAIS...
YEAH...WE DON'T REALLY SEE THEM OUTSIDE OF EVENTS LIKE THIS.
IT'S A BIG SCHOOL AND ALL.
OUR POINTS COMBINE WITH THE SECOND-YEARS', RIGHT?
ALL RIGHTY! LET'S DO THIS!!

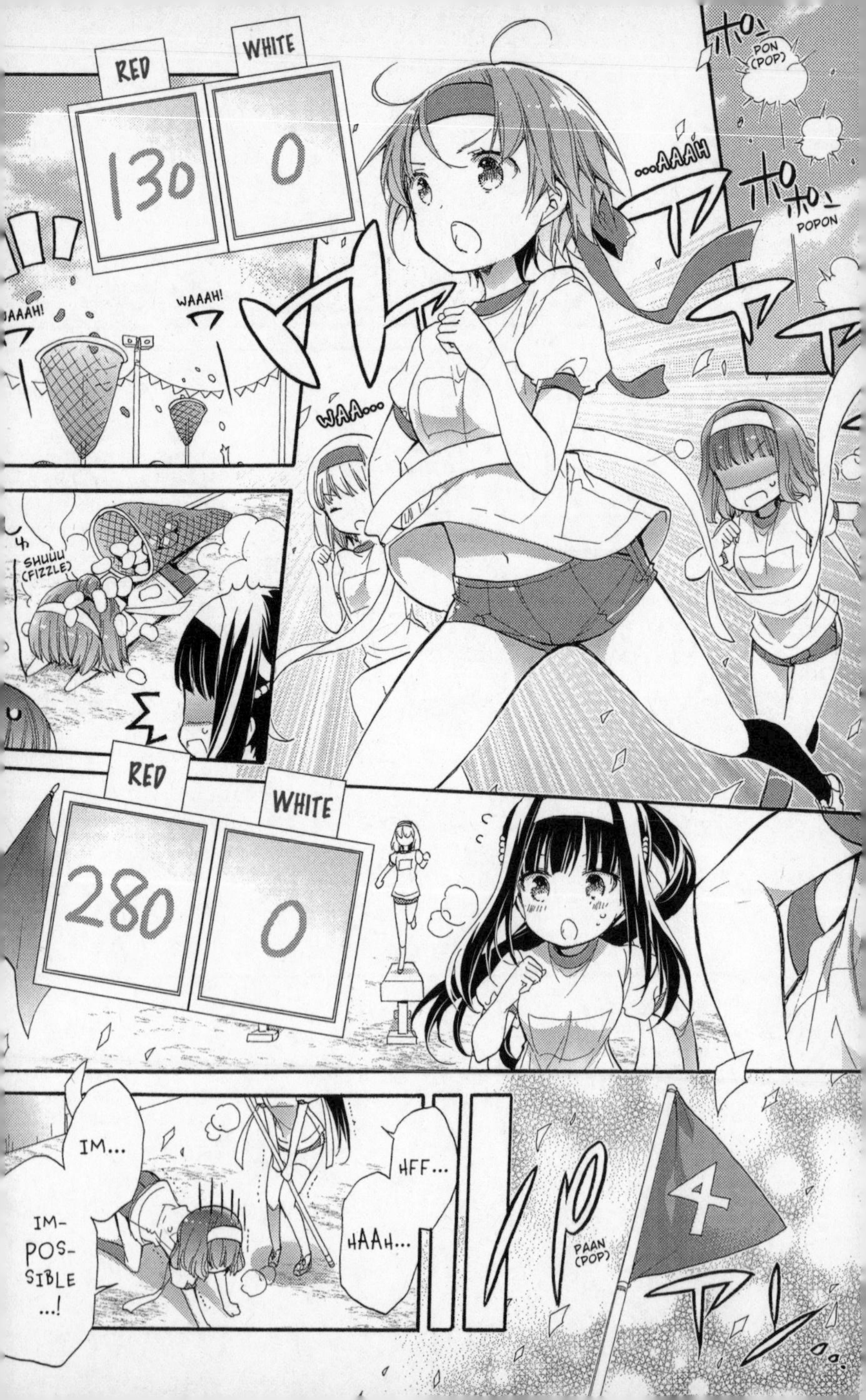
PON (POP)
...AAAH
POPON
WAA...
RED
WHITE
130
0
WAAAH!
AAAH!
SHUUU (FIZZLE)
RED
WHITE
280
0
PAAN (POP)
4
HFF...
HAAH...
IM...
IM-POS-SIBLE ...!

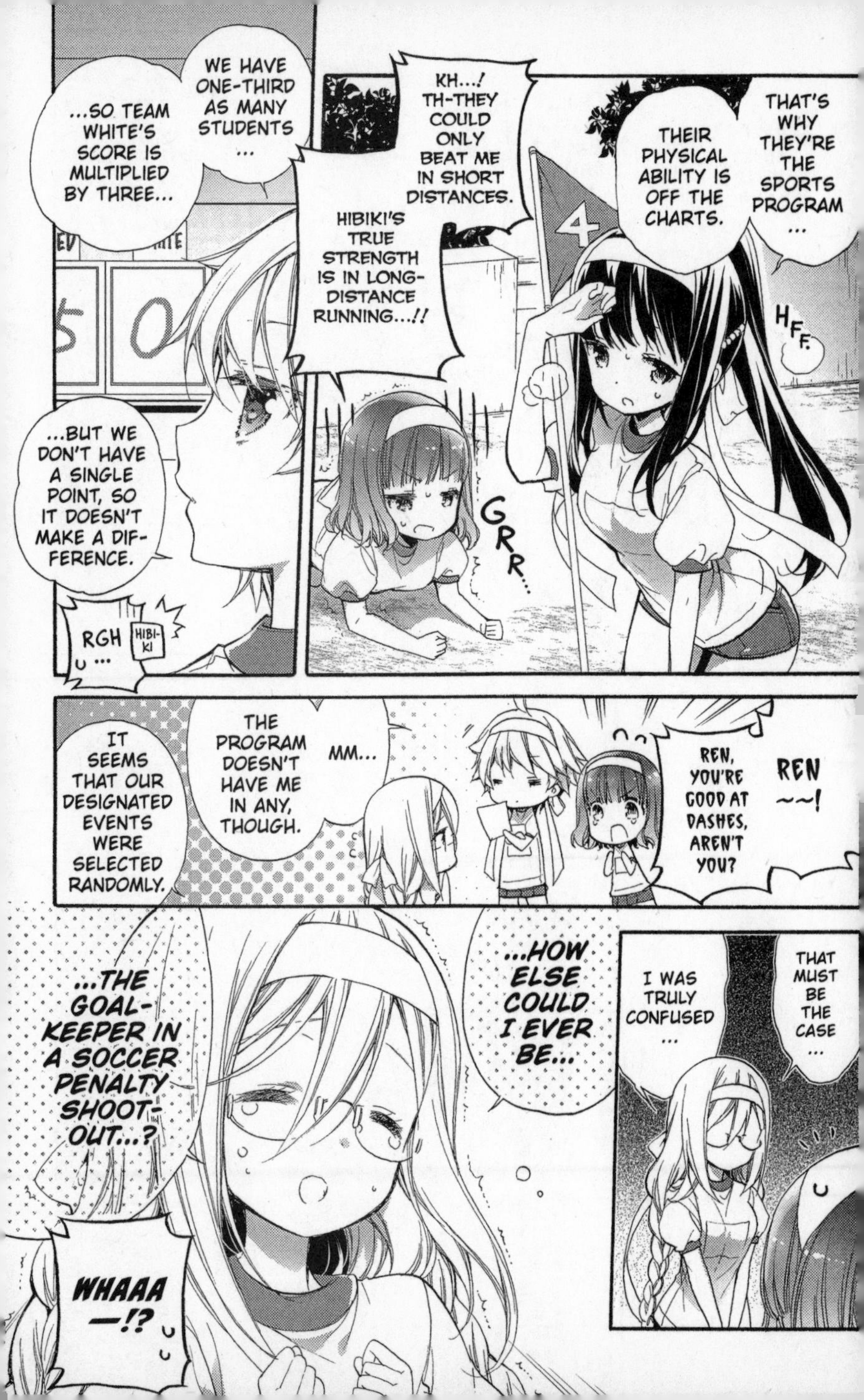
THAT'S WHY THEY'RE THE SPORTS PROGRAM...
THEIR PHYSICAL ABILITY IS OFF THE CHARTS.
HFF.
KH...! TH-THEY COULD ONLY BEAT ME IN SHORT DISTANCES.
HIBIKI'S TRUE STRENGTH IS IN LONG-DISTANCE RUNNING...!!
GRR...
WE HAVE ONE-THIRD AS MANY STUDENTS...
...SO TEAM WHITE'S SCORE IS MULTIPLIED BY THREE...
...BUT WE DON'T HAVE A SINGLE POINT, SO IT DOESN'T MAKE A DIFFERENCE.
HIBIKI
RGH...
REN ~~!
REN, YOU'RE GOOD AT DASHES, AREN'T YOU?
MM...
THE PROGRAM DOESN'T HAVE ME IN ANY, THOUGH.
IT SEEMS THAT OUR DESIGNATED EVENTS WERE SELECTED RANDOMLY.
THAT MUST BE THE CASE...
I WAS TRULY CONFUSED...
...HOW ELSE COULD I EVER BE...
...THE GOALKEEPER IN A SOCCER PENALTY SHOOTOUT...?
WHAAA—!?

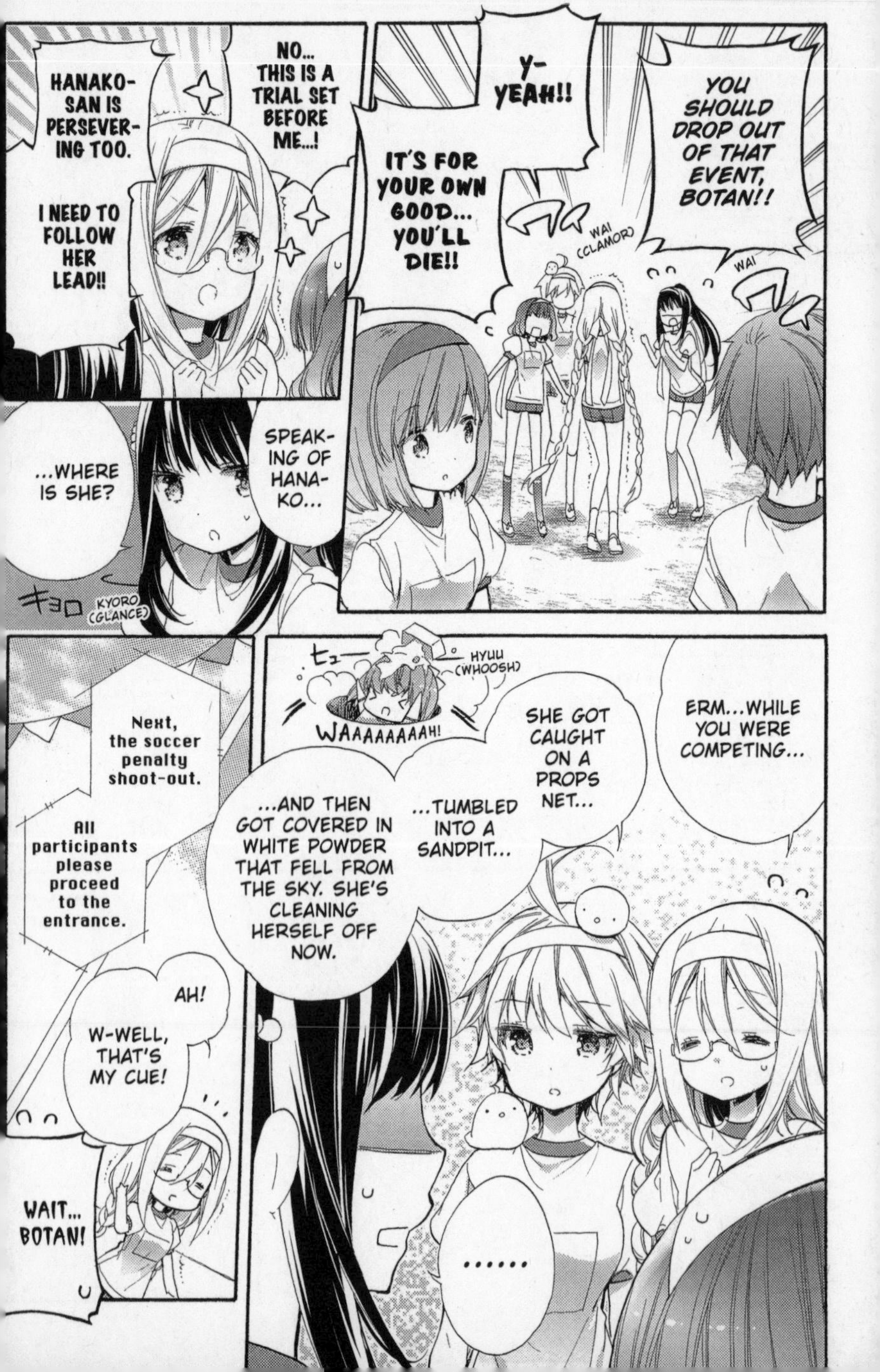
YOU SHOULD DROP OUT OF THAT EVENT, BOTAN!!
WAI
Y-YEAH!!
IT'S FOR YOUR OWN GOOD... YOU'LL DIE!!
WAI (CLAMOR)
NO... THIS IS A TRIAL SET BEFORE ME...!
HANAKO-SAN IS PERSEVERING TOO.
I NEED TO FOLLOW HER LEAD!!
SPEAKING OF HANAKO...
...WHERE IS SHE?
KYORO (GLANCE)
ERM...WHILE YOU WERE COMPETING...
SHE GOT CAUGHT ON A PROPS NET...
HYUU (WHOOSH)
WAAAAAAAAH!
...TUMBLED INTO A SANDPIT...
...AND THEN GOT COVERED IN WHITE POWDER THAT FELL FROM THE SKY. SHE'S CLEANING HERSELF OFF NOW.
......
Next, the soccer penalty shoot-out.
All participants please proceed to the entrance.
AH!
W-WELL, THAT'S MY CUE!
WAIT... BOTAN!

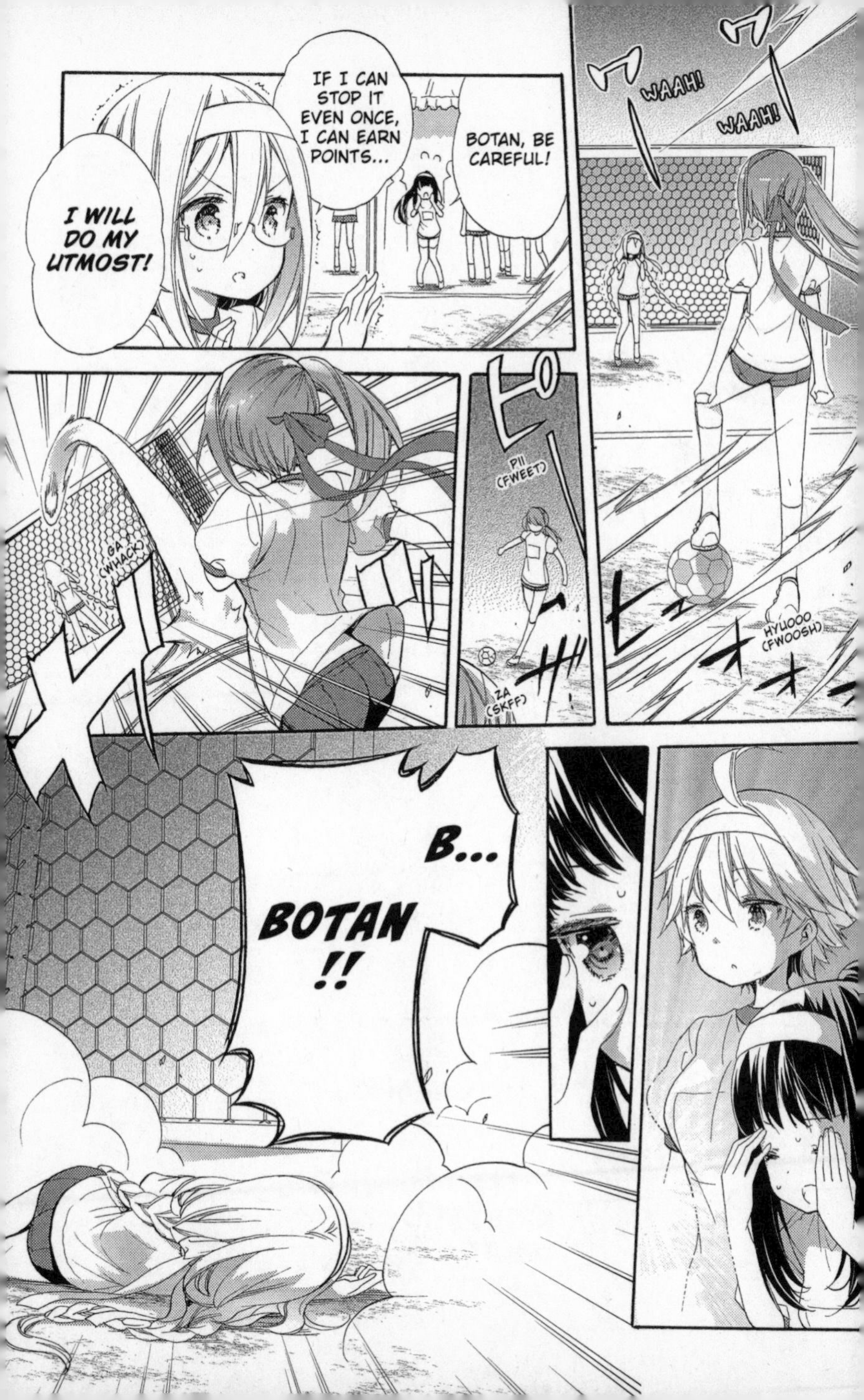
WAAH!
WAAH!
HYUOOO (FWOOSH)
BOTAN, BE CAREFUL!
IF I CAN STOP IT EVEN ONCE, I CAN EARN POINTS...
I WILL DO MY UTMOST!
PII (FWEET)
ZA (SKFF)
GA (WHACK)
B... BOTAN!!

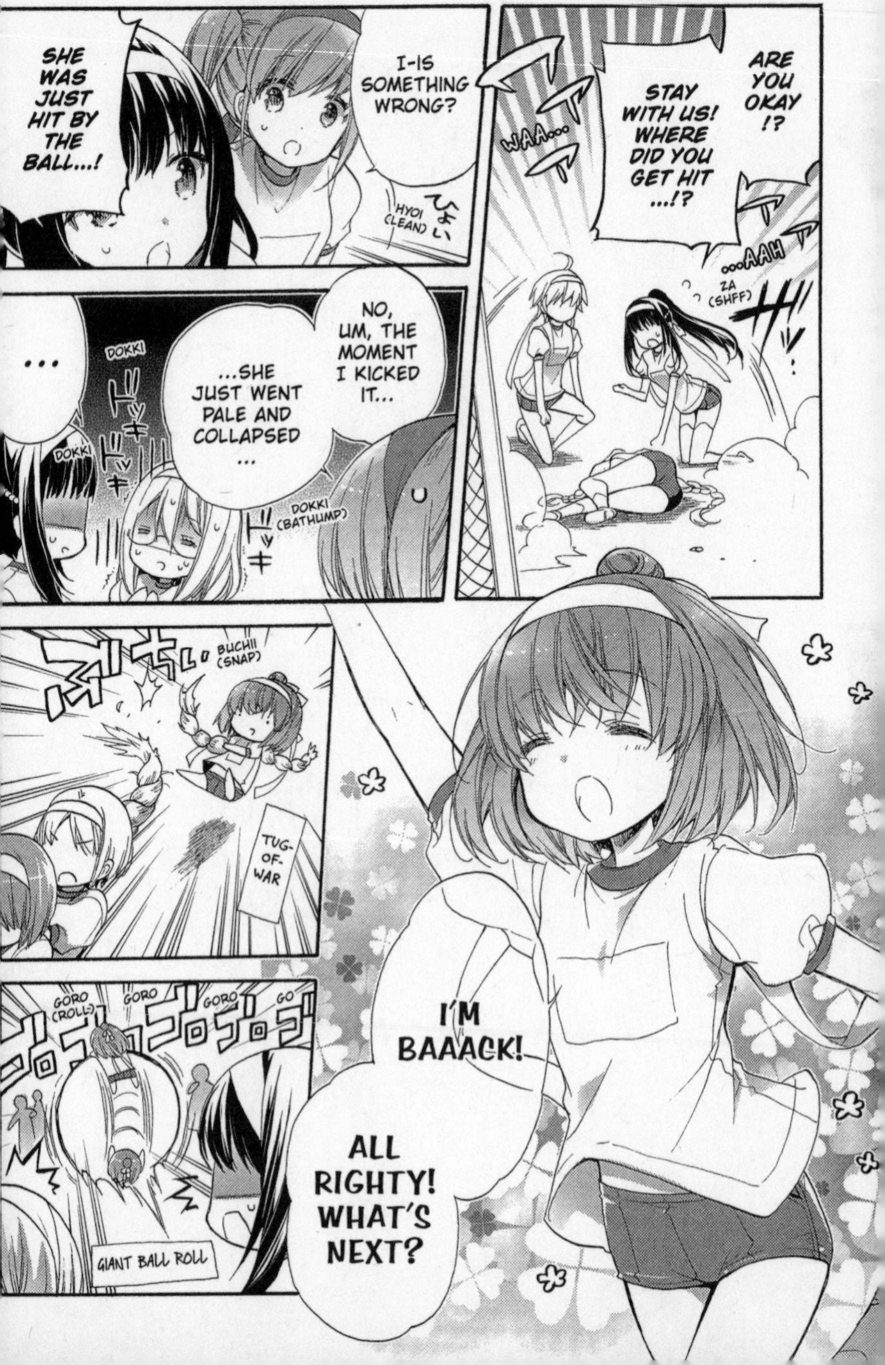

ARE YOU OKAY!?
STAY WITH US! WHERE DID YOU GET HIT ...!?
WAA...
...AAH
ZA (SHFF)
I-IS SOMETHING WRONG?
HYOI (LEAN)
ひょい
SHE WAS JUST HIT BY THE BALL...!
NO, UM, THE MOMENT I KICKED IT...
...SHE JUST WENT PALE AND COLLAPSED...
DOKKI (BATHUMP)
DOKKI
DOKKI
...
I'M BAAACK!
ALL RIGHTY! WHAT'S NEXT?
BUCHII (SNAP)
TUG-OF-WAR
GO
GORO
GORO
GORO (ROLL)
GIANT BALL ROLL

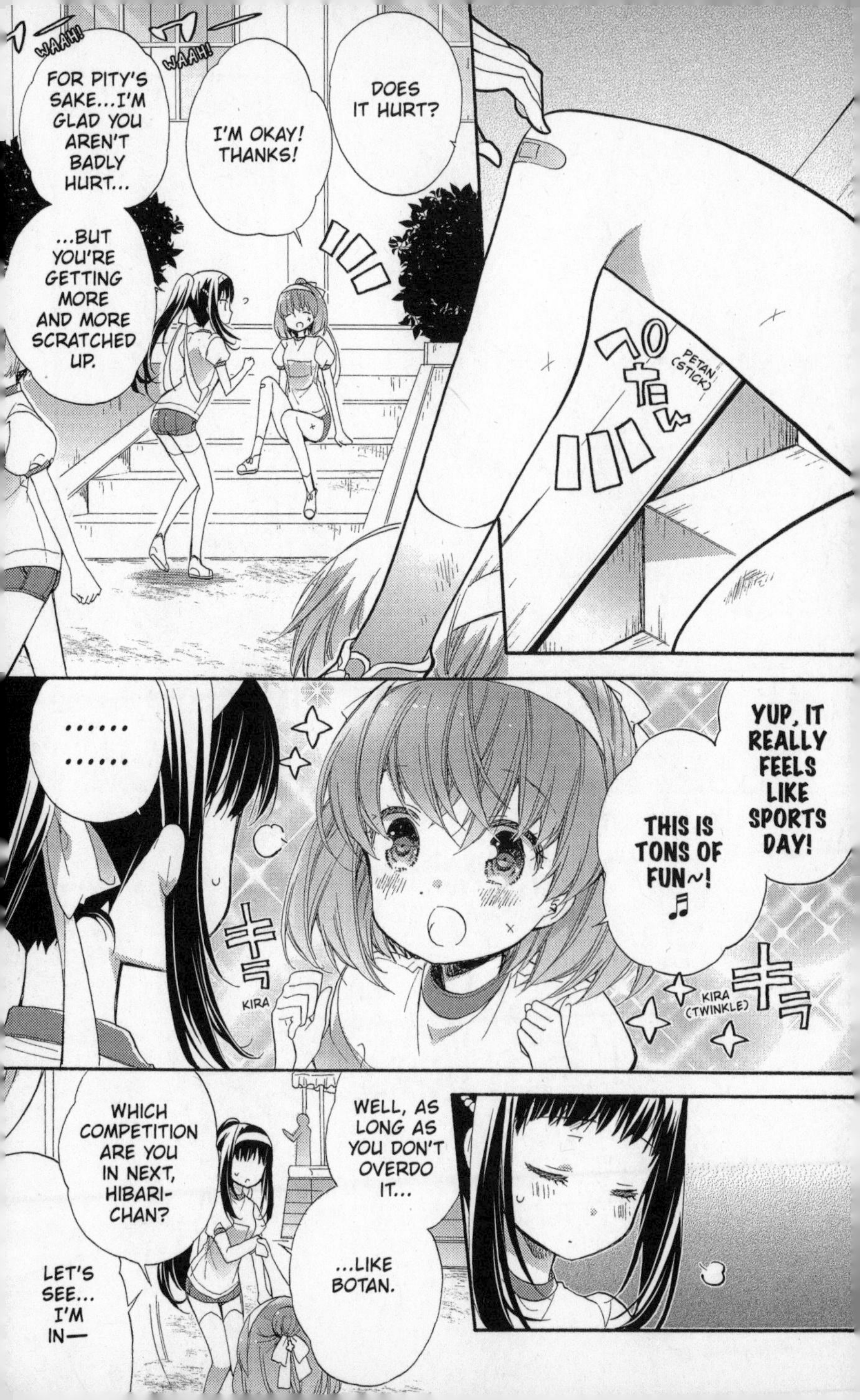
PETAN (STICK)
DOES IT HURT?
I'M OKAY! THANKS!
WAAAH!
WAAAH!
FOR PITY'S SAKE...I'M GLAD YOU AREN'T BADLY HURT...
...BUT YOU'RE GETTING MORE AND MORE SCRATCHED UP.
YUP, IT REALLY FEELS LIKE SPORTS DAY!
THIS IS TONS OF FUN~! ♬
KIRA (TWINKLE)
KIRA
......
......
WELL, AS LONG AS YOU DON'T OVERDO IT...
...LIKE BOTAN.
WHICH COMPETITION ARE YOU IN NEXT, HIBARI-CHAN?
LET'S SEE... I'M IN—

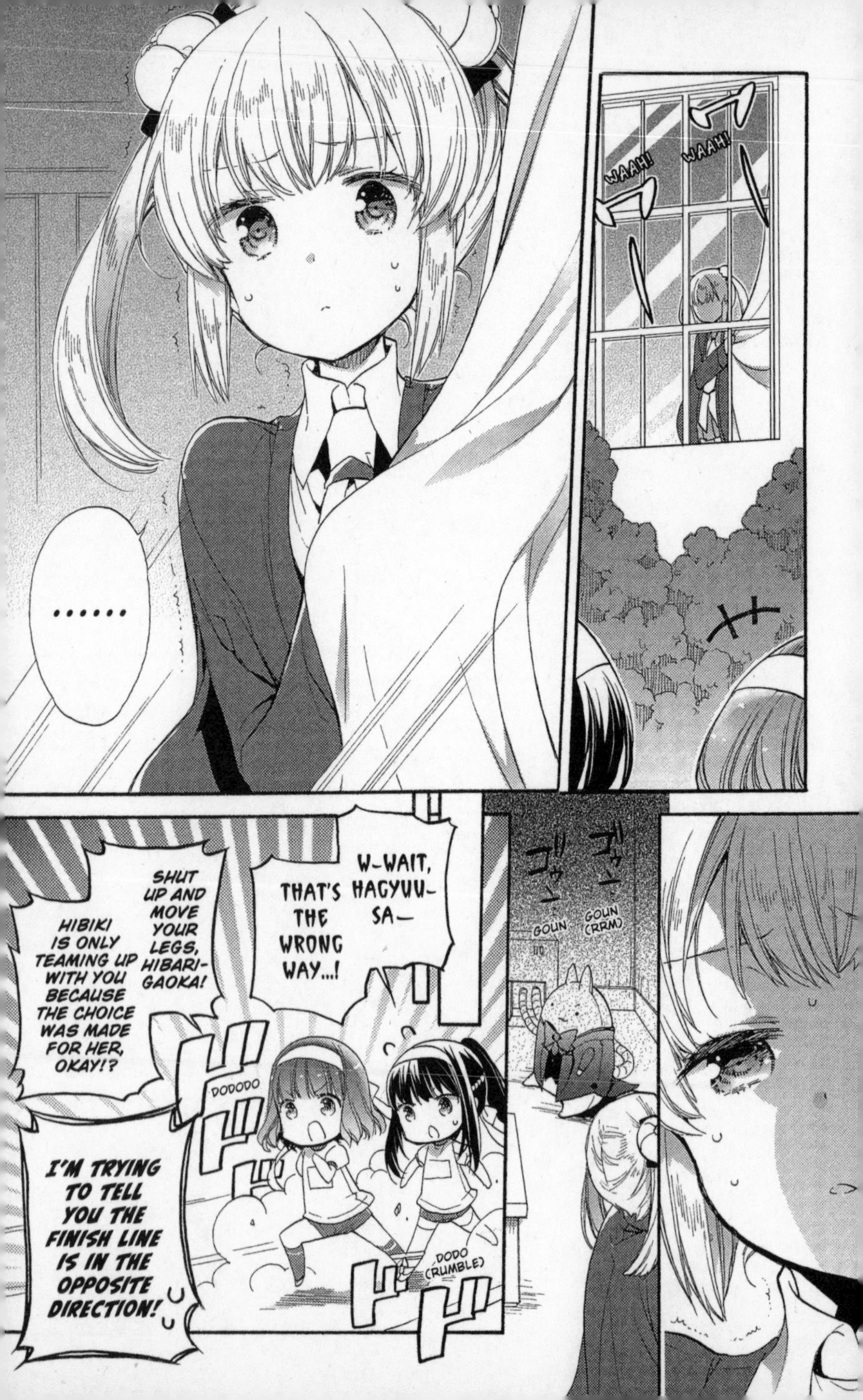
WAAH!
WAAH!
......
GOUN
GOUN (RRM)
W-WAIT, HAGYUU-SA—
THAT'S THE WRONG WAY...!
SHUT UP AND MOVE YOUR LEGS, HIBARIGAOKA!
HIBIKI IS ONLY TEAMING UP WITH YOU BECAUSE THE CHOICE WAS MADE FOR HER, OKAY!?
DODODO
I'M TRYING TO TELL YOU THE FINISH LINE IS IN THE OPPOSITE DIRECTION!
DODO (RUMBLE)

Anne Happy

unhappy go lucky!

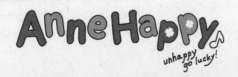

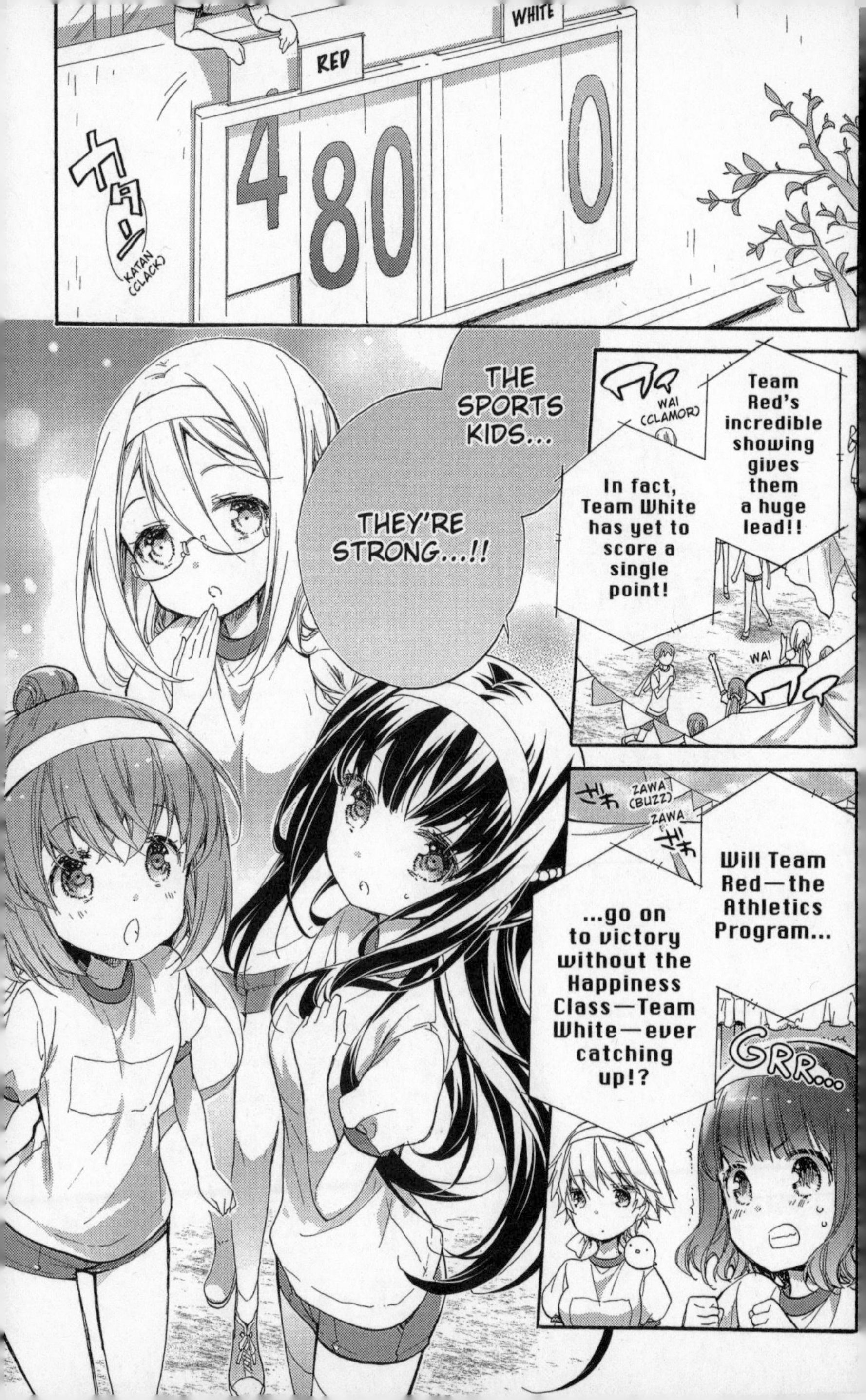
WHITE
RED
480
0
KATAN (CLACK)
Team Red's incredible showing gives them a huge lead!!
WAI (CLAMOR)
In fact, Team White has yet to score a single point!
WAI
Will Team Red—the Athletics Program...
ZAWA (BUZZ)
ZAWA
...go on to victory without the Happiness Class—Team White—ever catching up!?
GRR...
THE SPORTS KIDS...
THEY'RE STRONG...!!

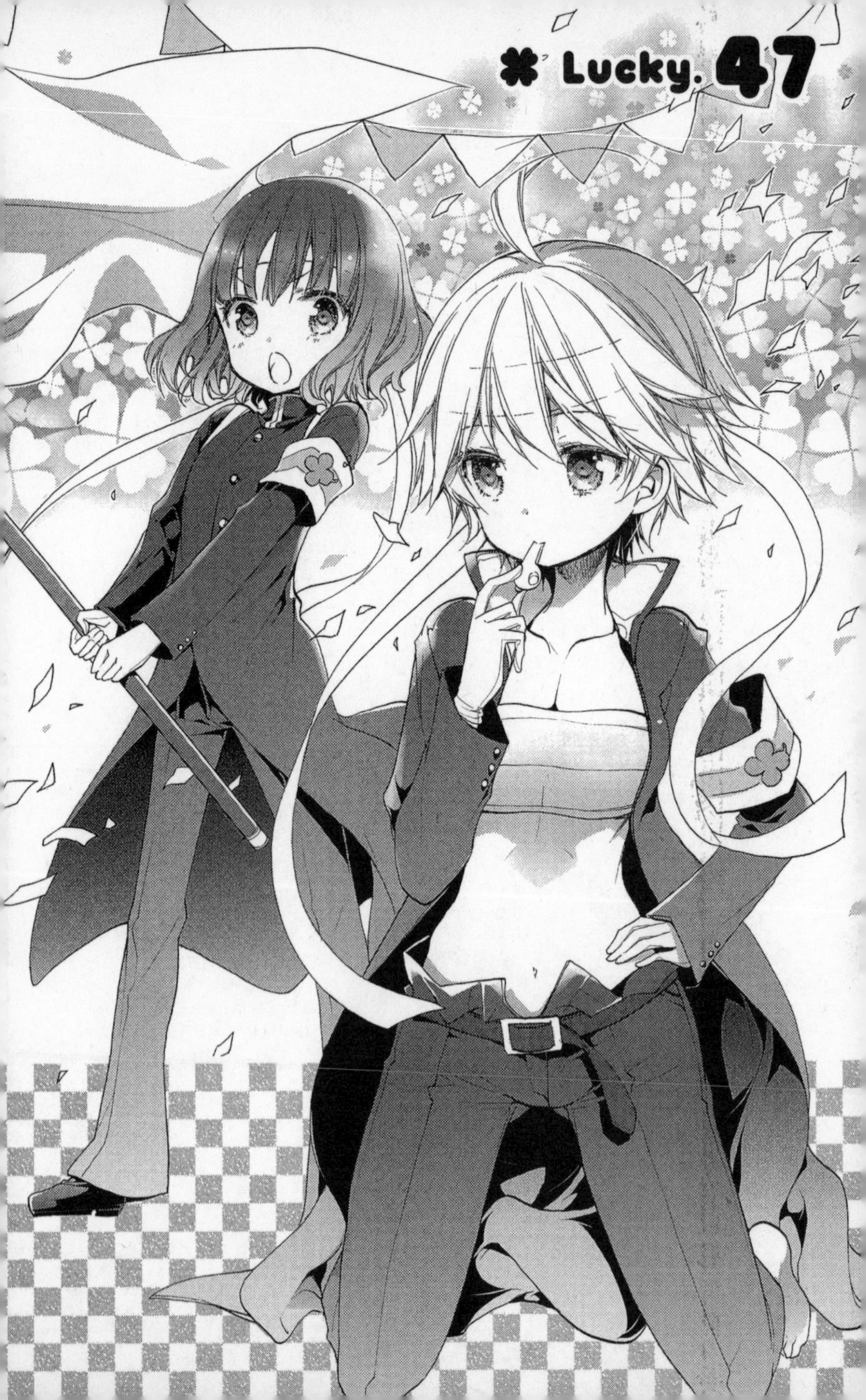
Lucky. 47

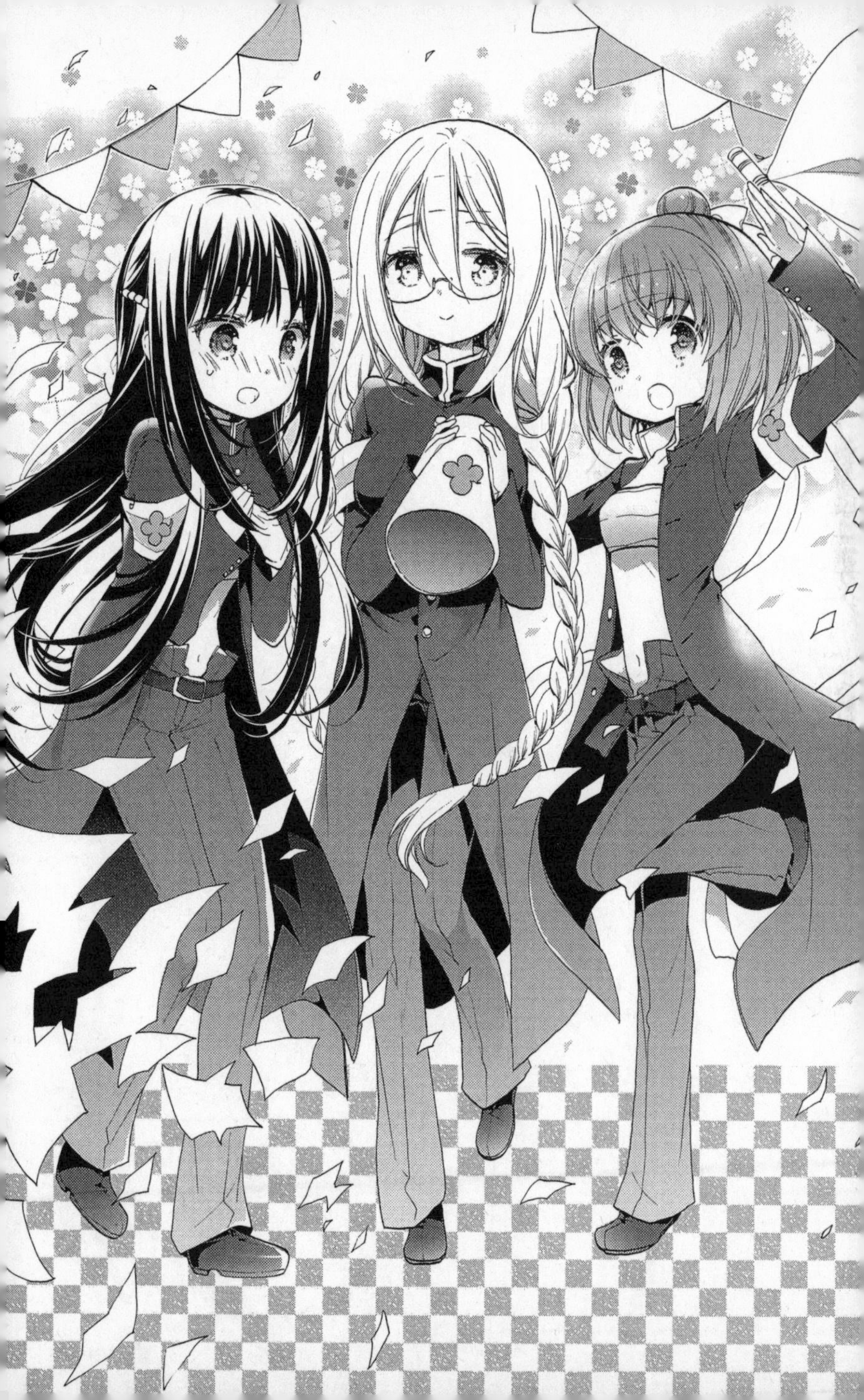

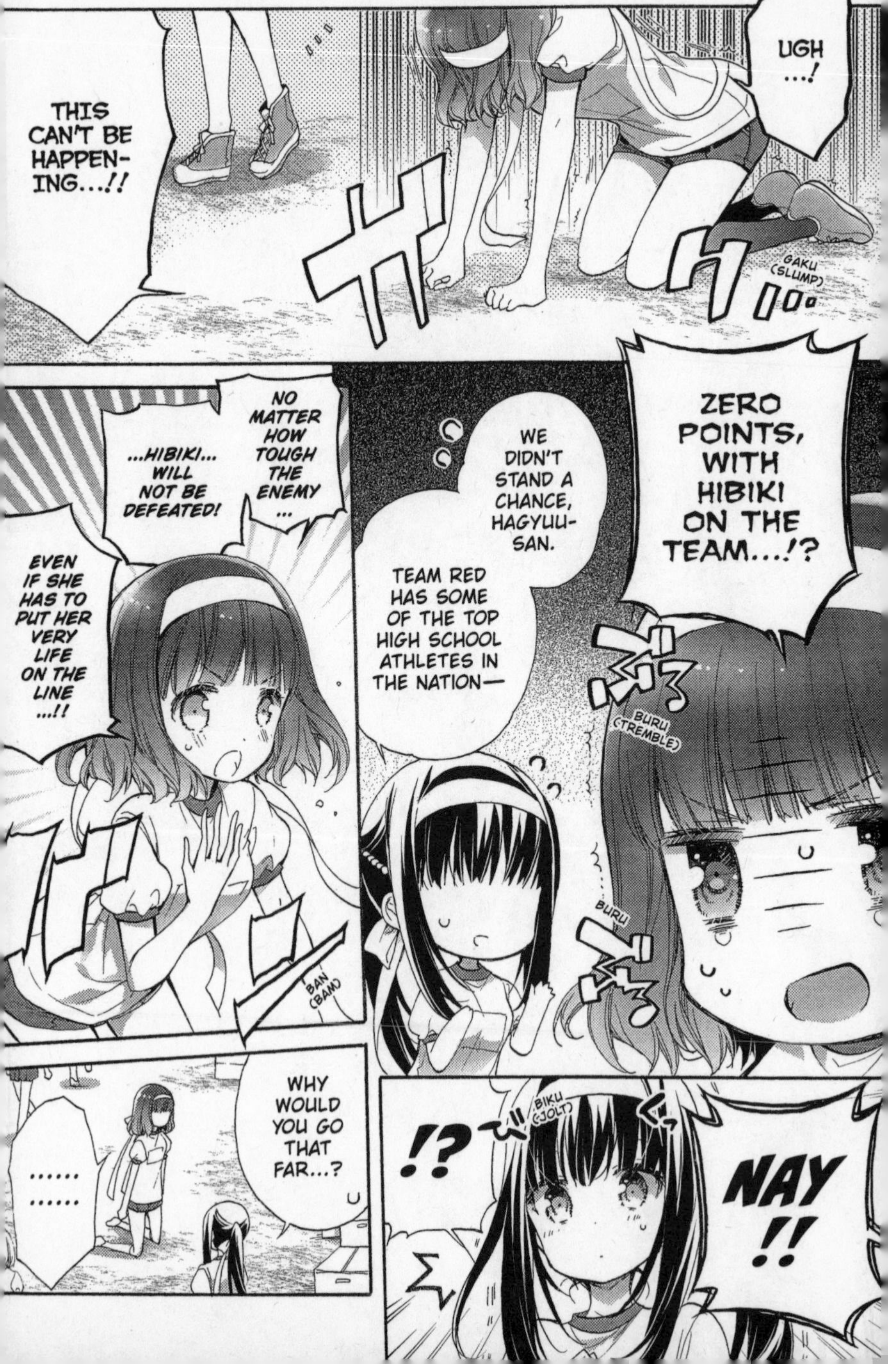
UGH...!
GAKU (SLUMP)
THIS CAN'T BE HAPPENING...!!
ZERO POINTS, WITH HIBIKI ON THE TEAM...!?
BURU (TREMBLE)
WE DIDN'T STAND A CHANCE, HAGYUU-SAN.
TEAM RED HAS SOME OF THE TOP HIGH SCHOOL ATHLETES IN THE NATION—
BURU
NO MATTER HOW TOUGH THE ENEMY...
...HIBIKI... WILL NOT BE DEFEATED!
EVEN IF SHE HAS TO PUT HER VERY LIFE ON THE LINE...!!
BAN (BAM)
NAY!!
BIKU (JOLT)
!?
WHY WOULD YOU GO THAT FAR...?
....

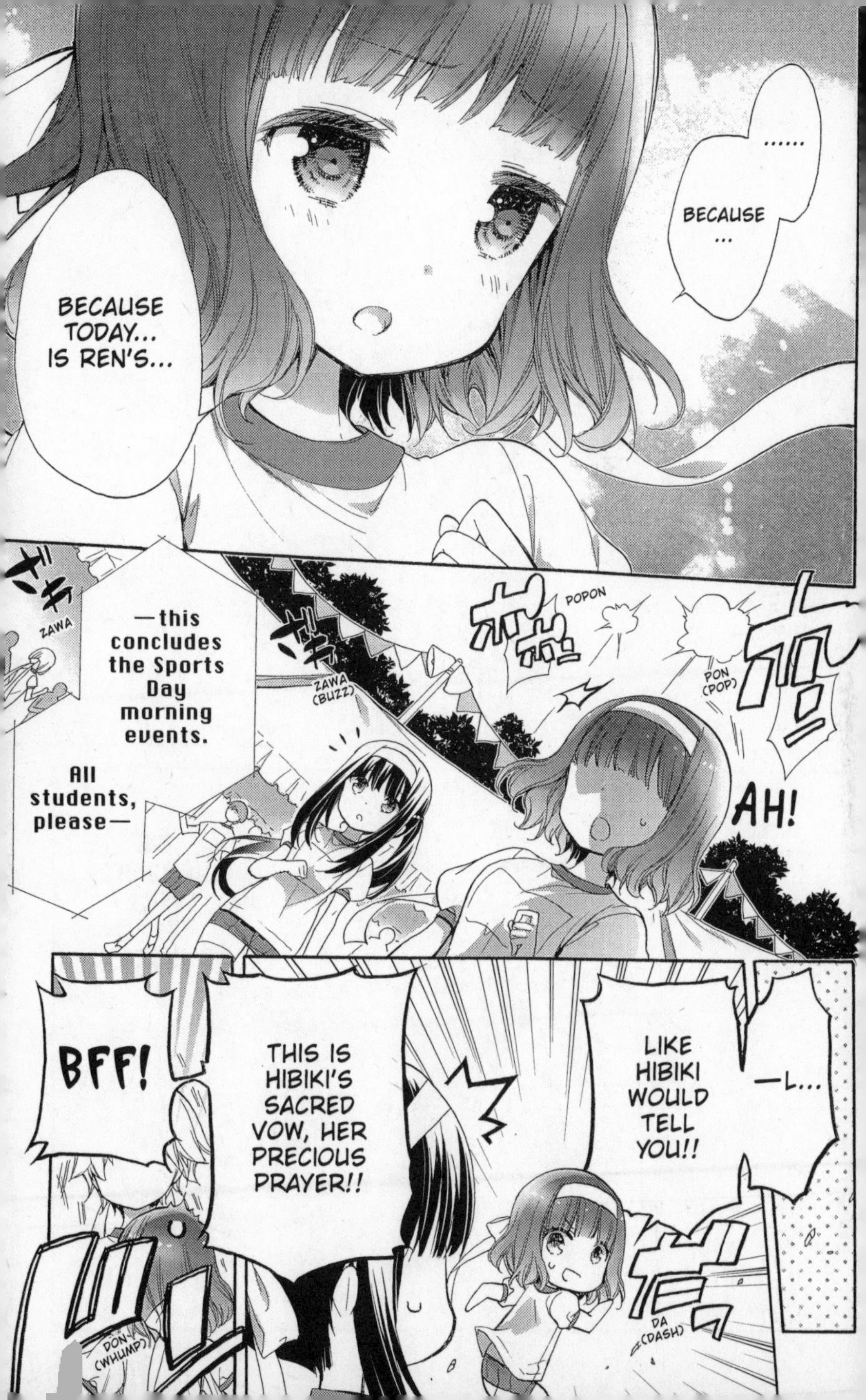
......
BECAUSE ...
BECAUSE TODAY... IS REN'S...
PON (POP)
POPON
AH!
ZAWA (BUZZ)
—this concludes the Sports Day morning events.
All students, please—
ZAWA
—L...
LIKE HIBIKI WOULD TELL YOU!!
DA (DASH)
THIS IS HIBIKI'S SACRED VOW, HER PRECIOUS PRAYER!!
BFF!
DON (WHUMP)

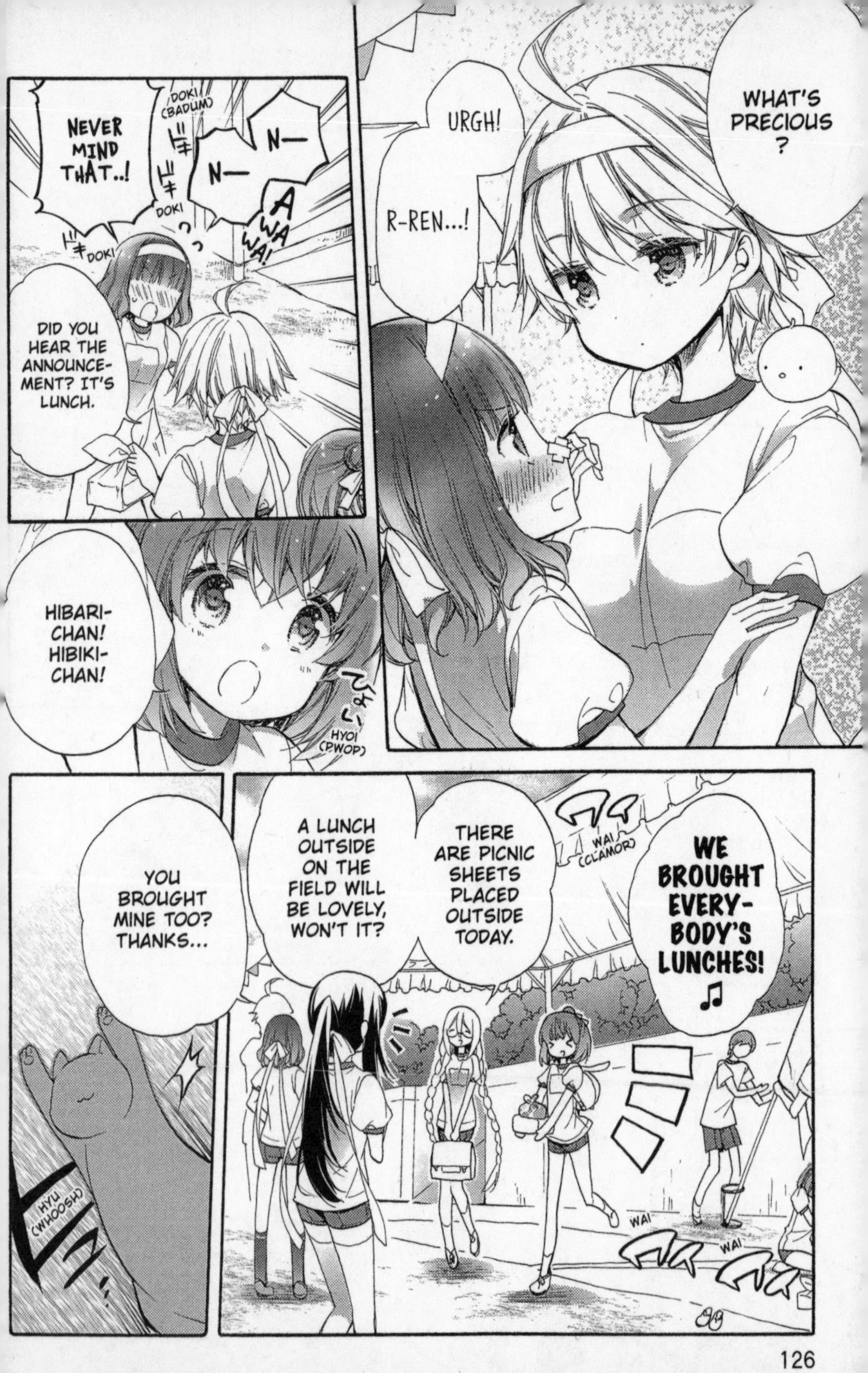
WHAT'S PRECIOUS?
URGH!
R-REN...!
N— N—
AWAWA!
DOKI (BADUM)
NEVER MIND THAT..!
DOKI
DOKI
DID YOU HEAR THE ANNOUNCEMENT? IT'S LUNCH.
HIBARI-CHAN! HIBIKI-CHAN!
HYOI (PWOP)
WE BROUGHT EVERYBODY'S LUNCHES! ♫
WAI (CLAMOR)
THERE ARE PICNIC SHEETS PLACED OUTSIDE TODAY.
A LUNCH OUTSIDE ON THE FIELD WILL BE LOVELY, WON'T IT?
WAI
WAI
YOU BROUGHT MINE TOO? THANKS...
HYU (WHOOSH)

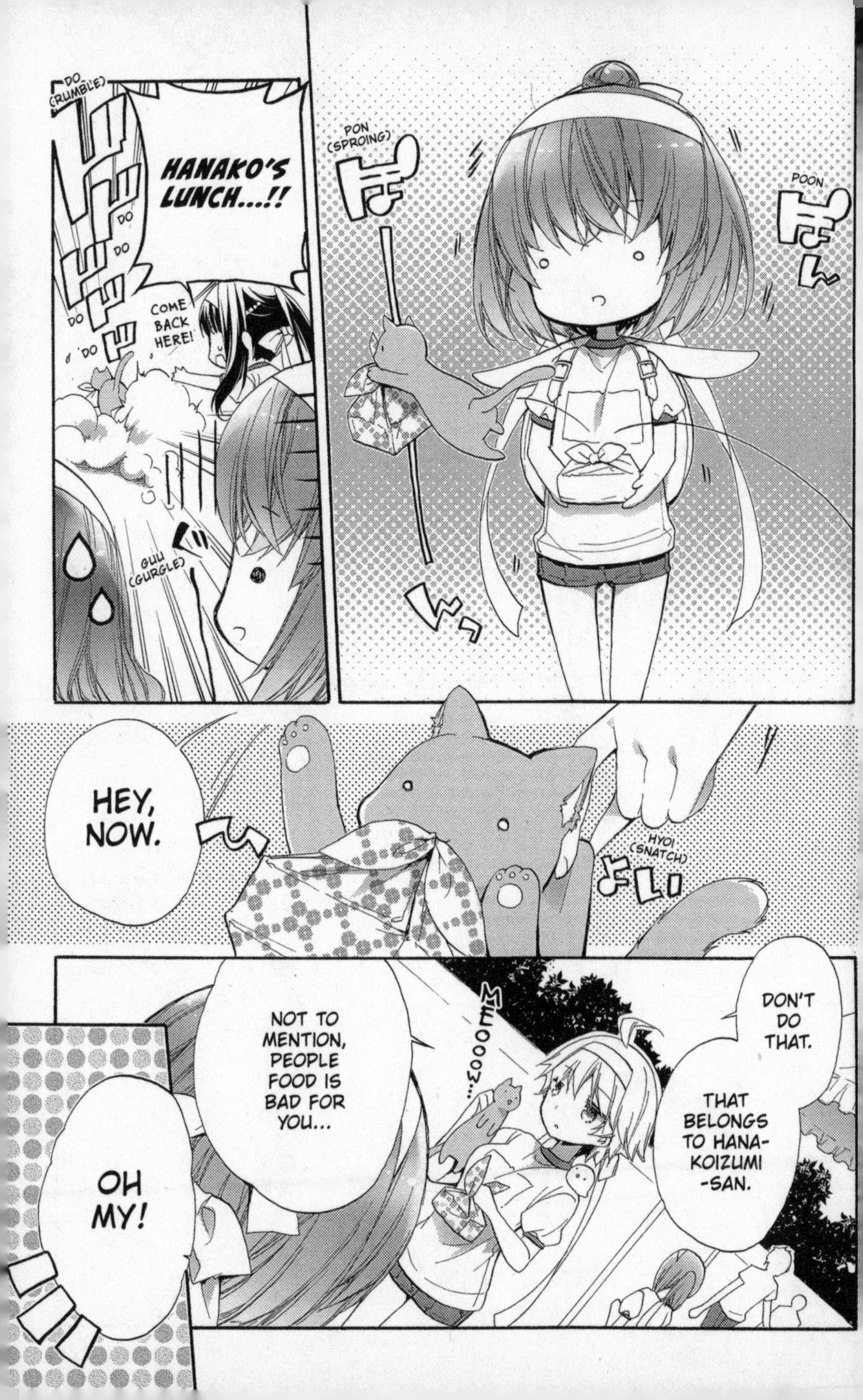
PON (SPROING)
POON
DO (RUMBLE)
HANAKO'S LUNCH...!!
DO
DO
DO
DO
COME BACK HERE!
GUU (GURGLE)
HEY, NOW.
HYOI (SNATCH)
DON'T DO THAT.
THAT BELONGS TO HANA-KOIZUMI -SAN.
MEOOOW...
NOT TO MENTION, PEOPLE FOOD IS BAD FOR YOU...
OH MY!

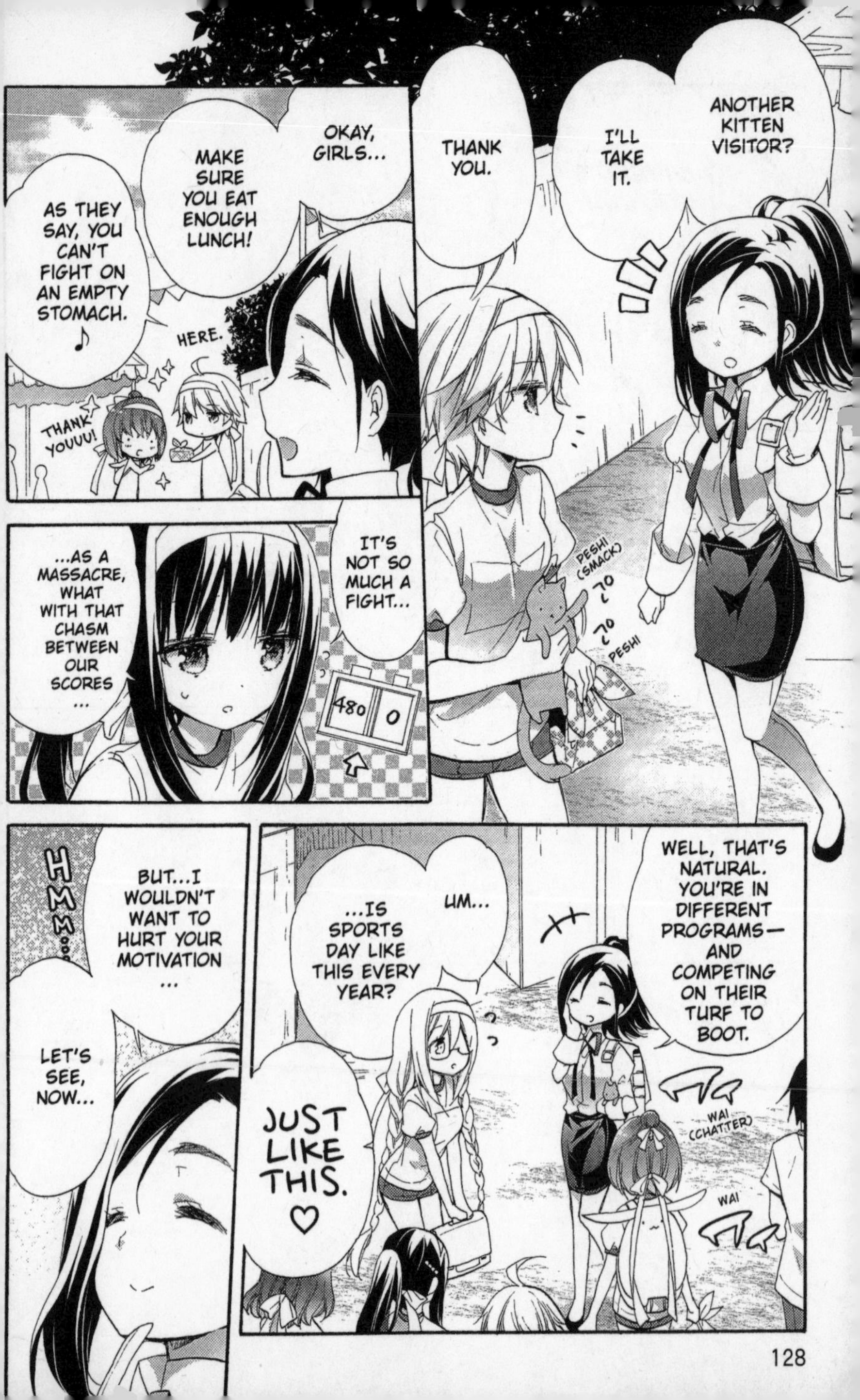
ANOTHER KITTEN VISITOR?
I'LL TAKE IT.
THANK YOU.
PESHI (SMACK)
PESHI
OKAY, GIRLS...
MAKE SURE YOU EAT ENOUGH LUNCH!
AS THEY SAY, YOU CAN'T FIGHT ON AN EMPTY STOMACH. ♪
HERE.
THANK YOUUU!
IT'S NOT SO MUCH A FIGHT...
...AS A MASSACRE, WHAT WITH THAT CHASM BETWEEN OUR SCORES...
480
0
WELL, THAT'S NATURAL. YOU'RE IN DIFFERENT PROGRAMS—AND COMPETING ON THEIR TURF TO BOOT.
UM...
...IS SPORTS DAY LIKE THIS EVERY YEAR?
JUST LIKE THIS. ♡
WAI (CHATTER)
WAI
HMM...
BUT...I WOULDN'T WANT TO HURT YOUR MOTIVATION...
LET'S SEE, NOW...

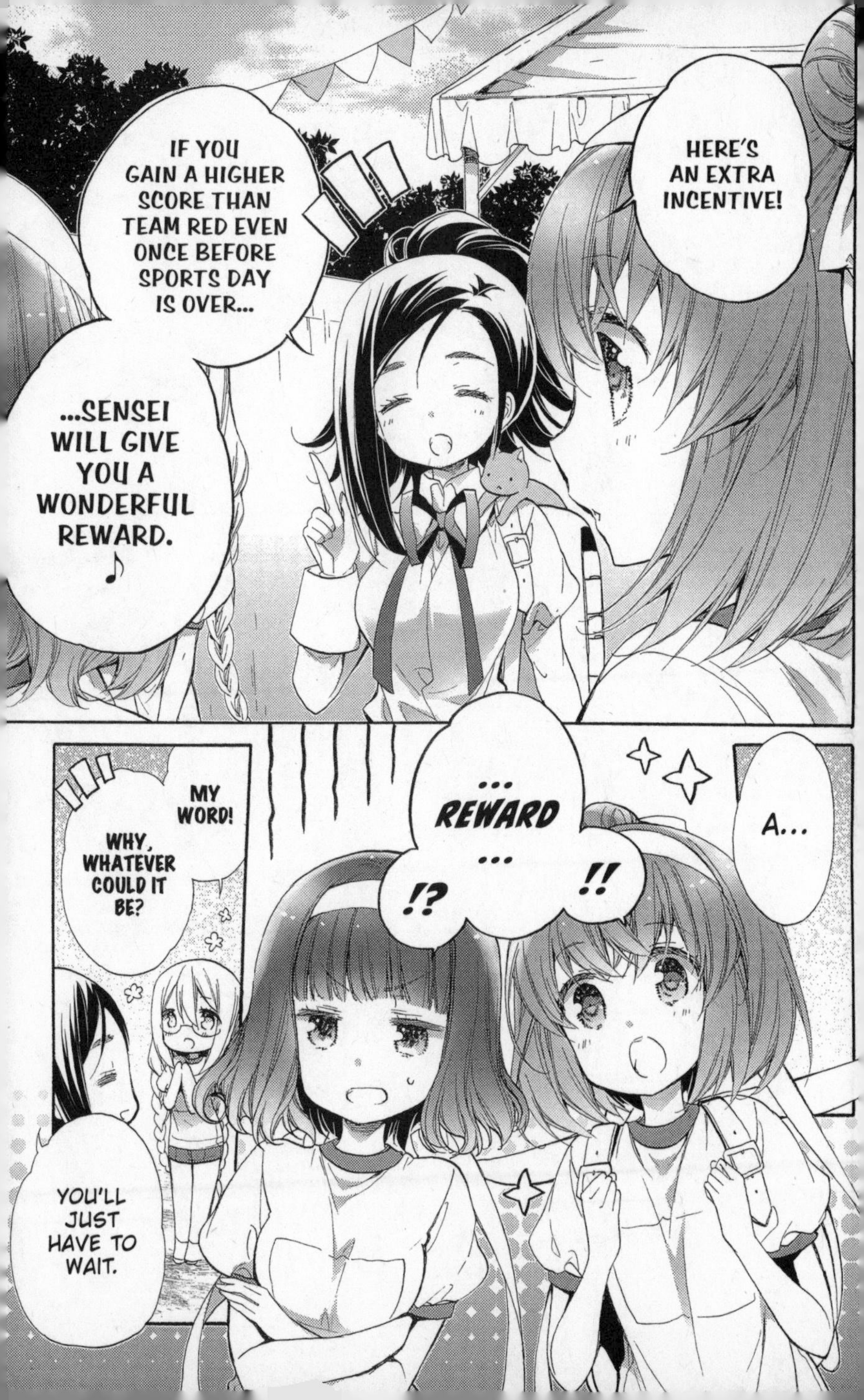
HERE'S AN EXTRA INCENTIVE!
IF YOU GAIN A HIGHER SCORE THAN TEAM RED EVEN ONCE BEFORE SPORTS DAY IS OVER...
...SENSEI WILL GIVE YOU A WONDERFUL REWARD. ♪
A...
...REWARD...
!!
!?
MY WORD!
WHY, WHATEVER COULD IT BE?
YOU'LL JUST HAVE TO WAIT.

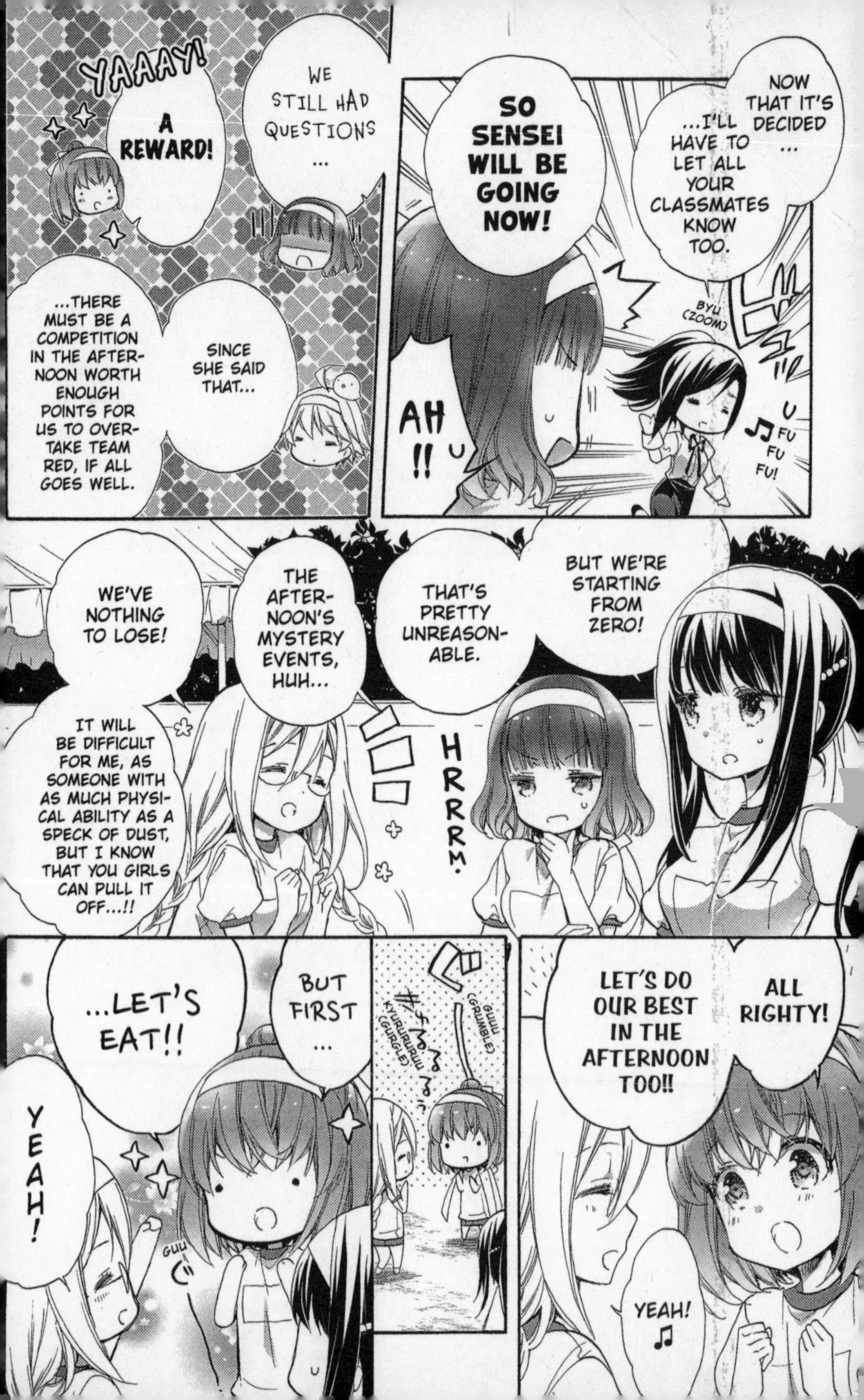
NOW THAT IT'S DECIDED ...
...I'LL HAVE TO LET ALL YOUR CLASSMATES KNOW TOO.
BYU (ZOOM)
U FU FU FU!
SO SENSEI WILL BE GOING NOW!
AH !!
YAAAAY!
A REWARD!
WE STILL HAD QUESTIONS ...
SINCE SHE SAID THAT...
...THERE MUST BE A COMPETITION IN THE AFTER-NOON WORTH ENOUGH POINTS FOR US TO OVER-TAKE TEAM RED, IF ALL GOES WELL.
BUT WE'RE STARTING FROM ZERO!
THAT'S PRETTY UNREASON-ABLE.
HRRRM.
THE AFTER-NOON'S MYSTERY EVENTS, HUH...
WE'VE NOTHING TO LOSE!
IT WILL BE DIFFICULT FOR ME, AS SOMEONE WITH AS MUCH PHYSI-CAL ABILITY AS A SPECK OF DUST, BUT I KNOW THAT YOU GIRLS CAN PULL IT OFF...!!
ALL RIGHTY!
LET'S DO OUR BEST IN THE AFTERNOON TOO!!
YEAH! ♪
GUUU (GRUMBLE)
KYURURURUU (GURGLE)
BUT FIRST ...
...LET'S EAT!!
YEAH!
GUU

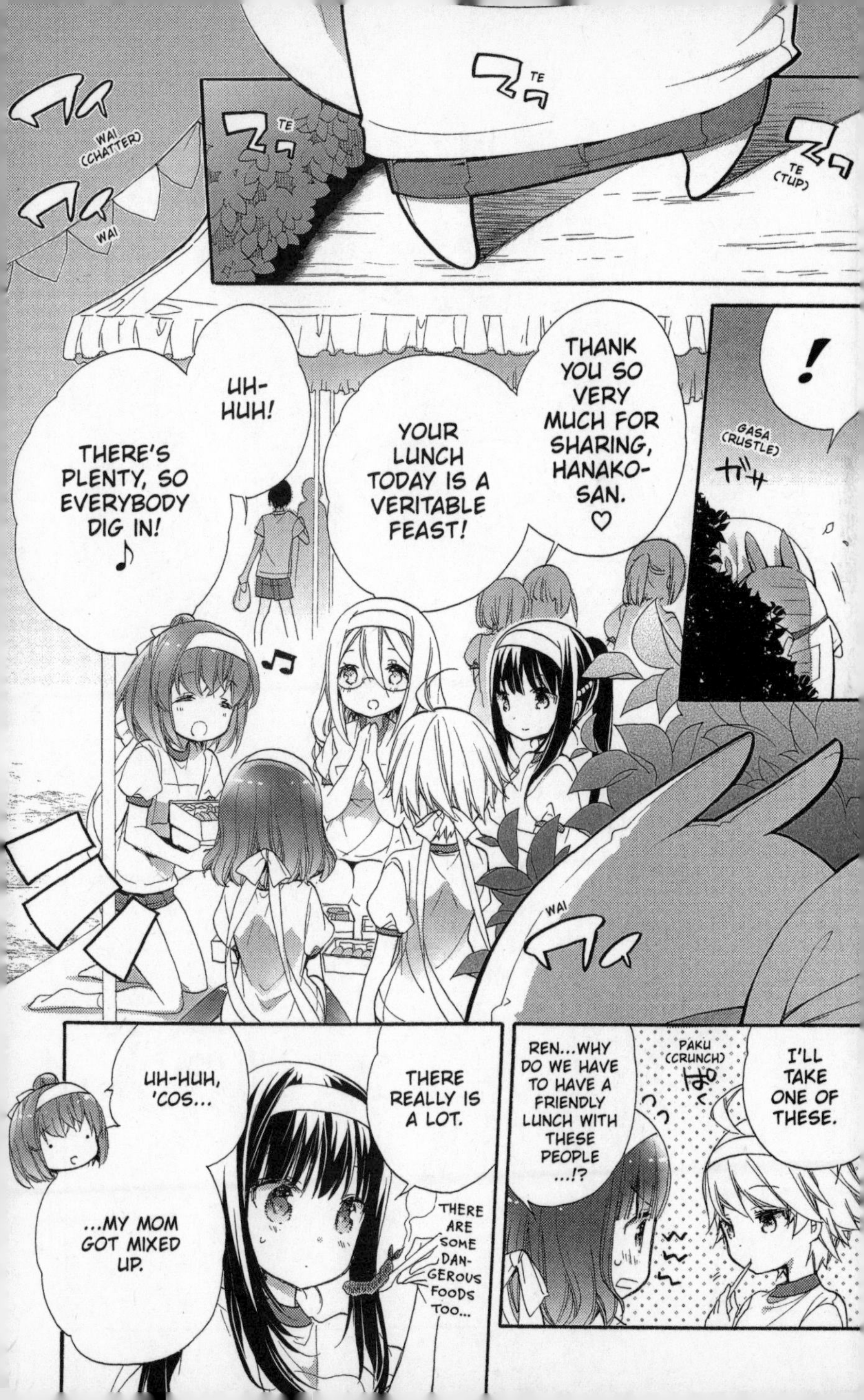
TE
(TUP)
TE
TE
WAI
(CHATTER)
WAI
!
GASA
(RUSTLE)
THANK YOU SO VERY MUCH FOR SHARING, HANAKO-SAN. ♡
YOUR LUNCH TODAY IS A VERITABLE FEAST!
UH-HUH!
THERE'S PLENTY, SO EVERYBODY DIG IN! ♪
WAI
I'LL TAKE ONE OF THESE.
PAKU
(CRUNCH)
REN...WHY DO WE HAVE TO HAVE A FRIENDLY LUNCH WITH THESE PEOPLE ...!?
THERE REALLY IS A LOT.
UH-HUH, 'COS...
...MY MOM GOT MIXED UP.
THERE ARE SOME DAN-GEROUS FOODS TOO...

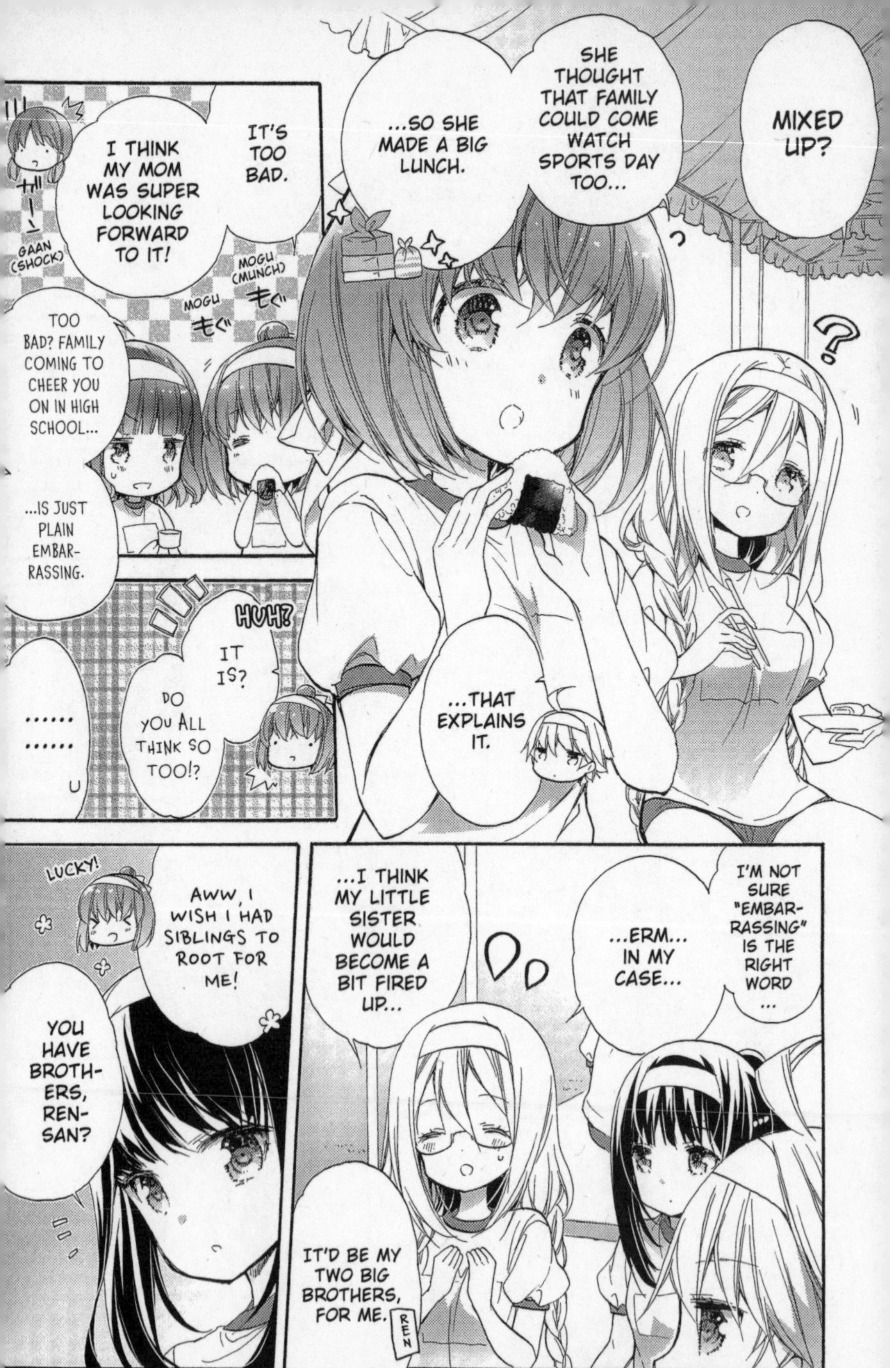
MIXED UP?
SHE THOUGHT THAT FAMILY COULD COME WATCH SPORTS DAY TOO...
...SO SHE MADE A BIG LUNCH.
...THAT EXPLAINS IT.
IT'S TOO BAD.
I THINK MY MOM WAS SUPER LOOKING FORWARD TO IT!
GAAN (SHOCK)
MOGU (MUNCH)
MOGU
TOO BAD? FAMILY COMING TO CHEER YOU ON IN HIGH SCHOOL...
...IS JUST PLAIN EMBARRASSING.
HUH?
IT IS?
DO YOU ALL THINK SO TOO!?
....
I'M NOT SURE "EMBARRASSING" IS THE RIGHT WORD...
...ERM... IN MY CASE...
...I THINK MY LITTLE SISTER WOULD BECOME A BIT FIRED UP...
IT'D BE MY TWO BIG BROTHERS, FOR ME.
REN
AWW, I WISH I HAD SIBLINGS TO ROOT FOR ME!
LUCKY!
YOU HAVE BROTHERS, REN-SAN?

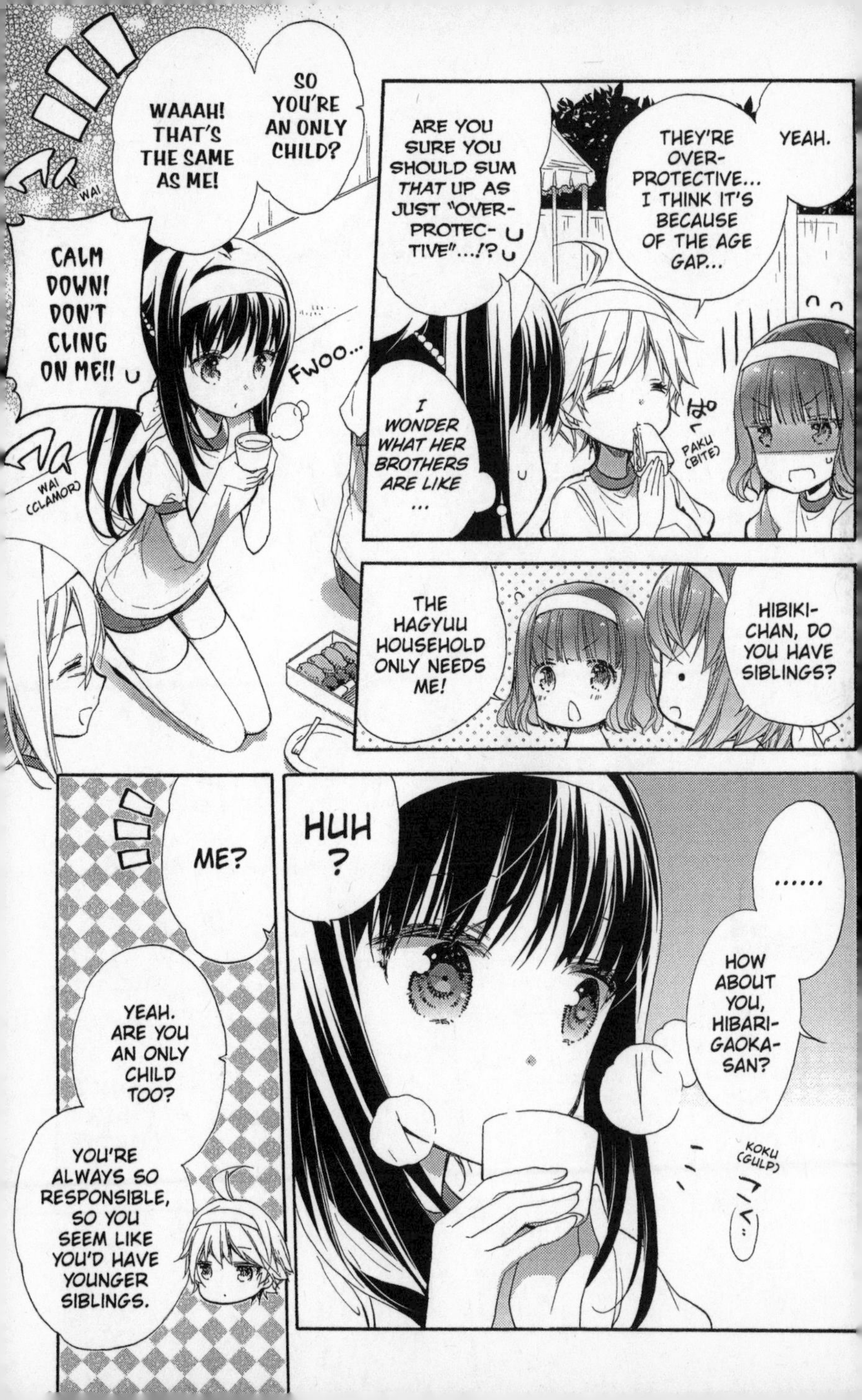
YEAH.
THEY'RE OVER-PROTECTIVE... I THINK IT'S BECAUSE OF THE AGE GAP...
ARE YOU SURE YOU SHOULD SUM THAT UP AS JUST "OVER-PROTECTIVE"...!?
PAKU (BITE)
I WONDER WHAT HER BROTHERS ARE LIKE...
HIBIKI-CHAN, DO YOU HAVE SIBLINGS?
THE HAGYUU HOUSEHOLD ONLY NEEDS ME!
SO YOU'RE AN ONLY CHILD?
WAAAH! THAT'S THE SAME AS ME!
WAI
CALM DOWN! DON'T CLING ON ME!!
FWOO...
WAI (CLAMOR)
......
HOW ABOUT YOU, HIBARIGAOKA-SAN?
KOKU (GULP)
HUH?
ME?
YEAH. ARE YOU AN ONLY CHILD TOO?
YOU'RE ALWAYS SO RESPONSIBLE, SO YOU SEEM LIKE YOU'D HAVE YOUNGER SIBLINGS.

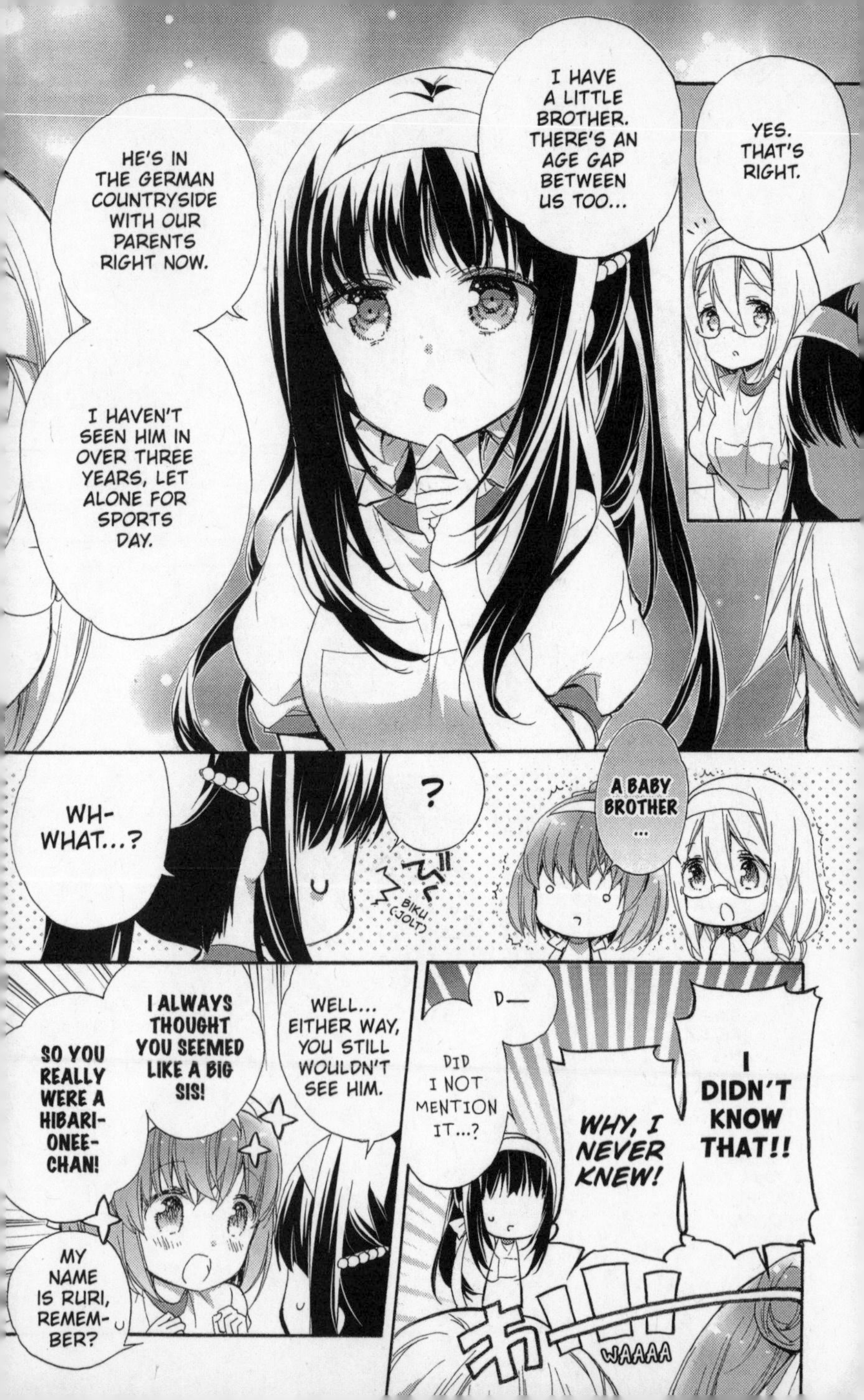
YES. THAT'S RIGHT.
I HAVE A LITTLE BROTHER. THERE'S AN AGE GAP BETWEEN US TOO...
HE'S IN THE GERMAN COUNTRYSIDE WITH OUR PARENTS RIGHT NOW.
I HAVEN'T SEEN HIM IN OVER THREE YEARS, LET ALONE FOR SPORTS DAY.
A BABY BROTHER ...
?
BIKU (JOLT)
WH- WHAT...?
I DIDN'T KNOW THAT!!
WHY, I NEVER KNEW!
D—
DID I NOT MENTION IT...?
WAAAA
WELL... EITHER WAY, YOU STILL WOULDN'T SEE HIM.
I ALWAYS THOUGHT YOU SEEMED LIKE A BIG SIS!
SO YOU REALLY WERE A HIBARI-ONEE-CHAN!
MY NAME IS RURI, REMEMBER?

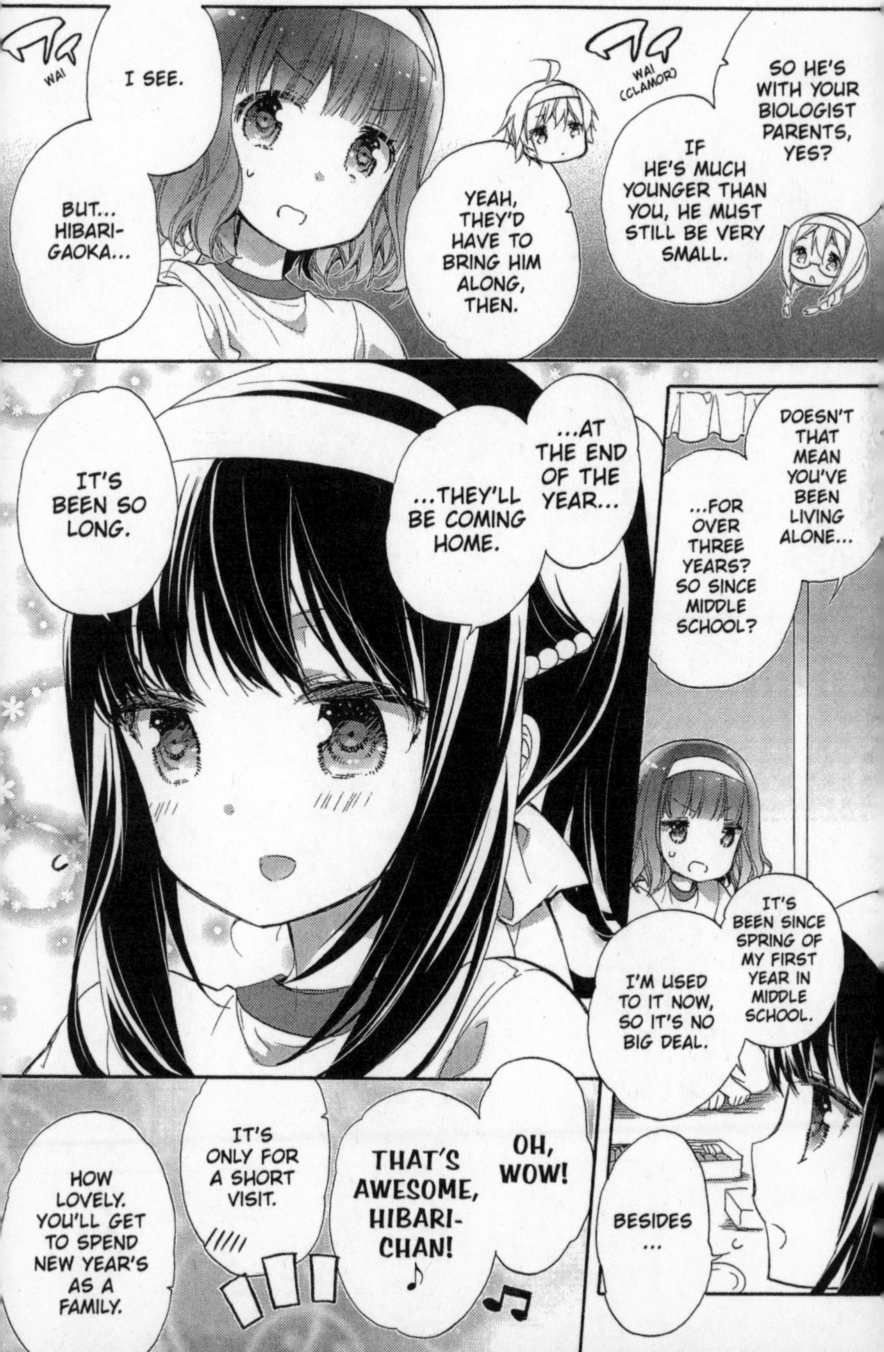
SO HE'S WITH YOUR BIOLOGIST PARENTS, YES?
WAI (CLAMOR)
IF HE'S MUCH YOUNGER THAN YOU, HE MUST STILL BE VERY SMALL.
YEAH, THEY'D HAVE TO BRING HIM ALONG, THEN.
WAI
I SEE.
BUT... HIBARI-GAOKA...
DOESN'T THAT MEAN YOU'VE BEEN LIVING ALONE...
...FOR OVER THREE YEARS? SO SINCE MIDDLE SCHOOL?
IT'S BEEN SINCE SPRING OF MY FIRST YEAR IN MIDDLE SCHOOL.
I'M USED TO IT NOW, SO IT'S NO BIG DEAL.
...AT THE END OF THE YEAR...
...THEY'LL BE COMING HOME.
IT'S BEEN SO LONG.
BESIDES...
OH, WOW!
THAT'S AWESOME, HIBARI-CHAN! ♪
IT'S ONLY FOR A SHORT VISIT.
HOW LOVELY. YOU'LL GET TO SPEND NEW YEAR'S AS A FAMILY.

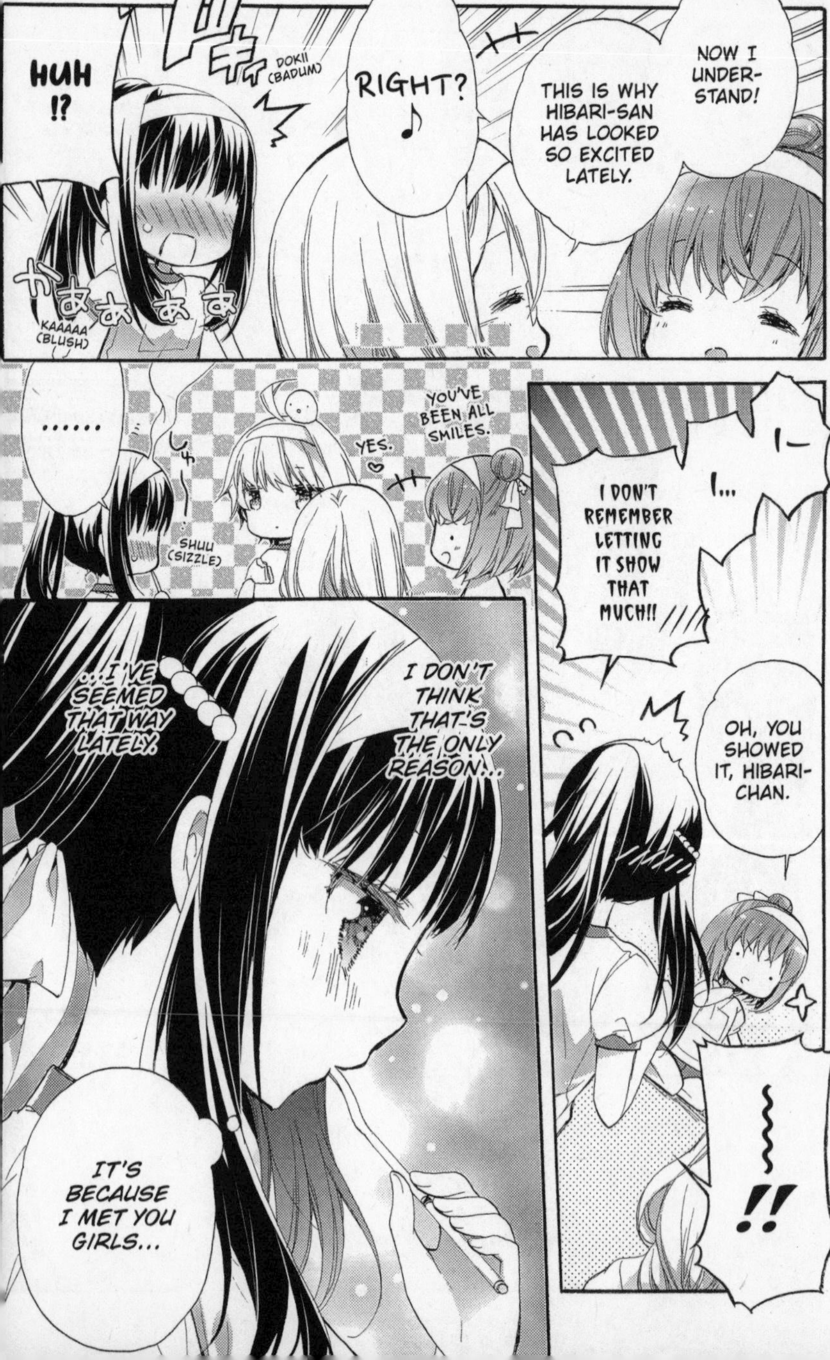
NOW I UNDER-STAND!
THIS IS WHY HIBARI-SAN HAS LOOKED SO EXCITED LATELY.
RIGHT? ♪
ドキィ
DOKII (BADUM)
HUH !?
かぁぁぁぁ
KAAAAA (BLUSH)
I-
I...
I DON'T REMEMBER LETTING IT SHOW THAT MUCH!!
OH, YOU SHOWED IT, HIBARI-CHAN.
~~~!!
YOU'VE BEEN ALL SMILES.
YES. ♡
......
しゅ~
SHUU (SIZZLE)
I DON'T THINK THAT'S THE ONLY REASON...
...I'VE SEEMED THAT WAY LATELY.
IT'S BECAUSE I MET YOU GIRLS...
~~~

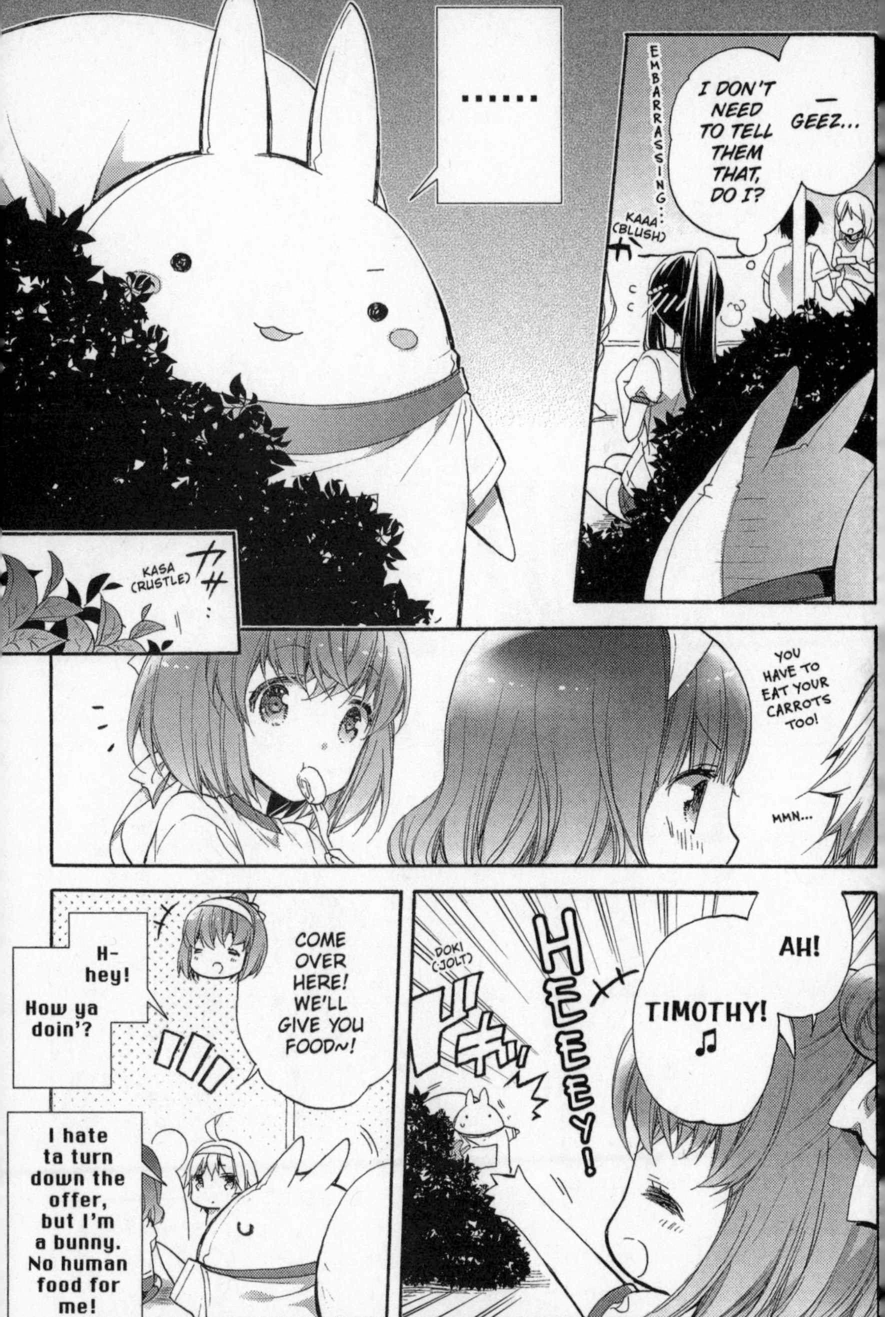
—GEEZ...
I DON'T NEED TO TELL THEM THAT, DO I?
EMBARRASSING...
KAAA (BLUSH)
......
KASA (RUSTLE)
YOU HAVE TO EAT YOUR CARROTS TOO!
MMN...
AH!
TIMOTHY! ♫
HEEEEY!
DOKI (JOLT)
COME OVER HERE! WE'LL GIVE YOU FOOD~!
H-hey!
How ya doin'?
I hate ta turn down the offer, but I'm a bunny. No human food for me!

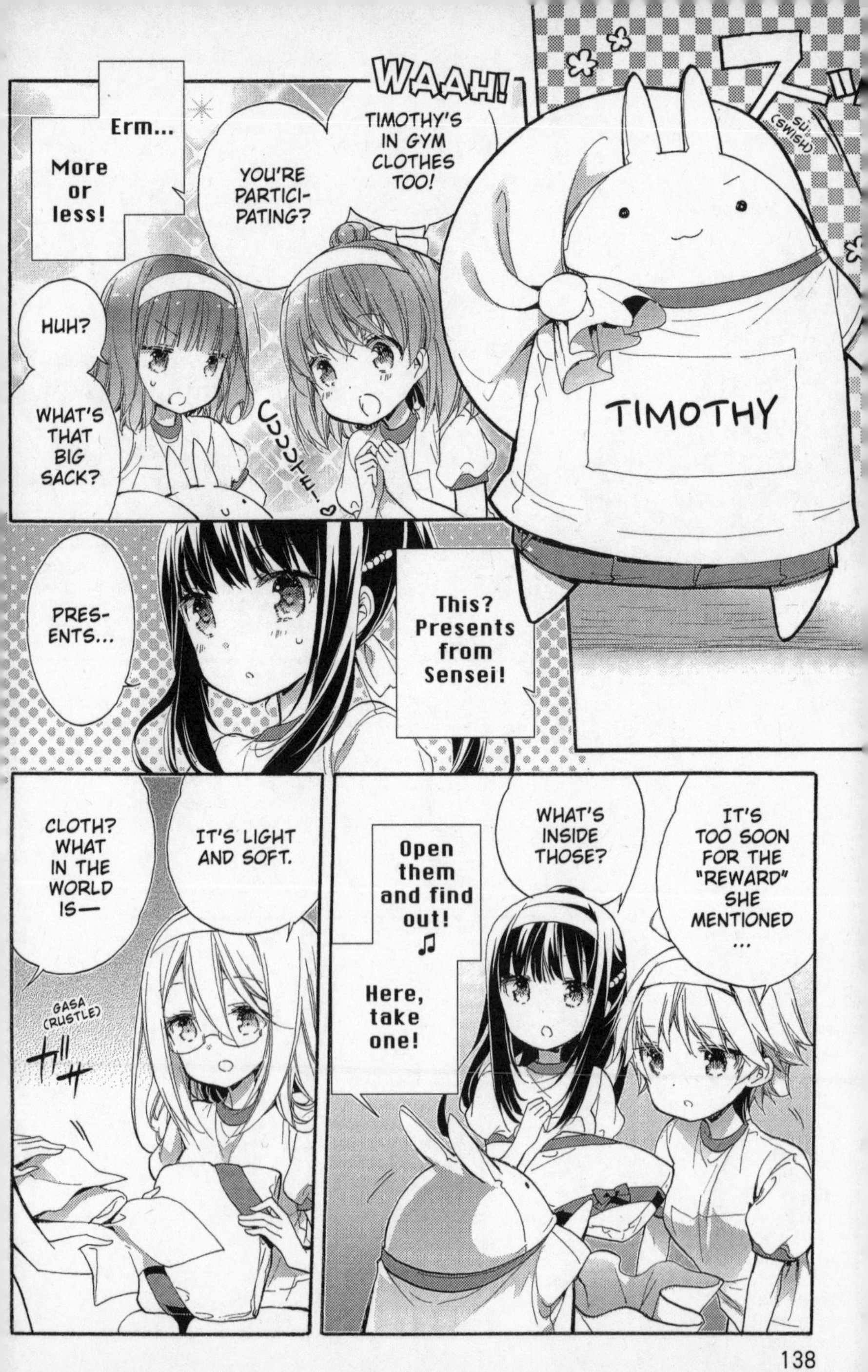
SU (SWISH)
TIMOTHY
WAAH!
TIMOTHY'S IN GYM CLOTHES TOO!
YOU'RE PARTICI-PATING?
Erm... More or less!
CUUUTE!♡
HUH?
WHAT'S THAT BIG SACK?
This? Presents from Sensei!
PRES-ENTS...
IT'S TOO SOON FOR THE "REWARD" SHE MENTIONED ...
WHAT'S INSIDE THOSE?
Open them and find out! ♫
Here, take one!
IT'S LIGHT AND SOFT.
CLOTH? WHAT IN THE WORLD IS—
GASA (RUSTLE)

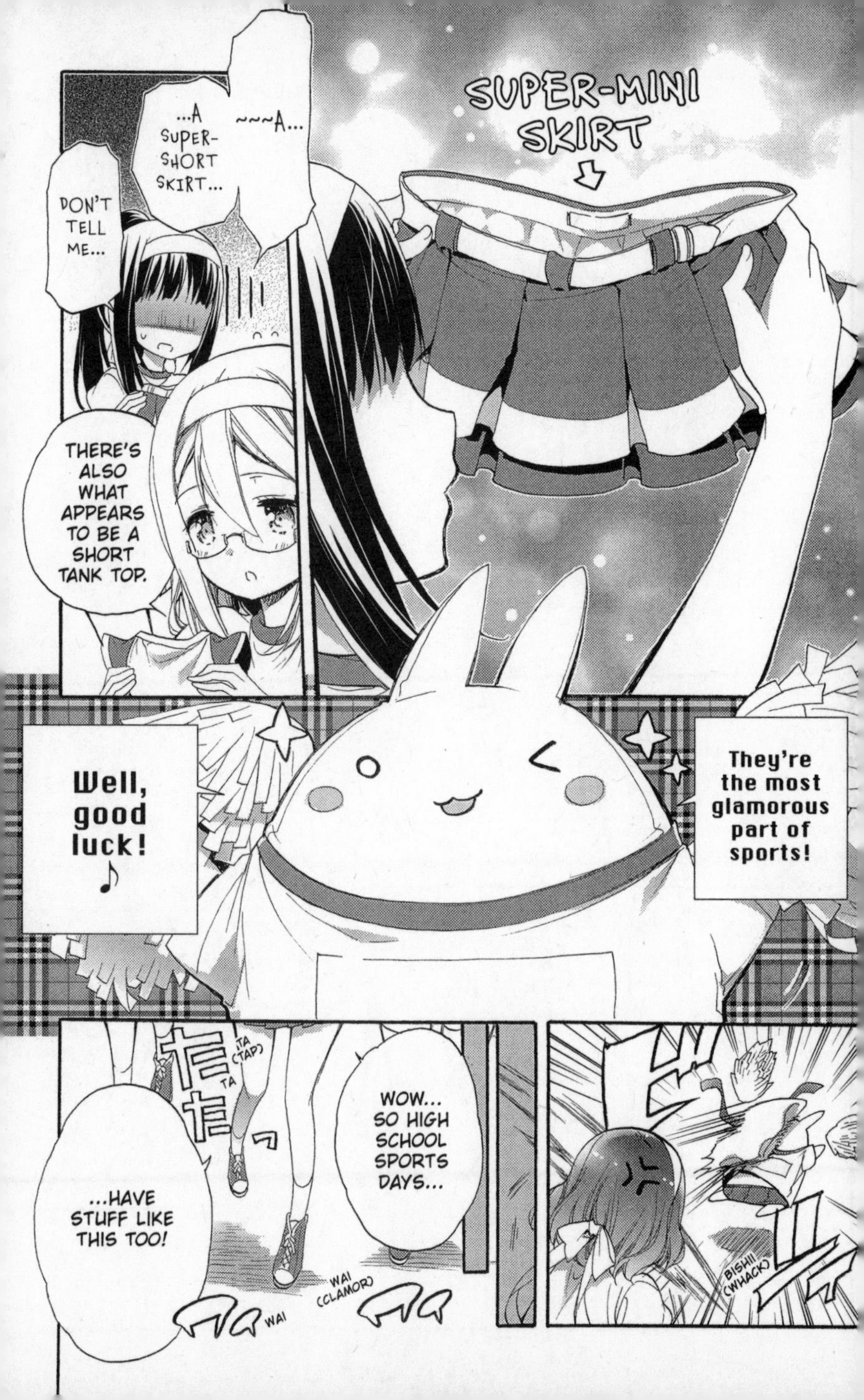
SUPER-MINI SKIRT
~~~A...
...A SUPER-SHORT SKIRT...
DON'T TELL ME...
THERE'S ALSO WHAT APPEARS TO BE A SHORT TANK TOP.
They're the most glamorous part of sports!
Well, good luck! ♪
BISHII (WHACK)
TA (TAP) TA
WOW... SO HIGH SCHOOL SPORTS DAYS...
...HAVE STUFF LIKE THIS TOO!
WAI (CLAMOR)
WAI
~~~

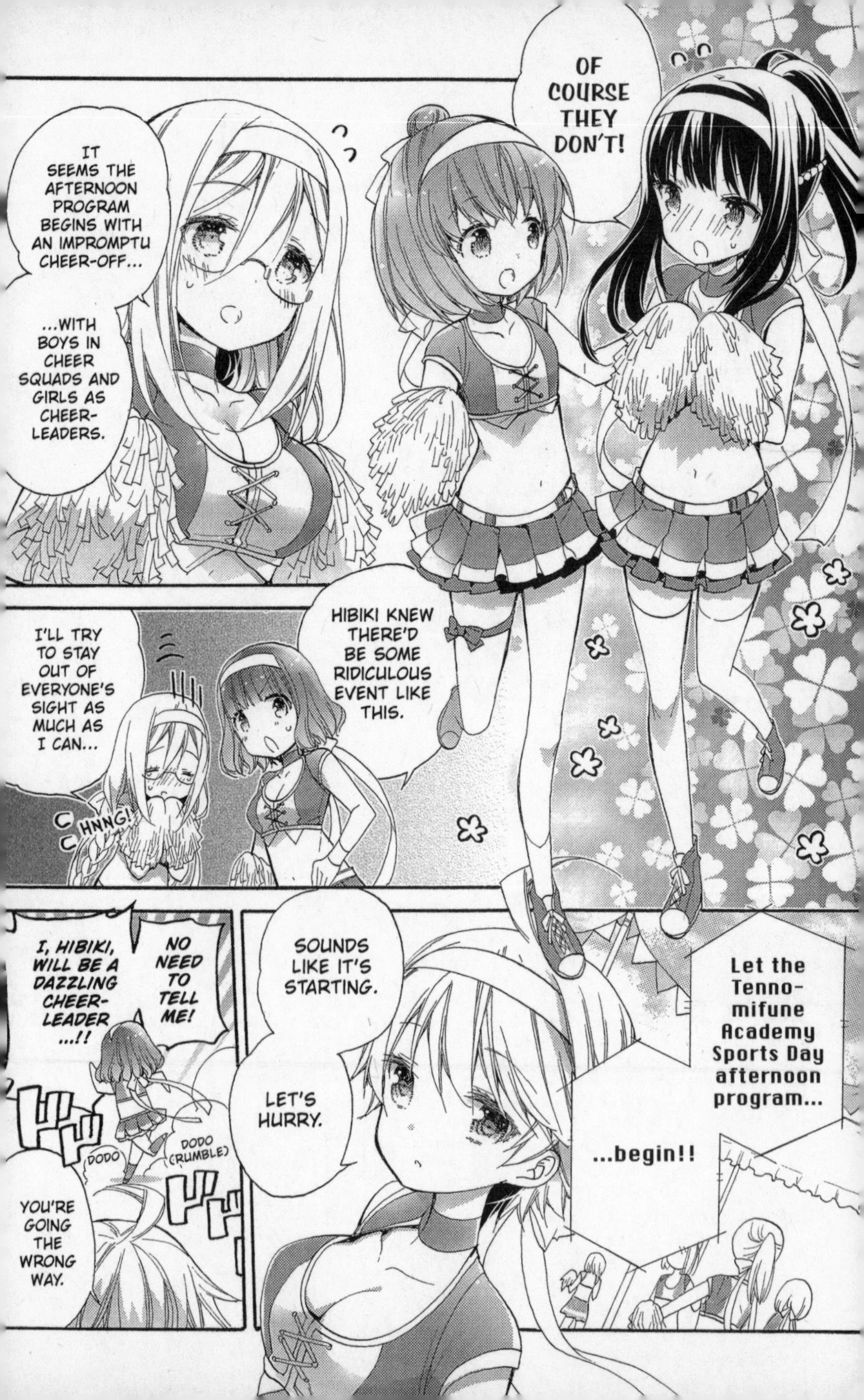
OF COURSE THEY DON'T!
IT SEEMS THE AFTERNOON PROGRAM BEGINS WITH AN IMPROMPTU CHEER-OFF...
...WITH BOYS IN CHEER SQUADS AND GIRLS AS CHEER-LEADERS.
HIBIKI KNEW THERE'D BE SOME RIDICULOUS EVENT LIKE THIS.
I'LL TRY TO STAY OUT OF EVERYONE'S SIGHT AS MUCH AS I CAN...
HNNG!
Let the Tenno-mifune Academy Sports Day afternoon program...
...begin!!
SOUNDS LIKE IT'S STARTING.
LET'S HURRY.
NO NEED TO TELL ME!
I, HIBIKI, WILL BE A DAZZLING CHEER-LEADER ...!!
DODO (RUMBLE)
DODO
YOU'RE GOING THE WRONG WAY.

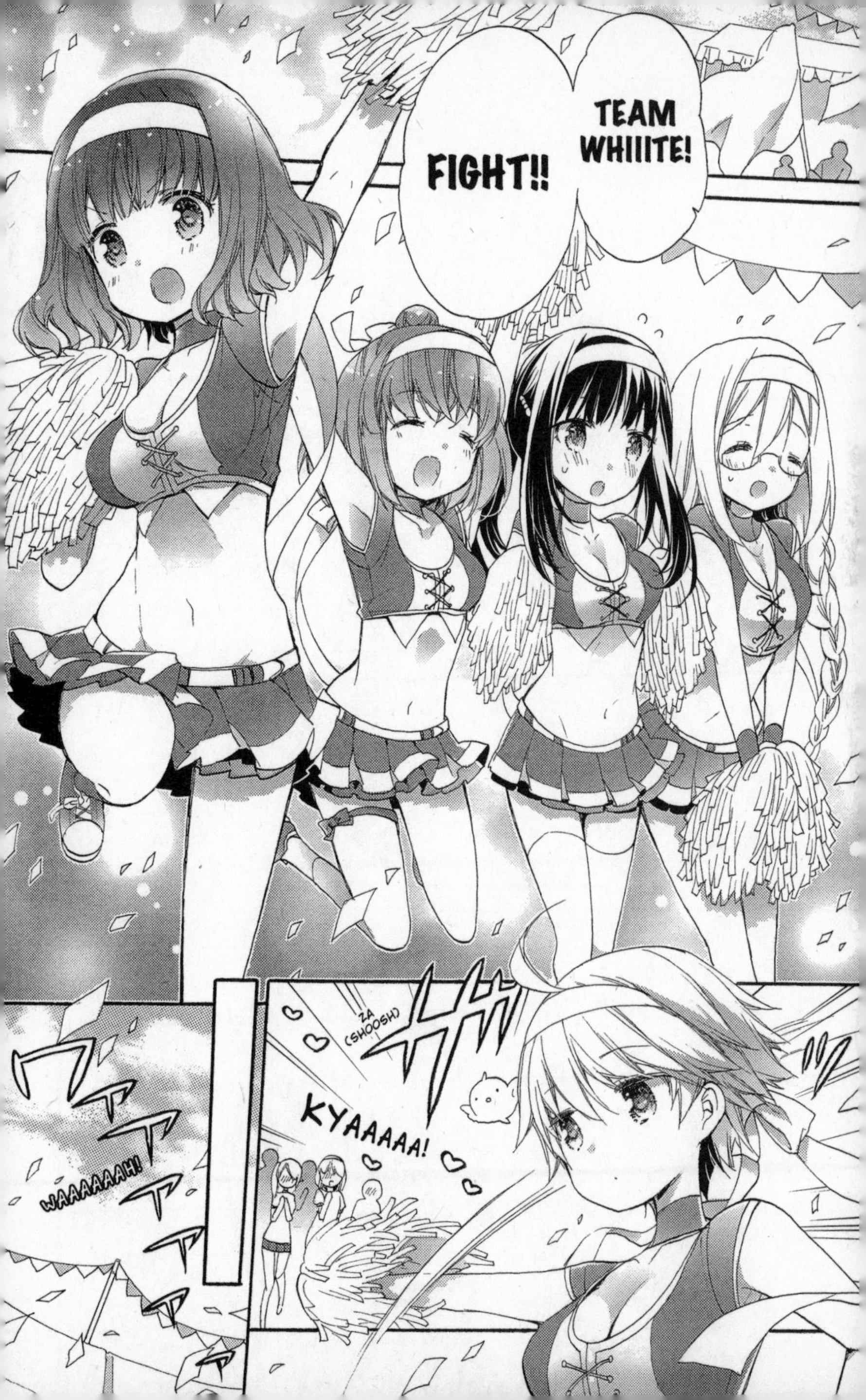
TEAM WHIIITE!
FIGHT!!
ZA (SHOOSH)
KYAAAAAA!
WAAAAAAH!

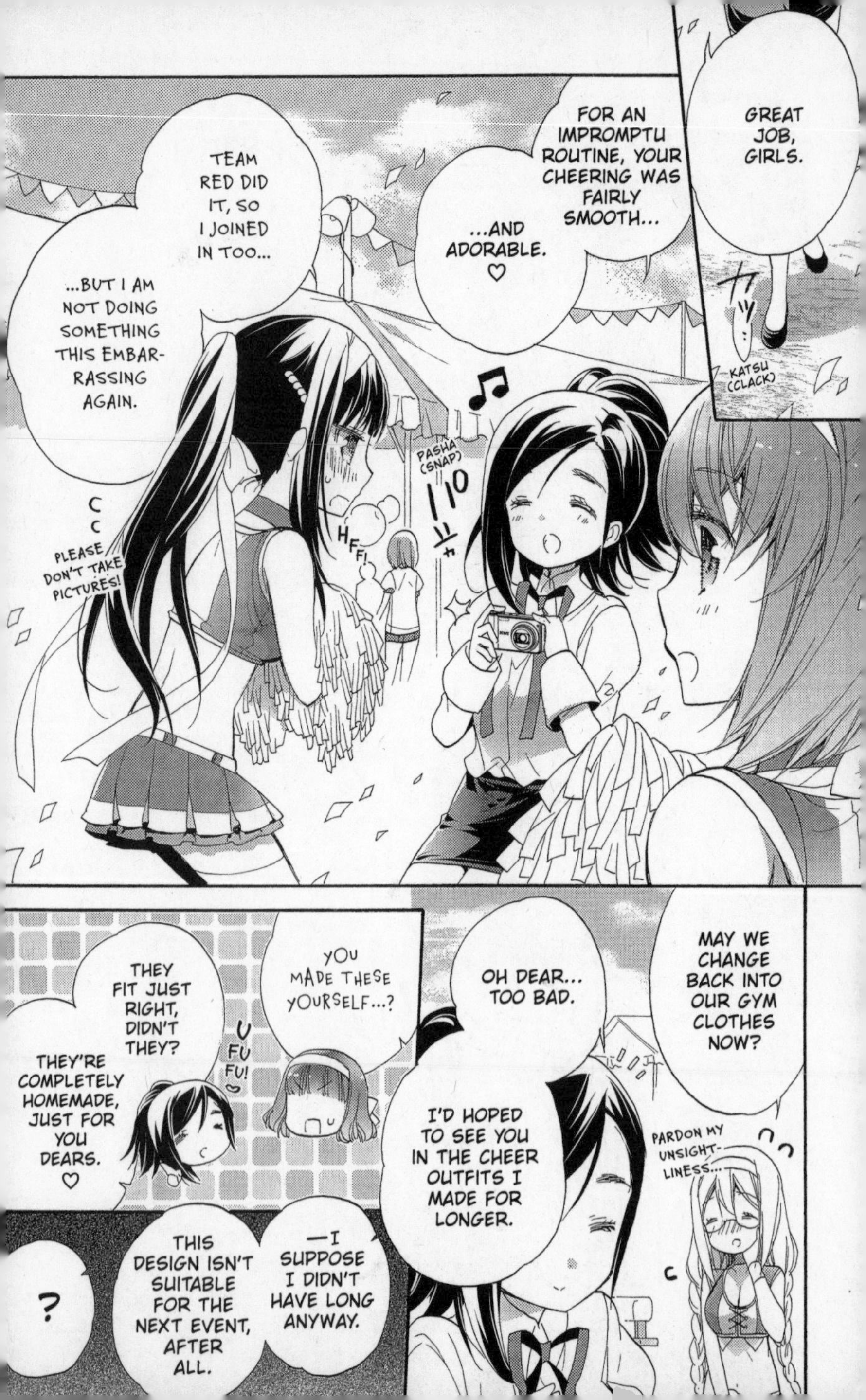
GREAT JOB, GIRLS.
KATSU (CLACK)
FOR AN IMPROMPTU ROUTINE, YOUR CHEERING WAS FAIRLY SMOOTH...
...AND ADORABLE. ♡
TEAM RED DID IT, SO I JOINED IN TOO...
...BUT I AM NOT DOING SOMETHING THIS EMBARRASSING AGAIN.
PASHA (SNAP)
HFF!
PLEASE DON'T TAKE PICTURES!
MAY WE CHANGE BACK INTO OUR GYM CLOTHES NOW?
OH DEAR... TOO BAD.
PARDON MY UNSIGHTLINESS...
I'D HOPED TO SEE YOU IN THE CHEER OUTFITS I MADE FOR LONGER.
YOU MADE THESE YOURSELF...?
THEY FIT JUST RIGHT, DIDN'T THEY?
UFUFU!
THEY'RE COMPLETELY HOMEMADE, JUST FOR YOU DEARS. ♡
—I SUPPOSE I DIDN'T HAVE LONG ANYWAY.
THIS DESIGN ISN'T SUITABLE FOR THE NEXT EVENT, AFTER ALL.
?

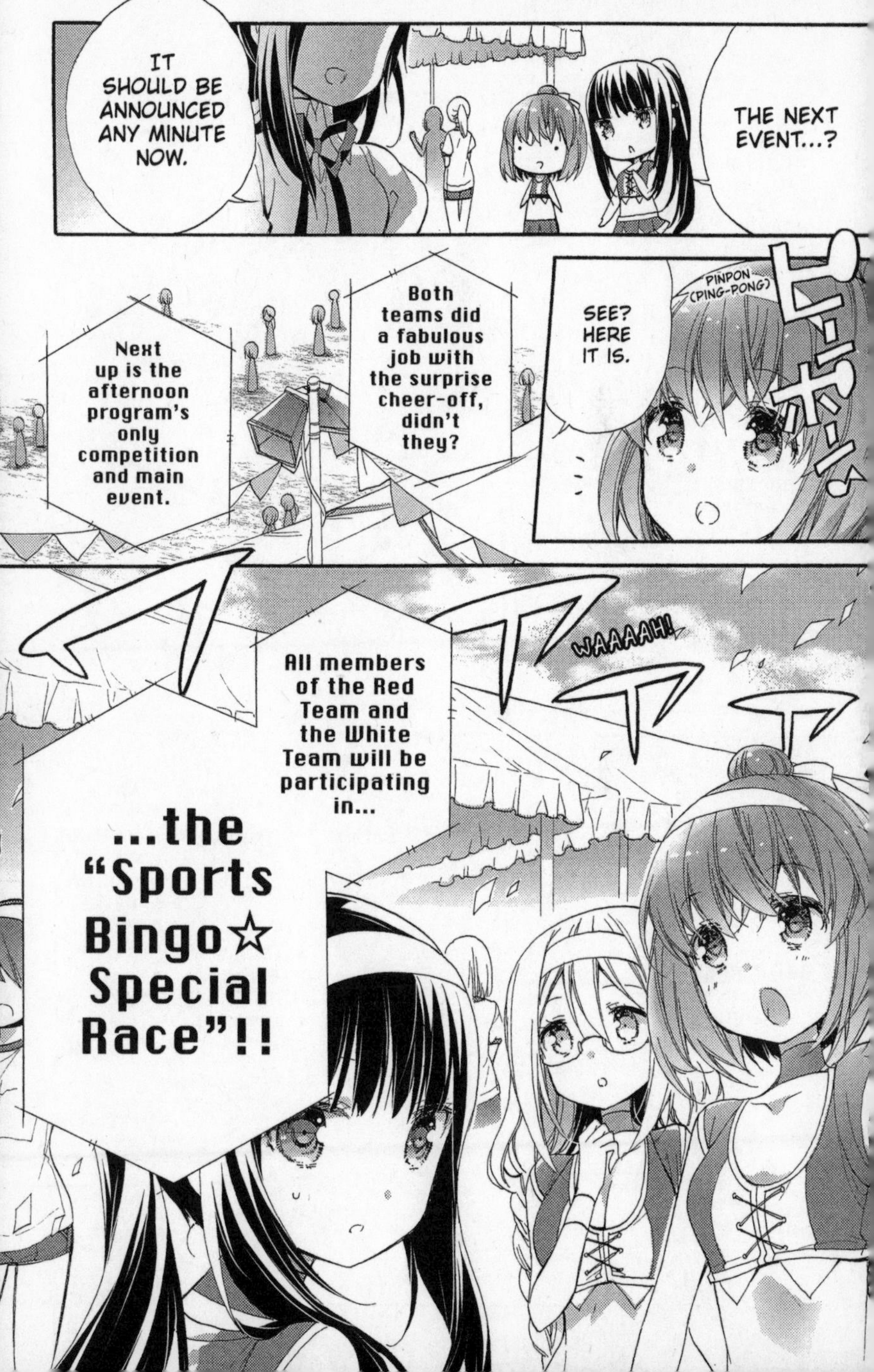
THE NEXT EVENT...?
IT SHOULD BE ANNOUNCED ANY MINUTE NOW.
PINPON (PING-PONG)
SEE? HERE IT IS.
Both teams did a fabulous job with the surprise cheer-off, didn't they?
Next up is the afternoon program's only competition and main event.
WAAAAH!
All members of the Red Team and the White Team will be participating in...
...the "Sports Bingo☆ Special Race"!!

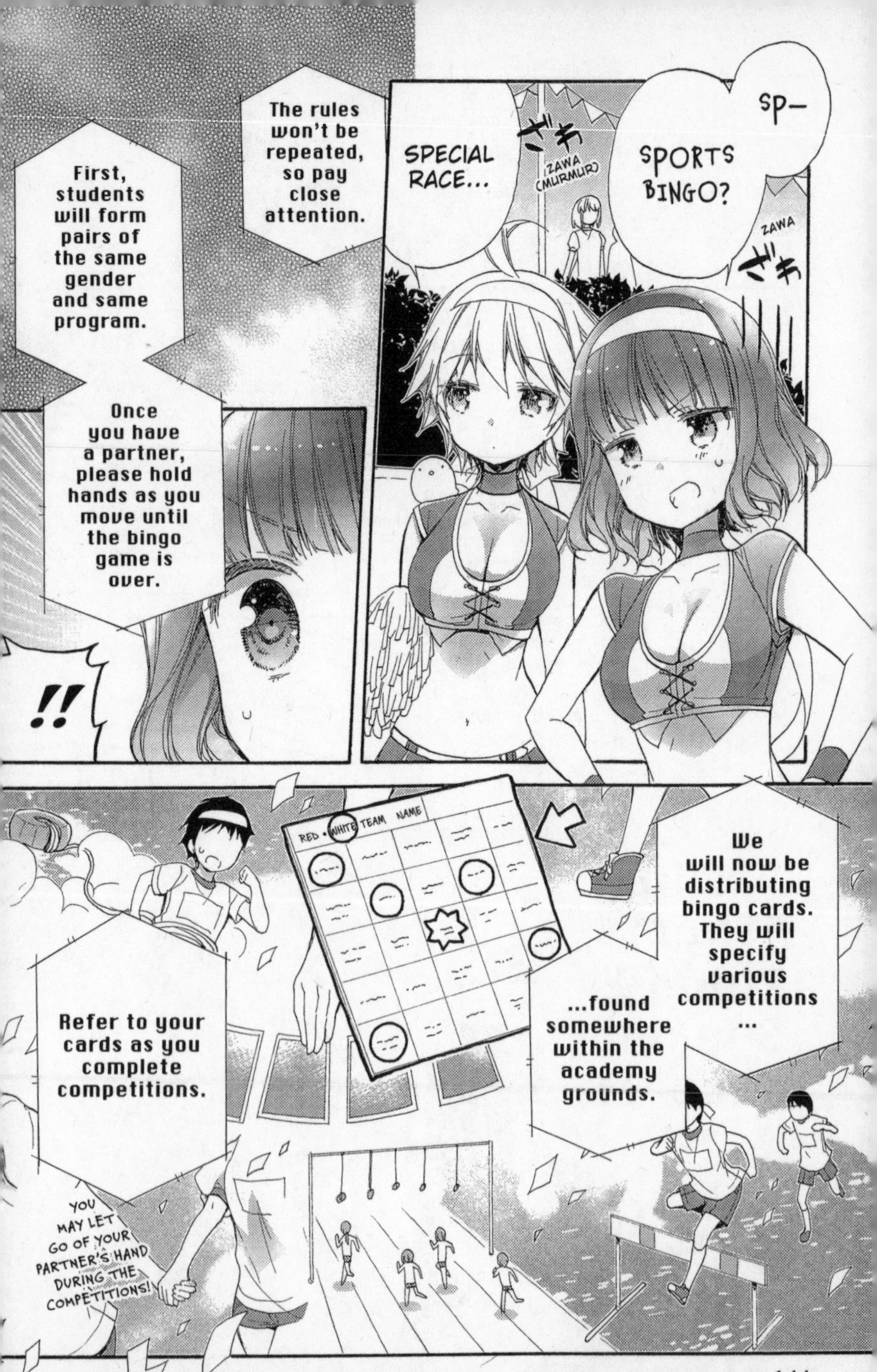
Sp—
Sports bingo?
ZAWA
ZAWA (MURMUR)
Special race...
The rules won't be repeated, so pay close attention.
First, students will form pairs of the same gender and same program.
Once you have a partner, please hold hands as you move until the bingo game is over.
!!
We will now be distributing bingo cards. They will specify various competitions...
...found somewhere within the academy grounds.
RED • WHITE TEAM NAME
Refer to your cards as you complete competitions.
You may let go of your partner's hand during the competitions!

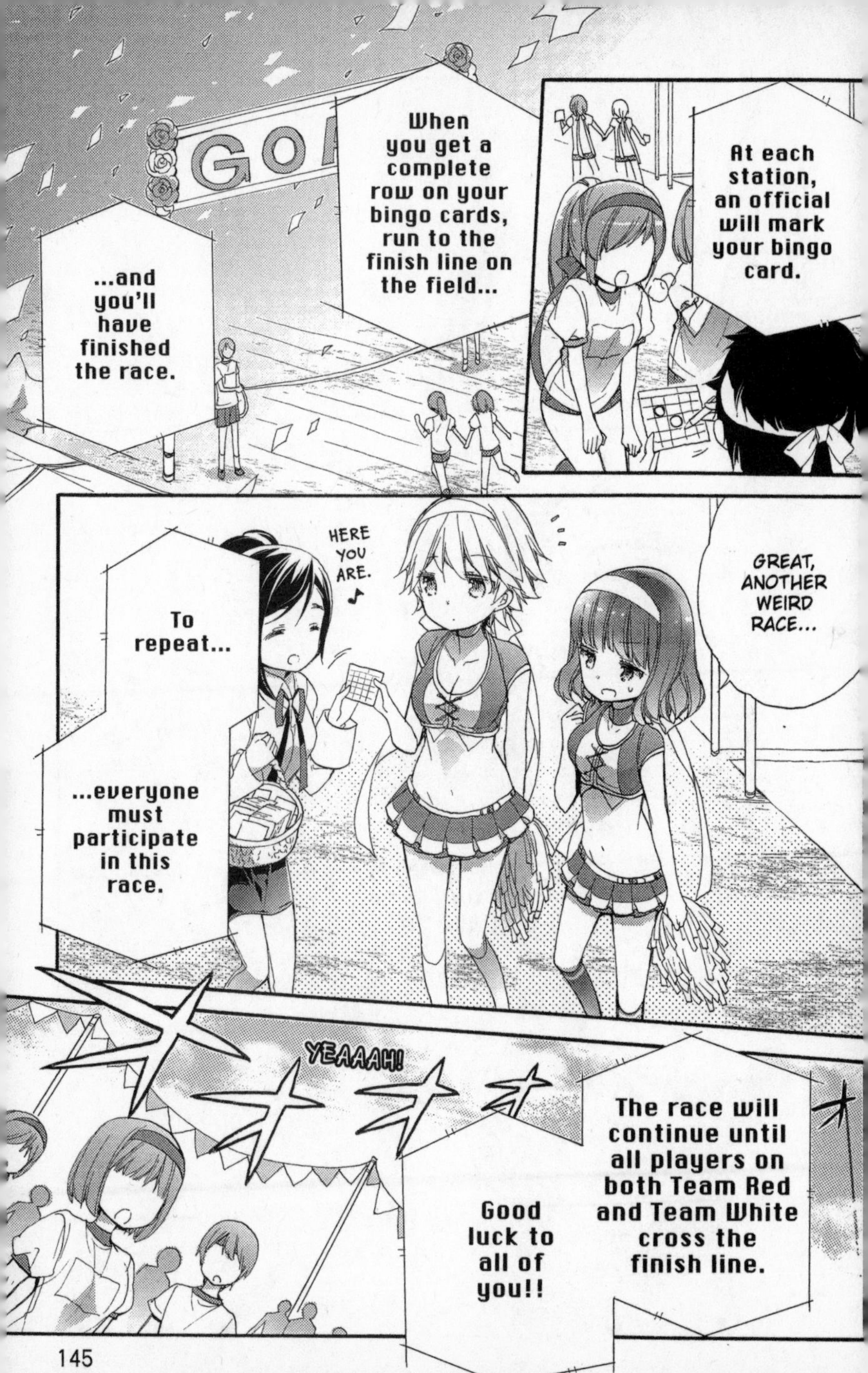
At each station, an official will mark your bingo card.
When you get a complete row on your bingo cards, run to the finish line on the field...
...and you'll have finished the race.
GO
GREAT, ANOTHER WEIRD RACE...
HERE YOU ARE. ♪
To repeat...
...everyone must participate in this race.
The race will continue until all players on both Team Red and Team White cross the finish line.
Good luck to all of you!!
YEAAAH!

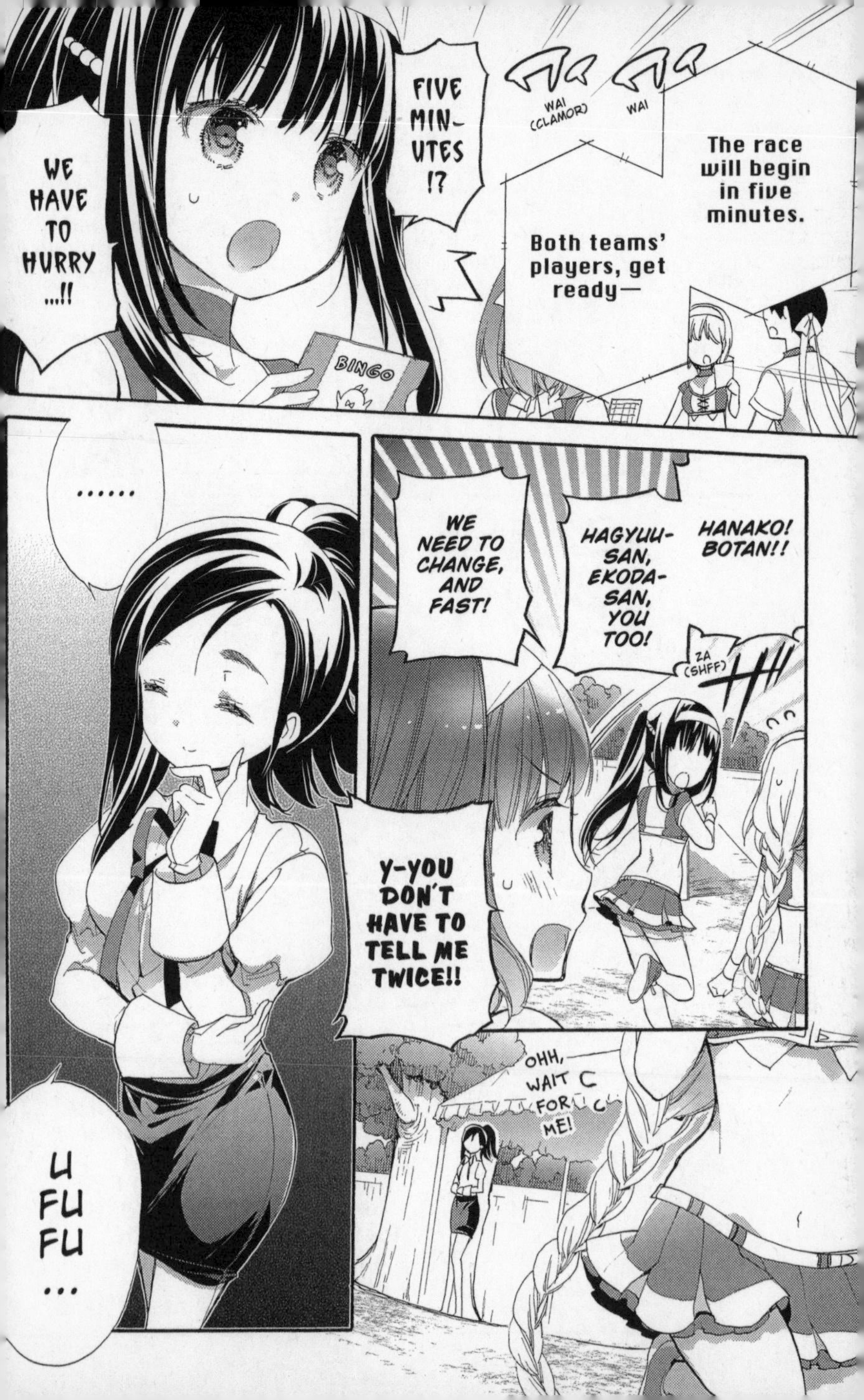
WAI
WAI (CLAMOR)
The race will begin in five minutes.
Both teams' players, get ready—
FIVE MINUTES!?
WE HAVE TO HURRY...!!
HANAKO! BOTAN!!
HAGYUU-SAN, EKODA-SAN, YOU TOO!
WE NEED TO CHANGE, AND FAST!
ZA (SHFF)
Y-YOU DON'T HAVE TO TELL ME TWICE!!
OHH, WAIT FOR ME!
......
UFUFU...

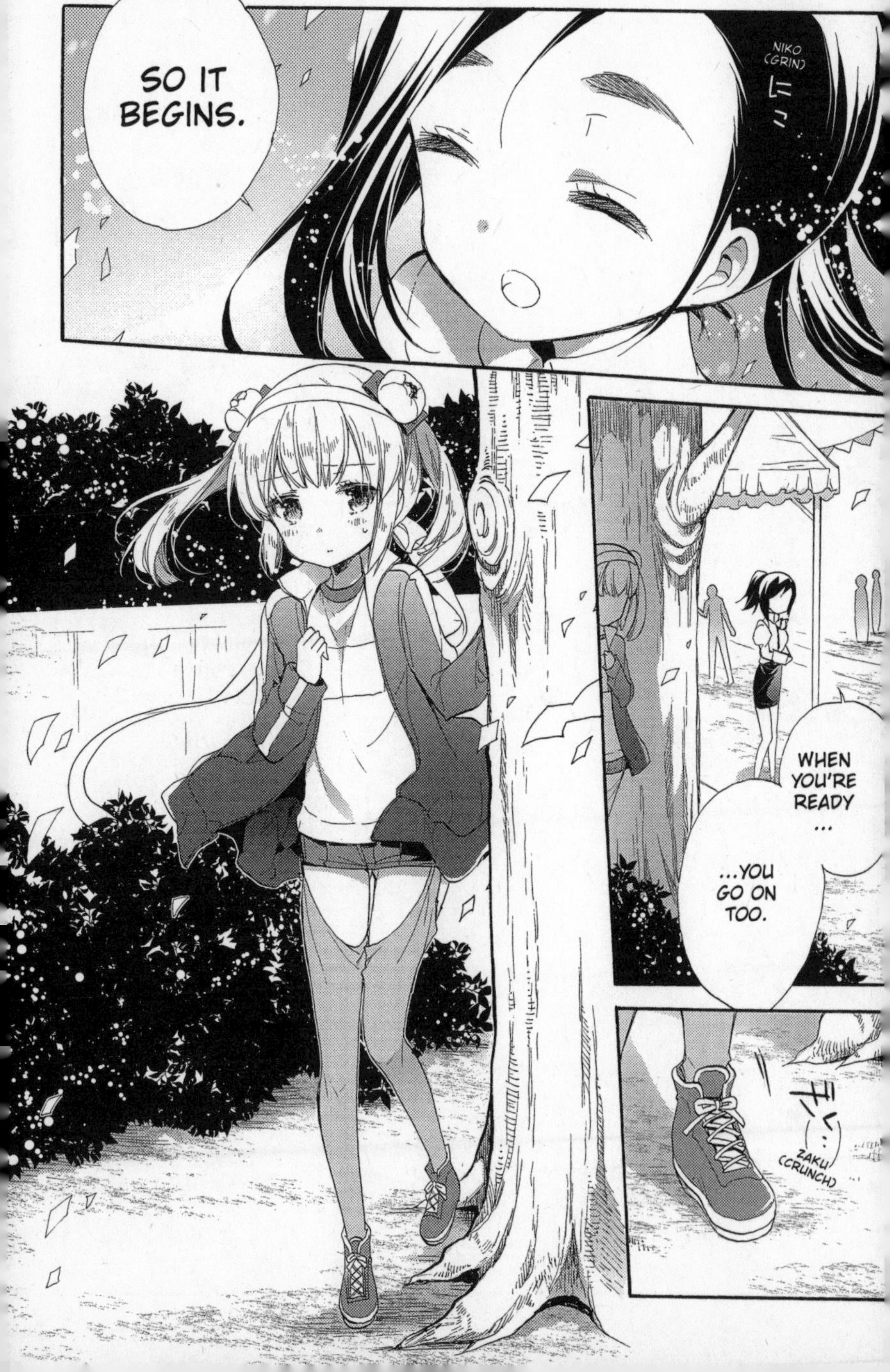
NIKO (GRIN)
SO IT BEGINS.
WHEN YOU'RE READY ...
...YOU GO ON TOO.
ZAKU (CRUNCH)

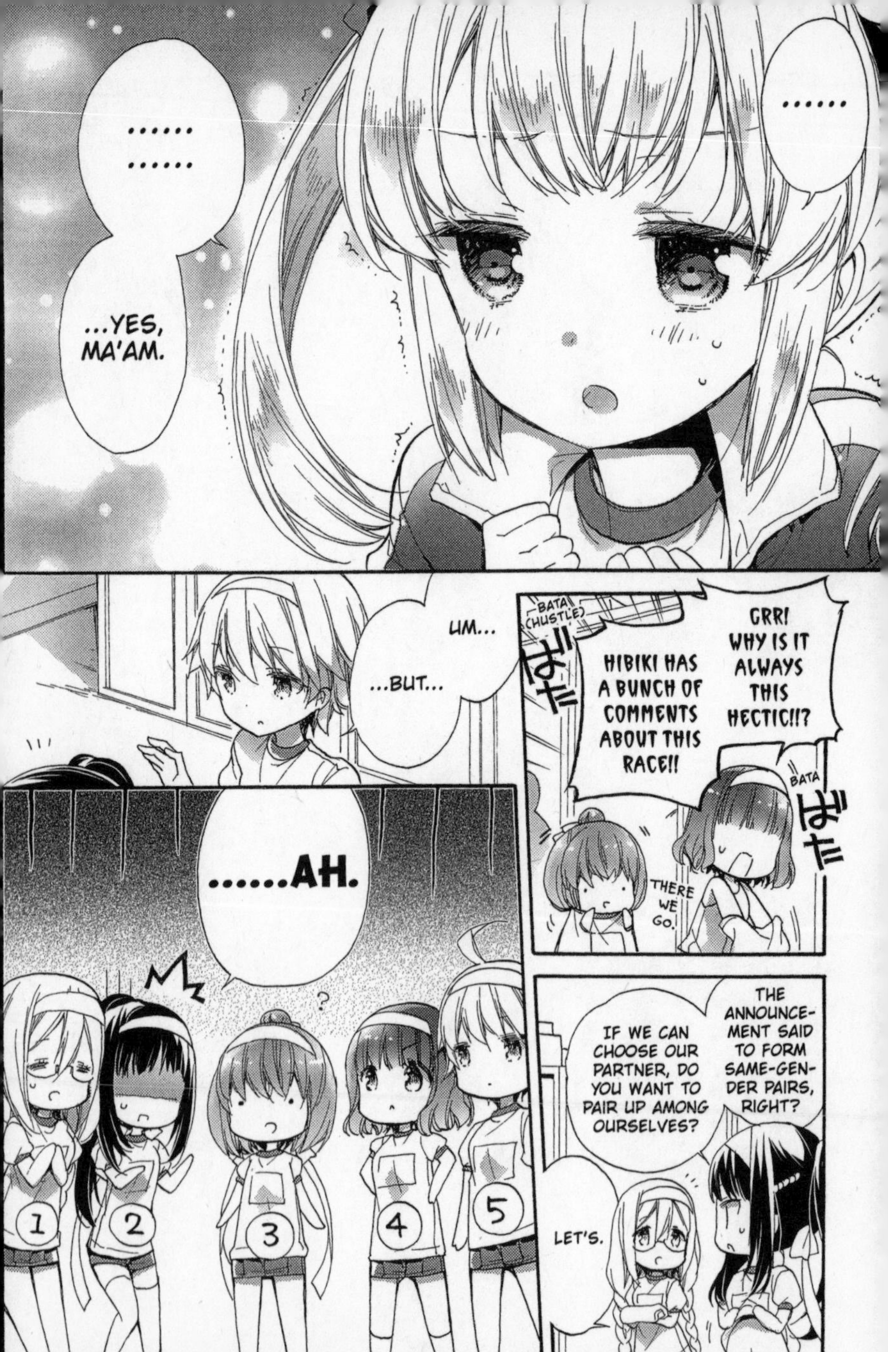

......
......
......
...YES, MA'AM.
GRR! WHY IS IT ALWAYS THIS HECTIC!!?
HIBIKI HAS A BUNCH OF COMMENTS ABOUT THIS RACE!!
BATA (HUSTLE)
BATA
THERE WE GO.
UM...
...BUT...
THE ANNOUNCEMENT SAID TO FORM SAME-GENDER PAIRS, RIGHT?
IF WE CAN CHOOSE OUR PARTNER, DO YOU WANT TO PAIR UP AMONG OURSELVES?
LET'S.
......AH.
1
2
3
4
5

AnneHappy♪

unhappy
go lucky!

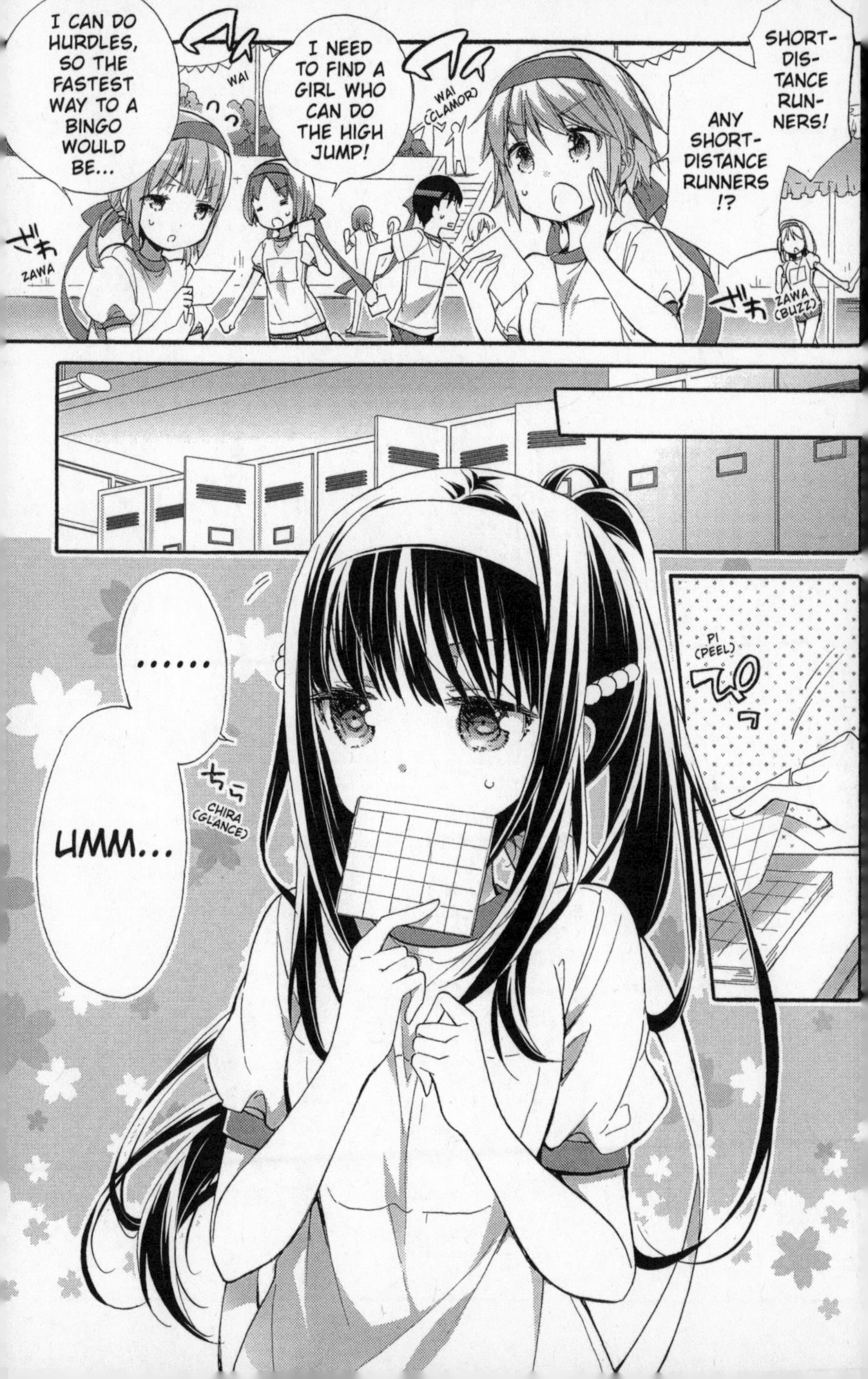

ZAWA (BUZZ)
SHORT-DISTANCE RUNNERS!
ANY SHORT-DISTANCE RUNNERS!?
WAI (CLAMOR)
I NEED TO FIND A GIRL WHO CAN DO THE HIGH JUMP!
WAI
I CAN DO HURDLES, SO THE FASTEST WAY TO A BINGO WOULD BE...
ZAWA
PI (PEEL)
CHIRA (GLANCE)
...... UMM...

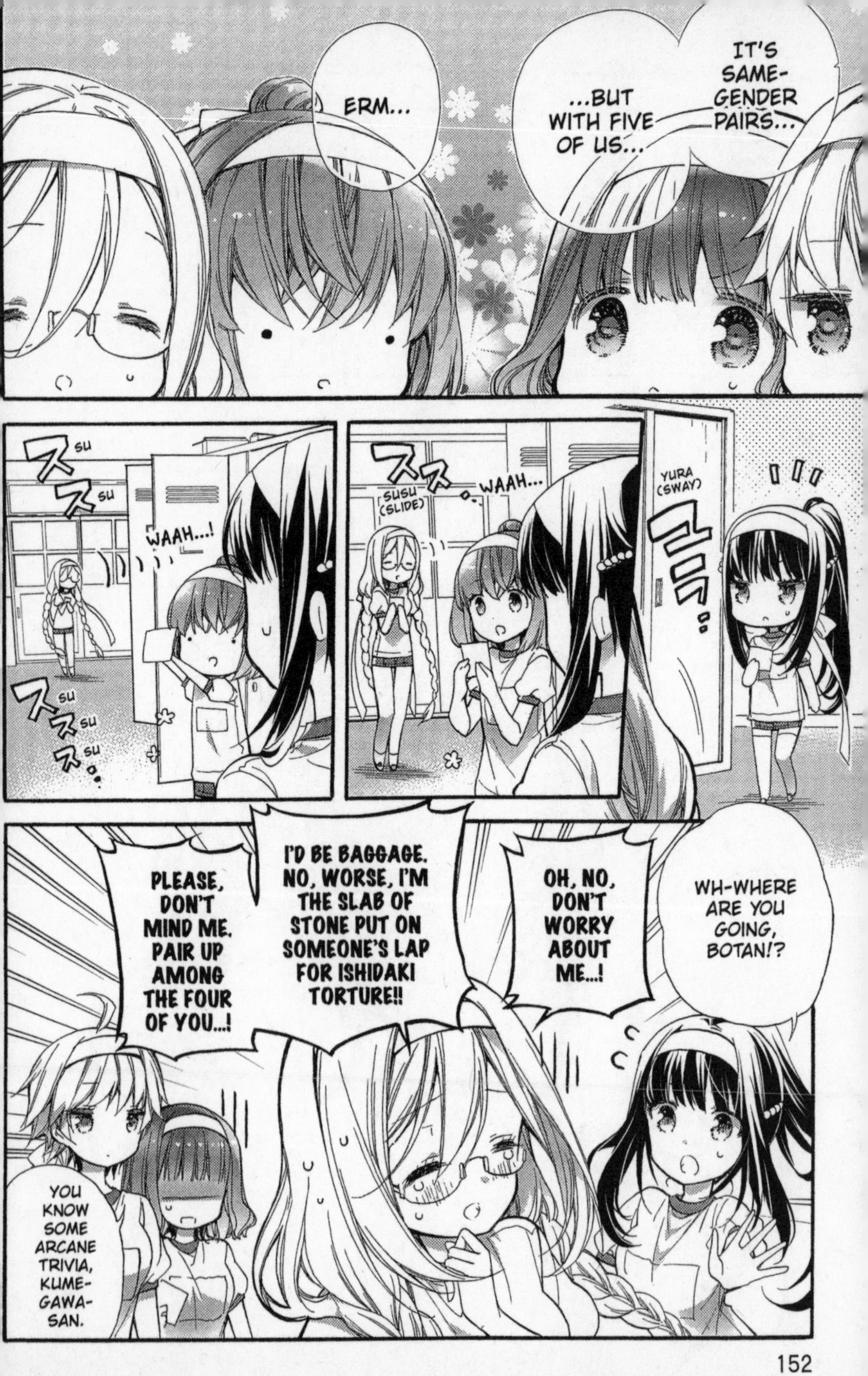
IT'S SAME-GENDER PAIRS...
...BUT WITH FIVE OF US...
ERM...
YURA (SWAY)
SUSU (SLIDE)
WAAH...
SU SU
WAAH...!
SU SU SU
WH-WHERE ARE YOU GOING, BOTAN!?
OH, NO. DON'T WORRY ABOUT ME...!
I'D BE BAGGAGE. NO, WORSE, I'M THE SLAB OF STONE PUT ON SOMEONE'S LAP FOR ISHIDAKI TORTURE!!
PLEASE, DON'T MIND ME. PAIR UP AMONG THE FOUR OF YOU...!
YOU KNOW SOME ARCANE TRIVIA, KUME-GAWA-SAN.

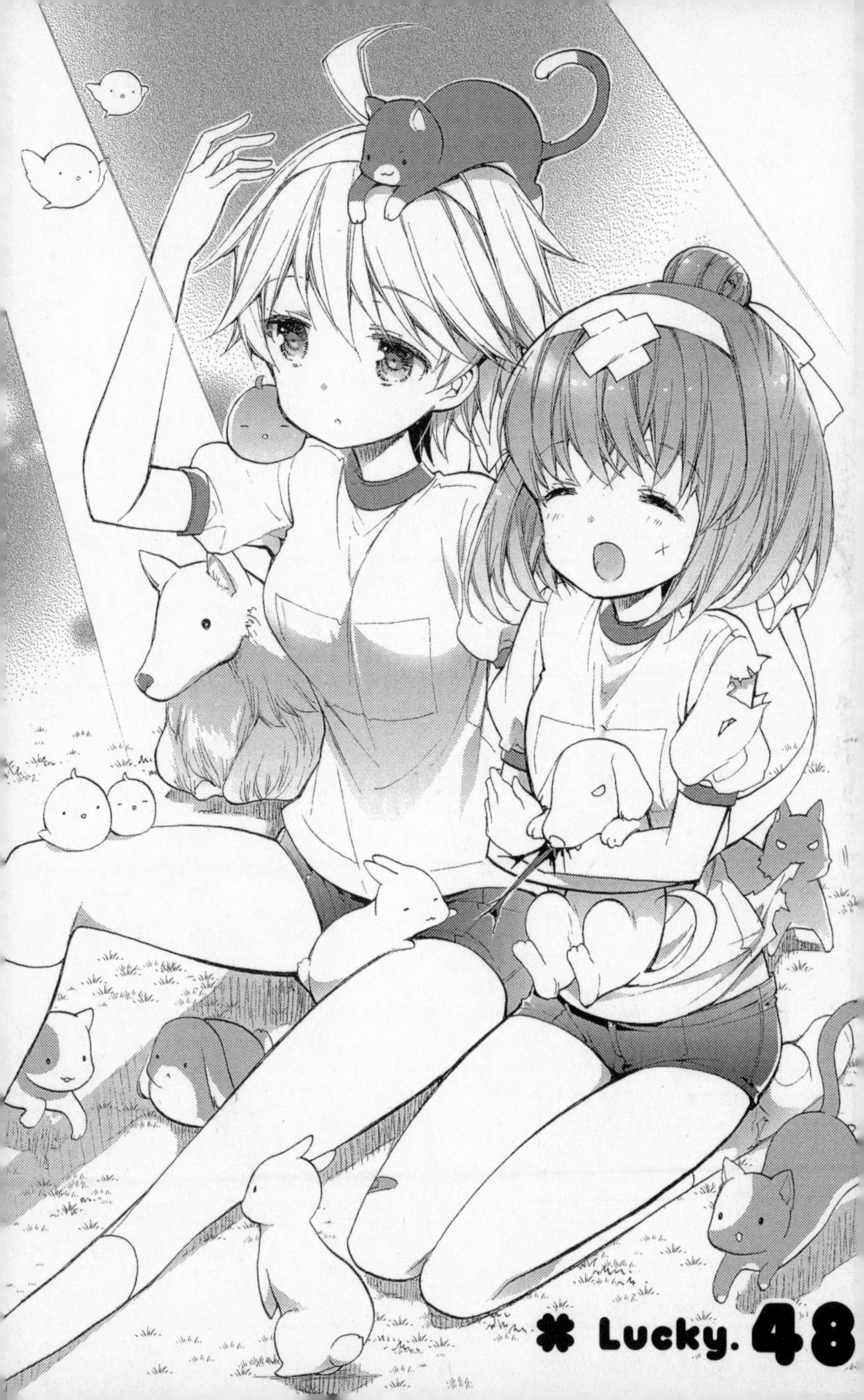
Lucky. 48

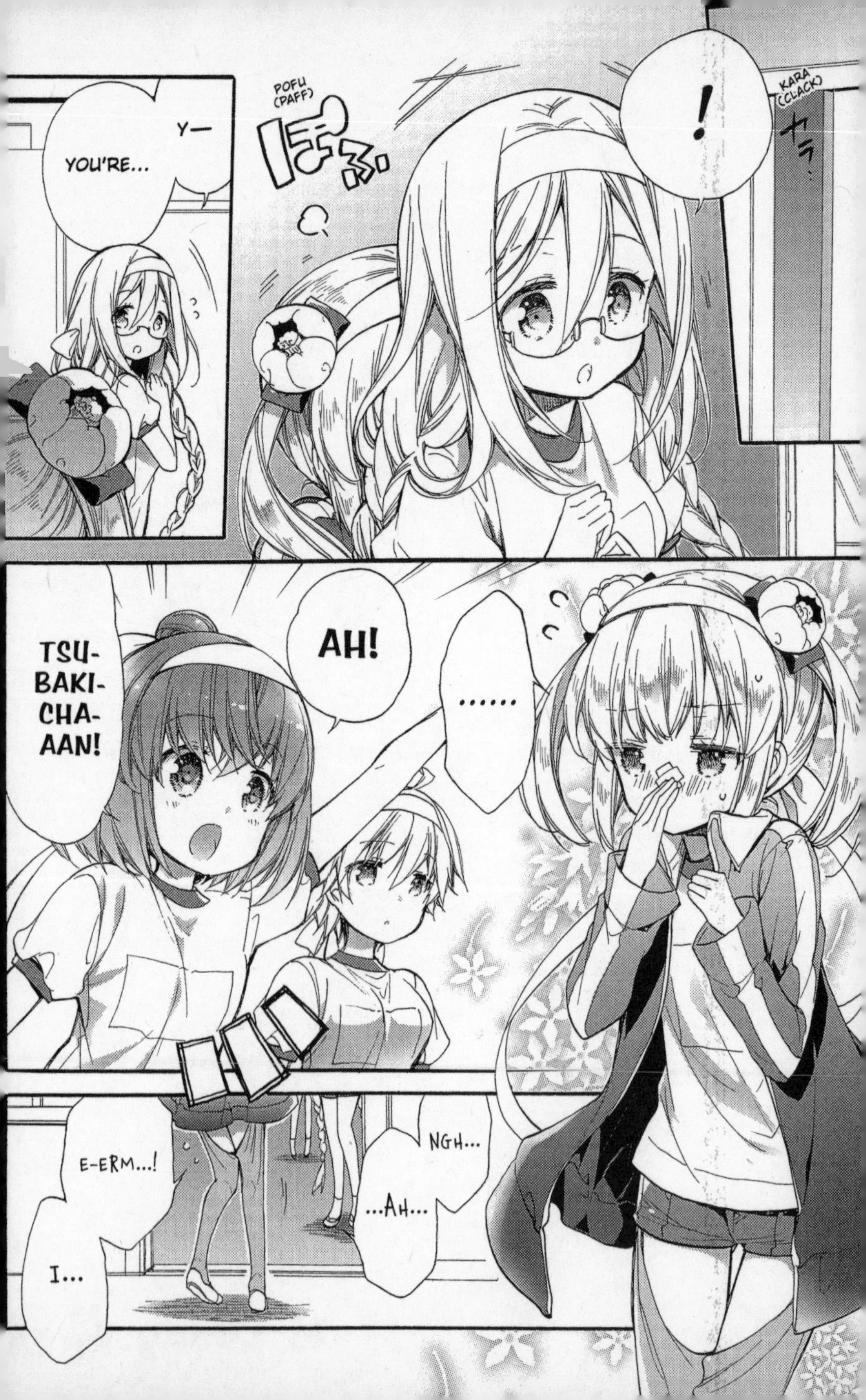
KARA (CLACK)
!
POFU (PAFF)
Y— YOU'RE...
......
AH!
TSU-BAKI-CHA-AAN!
NGH... ...AH...
E-ERM...! I...

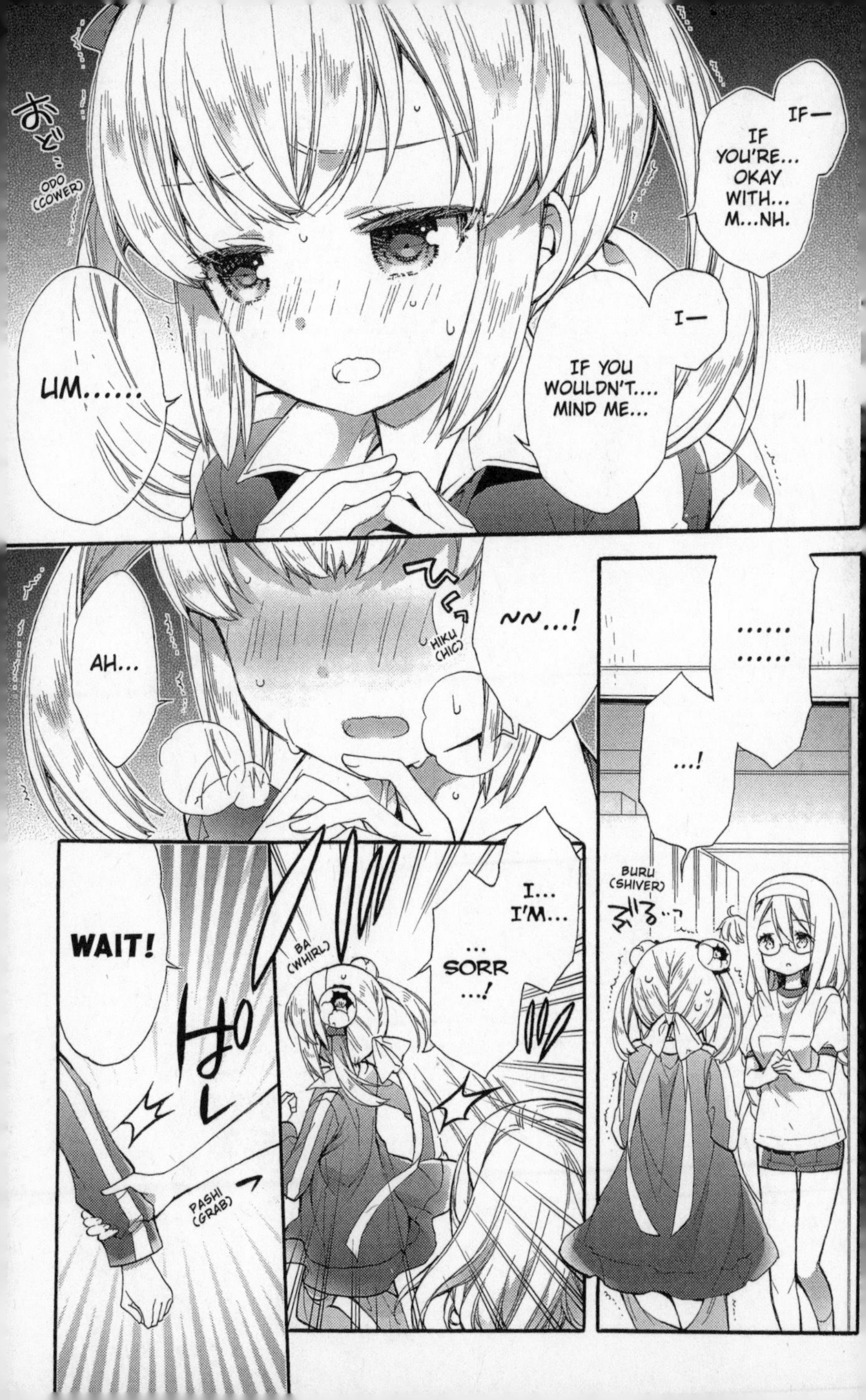

IF— IF YOU'RE... OKAY WITH... M...NH.
I— IF YOU WOULDN'T.... MIND ME...
おど…
ODO (COWER)
UM......
....
...!
ぶる…
BURU (SHIVER)
NN...!
ひく
HIKU (HIC)
AH...
I... I'M...
BA (WHIRL)
... SORR ...!
WAIT!
ぱし
PASHI (GRAB)

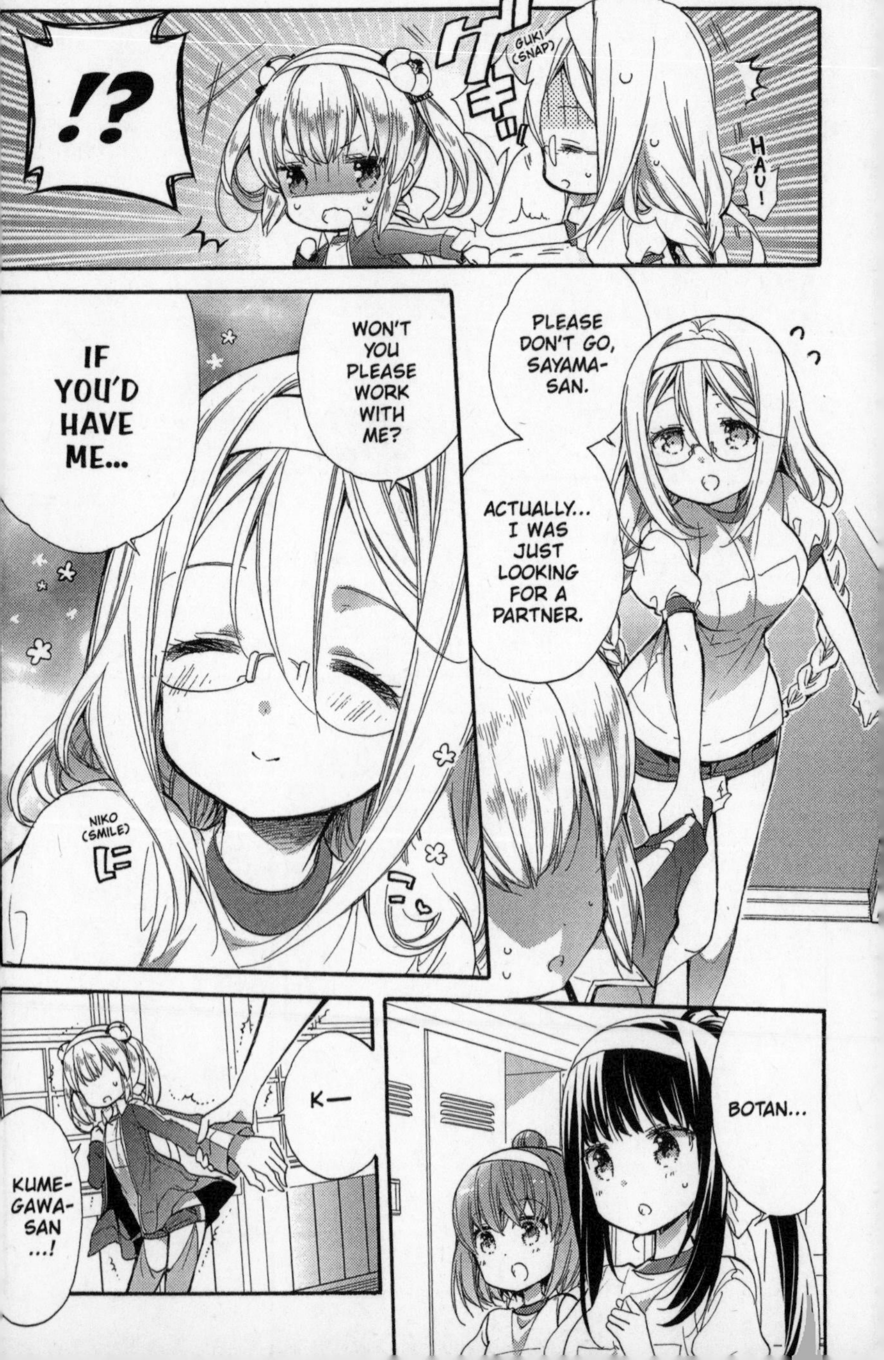
GUKI (SNAP)
HAU!
!?
PLEASE DON'T GO, SAYAMA-SAN.
ACTUALLY... I WAS JUST LOOKING FOR A PARTNER.
WON'T YOU PLEASE WORK WITH ME?
IF YOU'D HAVE ME...
NIKO (SMILE)
BOTAN...
K—
KUME-GAWA-SAN ...!

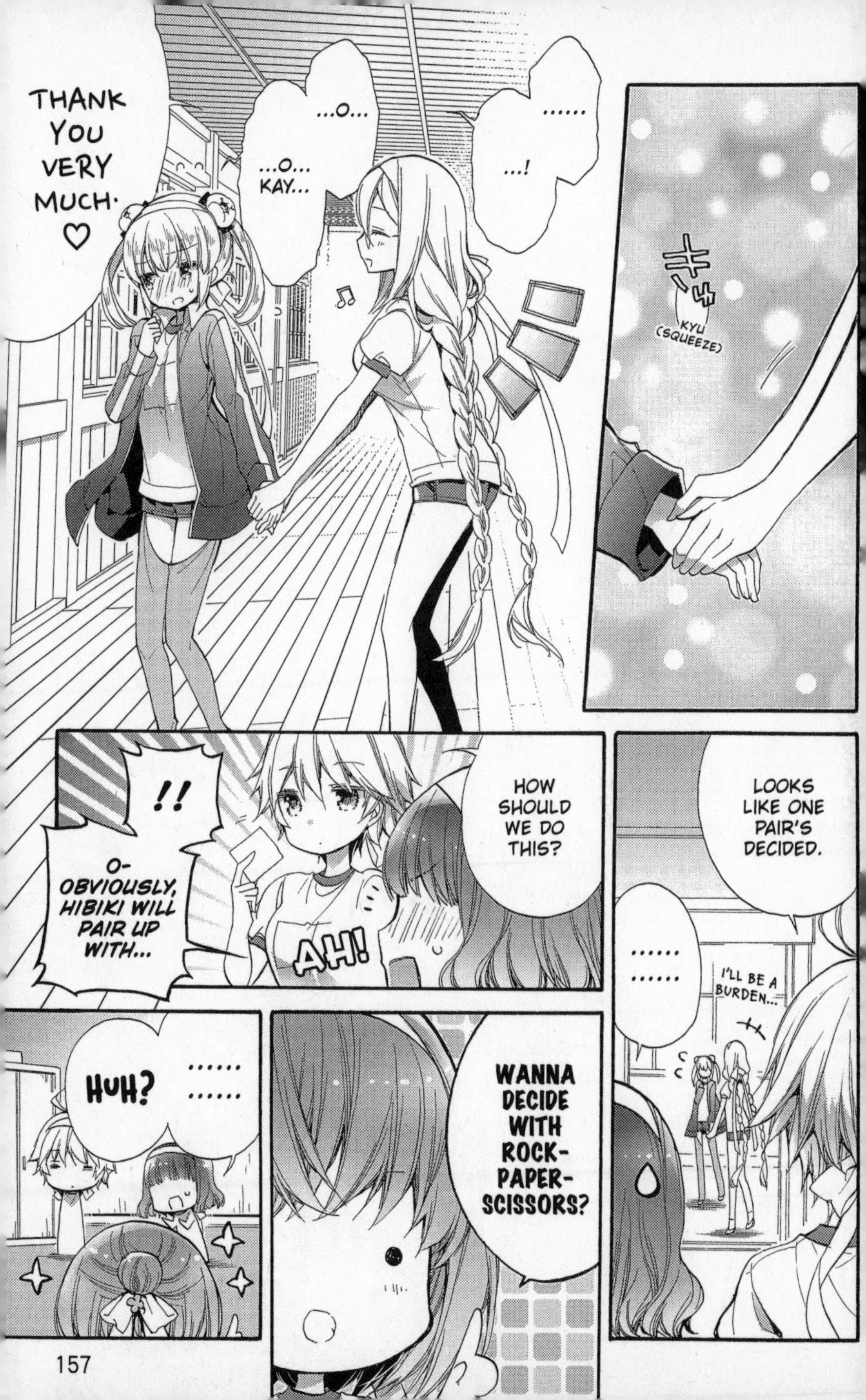
キュ
KYU (SQUEEZE)
......
...!
...O...
...O... KAY...
THANK YOU VERY MUCH♡
LOOKS LIKE ONE PAIR'S DECIDED.
....
I'LL BE A BURDEN...
HOW SHOULD WE DO THIS?
!!
AH!
O-OBVIOUSLY, HIBIKI WILL PAIR UP WITH...
WANNA DECIDE WITH ROCK-PAPER-SCISSORS?
HUH?
....

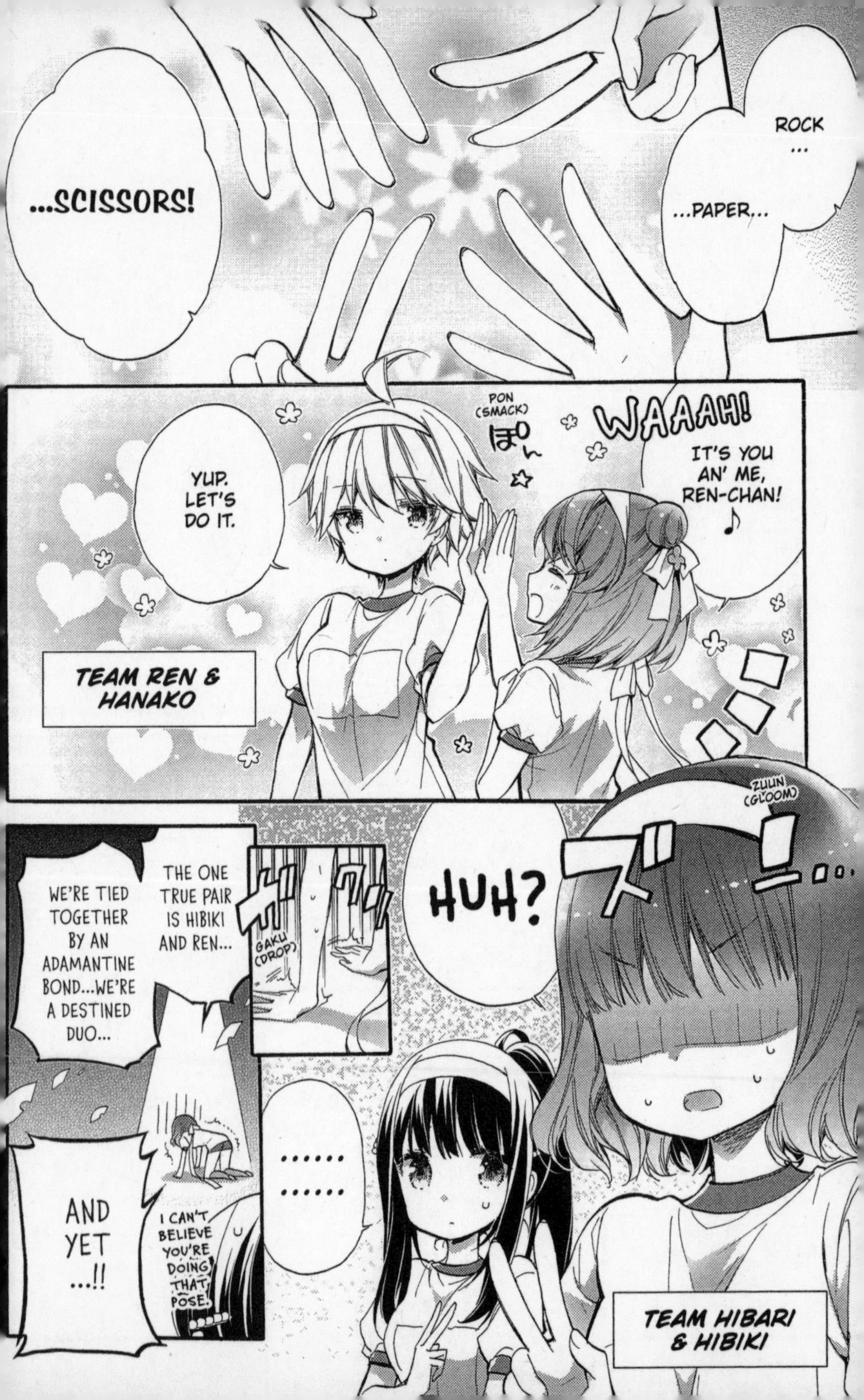
ROCK ...
...PAPER...
...SCISSORS!
WAAAH!
IT'S YOU AN' ME, REN-CHAN! ♪
PON (SMACK)
ぽん
YUP. LET'S DO IT.
TEAM REN & HANAKO
ZUUN (GLOOM)
HUH?
GAKU (DROP)
THE ONE TRUE PAIR IS HIBIKI AND REN...
WE'RE TIED TOGETHER BY AN ADAMANTINE BOND...WE'RE A DESTINED DUO...
TEAM HIBARI & HIBIKI
......
......
I CAN'T BELIEVE YOU'RE DOING THAT POSE.
AND YET ...!!

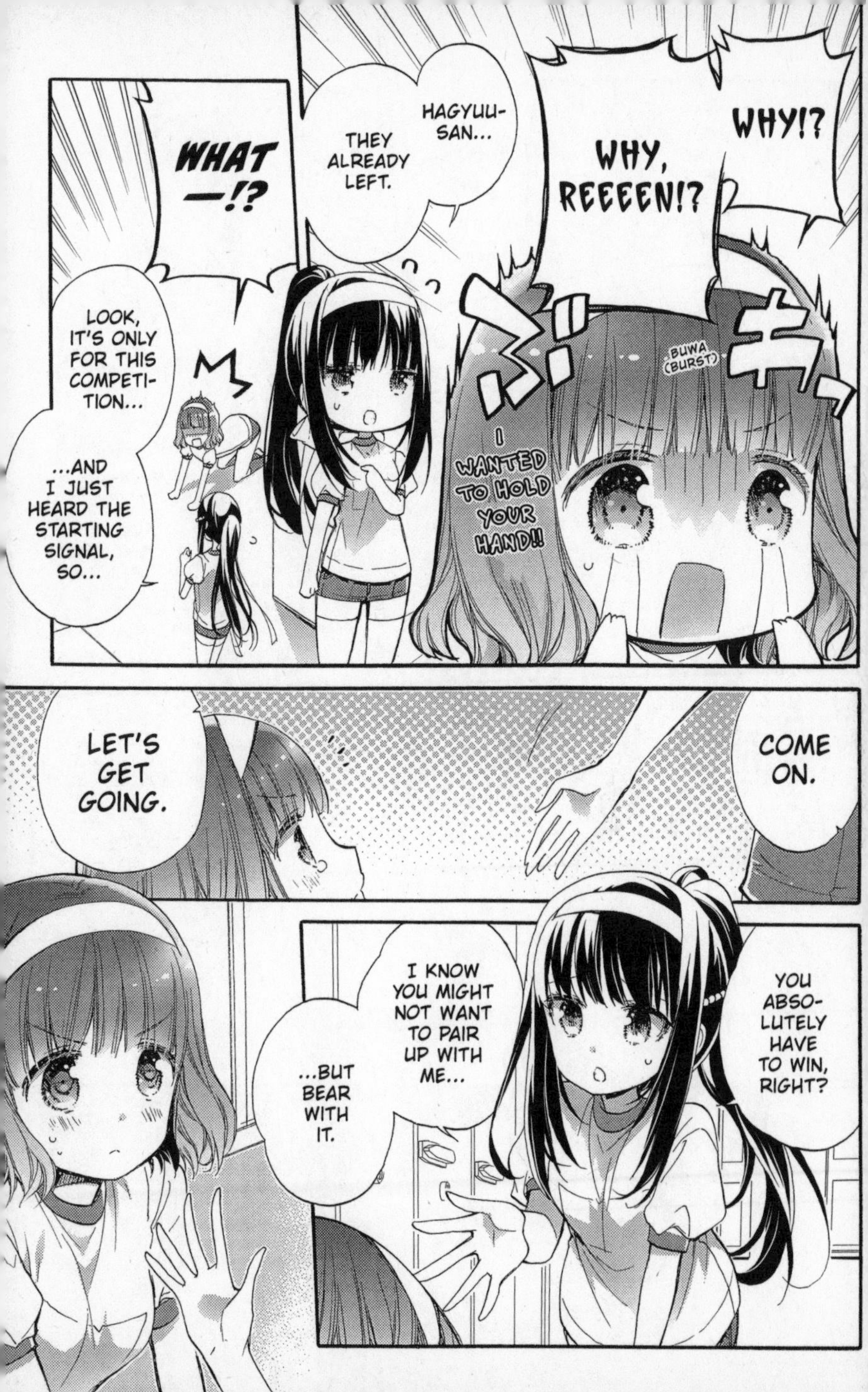
WHY!?
WHY, REEEEN!?
HAGYUU-SAN... THEY ALREADY LEFT.
WHAT—!?
BUWA (BURST)
I WANTED TO HOLD YOUR HAND!!
LOOK, IT'S ONLY FOR THIS COMPETITION...
...AND I JUST HEARD THE STARTING SIGNAL, SO...
COME ON.
LET'S GET GOING.
YOU ABSOLUTELY HAVE TO WIN, RIGHT?
I KNOW YOU MIGHT NOT WANT TO PAIR UP WITH ME...
...BUT BEAR WITH IT.

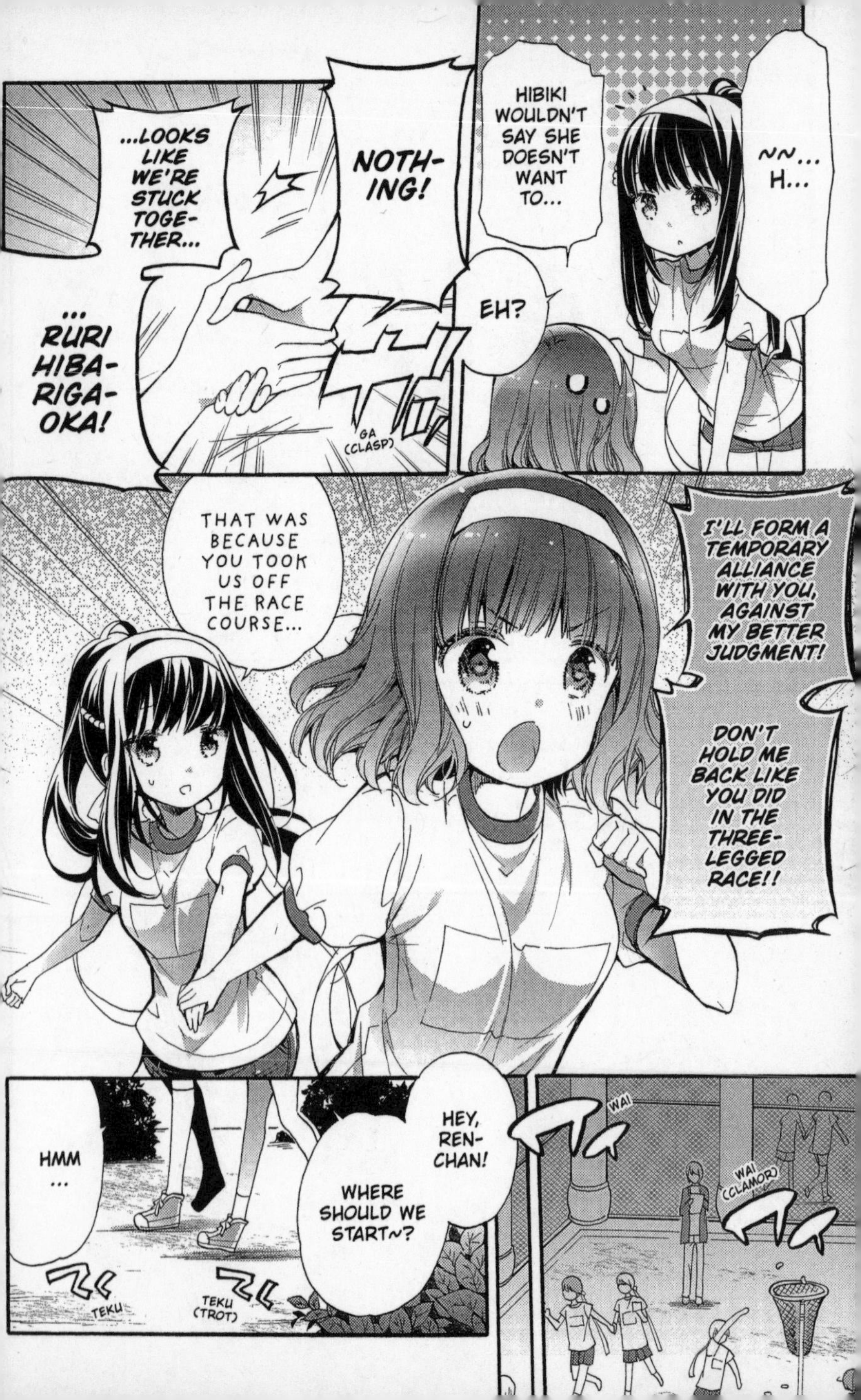
~~... H...
HIBIKI WOULDN'T SAY SHE DOESN'T WANT TO...
EH?
NOTHING!
...LOOKS LIKE WE'RE STUCK TOGETHER...
GA (CLASP)
...RURI HIBARIGAOKA!
I'LL FORM A TEMPORARY ALLIANCE WITH YOU, AGAINST MY BETTER JUDGMENT!
DON'T HOLD ME BACK LIKE YOU DID IN THE THREE-LEGGED RACE!!
THAT WAS BECAUSE YOU TOOK US OFF THE RACE COURSE...
WAI
WAI (CLAMOR)
HEY, REN-CHAN!
WHERE SHOULD WE START~?
HMM ...
TEKU (TROT)
TEKU

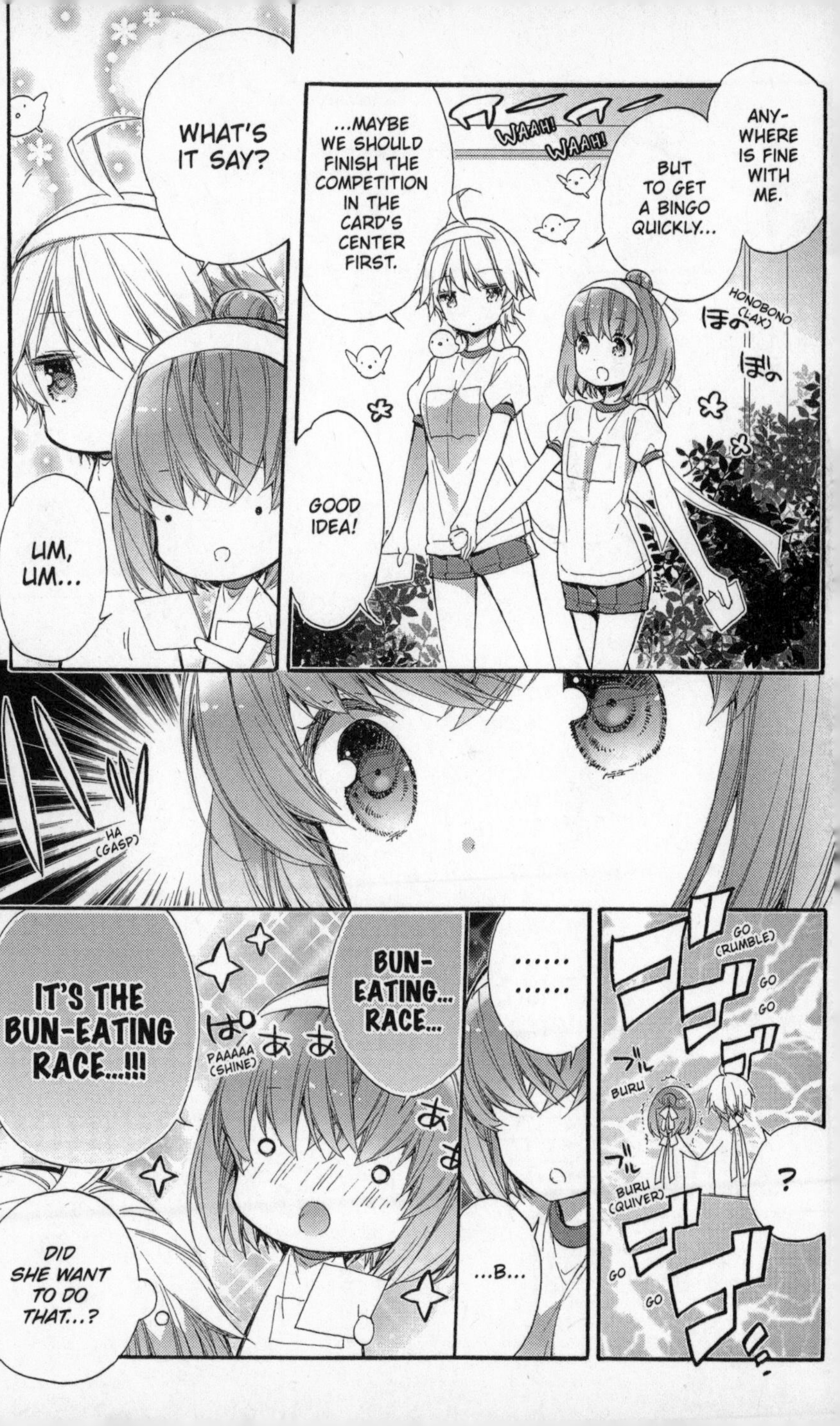

ANY-WHERE IS FINE WITH ME.
BUT TO GET A BINGO QUICKLY...
WAAAH! WAAAH!
...MAYBE WE SHOULD FINISH THE COMPETITION IN THE CARD'S CENTER FIRST.
HONOBONO (LAX)
GOOD IDEA!
WHAT'S IT SAY?
UM, UM...
HA (GASP)
GO (RUMBLE) GO GO
BURU BURU (QUIVER)
?
GO GO
......
......
...B...
BUN-EATING... RACE...
IT'S THE BUN-EATING RACE...!!!
PAAAAA (SHINE)
DID SHE WANT TO DO THAT...?

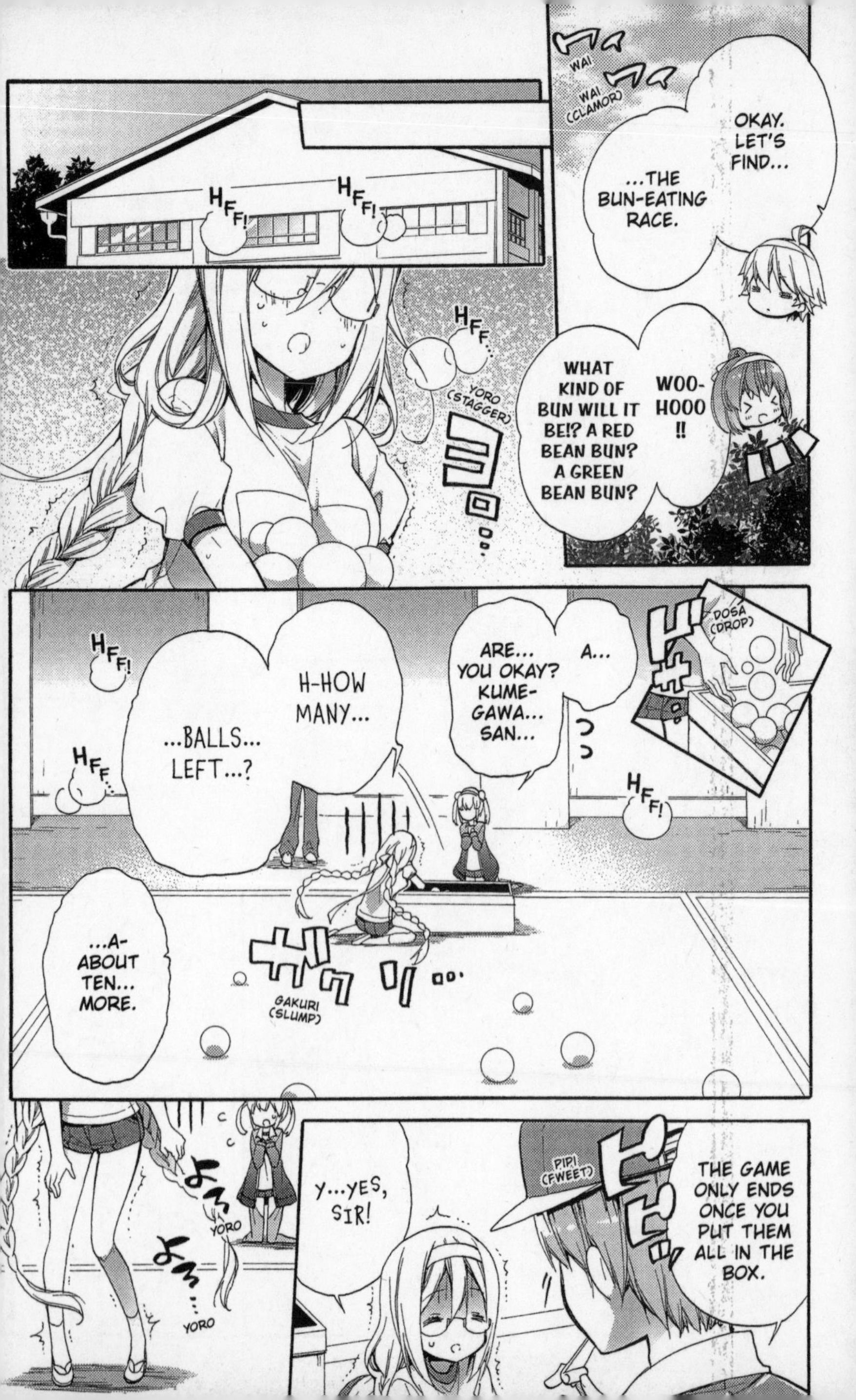
WAI
WAI (CLAMOR)
OKAY. LET'S FIND...
...THE BUN-EATING RACE.
WOO-HOOO!!
WHAT KIND OF BUN WILL IT BE!? A RED BEAN BUN? A GREEN BEAN BUN?
HFF!
HFF!
HFF...
YORO (STAGGER)
DOSA (DROP)
A...
ARE... YOU OKAY? KUME-GAWA... SAN...
HFF!
H-HOW MANY...
...BALLS... LEFT...?
HFF!
HFF...
...A-ABOUT TEN... MORE.
GAKURI (SLUMP)
PIPI (FWEET)
THE GAME ONLY ENDS ONCE YOU PUT THEM ALL IN THE BOX.
Y...YES, SIR!
YORO
YORO

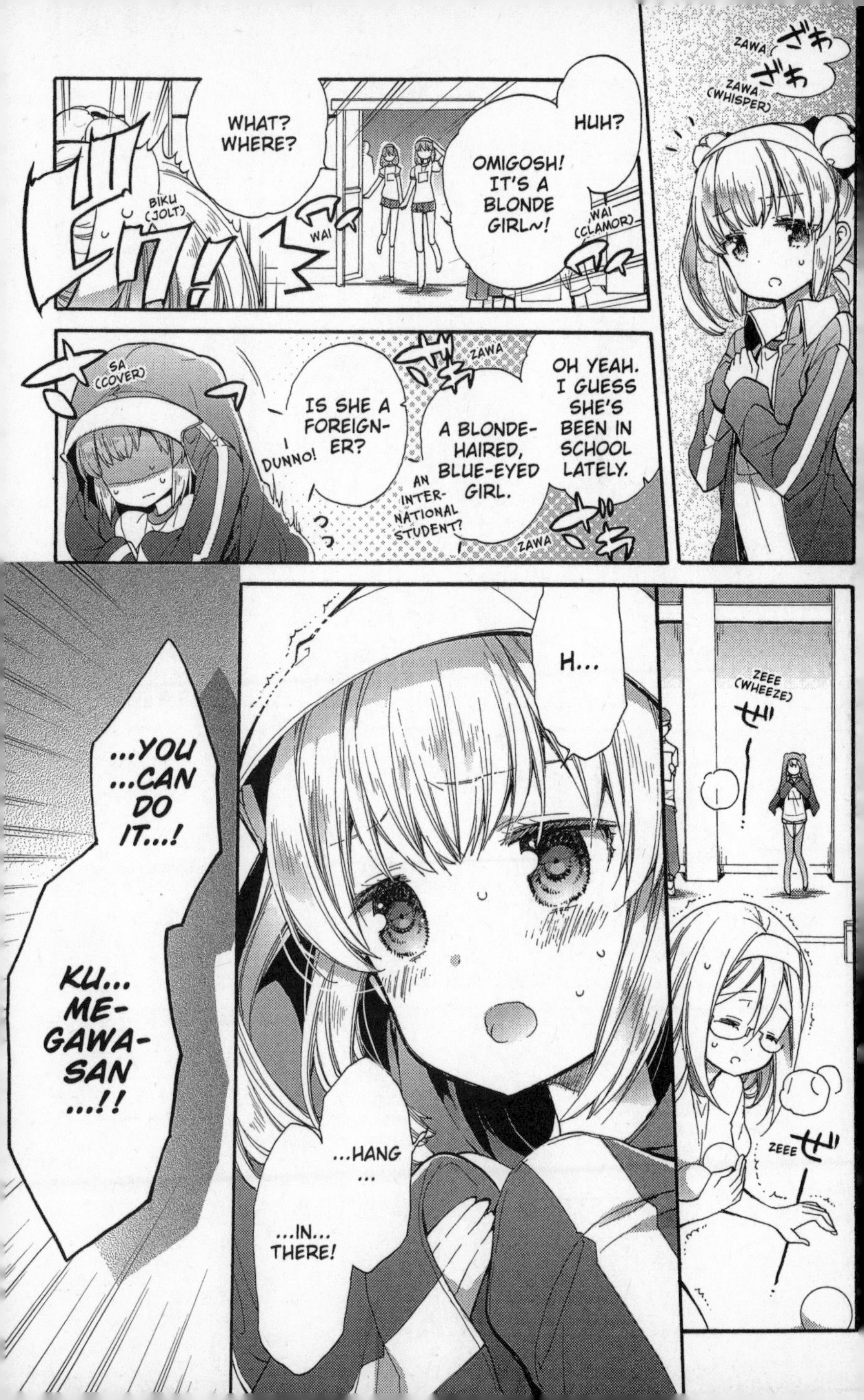
ZAWA
ZAWA (WHISPER)
HUH?
OMIGOSH! IT'S A BLONDE GIRL~!
WAI (CLAMOR)
WHAT? WHERE?
WAI
BIKU (JOLT)
OH YEAH. I GUESS SHE'S BEEN IN SCHOOL LATELY.
ZAWA
A BLONDE-HAIRED, BLUE-EYED GIRL.
ZAWA
AN INTERNATIONAL STUDENT?
IS SHE A FOREIGNER?
I DUNNO!
SA (COVER)
ZEEE (WHEEZE)
ZEEE
H...
...HANG...
...IN... THERE!
...YOU ...CAN DO IT...!
KU... ME-GAWA-SAN ...!!

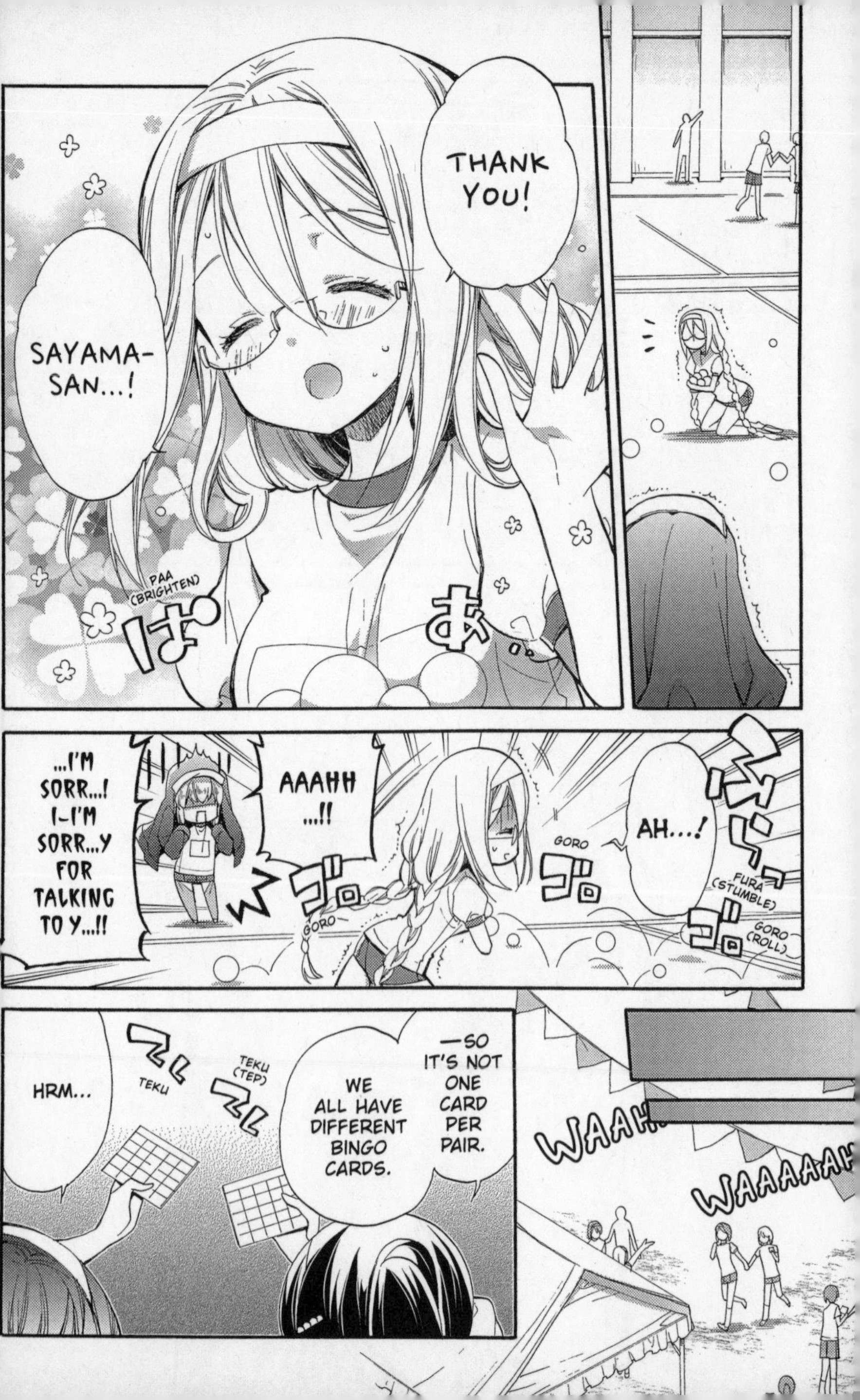
THANK YOU!
SAYAMA-SAN...!
PAA (BRIGHTEN)
ぱあ。。
ふらっ
FURA (STUMBLE)
AH...!
ゴロ
GORO (ROLL)
ゴロ
GORO
ゴロ
GORO
AAAHH...!!
...I'M SORR...! I-I'M SORR...Y FOR TALKING TO Y...!!
WAAAAAAH
WAAH
—SO IT'S NOT ONE CARD PER PAIR.
WE ALL HAVE DIFFERENT BINGO CARDS.
てく
TEKU (TEP)
てく
TEKU
HRM...

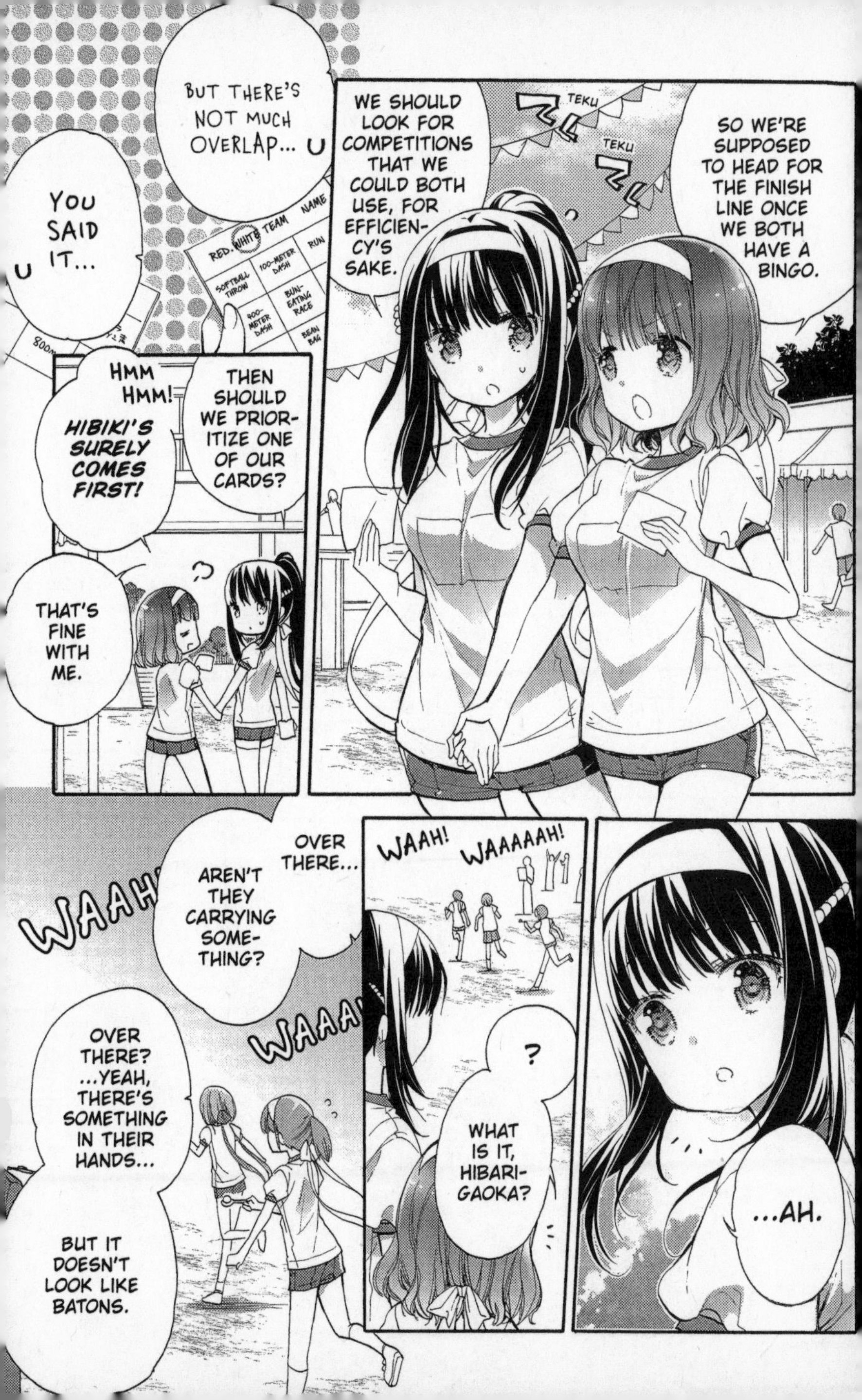
SO WE'RE SUPPOSED TO HEAD FOR THE FINISH LINE ONCE WE BOTH HAVE A BINGO.
TEKU
TEKU
WE SHOULD LOOK FOR COMPETITIONS THAT WE COULD BOTH USE, FOR EFFICIENCY'S SAKE.
BUT THERE'S NOT MUCH OVERLAP...
YOU SAID IT...
RED. WHITE TEAM NAME
RUN
100-METER DASH
SOFTBALL THROW
BUN-EATING RACE
400-METER DASH
BEAN BAG
800m
THEN SHOULD WE PRIORITIZE ONE OF OUR CARDS?
HMM HMM! HIBIKI'S SURELY COMES FIRST!
THAT'S FINE WITH ME.
...AH.
WAAH!
WAAAAAH!
?
WHAT IS IT, HIBARIGAOKA?
OVER THERE...
AREN'T THEY CARRYING SOMETHING?
OVER THERE? ...YEAH, THERE'S SOMETHING IN THEIR HANDS...
BUT IT DOESN'T LOOK LIKE BATONS.

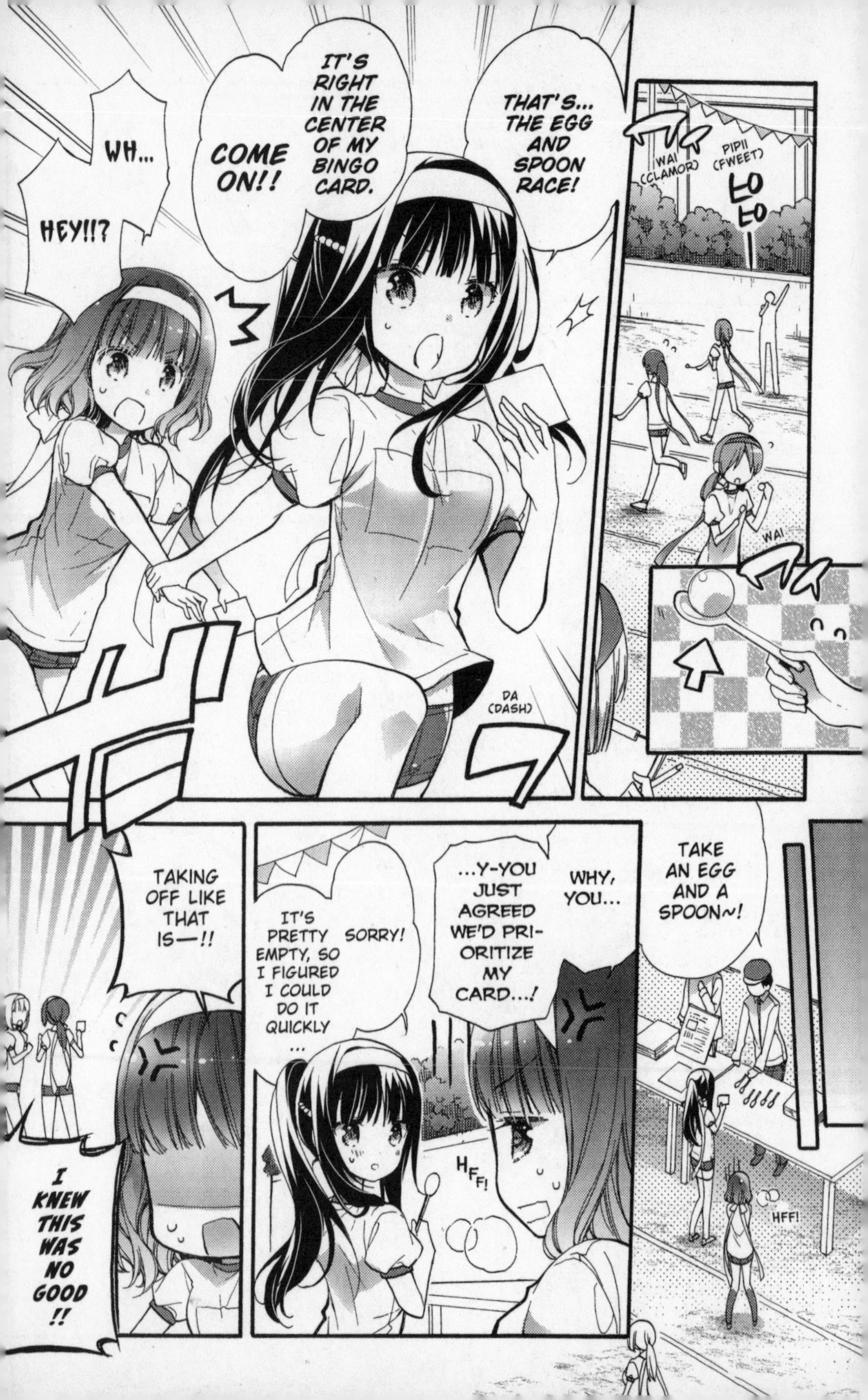
WAI (CLAMOR)
PIPII (FWEET)
WAI
THAT'S... THE EGG AND SPOON RACE!
IT'S RIGHT IN THE CENTER OF MY BINGO CARD.
COME ON!!
WH...
HEY!!?
DA (DASH)
TAKE AN EGG AND A SPOON~!
HFF!
WHY, YOU...
...Y-YOU JUST AGREED WE'D PRI-ORITIZE MY CARD...!
SORRY!
IT'S PRETTY EMPTY, SO I FIGURED I COULD DO IT QUICKLY...
HFF!
TAKING OFF LIKE THAT IS—!!
I KNEW THIS WAS NO GOOD!!

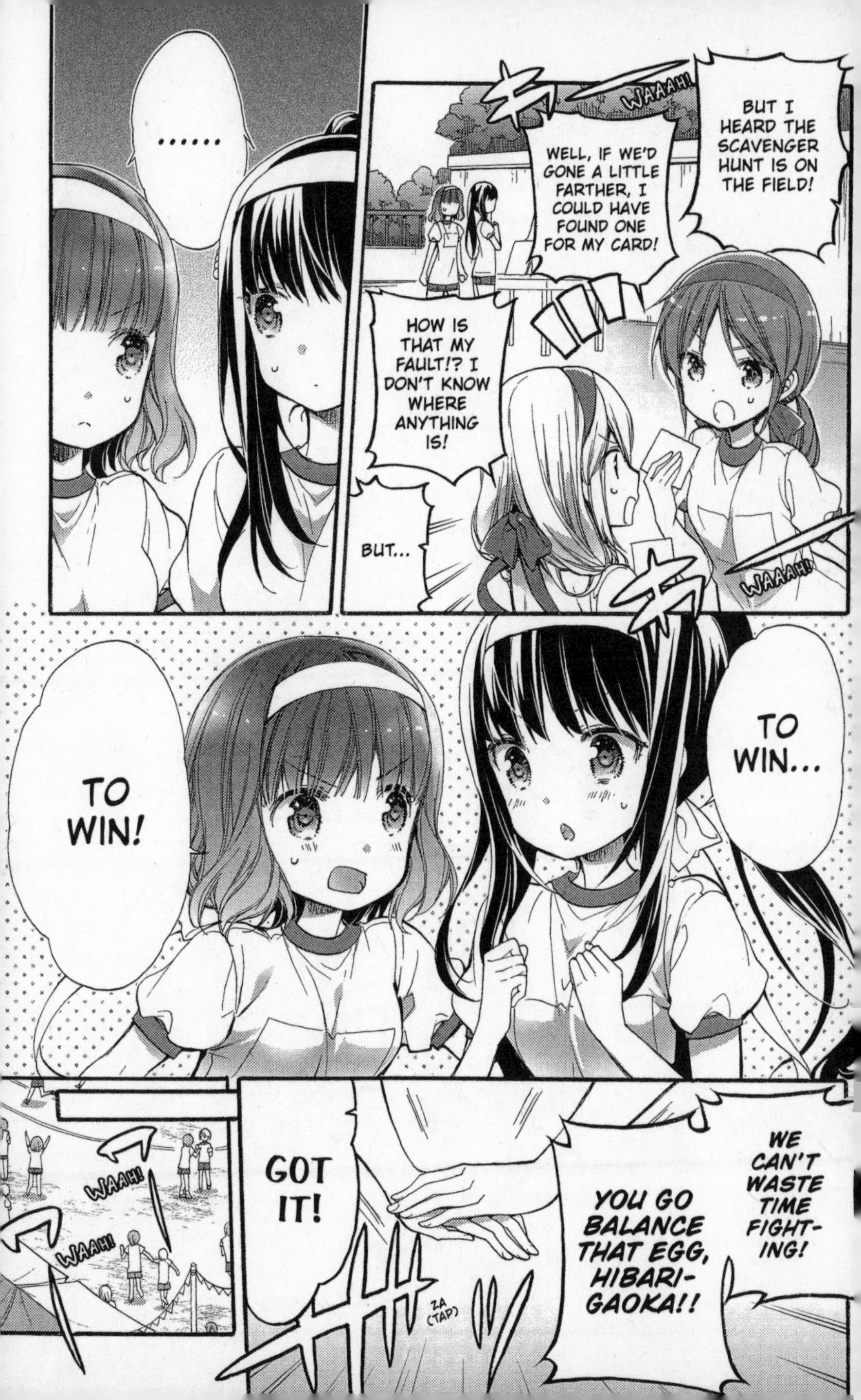
BUT I HEARD THE SCAVENGER HUNT IS ON THE FIELD!
WAAAH!
WELL, IF WE'D GONE A LITTLE FARTHER, I COULD HAVE FOUND ONE FOR MY CARD!
HOW IS THAT MY FAULT!? I DON'T KNOW WHERE ANYTHING IS!
BUT...
WAAAH!
......
TO WIN...
TO WIN!
WE CAN'T WASTE TIME FIGHT-ING!
YOU GO BALANCE THAT EGG, HIBARI-GAOKA!!
GOT IT!
ZA (TAP)
WAAH!
WAAH!

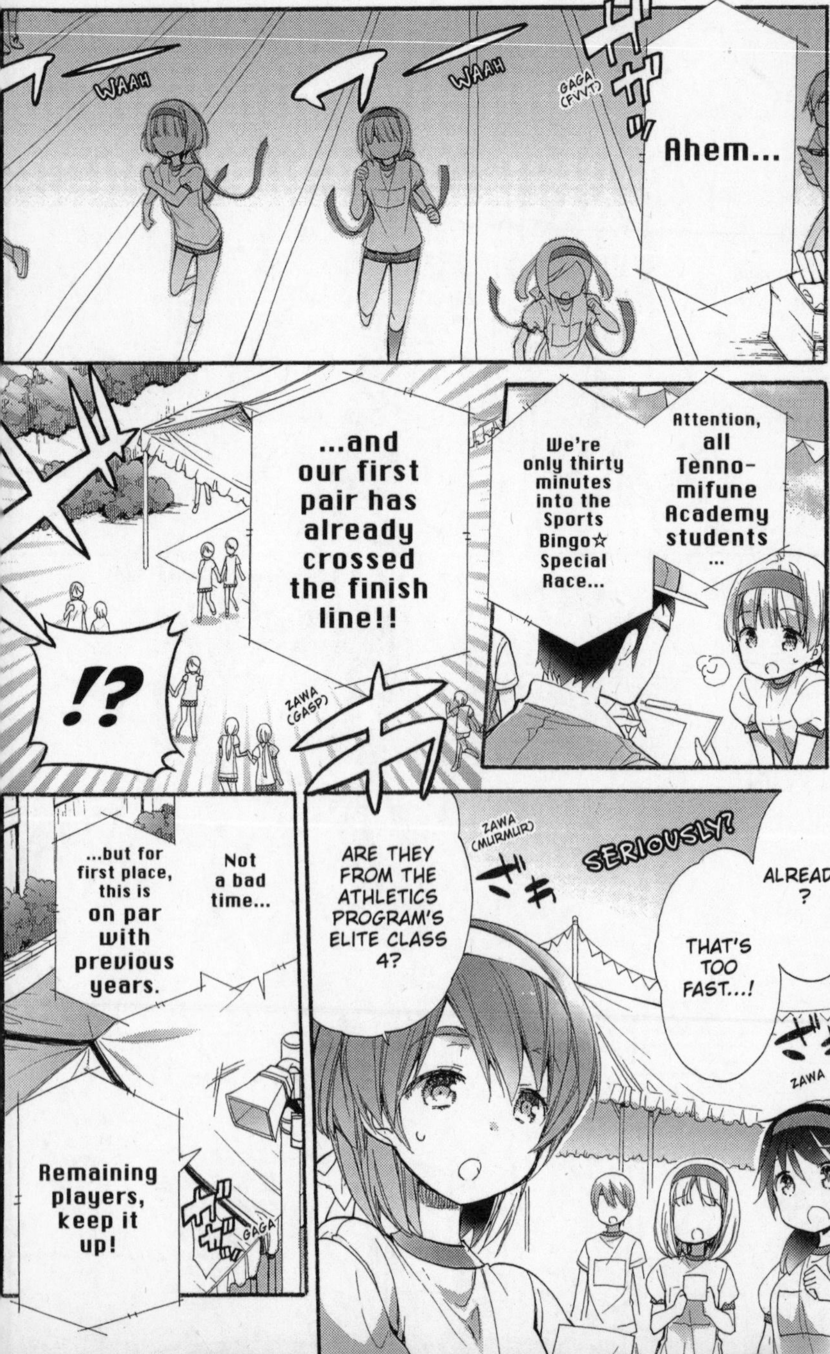
GAGA (FVVT)
Ahem...
WAAH
WAAH
Attention, all Tennomifune Academy students...
We're only thirty minutes into the Sports Bingo☆ Special Race...
...and our first pair has already crossed the finish line!!
ZAWA (GASP)
!?
ALREADY?
THAT'S TOO FAST...!
SERIOUSLY?
ZAWA (MURMUR)
ARE THEY FROM THE ATHLETICS PROGRAM'S ELITE CLASS 4?
ZAWA
Not a bad time...
...but for first place, this is on par with previous years.
Remaining players, keep it up!
GAGA

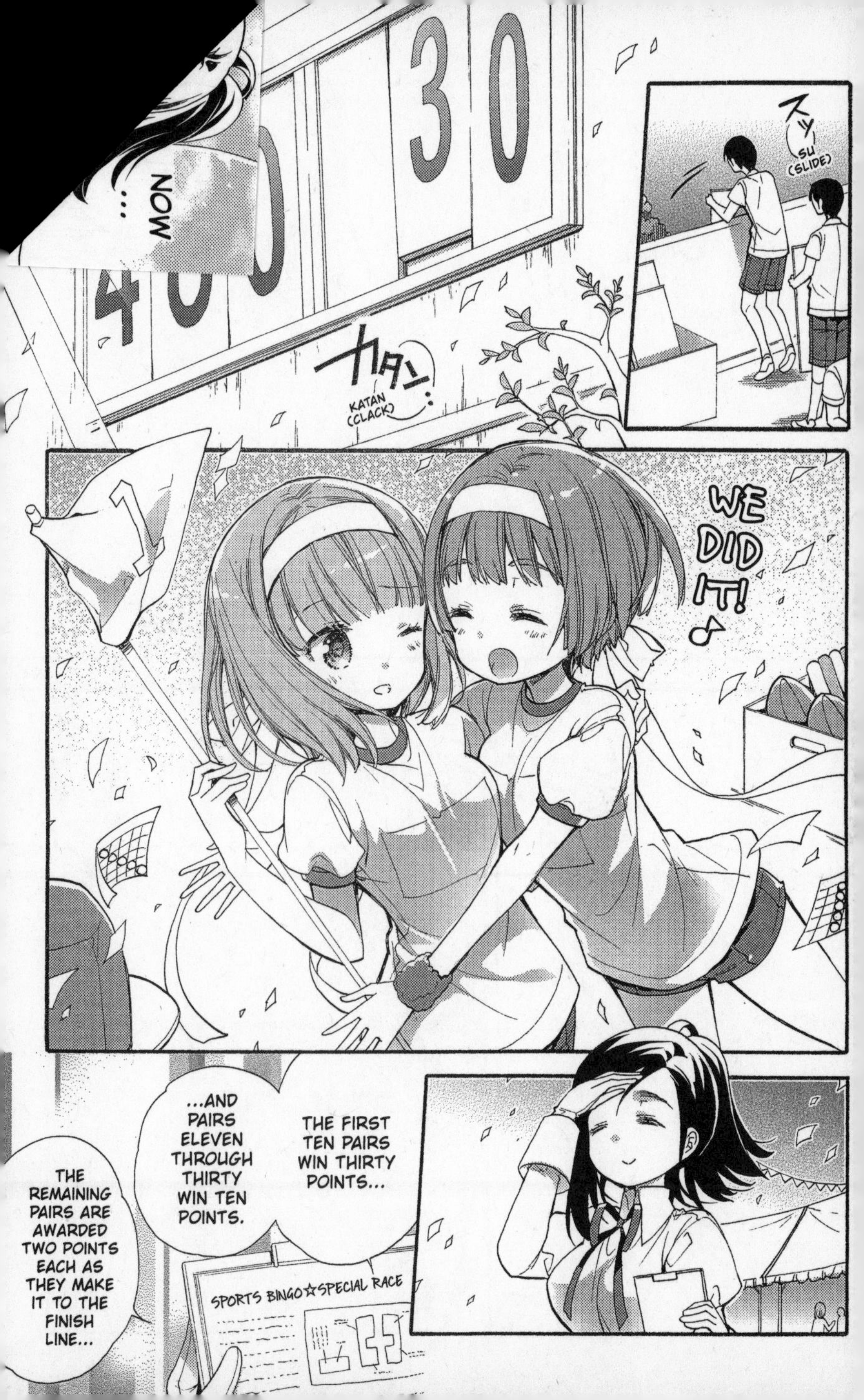
スッ
SU (SLIDE)
40
30
カタン
KATAN (CLACK)
WE DID IT! ♪
THE FIRST TEN PAIRS WIN THIRTY POINTS...
...AND PAIRS ELEVEN THROUGH THIRTY WIN TEN POINTS.
THE REMAINING PAIRS ARE AWARDED TWO POINTS EACH AS THEY MAKE IT TO THE FINISH LINE...
SPORTS BINGO☆SPECIAL RACE

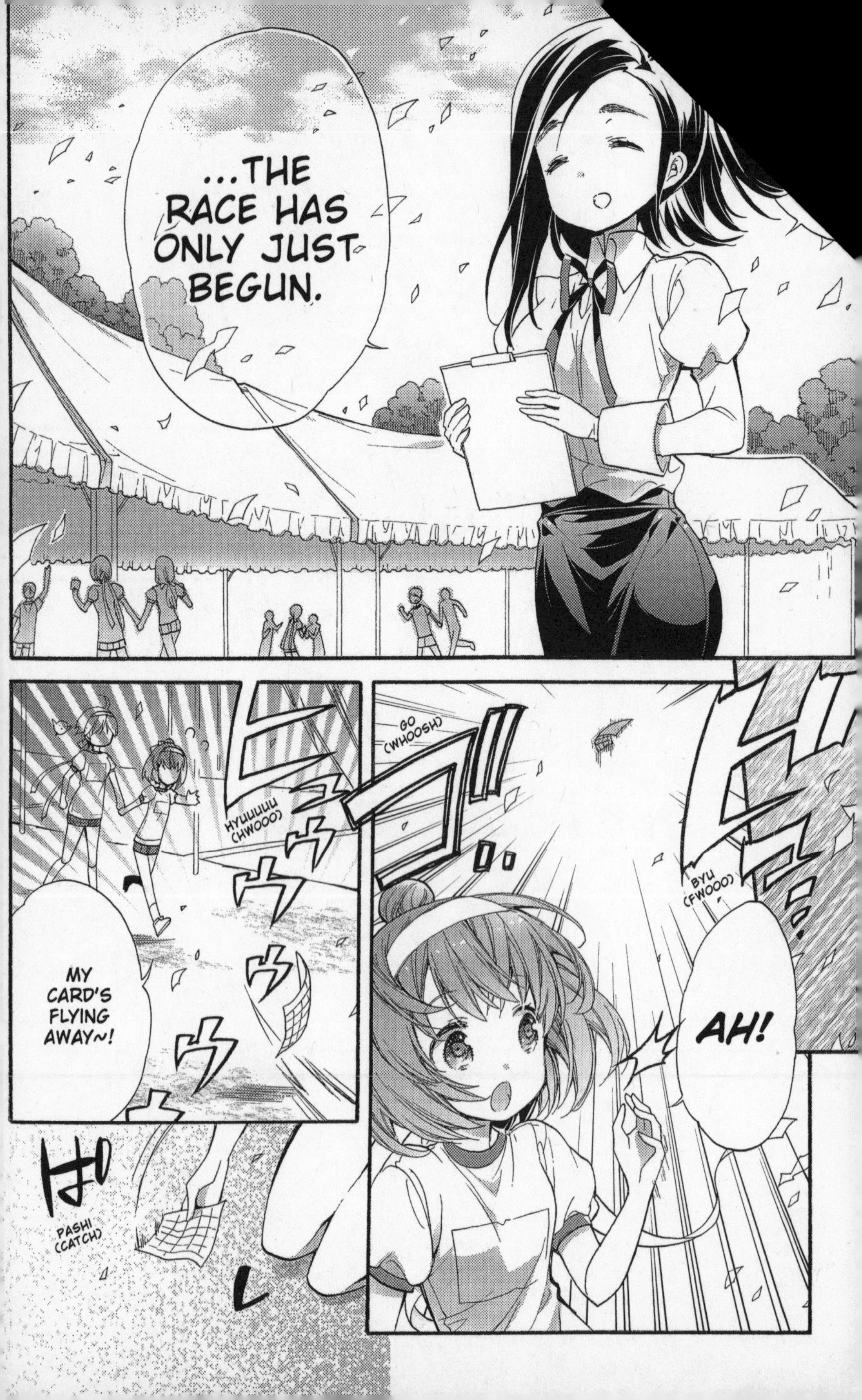
...THE RACE HAS ONLY JUST BEGUN.
GO (WHOOSH)
BYU (FWOOO)
AH!
HYUUUUU (HWOOO)
MY CARD'S FLYING AWAY~!
PASHI (CATCH)

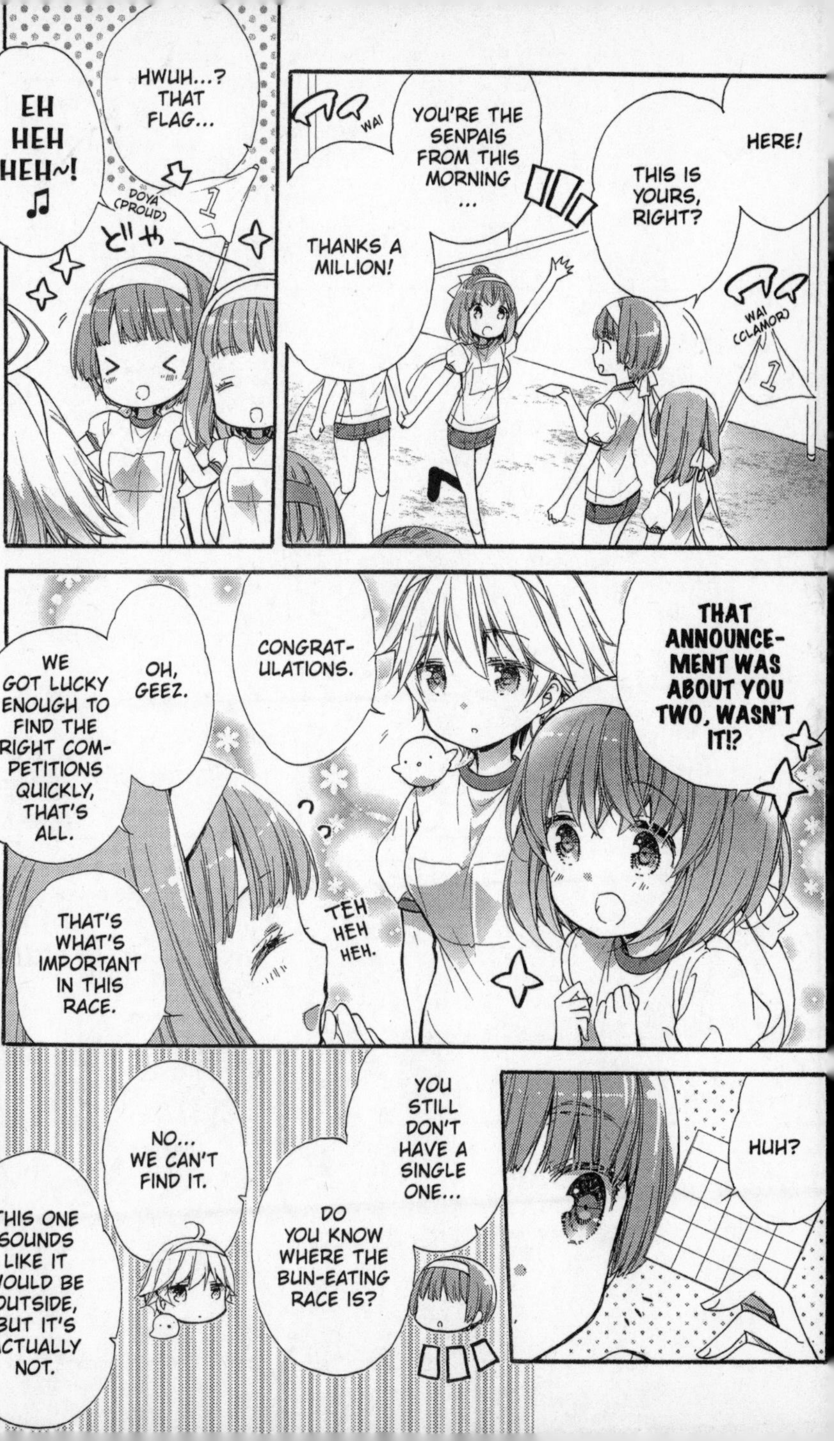
HERE!
THIS IS YOURS, RIGHT?
WAI (CLAMOR)
YOU'RE THE SENPAIS FROM THIS MORNING ...
THANKS A MILLION!
WAI
HWUH...? THAT FLAG...
EH HEH HEH~! ♫
DOYA (PROUD)
どや
THAT ANNOUNCEMENT WAS ABOUT YOU TWO, WASN'T IT!?
CONGRATULATIONS.
OH, GEEZ.
WE GOT LUCKY ENOUGH TO FIND THE RIGHT COMPETITIONS QUICKLY, THAT'S ALL.
TEH HEH HEH.
THAT'S WHAT'S IMPORTANT IN THIS RACE.
HUH?
YOU STILL DON'T HAVE A SINGLE ONE...
DO YOU KNOW WHERE THE BUN-EATING RACE IS?
NO... WE CAN'T FIND IT.
THIS ONE SOUNDS LIKE IT WOULD BE OUTSIDE, BUT IT'S ACTUALLY NOT.

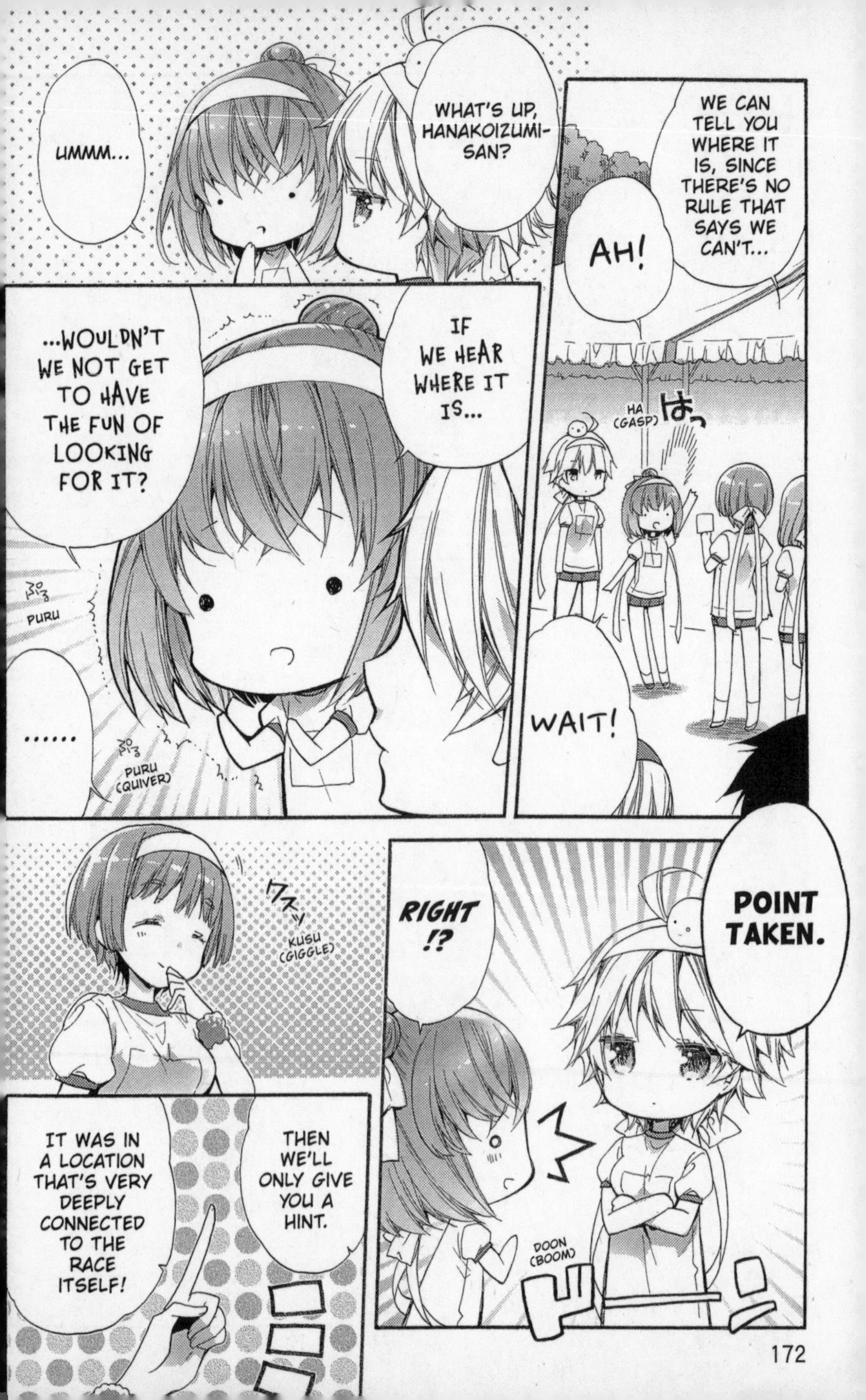
WE CAN TELL YOU WHERE IT IS, SINCE THERE'S NO RULE THAT SAYS WE CAN'T...
AH!
はっ
HA (GASP)
WAIT!
WHAT'S UP, HANAKOIZUMI-SAN?
UMMM...
IF WE HEAR WHERE IT IS...
...WOULDN'T WE NOT GET TO HAVE THE FUN OF LOOKING FOR IT?
ぷる
PURU
......
ぷる
PURU (QUIVER)
POINT TAKEN.
RIGHT !?
DOON (BOOM)
クスッ
KUSU (GIGGLE)
THEN WE'LL ONLY GIVE YOU A HINT.
IT WAS IN A LOCATION THAT'S VERY DEEPLY CONNECTED TO THE RACE ITSELF!

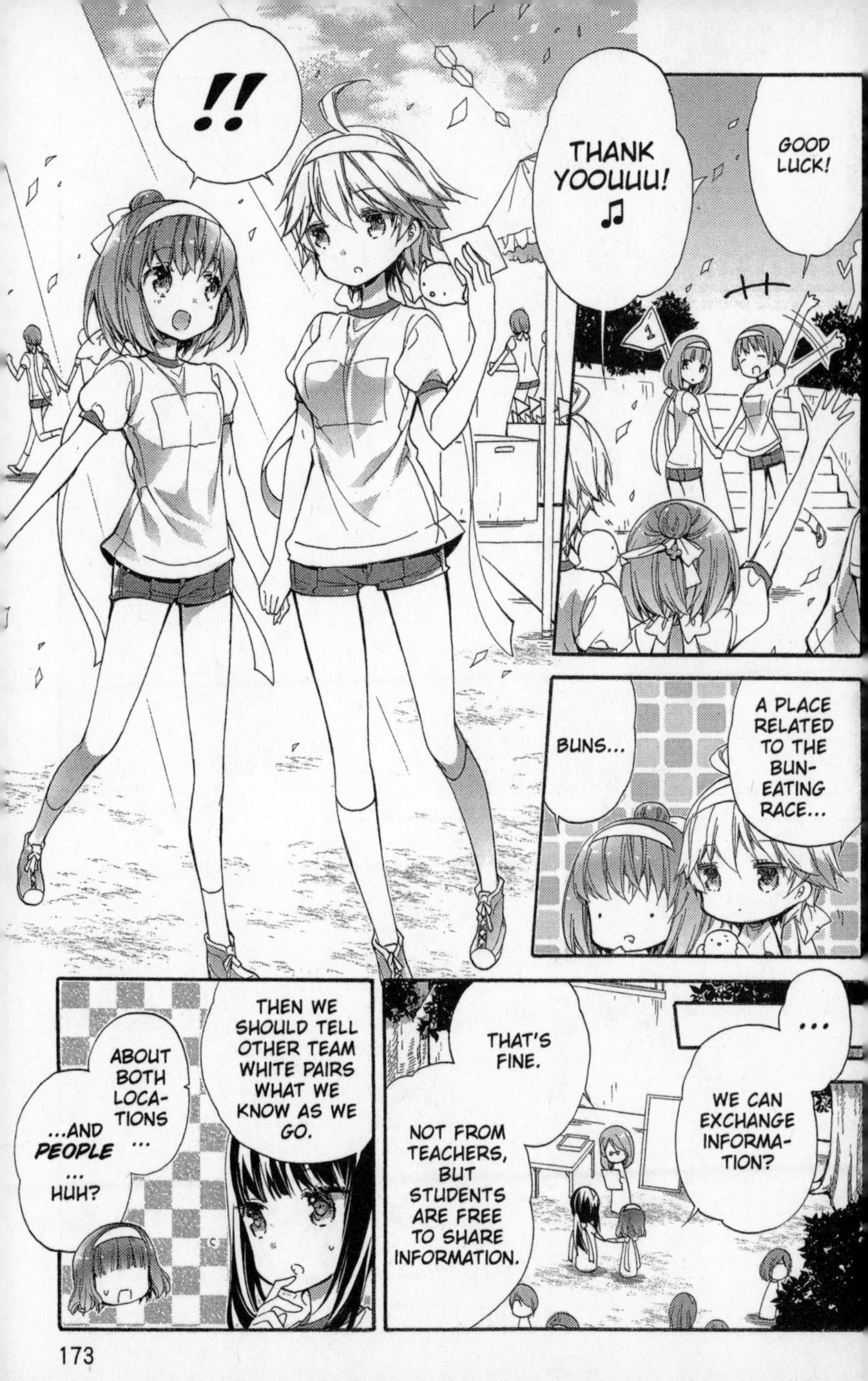
GOOD LUCK!
THANK YOOUUU! ♫
A PLACE RELATED TO THE BUN-EATING RACE...
BUNS...
!!
...
WE CAN EXCHANGE INFORMATION?
THAT'S FINE.
NOT FROM TEACHERS, BUT STUDENTS ARE FREE TO SHARE INFORMATION.
THEN WE SHOULD TELL OTHER TEAM WHITE PAIRS WHAT WE KNOW AS WE GO.
ABOUT BOTH LOCATIONS...
...AND *PEOPLE*... HUH?

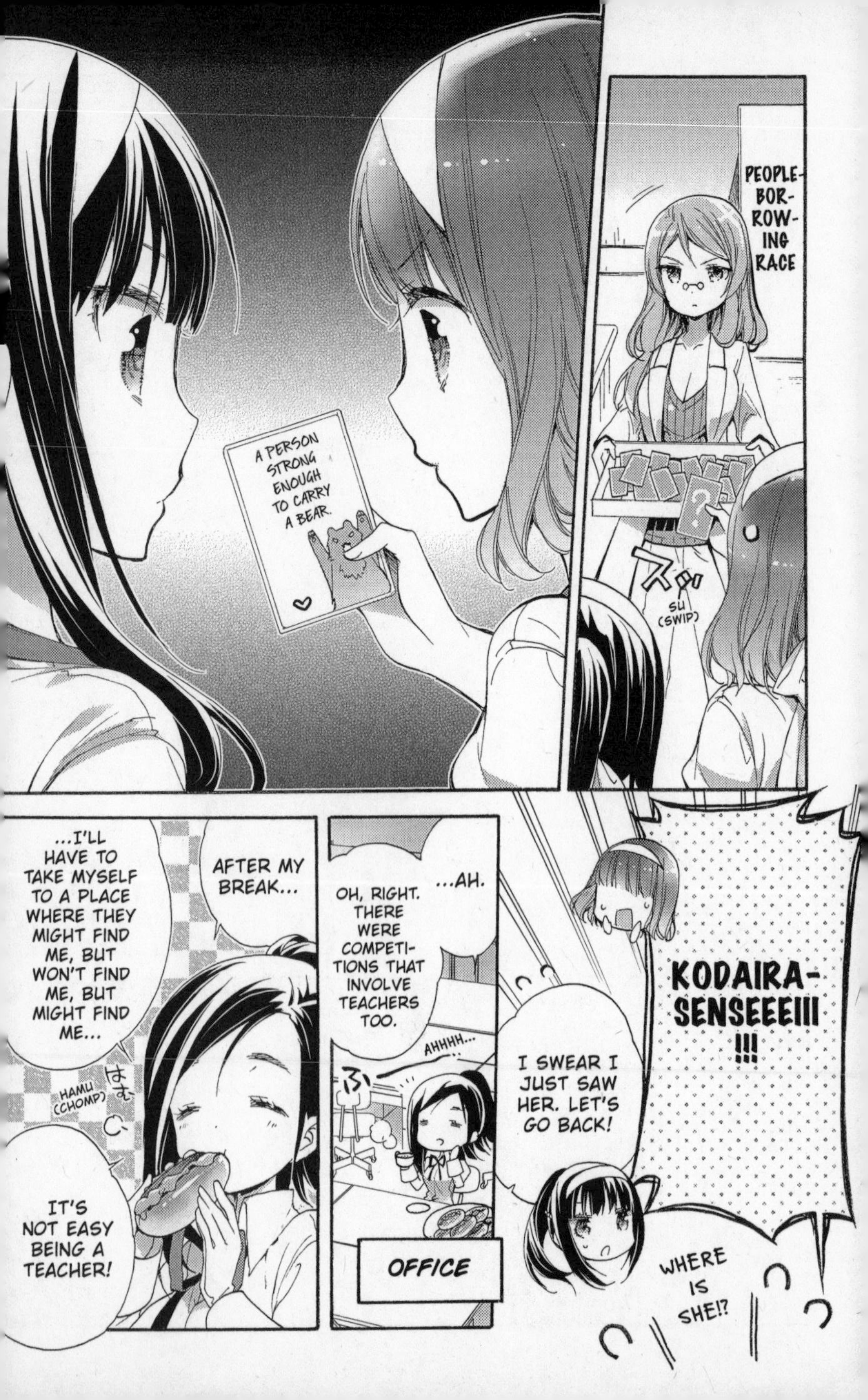
PEOPLE-BORROWING RACE
スッ
SU (SWIP)
A PERSON STRONG ENOUGH TO CARRY A BEAR.
KODAIRA-SENSEEEIIII!!!
I SWEAR I JUST SAW HER. LET'S GO BACK!
WHERE IS SHE!?
...AH.
OH, RIGHT. THERE WERE COMPETITIONS THAT INVOLVE TEACHERS TOO.
AHHHH...
OFFICE
AFTER MY BREAK...
...I'LL HAVE TO TAKE MYSELF TO A PLACE WHERE THEY MIGHT FIND ME, BUT WON'T FIND ME, BUT MIGHT FIND ME...
HAMU (CHOMP)
IT'S NOT EASY BEING A TEACHER!

Anne Happy
unhappy go lucky!

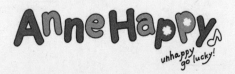

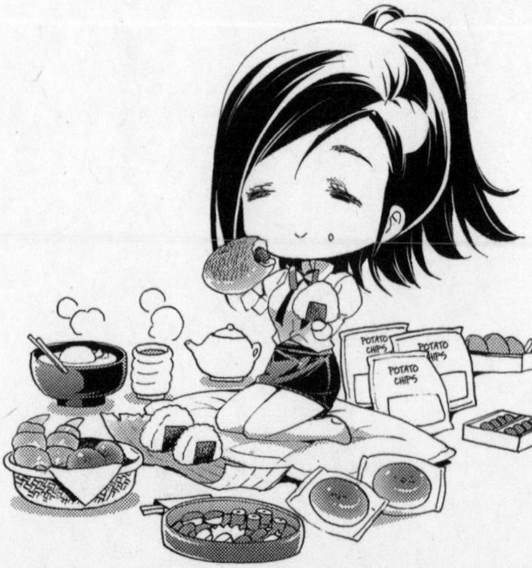
POTATO CHIPS
POTATO CHIPS
POTATO CHIPS

Page 76
Mochi is a soft, sticky rice cake. It can be different shapes, but a common one is a round shape that's flat on the bottom. It's not a stretch to imagine a bunny in that shape.

Page 122
On the chapter opener illustration for Lucky. 27, the girls are wearing *ouendan* ("cheer squad") uniforms, an activity similar to cheerleading but typically associated with male performers.

Page 152
Ishidaki is an old torture technique in which very heavy stone weights are placed on a kneeling subject's lap.

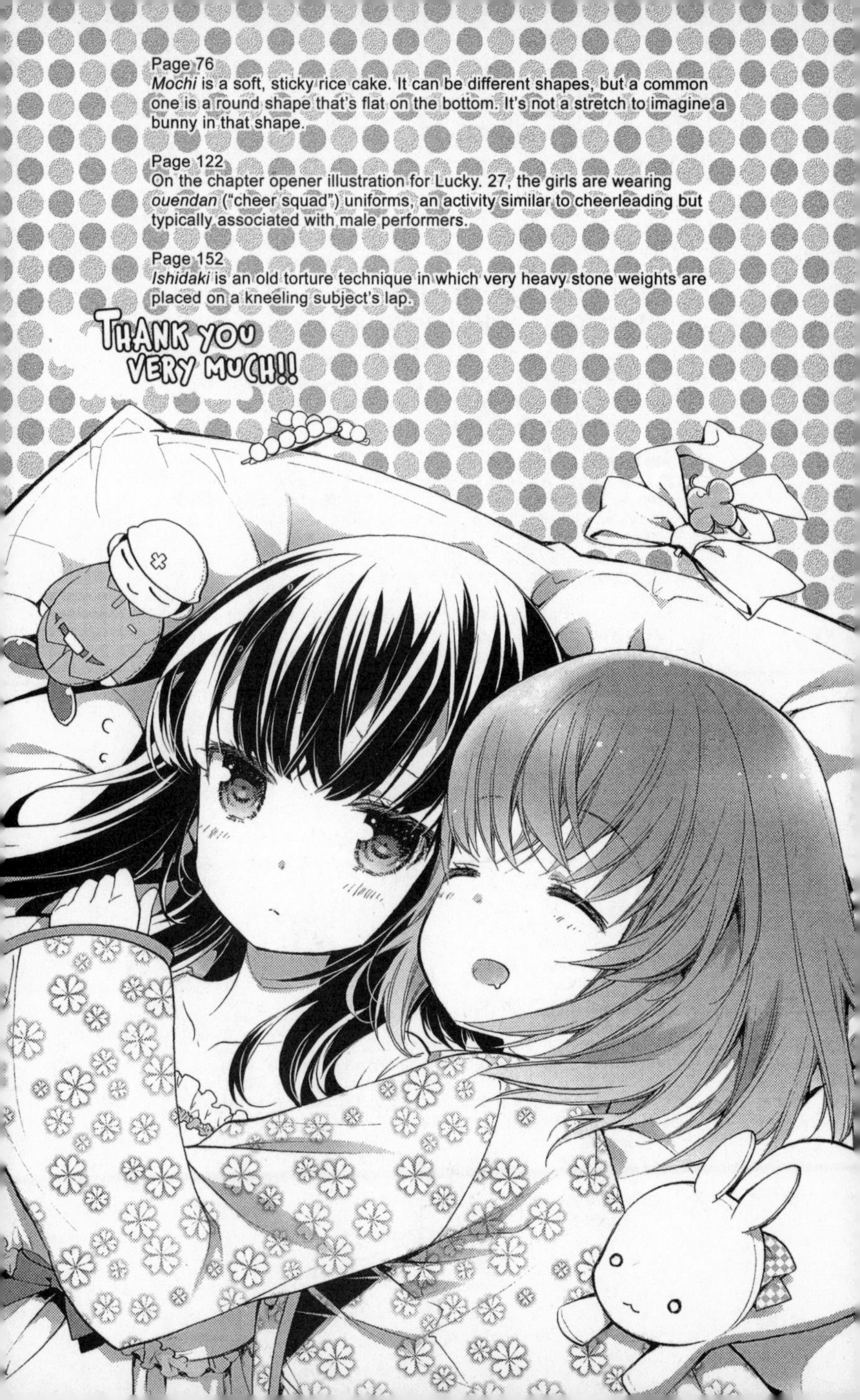
THANK YOU VERY MUCH!!

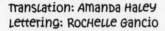

Translation: Amanda Haley
Lettering: Rochelle Gancio

ANNE HAPPY ♪ VOL. 7
© 2017 Cotoji. All rights reserved. First published in Japan in 2016 by HOUBUNSHA CO., LTD., TOKYO. English translation rights in United States, Canada, and United Kingdom arranged with HOUBUNSHA CO., LTD. through Tuttle-Mori Agency, Inc., TOKYO.

Yen Press
1290 Avenue of the Americas
New York, NY 10104

Visit us at yenpress.com
facebook.com/yenpress
twitter.com/yenpress
yenpress.tumblr.com
instagram.com/yenpress

First Yen Press Edition: November 2017

Yen Press is an imprint of Yen Press, LLC.
The Yen Press name and logo are trademarks of Yen Press, LLC.

The publisher is not responsible for websites (or their content) that are not owned by the publisher.

Library of Congress Control Number: 2016931012

ISBNs: 978-0-316-41277-3 (paperback)
       978-0-316-44831-4 (ebook)

10 9 8 7 6 5 4 3 2 1

BVG

Printed in the United States of America

CONTENTS
ANNE HAPPY
VOLUME SEVEN
COTOJI

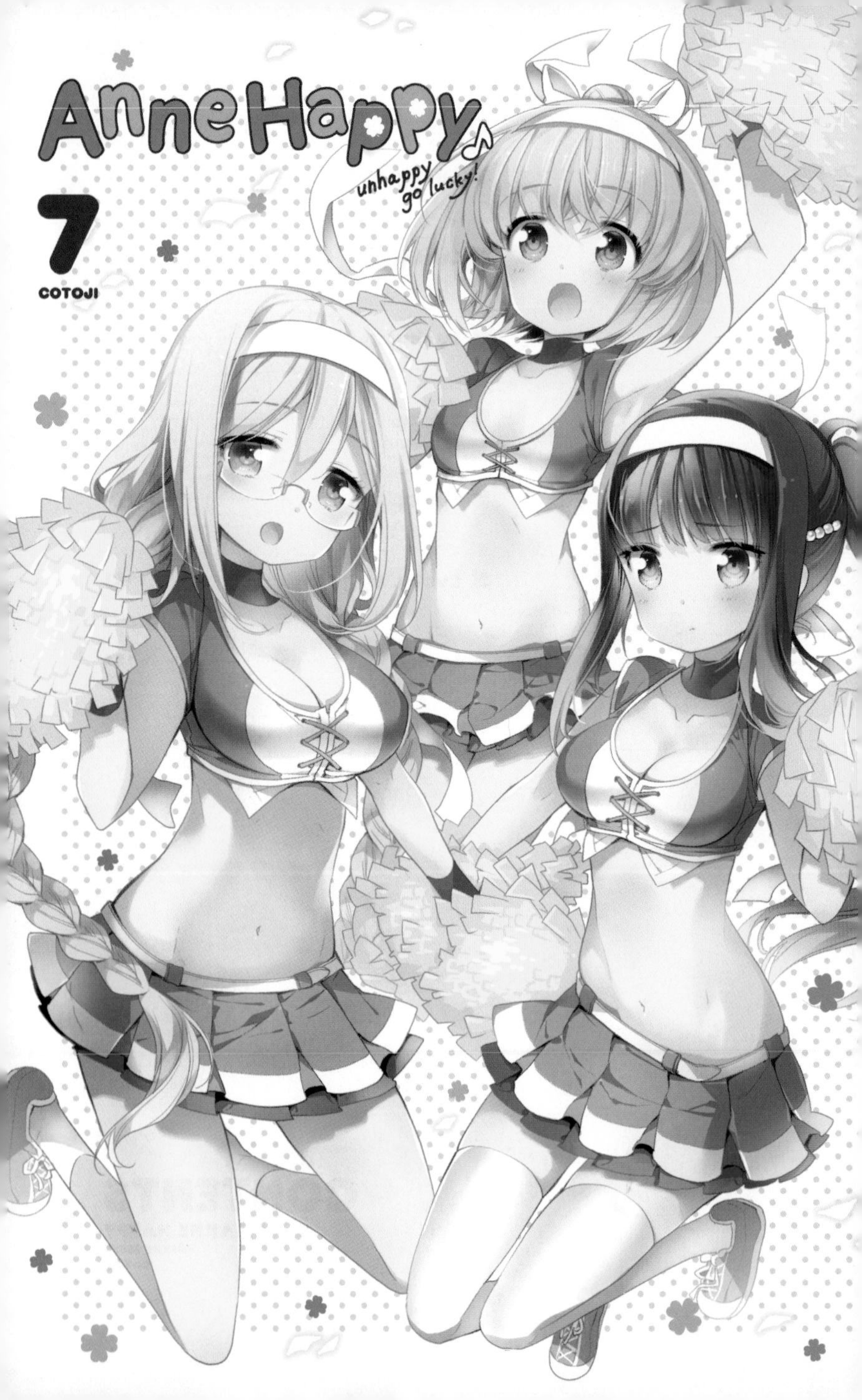
Anne Happy♪
unhappy go lucky!
7
COTOJI